Dreams as a Tool in Psychodynamic Psychotherapy

Dreams as a Tool in Psychodynamic Psychotherapy:
Traveling the Royal Road to the Unconscious

Vincenzo Conigliaro, M.D.

INTERNATIONAL UNIVERSITIES PRESS, INC.
Madison   Connecticut

Library of Congress Cataloging-in-Publication Data

Conigliaro, Vincenzo.
   Dreams as a tool in psychotherapy : traveling the royal road to the unconscious / Vincenzo Conigliaro.
      p.   cm.
   Includes bibliographical references and index.
   ISBN 0-8236-1439-5
   1. Dreams.   2. Dreams—Therapeutic use.   3. Dream interpretation.
I. Title.
   [DNLM: 1. Dreams—psychology. 2. Unconscious (Psychology)
3. Psychoanalytic Interpretation. 4. Psychoanalytic Therapy-
-methods.   WM 460.5.D8 C751d 1997]
RC489.D74C66 1997
616.89'14—dc20
DNLM/DLC
for Library of Congress   96-29393
                                              CIP

Manufactured in the United States of America

Contents

Appendix: Connections between and among Dreams,
    REM Sleep, Primary Process Functions, and States of
    Sensory Privation and Cortical Deafferentiation   361

The interpretation of dreams is the royal road to a knowledge of the unconscious activities of the mind.
[Freud, 1900]

Preface

Freud understood dreams as derivatives of the unconscious, along with neurotic and psychotic symptoms. To Freud dreams were the counterpart, during sleep, of the neurotic and psychotic symptoms that may exist during periods of wakefulness. According to Freud, both in dreams and in neurotic and psychotic symptoms, one sees the adaptive steps taken by the psyche to protect the socialized ego from too direct an encounter with the unconscious; and in both dream analysis and psychoanalysis, the analyst retraces the steps which the psyche has taken as it embellished the harsh unconscious contents of either dreams or symptoms. Because of this close connection between dreams and symptoms of emotional and mental distress, this book, while mainly a book about working with dreams, is also, inevitably, a book about working with symptoms of emotional and mental distress.

In *The Interpretation of Dreams,* Freud wrote, "*The interpretation of dreams is the royal road to a knowledge of the unconscious activities of the mind.* By analysing dreams we can take a step forward in our understanding of the composition of that most marvellous and most mysterious of all instruments" (1900, p. 608). When I first read that sentence as a young analytic student of Alessandra Tomasi di Palma in Palermo, Italy, I was moved by Freud's admiration for the human mind, his appreciation for the power of the unconscious, and his courage in wanting to encounter his own unconscious. Augustine's and Rousseau's *Confessions* were also

courageous skirmishes with the activities of the authors' own unconscious minds. I understood that Rudolph Otto's "numinosum" (1917, cited by Jung, 1938, p. 7), was an alteration of
consciousness occurring whenever the conscious mind was even
touched by the unconscious. Later on, as I read works by historians such as Barbara Tuchman's *The March of Folly* (1985), those
of philosophical anthropologists such as J. G. Frazer's *The Perils
of the Soul* (1911), the studies of contemporary neuroscientists
such as Nobel Prize Laureate Gerald M. Edelman, my awe for the
unconscious continued to grow. Emotional and mental diseases
are indeed the result of small or large forays by the unconscious
upon consciousness; states of dis-ease, un-ease, ill-at-ease-ness (or
states of manic or hypomanic joy or ecstasy) are produced whenever the unconscious impinges upon or even slightly brushes with
consciousness. Dream analysis and psychoanalysis are a truly fantastic voyage, because through them one has a chance of catching
a glimpse of the activities of the immeasurably deep, magnificent,
intimidating, awesome human unconscious.

The "royal road to a knowledge of the unconscious activities
of the mind" (Freud, 1900, p. 608) should not be seen, literally
or anthropomorphically, as a highway leading to a cave where a
huge beast, the id, lurks. Nevertheless, the human mind does
contain suppressed memories of powerful events usually experienced in infancy and childhood, kept away from consciousness
through a variety of means, mechanisms of defense. These memories have a dynamic influence, positive or negative, on the person's conscious feelings and behavior. Skillfully unearthing these
memories, as one does in well-conducted psychoanalytic psychotherapy, results in greater health. Carelessly excavating them, as
is done in "wild psychoanalysis" (Freud, 1910b), may fragment
and shatter the person. Dream analysis and psychoanalysis are
the royal road to a better understanding of the mind; traveling
down that road can exorcise dangerous skeletons in our psychic
closets, and effect what Freud advocated, "Where id was, there
ego shall be" (1933, p. 80).

This book is about traveling the royal road to the unconscious and the insights into the unconscious one may gain
through listening with our conscious and unconscious mind, our
"third ear," to our patients' dreams and symptoms. It is dedicated

to Sigmund Freud, who first spoke about the royal road to the unconscious and traveled down that road to his own unconscious; and to my patients, who trusted me as their guide to their unconscious and in so doing helped me continue to travel to my own.

Acknowledgments

I wish to thank my patients for having allowed me to travel with them down the road to their unconscious.

This book would not have been written "but for Deborah," my wife. After hearing my thousandth dream (I dream prolifically), she said (maybe in self-defense?), "Why don't you write a book on dreams?" I want to thank her for her inspiration, encouragement, support, patience—and occasional impatience—that helped, too.

I wish to thank Ms. Beatrice Saunders, for editorial assistance early on in the writing of this book; and Ms. Paula Fortunato, for very valuable editorial help, painstaking computer work on the manuscript, and infinite tolerance of this author's perfectionist tendencies.

Very special thanks to Lois Cipriano for assistance concerning style, accuracy in quotations, and her priceless and rich contribution in content to chapter 1.

I also want to thank Mary Ann Quaranta, Dean, Fordham University Graduate School of Social Work for generous and continuous encouragement and support.

And this book might not have been written had my young friend Drew Souza not convinced me (against my best *conscious* wishes) to enter the twentieth century and buy a computer.

Introduction

This is a book about Freud's theories on dreams and dreaming and about my clinical applications and utilization of these theories. On the subject of dreams, Freud wrote *The Interpretation of Dreams* (1900), "On Dreams" (1901a), and, between 1895 and 1938, twenty-three additional monographs having to do with dreams exclusively or predominantly: truly a plenitude of seminal contributions on the subject. As Strachey commented in an editorial note, "It would scarcely be an exaggeration to say that dreams are alluded to in the majority of Freud's writings" (1900, p. 626). Why, then, one more book on Freud's theory of dreams? Why this book?

This book is intended for psychoanalytic trainees, beginning practitioners in psychoanalysis, graduates of social work or clinical psychology programs who are becoming clinical social workers or clinical psychologists, and for those mental health practitioners who, while not interested in pursuing formal psychoanalytic training, nevertheless wish to understand their patients' dreams in the light of Freud's theories on dreams. Its usefulness is twofold. First, this book summarizes but also considerably elaborates on Freud's thoughts upon dreams. It elucidates and clarifies his thoughts when his unique cognitive style makes those thoughts difficult to understand. In some instances, most notably concerning "primary process" and "dramatization," this book interprets and extrapolates from Freud's thoughts, but is faithful to Freud's implicit meanings. Finally, by arranging Freud's thoughts on dreams into two major themes, dream formation and dream interpretation, his entire work on dreams is made more accessible.

This book cannot be a substitute for Freud's works on dreams, but it can complement and supplement his work, as well as aid in understanding it better.

Second, this book, in presenting interpretation of dreams through my personal way of applying and utilizing Freud's theories on dreams, demonstrates how one can "personalize" one's work with dreams and still remain faithful to basic Freudian theory and techniques of dream interpretation.

Freud believed that dream analysis occupies a central place in psychoanalysis, that "the interpretation of dreams is the royal road to a knowledge of the unconscious activities of the mind" (1900, p. 608), and that dream analysis is, in effect, a micropsychoanalysis. As already indicated in the *Preface*, dream analysis and psychoanalysis are inextricably interconnected, symptom formation and dream formation have many parallels, as do the techniques of psychoanalysis and those of dream analysis. Although mainly concerned with Freud's theories about dreams, this book also discusses general philosophical, theoretical, and clinical aspects of Freudian psychoanalysis. It will attempt to demonstrate how knowledge of the unconscious activities of the mind is gained in both psychoanalysis and dream analysis. It will be helpful to an understanding both of dreams and of neurotic and psychotic symptoms.

This book is divided into three parts: Part I (chapters 1 through 3) consists of preliminary but basic considerations relevant to dreams and dreaming. Part II (chapters 4 and 5) deals with dream formation. Part III (chapters 6 through 9) is about dream interpretation.

Chapter 1 presents an overview of dreams and dreaming. It begins with some general observations which show the conceptual continuity and kinship of ideas that exist (latently, if not always patently) between Freudian psychoanalysts on the one hand, and, on the other hand, romantics, artists, existential and Jungian psychologists, neurologists, and biologists. This is followed by a short history of ideas about dreams and dreaming from antiquity to Freud. The chapter concludes with a review of neurological findings on dreams and dreaming after Freud.

Freud's dream theories and general psychoanalytic theories are intimately related. *The Interpretation of Dreams* is not just a book about dreams; it is a book about psychoanalysis and psychodynamic psychology. The first five editions, which were published before 1919, contained most of the theoretical and clinical concepts of psychoanalysis Freud had already developed as well as hints and allusions to discoveries still to come. The last three editions, published after 1921, included more of Freud's later ideas on the mind's structure and functioning. One cannot discuss or understand Freud's theories on dreams without a solid understanding of Freud's basic psychoanalytic postulates. *Chapter 2* is about basic Freudian theory on personality and personality structure; it summarizes Freud's thoughts on drive theory, topographic theory, and structural theory as they bear upon dreams and dreaming. *Chapter 3* is concerned with basic Freudian theory on symptom formation as it relates to dream formation.

In Part II, chapters 4 and 5 discuss dream formation. *Chapter 4* discusses the conception, gestation, and birth of dreams from three perspectives: in terms of the theory of the neurotic conflict, the sources and the content of dreams, and "the wish to sleep." *Chapter 5* discusses the dream work operations.

In Part III, chapters 6 through 9 discuss dream interpretation. As this writer sees it, when the patient tells the analyst a dream, the analyst has three tasks: (1) understanding the session, understanding it psychodynamically with the third ear, connecting it, psychodynamically, to the dream; (2) understanding the dream, understanding it, again, psychoanalytically, deciphering it internally, within one's own mind (i.e., knowing what the patient's dream says); and (3) responding to the patient's dream, knowing which of the three possible kinds of responses (silence, interventions, interpretation) one should choose; that is, knowing what to say to the patient about the dream (if anything).

A valid distinction can be made between the *theory* of technique of dream interpretation and *technique* of dream interpretation. The theory of technique of dream interpretation helps analysts decode dreams, each dream being regarded as a single, discrete psychic phenomenon. Technique of dream interpretation helps analysts truly understand dreams, each dream being regarded as an integral part of the patient's whole psychic life. The theory of technique of dream interpretation decodes dreams, mainly through knowledge of dream theory; to accomplish the second of the three tasks mentioned above, knowing what patients' dreams say, the theory of technique of dream interpretation is enough; one only needs a thorough grasp and understanding of dream theory, and, especially, of the psychological operations of the dream work. Barring cases of strong countertransference, one can decode most dreams just by reversing the steps the dream work had taken in transforming the latent dream into the manifest dream. But to accomplish the third task, knowing what to say to patients about their dreams, the theory of technique of dream interpretation is not enough, and the technique of dream interpretation is needed: with the latter, analysts use not only thorough knowledge of dream theory, but also a reliable understanding of their patient's unconscious and their own unconscious self.

Chapter 6 discusses in detail the three tasks mentioned above, as well as the two basic technical principles governing the science and art of Freudian dream interpretation. These are: (1) ultimately, it is the dream's latent, not semilatent or manifest content, that must be analyzed (this being the cardinal rule of Freudian dream interpretation); and (2) dreams can be analyzed on the level of the defenses, on the level of the drives, and within the context of the transference. The chapter also introduces my use of the internal soliloquy technique, which is nothing more than listening with the third ear, listening to oneself as well as to one's patient, listening to all resonances from within one's conscious and unconscious self to the patient's conscious and unconscious material, letting all kinds of conjectures, speculations, and fantasies bubble up to one's consciousness. *Chapter 6* also discusses when to apply and when to suspend the cardinal rule.

Chapter 7 presents at length the actual application of the above-mentioned tasks and principles through an extensive discussion of my patients' dreams. It illustrates in detail the analyst's internal thinking, the internal soliloquy, in working with dreams.

Chapter 8 discusses various clinical scenarios in which the cardinal rule of Freudian dream interpretation should and should not be applied, and presents a number of dreams dreamed in clinical circumstances which warranted the total or partial suspension of the rule: first dreams, early dreams, dreams presented in a consultation session, dreams dreamed in conjunction with severe psychic crises, and "special purpose" dreams. *Chapter 9* revisits three dreams presented by Freud, "Medical Student and Hospital," "The Dream of Irma's Injection," and "Three Theatre Tickets." The chapter examines how Freud interpreted these dreams before 1900, and then discusses how I would interpret them now.

Finally, the *Appendix* discusses recent findings on intriguing connections between Freud's dream theory and primary process functions on the one hand, and on the other hand, daydreams, hallucinations, sensory privation, and states of cortical deafferentiation.

Although this book is on and about Freud's theories on dreams, my own personal, ideological, and clinical leanings visibly and inevitably manifest themselves in the techniques I use in interpreting dreams. Within the continuum of Freudian psychoanalytical technique, one finds, at one extreme, analysts who believe that psychoanalysis should be like an obstetrical procedure (the analyst should intervene only when the analytical process is truly stalled and the patient is truly "stuck"); and, at the other extreme, analysts who are somewhat more active (and not because of countertransference). Although still firmly rooted in Freud's theory of psychoanalysis, I have become more phenomenological and existential in my psychoanalytic technique. These ideological propensities, and my analytical style—something that is never just related to type of training, Freudian or non-Freudian, but also to character, temperament, and the analytical style of the analyst's own analyst—explain my somewhat active, "Freudian, but" approach to dream interpretation.

Also, paraphrasing Oliver Sacks (1991), I believe that a psychoanalysis starts and ends with "stories." Patients have a story, dreams are a story. Patients tell analysts their stories and their dreams, and these stories and dreams may not make much sense to the patient; but the analyst helps the patient make more sense of them, and in the process of doing so, analysts bring their own internal stories. My internal soliloquies are the first step in the process.

Part I

PRELIMINARY CONSIDERATIONS RELEVANT TO DREAMS AND DREAMING

1

Overview

DREAMS TO NONPSYCHOANALYSTS AND PSYCHOANALYSTS

To a romantic, dreams are a way of beautifying life and embellishing reality, a way of being a hero rather than a villain, beautiful rather than ordinary, a saint rather than a devil, a wizard rather than a fool. This is truer of daydreams, but it also applies to night dreams: we have all dreamed our impossible dreams in which we were unbelievably, and possibly, uncharacteristically vibrant and heroic, dreams from which we hated to awaken, dreams that we wished would continue forever. To the Freudian psychoanalyst too, through the magic of primary process thinking, dreams are a way of beautifying reality, a way of embellishing one's psychic life, a way of beautifying and embellishing ("distorting") a life made unpleasant and frightening by unconscious intrapsychic conflicts. The word *magic* is used advisedly. Dream thinking is magic thinking, which is one of the characteristics of primary process thinking and feeling, the thinking and feeling of the unconscious id, and of the earliest stages in the birth of a dream. In dreams, through primary process thinking, we recreate psychological reality as we wish it to be by hallucinating the memory images of those objects, object relations, and interpersonal relationships the lack of which has made life ugly or unbearable. This is also demonstrable empirically. While one *always* dreams,[1] the

---

[1]Dreams may not occur in comatose states or if one goes to sleep in a chemically altered state because of alcohol or drugs reaching the brain.

less frustrating the day has been, the less will one dream that night. On a pleasant vacation, with its potential outlets to express conflicted drives through culturally and psychologically acceptable symbolic behavior (exhibitionism, through swimming in the nude; oral drives, through drinking and eating more than usual; generalized regressions in the service of the ego by sleeping late, napping in the afternoon or daydreaming), one dreams less.

To artists, at least abstract artists, reality is seen and represented differently from the way the eye sees it, or naturalistic painters and conventional photographers depict it. Picasso's profile of a person may clearly show both eyes, as if the subject were seen not from the side, but frontally. Artistic renderings, of course, are distortions of "real reality," but they may give a view into the inner fabric of reality; art, rather than representing the outward appearance of things, may give their inward significance. To Freudian psychoanalysts too, dreams are the dreamer's way of seeing reality's deeper aspects. Dreams depict the dreamer's psychological, subjective reality, which is the only reality "true" to that person. After all, psychologically, all persons are as two-faced as figures in a Picasso painting seem to be; all persons have the two-facedness of conscious and unconscious feelings, overt behavior and covert motivations, inner character and outer personality. It may take a dream for the dreamer to realize that he or she is seeing someone else as two-faced. In dreams too, as in abstract art, there are distortions. In the latent dream, before the dream work distorts it, there lie reality's other faces, reality as the dreamer sees and experiences it unconsciously. In the manifest dream, after the dream work's distortions, there is reality as the dreamer sees and experiences it in conscious reality, as psychological, social, or aesthetic conventions disguise it for him or her. As a brief example, the overprotective behavior of a young woman's father was a cover of his unconscious hostility. He was protecting her from the harm he unconsciously wished on her. His daughter consciously believed her father loved her but unconsciously knew of his hostility, and only in her dreams saw him, disguised of course, as murderous. Her manifest dreams about hostile men (i.e., her father), were not only a well-disguised representation of her projected hostility against them (father), but also a disguised representation of her inner perception of her father's hostility.

To existential and Jungian psychoanalysts, dreams are a way of achieving authenticity and wholeness. The dream is secondary, the dreamer is primary; the dreamer determines the ultimate value of the dream, determines whether the dream is goal or escape, objective or refuge. To the Freudian psychoanalyst, too, each dream's significance is determined by the dreamer. Freud was the first to see that dreams cannot be analyzed without the dreamer's associations and without knowing the dreamer, thus removing dream analysis from numerology and cabalism.[2]

To biologists and neurologists, dreams are phenomena inherent in and characteristic of the brain cells, as breathing is for the pulmonary cells, and as the production of urine is for the kidneys, and as essential to the person's physical and mental health as the normal functioning of lungs and kidneys. And to the Freudian psychoanalyst too, dreams are essential to mental health; Freud saw dreams as cleansing the mind after a day of civilized living and its discontents. This has been confirmed by more recent studies on sleep deprivation (Gaer Luce, 1974a) and dream deprivation (Dement, 1960; Gaer Luce, 1974b). Moreover, to biologists, dreams are the remnants of evolutionary processes essential for physical survival thousands of years ago and the product of mutations, preserved through natural selections. As a result of these evolutionary occurrences, a self-awakening metronome developed in the brain. For obvious reasons, at the dawn of human evolution, it was highly adaptive for humans not to sleep deeply for too long at a time, and only those ancestors of ours survived in whom this self-awakening pacemaker had developed. Therefore dreams and dreaming go back to the early days of our philogenetic past, our past in terms of our development as a species. But to the Freudian psychoanalyst too, dreams are the expression of processes going back to the early days of our past, our ontogenetic past, the early days in the infancy and childhood of our individual personal development.

To the Freudian psychoanalyst, dreams are indeed some of all of the above: some of what dreams are to the romantically

---

[2]Cabalism was an esoteric theosophy developed by rabbis from the seventh to the eleventh century, which also influenced medieval Christian thinkers. Originally cabalism was primarily a mystical method, which only its initiates mastered, for interpreting sacred mysteries. Cabalists also dabbled with foretelling the future and with dream analysis.

minded, the artist, the existential psychoanalyst, the Jungian psychologist, the biologist, and the neurologist. And, of course, they are something more: they are the equivalent of the psychoneurotic and psychotic symptoms we would develop if we did not dream; they are the royal road to a knowledge of the unconscious activities of the mind. They are the best way to understand our patients' psychodynamics, symptoms, and psychic pain; and the best way to help toward changing those symptoms and relieving that pain.

HISTORICAL OBSERVATIONS: FROM ANTIQUITY TO FREUD

In every known culture, human beings have always wondered about the often bizarre drama that unfolded in their minds as they slept. Generally speaking, our ideas about dreams have been influenced by our philosophical conceptions about the world and its nature. People who understand the world in supernatural, theistic terms, view dreams as supernatural products; for instance, as visitations from gods or demons. In some cultures, it is believed that the "soul" (i.e., the mind) travels away from the body when the body sleeps, and visits those places and experiences those events which later appear in dreams. It is thought that dead persons or gods and demons visit the body while it is asleep with warnings and instructions. In Western cultures, as the philosophical pendulum swung from the supernatural to the scientific, dreams came to be understood in solely biological and physiological terms or in a purely mechanistic fashion.

Freud (1900) acknowledged that he was not the first writer to understand dreams as derived from wishes. He noted that Herophilus, a Greek physician who lived under Ptolemy around 329 B.C., was the first to do so. Citing Büschenshutz (1868, p. 33), Freud, in a footnote added in 1914, said that Herophilus distinguished among three kinds of dreams: "those which are sent by the gods, those which are natural and arise when the mind forms a picture of something that is agreeable to it and will come about, and those which are of a mixed nature and which arise of their own accord from the emergence of pictures in which we see what we wish for" (Freud, 1900, p. 132n). Freud also referred to Artemidorus of Daldis, born at the beginning of the second century

A.D., whose book Freud considered one of the most authoritative in antiquity (Freud, 1900, pp. 98–99). But an even earlier source of thinking about dreams and dreaming, according to Lorand, is the Babylonian Talmud (Lorand, 1974). As a written text, the Babylonian Talmud was compiled between 200 B.C. and 300 A.D., but it contains references which had been orally transmitted, going back to 1500 B.C. Of the Talmud's two main sections, the *Halakah* and the *Haggadah*, the former dealt mainly with the law, the latter with theology, philosophy, mathematics, history, and psychology. The psychological parts have at least two hundred substantive references to dreams. If assembled separately, Lorand remarks, they would make an impressive book on dreams (1974, pp. 150–158).

Two trends can be discerned in the Talmud's sections on dreams: one religious–political and the other psychological. Within the religious–political trend, the Talmudic writers viewed dreams as visions revealing God's will to his people and understood dreams as having an external source, the Deity. Of course, the sages of the time knew, or thought they knew, what was good for the Israelites. When they interpreted their people's dreams in prophetic terms, they wanted, consciously or unconsciously, to mold and direct their religious–political thought and behavior. The function of the prophet is not simply to foretell the future, but to determine it as well. Within the psychological trend, dreams were viewed as having an internal source, the dreamer's mind, and were interpreted symbolically. References are found to "antagonistic forces in the soul" as being the chief source of dreams (analogous to what was later to be termed *conflict theory*). Struggles in man's soul between "higher ambitions" and "immoral impulses" are discussed, and this struggle was seen as finding expression in dreams. Symbols were similar to our own: birds, houses, and fruits representing, respectively, men, women, and sexual organs. Incestuous wishes in dreams were correctly recognized. Interpretation was done solely by the interpreter.

Many references to dreams are found in the Bible: the Jacob's ladder dream (Gen. 28:10–17), Nebuchadnezzar's dreams as interpreted by Daniel (Dan 2:1–49; 4:1–33), dreams recorded in the New Testament, such as Joseph's dream of the angel telling him to marry Mary (Matt. 1:18–25), and later urging him to flee into Egypt (Matt. 2:12–13); and of course in the Old Testament the famous dreams of the earlier Joseph (Gen. 37:5–11). Freud himself referred to this Joseph as "a man famous in the Bible as an interpreter of dreams" (1900, p. 484). Twice earlier, he had referred to how Joseph had interpreted dreams (1900, pp. 97, 334). Dream historians have elicited descriptions of Joseph from the Book of Genesis. Joseph was Jacob's next to youngest son, and his favorite, being a "son of his old age" (Gen. 37:3). He was also his mother's favorite, and this double good fortune made him quite cocky (a phallic character?). Sibling rivalry by his sisters and brothers was considerable: "they hated him, and could not speak peaceably to him. Now Joseph had a dream, and when he told it to his brothers, they only hated him the more" (Gen, 37: 4–5). Joseph recounted his dream: "Behold, we were binding sheaves in the field and, lo, my sheaf arose, and stood upright; and behold, your sheaves gathered round it, and bowed down to my sheaf" (Gen. 37:7). Subsequently, he dreamed that "the sun, the moon, and the eleven stars were bowing down to me" (Gen. 37:9).

The Egyptians thought that through prayer one might be rewarded with a dream in which God gives the dreamer good advice (in psychoanalytic terms: propitiatory behavior during the day could soften the superego; the result of that might be a pleasant, optimistic dream). The Greeks believed that their pleasant or frightening dreams were divine omens of good health or illness, good or bad fortune. While the ancient Greeks had a true cult of dreams and an elaborate art of divination, the classical Greeks had a more sophisticated understanding of dreams. Plato quoted Socrates as saying: "When the rest of the soul, which is rational and mild, is asleep, that part of the soul which is savage and rude frisks about, drives sleep away and seeks to go and accomplish its practices. It dares to do everything, because it has no modesty or prudence, even embracing one's mother, or a man, or committing murder" (Plato, *Republic*). One has only to translate "soul" to "mind" to recognize in the "rational and mild soul" the rational and reality-oriented ego; in the "savage and rude soul," the amoral and asocial id and its incestuous, homosexual, and murderous drives.

In agricultural societies today, one finds ideas on dreams that duplicate ideas held in antiquity. For instance, the Senoi on the Malay peninsula practice "dream therapy" at breakfast time every morning. The family assembles, the dreams of the night before are discussed, and an elder explains their meaning, deciphers their messages, or uses the dreams to give instructions that will benefit the dreamer or the dreamer's tribe. For instance, a child wakes up frightened by a dream in which a ferocious wild beast has entered his tent. He is instructed to dream the dream again. He is also told that this time he will dream that he will call out to his loving father who will chase the beast away. In his unconscious wisdom (i.e., his intuitive understanding of psychodynamics and in his being attuned to the child's unconscious), the elder understood that the child's rage had been displaced onto, and symbolized as a wild beast, or had been projected onto the child's father, who was then symbolized as a wild beast. By telling the child to see his father as loving, the child's anger was reduced and his fear of retaliation was defused. (Elders of agricultural or hunting and gathering cultures are the recipients of strong transferences and are, therefore, as powerful as the parents and the superego.)

Neuropsychiatrists in the mid to late nineteenth century proposed many scientific, materialistic, anatomic–physiologic theories about dreams, understandably naive because of the still rudimentary knowledge of brain physiology. Most of them are reported in Freud's extensive historical and scientific review of dreams in chapter 1 of *The Interpretation of Dreams*.

In 1900, physicist Otto Plank published the first of his works on quantum theory. What is relevant to psychoanalysis within this theory is the postulate according to which energy does not proceed in a *noninterrupted flow* of particles, but in quantum amounts interrupted by intervals, by, as it were, "spaces-in-between." Quantum theory demonstrates that the long honored scientific–philosophical dogma *natura non facit saltus*—nature makes no leaps—is not true. There are indeed discontinuities, intervals, interruptions in nature and in the natural order of things. Quantum theory, as all scientific principles do, has important philosophical implications as well as implications for other sciences. The idea that there are discontinuities in nature, paved the way for neo-Darwinism. Some of the existential psychoanalysts, while remaining firmly committed to Darwinian theories of evolution, believe that there is a discontinuity, an interval (the "existential jump") between the brightest of prehuman great apes, or even the brightest of hominids, and the least intelligent homo sapiens. And there are intervals, spaces-in-between, discontinuities between conscious and unconscious, id and ego, ego and superego.

On May 28, 1899, Freud decided to publish *The Interpretation of Dreams*. The book was put on sale on November 4, 1899, but the possibly superstitious or prophetic publisher had it dated "1900" (as if the book of the century?). While philosophers, theologians, psychologists, and the ancients had had intimations that dreams were self-revealing, not until Freud's book on dreams was the study of dreams put on a scientific basis, Freud's being the most comprehensive analysis of dreams up to that time. He showed that dreams are a mirror of the dreamer's *unconscious* mind. He was the first to stress the importance of the hidden or latent content of dreams. He demonstrated that dreams play a dynamic role in the psychological life of the dreamer. Freud was also the first to show how the dreamer's active participation in the analysis of the dream is indispensable. For almost one hundred years now, *The Interpretation of Dreams* has been a fundamental source book, not just for psychoanalysts, but for psychiatrists, social researchers, philosophers, theologians, artists, and indeed for everyone interested in ideas.

The science of dreams truly started with Freud; whether one agrees with it or not, his was the first real theory of dreams. Freud originally stated that he discovered the value and significance of dreams quite accidentally while analyzing Elisabeth von R, who told him not to interrupt her while she was trying to tell him one of her dreams (Breuer and Freud, 1893–1895, pp. 135–182). In reality, he had long been interested in dreams, and for years had written down his own dreams quite diligently; although later he came to believe that writing down dreams could be a manifestation of "resistance." Also, his understanding of dreams was intimately connected with his developing understanding of the neuroses, and this in turn was inextricably connected with his understanding of his own neurosis and its vicissitudes.

In 1885, Freud, then 29 years old, in a letter to Martha Bernays, his fiancée, commented that his future biographers would resent his having destroyed all of his previous notes, letters, and manuscripts (E. Freud, 1960, pp. 140–141). This was a prophetic fantasy in itself. He was fond of alluding to the biblical Joseph and, in a later letter to Fliess, playfully referred to his yet unfinished manuscript as "the Egyptian dream book" (Bonaparte, Freud, A., and Kris, 1954, p. 291). This suggests both his identification with Joseph as interpreter of dreams, and his long-held belief that dreams harbored secret messages, divine or otherwise. Early on, he suggested that the wish is the parent of the action, further elaborating this notion in another letter to Fliess where he compared dreams and neurotic symptoms (Bonaparte, Freud, A., and Kris, 1954, p. 277). Both are expressions of a wish; but in the dream the wish is kept apart from reality, while in the symptom it is expressed in action. In 1892, at age 36, he moved away from hypnosis, away from stroking his patient's head, from applying pressure to the forehead, and toward free associations. Left more and more on their own, his patients began telling him their dreams. Between 1892 and 1895, he underwent a period of resistance against self-exploration, focusing instead on more objective hypotheses. He sent Fliess his famous *Project for a Scientific Psychology* (Freud, 1895). Fliess was not impressed, and Freud returned to his attempts to find psychological explanations for "the neuroses."

In a letter to Fliess of March 4, 1895 (Freud, 1892–1899, p. 213), Freud, having been told about Rudi Kaufmann's dream (see chapter 9), first speculated about dreams having the purpose of preserving sleep. On July 23 to 24, 1895, when he was 39 years old, Freud had the famous dream of Irma's injection (see chapter 9). He wrote down his interpretation in a house near Bellevue, a suburb of Vienna where he was vacationing. As Strachey notes, some five years later, in a letter to Fliess of June 12, 1900, Freud reported the fantasy of a commemorative plaque being placed there one day (Freud, 1900, p. 121). It appears that, in his interpretation of this dream at Bellevue, Freud was aware of the magnitude of his insights into the meaning of dreams. In 1895, his father's illness took a turn for the worse. Freud was experiencing intense feelings of guilt and went through one more phase of resistance. After his father's death in 1896, he went back to self-analysis and in 1897 began to write *The Interpretation of Dreams*. Two years later, the book was completed.

There followed a period of intense ambivalence as to whether to publish the book. Freud wondered whether he had researched the subject sufficiently, worried as to where he should put his bibliography, decided to add an extremely abstract chapter on the "psychology of dreams" (a chapter Freud himself detested but which he felt he should insert for the sake of *academia*), and understandably worried about self-exposure (the book contained many of his own dreams). The book that was going to become one of the great classics of human thought was to achieve a disastrous and humiliating fate in its first edition. It was practically ignored for close to eighteen months, and it took eight years to sell the first printing of 600 copies; only 228 more were sold over the following two years. There were few comments on the book, and all were harsh and negative. Freud's own reaction was mixed: at times self-assured ("I am twenty years ahead of my time"), at others depressed ("The book is very incomplete"). *The Interpretation of Dreams* was hardly noticed for about ten years; then, nine new editions were published in the next ten years.

NEUROLOGICAL FINDINGS ON DREAMS AND DREAMING AFTER FREUD

In 1953, Eugene Aserinsky, a graduate student of physiology and assistant to Nathaniel Kleitman at the University of Chicago, noticed that the eyes of people who were asleep moved rapidly for periods of several minutes: rapid eye movement, REM sleep. Twenty of twenty-seven subjects who were awakened after a period of REM sleep recalled detailed dreams, while nineteen of twenty-three subjects who where awakened during a period of NREM (no REM) sleep recalled no dreams (Aserinsky and Kleitman, 1953).

Since Aserinsky and Kleitman's pioneering work, much has been written on dreams and dreaming from the perspectives of neuroscience. Some of these works flatly contradict Freud's findings. Some point out that in Freud's time too much was unknown about neurology and neuroscience for him to have an accurate or truly scientific understanding of dreams and dreaming. But many of these studies enrich and confirm many of Freud's insights on the subject; or they demonstrate scientifically what had only been hypotheses or speculations on Freud's part about dreams, dreaming, and the body–mind connection: precisely because of how little was known in Freud's day about neurology and neuroscience.

Edward Grey Walter found that during REM sleep, the sleeper is not as deeply asleep as during NREM sleep. He hypothesized that, eons ago, a self-awakening pacemaker developed through genetic mutation, and that only those survived in whom that pacemaker had been preserved through natural selection. Obviously, it was unsafe for primitive men and women to be deeply asleep for too long a period of time: the fire had to be tended and predators fended off. In the REM sleep state of shallower sleep, rudimentary, life-saving vigilance operations are possible; during REM sleep (i.e., while sleeping and dreaming), one may be awakened by sounds and smells more easily than during periods of NREM sleep (Grey Walter, 1953).

Utilizing EEG tracings, Loomis described five "Sleep Stage Gradations" (1957). Dement and Kleitman (1957) divided sleep into four stages and observed a consistent pattern of sleeping, dreaming, and REM states. They reported that REM bursts were found regularly in the first stage of sleep, that everyone dreams every night, that dream periods occur approximately every ninety minutes, each averaging about twenty minutes a period and lasting for lengths of time that become slightly longer as the night progresses. Each dream period consisted of several dreams, was usually separated by some body movements and a few seconds of partial wakefulness. Everyone has from four to seven dream periods a night, taking up about 20 percent of total sleeping time, and accounting for ten to twenty separate dreams.

Dement and Kleitman also found that external situations brought upon the sleeping person do not bring on a dream if the person is in a state of NREM sleep (deep sleep), but do evoke a dream if the person is in a state of REM sleep. In this case, the stimulations variously modify the dream, and the dream's content does reflect the stimulus in a metaphorical fashion. For example, if the researcher gently squirted some water on the sleeper, the sleeper would dream of rain, or of leaking roofs, or of a waterfall. Also, auditory and tactile stimulations were represented in the dream as visual stimulations: whatever provoked the sound or the touch was seen, rather than heard or felt. Dement and Kleitman also found a high degree of correlation between the dream narrative and the direction of REM scanning: the sleepers whose REM scanning had been vertical were dreaming, respectively, of standing at the foot of a cliff watching climbers going up and down, or of throwing basketballs into a net, or of a blimp dropping leaflets (Dement and Kleitman, 1957).

Dement studied dream deprivation in the sleep laboratory of Mount Sinai Hospital, New York, where volunteers were awakened as a REM period started, while control subjects were awakened in NREM periods; both groups slept a total of six hours a night. After five consecutive nights, the first group reported anxiety and depression and greater hunger for food. Allowed, later on, to sleep undisturbed, these same subjects dreamed 60 percent more than previously (Dement, 1960). A compensatory period of overdreaming was reported in amphetamine addicts and in alcoholics who had previously been on dream-suppressing drugs. This has also been reported in animal studies: in rabbits by Sawyer, and in cats by Jouvet (Gaer Luce, 1974b). Later studies by Dement and his colleagues suggested that central nervous system development may be related to, if not dependent upon, dreaming sleep (Roffwarg, Muzio, and Dement, 1966). Dement's studies thus confirmed the damaging effects of dream deprivation and offered positive evidence that we need to dream as much as we need to sleep. This suggested to him that we sleep so that we may dream rather than, as Freud believed, that we dream in order to sleep.

Such drives as hunger, sex, aggression, and fear originate in the philogenetically old cerebral cortex and its related nuclei, the limbic system: what MacLean refers to as "the old mammalian brain" as opposed to the neocortex, or "the new mammalian brain" (MacLean, 1963, cited by Ephron and Carrington, 1967, p. 88). "This section of the brain . . . is highly activated during REM sleep" (Ephron and Carrington, 1967, p. 88). As Fisher (1965) pointed out, the pontolimbic system, which regulates REM sleep, is closely related to the limbic circuits activating these drives (hunger, sex, aggression, fear). Thus, as elaborated by Ephron and Carrington, "a spread of limbic excitation during REM sleep may be reflected behaviorally in the sucking responses in infants seen at this time, penile erections, and other reactions suggesting a heightening of primary drive states. It seems likely, in fact, that limbic excitation supplies much of the drive force behind the REM dream" (1967, pp. 88–89). These researchers postulated: "The REM dream might be seen as taking the raw impulses released by limbic structures and converting them into concrete images and organized concepts of significance to the dreamer. The volcanic violence, the terror, the rampant sexuality, and the body hungers originating in primitive areas cannot serve the survival–adaptive process of man unless image-formation renders them manageable" (Ephron and Carrington, 1967, p. 89).

Rechtschaffen and Kales (1968) further revised the phases of sleep to what is in general use among sleep and dream researchers today. They correlated them with EEG characteristics and with general physiological states. *Stage 0, Wakefulness with Eyes Closed:* alpha waves in the EEG, high muscle tone; *stage 1, Falling Asleep:* beta and theta waves, slow eye movements, relaxed muscle tone; *stage 2, Sleep:* theta and delta waves, lower muscle tone; *stage 3, Deeper Sleep:* 20 to 50 percent of delta waves; *stage 4, Deepest Sleep:* above 50 percent of delta waves, highest threshold of arousal, lowest muscle tone, secretion of growth hormones. Stages 2 to 4 are NREM states. There are regular bursts of REM states during stage 1, and during those bursts there is increase in blood pressure, muscle tone and heart rate, and tumescence of the penis or clitoris. The cycle of sleep staging was found to be fairly constant within the eight-hour sleep period, with the average 25-year-old adult having from two to four cycles in the following sequence: 1-2-3-4-3-2-REM.

As it shall be seen in the course of this book, a majority of these findings confirm scientifically what had been solely speculative or conjectural insights on Freud's part. Freud believed that when a person is deeply asleep and not dreaming, external stimulations are either not responded to, or they awaken the sleeper (see chapter 4). He believed that the dream's thoughts are primarily rendered visually, through the dream work operation which he referred to, at various times, as "concrete pictorial representation," "plastic representation," and "dramatization" (see chapter 5). In this, Freud anticipated by over fifty years the findings of Aserinsky and Kleitman (1953) and those of Dement and

Kleitman (1957) regarding REM sleep. Freud believed that the latent dream is represented metaphorically in the manifest dream through the psychological operations of the dream work; there are neurological parallels of these psychodynamic processes in findings that lower brain structures interact with higher cortical areas during REM sleep, confirmed by the work of Roffwarg, Muzio, and Dement (1966), as well as contemporary studies cited below.

Freud believed that the drives of the raw id provide the main impetus for the formation of a dream (chapters 2 and 4). Ephron and Carrington (1967) believed that the REM dream originated from the raw impulses of the limbic system. Freud (see chapters 4 and 5) believed that the censorship and dream work shield the socialized conscious ego from too direct an experience of the primitive id drives. Ephron and Carrington (1967) postulated that image formation renders the violent feelings originating in the limbic areas more manageable, thereby insuring human survival and adaptive processes. The research of Roffwarg, Muzio, and Dement (1966), elaborating the ontogenetic development of the sleep–dream cycle and its functions for CNS development, in effect, ruled out the commonly held myth that gastrointestinal disturbances, or the food eaten the night before, produce dreams; Freud had said the same some fifty-two years earlier. While Dement (1960) postulated that we sleep so that we may dream (sleep as the guardian of the dream) and Freud believed that we dream in order to sleep (the dream as the guardian of sleep), Ephron and Carrington suggested that both statements are accurate. In one of their studies, they discussed the sleep-preserving function of dreams (1967, p. 90). In another, they took exception to the shift in emphasis away from this important dreaming function. They said: "The freudian [sic] hypothesis of the dream as the 'guardian of sleep' has fallen into increasing disfavor with sleep researchers. Little attention is now devoted to the possibility that dreaming *among other things* may represent an attempt to cope with concurrent stimuli so as to preserve sleep in a generalized sense" (1970).

Ephron and Carrington cited Head (1923) who had used the term *vigilance* to describe "a high-grade neurophysiological efficiency." Their research suggested that this vigilance "varies with the state of the organism, the level of vigilance being gauged by the extent to which at any given moment, the activity of a particular portion of the central nervous system exhibits signs of integration and purposive adaptation" (1966, p. 502). A state of vigilance (which includes a sense of orientation in space and time, processed sensory inputs, and goal directedness) is essential for survival. All of these vigilance functions are possible only with a degree of ego integration which is not found in NREM sleep (1967, pp. 85–87). During REM sleep, a degree of ego reintegration occurs (Ephron and Carrington, 1970, p. 88). They further suggested that the REM process "reinstates cortical tonus through providing afferentiation to the deafferentiated cortex following NREM sleep," and that "by means of imagery-formation, it sharpens the capacity of the organism to maintain a sense of orientation adequate for survival purposes. . . ." They continued: "[T]he REM dream might be seen as a compromise, providing the cortex with an arousal substitute while still permitting sleep to continue" (Ephron and Carrington, 1967, p. 90). This too is highly consistent with Freud's view of dreams as the guardian of sleep and his view of the dream as a compromise product.

The work of Ephron and Carrington (1966) is further correlated with Freud's theory of dreams. NREM sleep "is characterized by functional deafferentiation; lowered cortical tonus; reduced vigilance; general disorganization of associative processes." In contrast, during REM sleep there is "massive activation in the sensory receiving areas of the brain which occurs in the relative absence of any external sensory input." A few lines later they suggested that REM sleep "may approximate a state of endogenous afferentiation." They cited correlative findings which suggested that bursts of impulses emanating from a "REM Sleep Center" ascend to the thalamus, whence they go to the sensory receiving areas in the cortex (1966, pp. 510–511). This is neurophysiological confirmation of Freud's idea that the dreamer's consciousness (in neurophysiological terms: the sensory-receiving areas of the brain) is not open to external stimulations, but is open to stimulations from within; that is, from the id and the unconscious (in neurophysiological terms, the somatic–affective relay processes of the limbic system).

Ephron and Carrington (1966) continued: "Hallucinations (usually either visual or auditory) have been reported to occur in certain persons under conditions of experimental sensory deprivation . . . and it is not unusual for persons subjected to reduced sensory input to greet these visions as a form of welcome relief from monotony" (p. 511). Citing the work of Miller (Miller, 1962), they stated, "In similar manner, explorers, prisoners, and others in states of natural isolation are frequently reported to welcome their hallucinations" (1966, p. 511). Ephron and Carrington postulated that with diminished stimulation, stimulations of any kind may be avidly sought. They suggested that hallucinations may "perform a necessary *replacement function*. If so, an organism deprived of sensory input might be regarded as creating its own input." They concluded that in a similar manner, the experience of dreaming is a form of recovery, following upon the functional deafferentiation of NREM sleep (1966, pp. 511–512). This is consistent with Freud's view of dreams as originating from within the intrapsychic world.[3]

Freudian psychoanalysis and dream theory have been attacked as a theory, as a treatment technique, as a philosophy. One might criticize these critics for unilateral commitment to left-brain thinking, for lack of awareness about the importance of right-brain thinking, for their commitment to a post-Cartesian Cartesianism of "I measure, therefore I am." Or better, one can remind oneself that contemporary neurologists and neuroscientists are confirming many of Freud's basic tenets and many of Freud's intuitions, not only about dreams and dreaming, but also about the body–mind connection, proving on a neurological basis much of what Freud, limited by the unsophisticated neurology of his day, could only suggest conjecturally.

*In 1895, Freud had just begun to uncover the powerful role of unconscious processes and, as had most nineteenth century

---

[3]References to Ephron and Carrington may seem to have a disproportionately larger share than references to other authors. Although I had no part whatsoever in their research, Dr. Ephron, whom I knew personally, shared with me much of his thinking about their work.

*The remainder of this chapter was written almost entirely by Lois Ann Cipriano, M.S., M.S.W., psychoanalyst and member of the faculty of the Mount Sinai School of Medicine, New York City.

neuropsychiatrists, he first tried to understand the relationship between the unconscious and conscious behavior in neurological terms. But the connections between body and mind proposed by the neurologists and neurophysiologists of his time were not consistent with his evolving discoveries about the unconscious. In a noble attempt at resolving the Cartesian dualism dominating the world of science at the time, he began his *Project for a Scientific Psychology* (1895), in which he tried to explicate the relationship between the unconscious and conscious experience in neurological terms. Correlatively, in his clinical work with hysterics, he was trying to understand bodily symptomatology in psychological terms. His *Project* was a magnificent, heroic attempt, but a futile one: he hypothesized body–mind connections that the neuroscience of his time could not corroborate. Still, in December 1896, in a letter to Fliess, Freud addressed the ontological problem of body–mind integration (Bonaparte, Freud, A., and Kris, 1954, p. 181 n. 2). He alluded to Fliess's organological studies, paralleling them with his own psychological researches: the "in-between" he speculated, would require a hypothesis. In what many fail to recognize as a related initiative, he began *The Interpretation of Dreams*; a related endeavor, because today we may well regard this work also as Freud's attempt to understand the "in-between," to understand the dream precisely as the integrating road between body-brain and mind, the royal road of dreams and dreaming, capable of revealing the nature and meaning of pathways which integrate somatic and neurological processes in the ontological evolution of mind. The integrating hypotheses which Freud formulated speculatively in *The Project* and *The Interpretation of Dreams* nearly one hundred years ago are indeed now being discovered by late twentieth century neuroscience.

Of course, contemporary neuroscience has discovered a brain that the neurology of Freud's day knew little about. The brain written about today by Oliver Sacks or Gerald M. Edelman is not the brain of nineteenth century neurology. Those early neurologists were explicitly Cartesians, grounded in the physiology of brain. Sacks' brain is one with a "soul" (Sacks, 1990b), an unconscious mind; his neurology is a neurology of the whole person (body and "soul"), not just localized cerebral lesions. In these views, the brain is not a computer, but an ever evolving, self-organizing system, with infinite variability; not hardwired and precise as a computer, but even more capable of categorizing, abstracting, and generalizing with personal meaning. This recently "discovered" brain has ten billion nerve cells, the most specialized cells of the roughly two hundred different types of human cells, functioning through one million billion synapses. Many of these synapses are "silent": there are continuous changes in the patterning or mapping of their silent communications, enabling immense variability of human responses.

Despite the many integrating hypotheses which underscore and pervade all of Freud's thinking on dreams, early researchers after him, as well as more contemporary neuroscientists, reflecting the subtleties of Cartesian reductionism, have tended toward one or the other horn of a bifurcated view of dreams. In these views the dream either solves current problems or it expresses unconscious wish-fulfillment. The dream is either derived from higher cortical functions or it is a neurobiological frenzy generated by brain stem activity. The dream is either dependent on right-brain visualization during REM sleep or it is steered by left-brain rules of language and cognition. The dream is either a meaningful psychological product of unconscious mental activity or its purpose is to forget an overload of short-term remembrances.

These polarities are not consistent with a careful reading of Freud and his meaning. Freud's is a theory of mind-embodiment—not only in brain, but in body. A review of contemporary neuropsychological studies, if understood from the phenomenological perspective of mind-embodiment, in great measure supports Freud's hypotheses regarding the nature of dreams as a *compromise formation* between conscious and unconscious content; and as an *integration of body and mind*, soma and psyche, in the formulation of personal meaning.

When Wilder Penfield explored the neural substrates of consciousness, he postulated a neural mechanism of memory integration that "lies not in the new brain but in the old . . . between the cerebral cortex and above the midbrain" (1938, p. 442). He viewed memory as a passive process, often comparing the brain to the workings of a computer (Sacks, 1990b). He postulated what he called "fossilized memories," that may remain in the cortex, dormant, asleep, but which can become stimulated under specific conditions (Sacks, 1990a).This perspective, Oliver Sacks believes, fueled Penfield's persistent brain–spirit dualism, until his death in 1976 (Sacks, 1990b).

But not all neuropsychiatrists were guided by this dichotomy. For some, dormant memories might become dreams. Ostow (1954), in his research with organically impaired patients at Mount Sinai Hospital in New York, suggested that a fantasy or dream may participate integrally as both "part of a temporal lobe seizure, and simultaneously a nodal point in an extensive psychodynamic system." For Ostow, the patient is the *mindful* director of his or her physiology and psychology, trying to express personal meaning. Unique to his methodology, Ostow integrated ongoing psychological assessment of each patient with the organological diagnosis of neurological impairment.

In the early sixties, researchers at the University of Chicago demonstrated the interrelatedness of NREM content and REM mentation (Rechtschaffen, Vogel, and Shaikun, 1963). Freud believed that day residues connect, through trains of thought, to nodal points of latent content in the unconscious dream thoughts. The findings of Rechtschaffen and his associates suggested that one psychical function of the recurrent alternation of NREM and REM stages throughout the night is precisely to enable this connection between recent events in the dreamer's waking life and latent thoughts. These researchers did not regard dreams as isolated productions; rather they "emerge as the most vivid and memorable part of a larger fabric of interwoven mental activity during sleep." This confirms the compromise formation, notably of day residues with latent content, in the formation of the dream.

In a fascinating study by Roffwarg, Herman, Bowe-Anders, and Tauber (1978, cited by Winson, 1985, pp. 210–212), researchers asked subjects to wear red-tinted goggles continuously during waking hours. They found that red-tinted coloration pervaded dream images increasingly as days passed, and increasingly into levels of REM sleep through succeeding nights. This confirms Freud's thoughts about the integration of day residues with latent dream thoughts. Some dream sequences intermixed both red-tinted and noncolored images: indicating the integration of old

memories with new, and attesting to the complex processes involved in dreams (Winson, 1985).

The occurrence of hypnagogic "dreams" prompted several
studies regarding the nature of mentation during this period.
Foulkes and Vogel (1965) found similarities between hypnagogic
"dreams" (what they termed *hallucinated dramatic episodes)* and
nocturnal REM dreaming. These episodes included symbolism
and primary process indications.

Vogel, Foulkes, and Trosman (1966) found significant correlations between the degree of ego strength in their subjects and
the capacity to tolerate regressive mental content in early onset,
hypnagogic sleep states. It is probable that variations in character
structure impact on regression as well, although this was not a
focus of these studies. It is not an overstatement of these findings,
however, to suggest that the dreamer, by virtue of the relative
strength of his ego, determines his capacity to regress, the timing
of the regression, and his utilization of somatic–neurologic processes in the formation of a dream. In an integration of mind
and body, the dreamer is the "director" of his "movie." Freud
also contrasted and compared hypnagogic states and dreams (see
chapter 5). He noted that such "hypnagogic hallucinations" appeared "quite habitually in some people," alluding to a characteristic capacity in some individuals to produce these images (1900,
p. 31). Recounting the researches of Maury (1878), Freud also
distinguished between "hypnagogic hallucinations" and dreams,
the former being characterized by rapidly changing visual images
which differ from the associatively connected, more elaborated
scenes of the night's dream (1900, pp. 31–32).

Recent study at the University of Bologna suggests that the
same mechanisms of dream formation operate in REM and hypnagogic sleep states, but at different levels of cognitive engagement (Cicogna, Cavallero, and Bosinelli, 1991). Again, there is
confirmation of ego facilitation of the dream product, but at different levels of consciousness (preconscious through unconscious). Cicogna, the senior author in this study, elaborated their
hypothesis to suggest that the hypnagogic episodes are utilized
by the waking ego to adapt to sleep at sleep onset, and to consciousness upon awakening (1994). This is consistent with Freud's
regard for the role of the preconscious (1900, p. 507).

In the midseventies, hemispheric specialization became a focus in attempts to understand the dream's vivid visual imagery and its verbal narrative (Galin, 1974). Right hemispheric functions resemble primary process thinking; left hemispheric functions resemble secondary process thinking. While the speculation of diverse functions predominantly associated with each hemisphere has been affirmed, the findings are often elaborated to suggest a Cartesian and implicitly preferential segregation of the left hemispheric analytic, linear mode from the right holistic, globally impressionistic mode. Galin speculated that dreaming was a function of right hemispheric processing and suggested an anatomical localization of the unconscious processes of repression therein (1974). Greenwood, Wilson, and Gazzaniga (1977) failed to support Galin's hypothesis, observing callosum-sectioned patients who were able to report some visual dream content upon wakening.

On the other hand, Kerr and Foulkes (1981) posited that, since a patient with extensive right hemispheric lesions was able to report sequential narratives with only fragmentary visual references, the visual mediation of dream experience could well be attributed to right hemispheric functions, distinct from the narratives accompanying the reporting of the dream. Describing a congenitally impaired patient, with " 'pure' inborn defective revisualization," who tended to "dream 'words,' " a tcam of neuroresearchers in Montreal and Cleveland suggested that the neurological substrates of cognitive thought can indeed be dissociated from those of imagistic thought (Botez, Olivier, Vezina, Botez, and Kaufman, 1985). But an earlier work of Gazzaniga and Hillyard (1971) had demonstrated that language can be utilized by a patient who suffered total left hemispherectomy: while unable to construct a sentence from the words of a song, their patient was able, nonetheless, to sing the lyrics when accompanied by music.

Kerr and Foulkes highlighted the epistemological problem in these conflicting neurological studies. "At least part of the difficulty rests on failure to consider the fact that *dreaming is a complex and integrative process* whose several components may have disparate forms of neurocognitive mediation" (1981, p. 604; emphasis added). We are reminded of Sacks' patient, Frances D, of whom he said, "Only music which moved her 'soul' had this power to move her body" (1990a, p. 62n). The very disparity among these multiple studies points to Freud's view of dreaming as the dreamer's integrating creation, a compromise formation between latent and manifest, music and lyrics, the song of the soul.

Gabel (1987) believed that the increased influence of right hemispheric activity during REM (affording a uniquely nonverbal perspective for the dreamer of his inner life) is later integrated with left hemispheric reprocessing of stored memory. But he viewed this only as an adaptive function, as information-processing relevant to conscious life.

Even among psychodynamically oriented theorists, there has been a significant shift away from the dream as unconscious wish-fulfillment toward emphasis on the functional nature of the manifest dream as a means of current problem-solving (Hawkins, 1966, 1969, 1990; Greenberg and Pearlman, 1975; Fosshage, 1987; Greenberg, 1987; Busch, 1994). The concept of "problem-solving" by dreams was addressed by Freud in a footnote added to *The Interpretation of Dreams* in 1914 (1900, pp. 579–581). He saw this function as a secondary one of preconscious waking operation: the dreamer, after having dreamed the dream, utilizes its manifest content for conscious, adaptive purposes. In a note added in 1925, after he had elaborated the unconscious functions of ego in *The Ego and the Id* (1923), Freud stated definitively that dreams are "a particular *form* of thinking, made possible by the conditions of the state of sleep" (1900, p. 506). He concluded, "The fact that dreams concern themselves with attempts at solving the problems by which our mental life is faced is no more strange than that our conscious waking life should do so; beyond this it merely tells us that that activity can also be carried on in the preconscious—and this we already knew" (p. 507). Further he asserted that the preconscious wish (deriving its content from, let us say, a current life problem) in itself is insufficient to instigate a dream (p. 553). From a neurological point of view, why would this be so?

Ironically, it is in the formulation of McCarley and Hobson (1977), aimed precisely at countering Freud's concept of wish-fulfillment, that we find support for Freud's theory. Freud's frustration with his *Project* lay not only with limitations of nineteenth century neurology, but with those of nineteenth century biology. McCarley and Hobson (1977) took issue with Freud's energy economics as an attempt to explain psychical functions. They equated his terminology with neurological functions, yet they themselves excluded the biological, somatic–neurological integration which Freud intuited, but which he, albeit frustratedly, refused to posit for his psychology. Misinterpretations of his word usages as they evolved in his theoretical elaborations (Wasserman, 1984), and mistranslations of his implicit metaphorical meanings (Bettelheim, 1983), have contributed to faulty interpretations of Freud's neurobiological insights. Freud recognized the interaction of overcathected preconscious day residues with unconscious drives: he regarded these as the psychological elaborations of neurosomatic structures.While Hobson and McCarley (1977) equate mind with brain, Freud did not.

Hobson and McCarley's "activation-synthesis hypothesis" posits that an intense and sporadic activation of the forebrain by random signals from the brain stem, pontine-geniculate-occipital cortex spikes (PGO), instigate dreaming. These PGO spikes activate neuronal mechanisms in the forebrain to synthesize brain stem information with information stored in memory, thereby constructing the dream. For Hobson and McCarley, the dream-state instigator is a clock that enables sleep. Freud had stated that dreams are the product of the overcathecting of preconscious day residues in the forebrain by overcathected unconscious drives. But for Hobson and McCarley, the dream may be regarded as a fine-tuning mechanism, the static control on your television dial. Dreaming is *random* and physiological. In their view, any psychological or emotional meaning of the dream is secondary; and even then, its function is synthetic and organizing, not disguising, as Freud suggested (Hobson and McCarley, 1977). Who sets the clock, who tunes the television, what meaning the dream has in the total economy of body-brain-mind is not addressed. Wasserman (1984) accurately targeted the inherent contradictions in their approach: while denying reductionism to their theory, they nonetheless expound its tenets in their implicit denial of psychical–somatic integration.

Subsequent research expanded their hypothesis to a *selective* control by brainstem reticular formation in processing "hallucinatory perceptions" (dreams); but this processing is viewed mechanistically (Harth and Unnikrishnan, 1985). Singer Peggy Lee voices a response to such mechanization: "If that's all there is, my friend, then let's keep dancing" (1994). More recently, Hobson has revised his theory, acknowledging a psychological significance of dreams. Winson quotes him as now recognizing a sense or plot of dreams, which results from order that is imposed on the chaos of neural signals. "That order" Hobson now believes, "is a function of our personal view of the world, our remote memories" (Winson, 1990, p. 87). Similarly, Freud had said that secondary revision, another dream-work operation, rearranges the disordered latent dream into a more logical and coherent manifest dream.

With compelling experimental evidence, Vogel (1978) questions the pervasive application of the activation–synthesis hypothesis. His studies demonstrate that dreams can occur in the absence of PGO spiking; dreams in which there is participation of brain stem activity are not necessarily accompanied by bizarre distortion; cortical areas have input into dreams; and forebrain activity (and its mental correlates) are crucial to dream sleep. In a word, brain stem pontine structures may be a necessary, but not sufficient, cause for dream-state instigation. In a very recent review of studies with neurologically impaired patients, Solms (1995) asserts that REM sleep (associated with brain stem arousal) may be correlative to, but not sufficient for, dream instigation. He demonstrates that higher forebrain mediation is required for the psychological construction of the dream. For Freud, integration is the key. Crick and Mitchison (1983) suggested that bombardment by random PGO neural signals overloads the brain and that dreams serve the function of reducing this overload. While these theorists differ from Freud in the very dissimilar conclusions they reach about the nature and meaning of dreams and dreaming, their hypothesis affords a partial neural substrate for Freud's view that dreams are a substitute for neurotic symptoms: by dreaming out our overcathected unconscious conflicts, so to speak, we avoid developing neurotic symptoms.

Labruzza (1978) challenged purely physiological hypotheses, but then posited his own subtle dualism: because they speak two separate languages, he said, neurobiological data cannot be compared with psychological. They must remain "empirically parallel." Today, with the technology afforded by magnetic resonance imaging (MRI) and positron emission tomography (PET) scans, that is no longer the case.

Winson, a neuroscientist (1985), has focused on the hippocampus and its unique theta rhythm, which appears in some mammals and not in others. The echidna is a monotreme mammal which differs notably in two respects from the rest of mammalian species including man, but is the same as man and different from all other mammals in one respect. Unlike the rest of mammalians, the echidna does not evidence REM sleep and it has an unusually large prefrontal cortex. Winson suggested that this evolution was required to compensate for a process that for other mammals is enabled in REM sleep and in survival-oriented activities. During REM and survival-oriented activities, lower mammalian species demonstrate the theta rhythm. *But this theta rhythm is not present in the echidna, nor in man.* Winson concluded that the theta rhythm is a sign of information processing in the evolutionary, small prefrontal cortex of lower mammals. The echidna has a huge prefrontal cortex because it does not process memory patterns of survival. It uses this huge brain area to continually scan its environment to guard against danger and to insure survival. On the other hand, man has evolved a neural mechanism that does process information without the use of hippocampal theta rhythm. Man has selected, in the Darwinian sense, a hippocampal structure that is able to process information from a variety of sources and to route them ("hippocampal gating") to various areas in the cortex, in memory, to insure survival. Nature, Winson postulated, has found for man a solution for integration of new experiences with old: REM sleep dreams.

In a paper that summarizes his 1985 hypotheses and formulates important conclusions, Winson (1990) stated:

> Dreams are indeed meaningful. Studies of the hippocampus (a brain structure crucial to memory), of rapid eye movement (REM) sleep and of a brain wave called theta rhythm suggest that dreaming reflects a pivotal

aspect of the processing of memory. In particular, studies of theta rhythm in subprimate animals have provided an evolutionary clue to the meaning of dreams. They appear to be the nightly record of a basic mammalian memory process: the means by which animals form strategies for survival and evaluate current experience in light of those strategies. The existence of this process may explain the meaning of dreams in human beings [p. 86].

Affirming the value of Freud's intuitions, despite nineteenth century neurological limitations, Winson goes on to state: "For reasons he could not possibly have known, Freud set forth a profound truth in his work. There is an unconscious, and dreams are indeed the 'royal road' to its understanding" (1990, p. 96).

In fascinating elaborations of dream studies and of time-differentials in processing stimuli (1985), Winson affirmed Freud's notion of repression and the neurotic conflict. REM sleep dreaming provides neural excitation for continuous physiological development of the brain in infancy, notably during critical periods of learning. His continued research affirms the significance of hippocampal activity in integrating awake events with dream sleep (Pavlides and Winson, 1989). From his implicitly Darwinian perspective: we sleep to dream, and we dream to sleep. His understanding of the dream is one of information processing by the hippocampus during REM sleep in order to integrate current experiences with old (unconscious) memories. Consciousness raising, that is, from unconscious to conscious, enables and actualizes the evolution of the individual.

Damasio (1994) focuses on the body and its continuous integrative interaction with the brain. Feelings, in his view, are not "an elusive mental quality attached to an object, but rather the direct perception of a specific landscape: that of the *body*" (p. xiv; emphasis added). Mental representation of body states, emotions, are transmitted to cortical areas via the amygdala and related thalamic structures. These somatic experiences are "marked" in corresponding mental images, "acquired dispositional representations," categorized according to their personal and social meaning for survival. While Damasio believes that Freud's theory of superego formation is reflected in his neurological theory, it is also arguably true that his "*somatic marker hypothesis*" is consistent with Freud's theory of dream symbols as the

individually selected, personally meaningful, metaphorical correlates of infantile somatic experience. For Freud, the ego is "first
and foremost a body-ego" (1923, p. 27); for Damasio, because of
the integrated neural networking of every functional brain structure, bodily based emotion is part and parcel of every cortical
cognitive process. Referring to the fallacy of disembodied dualism, Damasio calls his book *Descartes' Error.*

Damasio does not delineate the relationship of hippocampal
memory storage in this body–brain interaction, while Winson
speculates about, but does not delineate, the role of the amygdala
in information processing. Perhaps neurological studies linking
their respective hypotheses (hippocampus and amygdala, memory processing and affect) may find validation of the somatic–affective sources of unconscious wishes, elaborated in the REM
sleep dream. Dreams evolve not only from the back of our head,
but from the bottom of our heart.

Nobel Laureate Gerald M. Edelman lays a foundation for
understanding body–brain–mind evolution (1992). Edelman's
theory of neuronal group selection is the neurobiology that Freud's
theory of dreams dreams of. For Edelman, the brain is an active
and creative organ, constructing and reconstructing itself into
ever higher levels of consciousness. Initially, Darwinian selection
moves the developing individual to make choices for survival
which are based in his genetic structure (developmental selection). As life evolves, so too does the nature of his selections, now
experientially driven toward survival. Guided by affective experience, these experiential selections make use of opportunities
based on their "value-laden" potential, their capacity to insure
survival. It is as though the ever evolving individual asks in his
or her biology-neurology, "Based on my comparison to previous
somatic–affective experiences, will this response evoke survival?"
We will be inclined to select those responses that do just that. For
Freud, the drive for life, libido, prompts us to do so.

As selections are made, categories of neurological responses—grounded in bodily experiences—are formed. These
categories, these neuronal group selections, then correlate with
other categories, in "maps." These maps are continually recon-
structed as new experiences are incorporated with previous ones.
These maps are capable of constructing maps among themselves,

of their own functioning, maps of maps, categorizing along multiple layers of meaning, in a personal evolution of consciousness. (Consider Freud's notion of the overdetermined meaning of each dream element; and the process of free association in perusing these layered landscapes of meaning, from manifest to latent.) And with each new experience, neuronal groups reconstruct themselves to adapt to the new input: what Edelman terms "reentrant mapping." Experience and memory are neither stale nor static: the mind, never a passive observer, is ever reconstructing the meaning of its own experience based on integration of old memory with current input.

Edelman distinguishes between primary consciousness (bodily based and affect driven) and higher order consciousness. Groups of neurons consolidate into maps that categorize somatic experiences which have boded well for survival. Edelman believes that this neuronal categorization of "concepts" is first experienced in a bodily, preverbal way (primary consciousness): it occurs before the development of language. (Baby *experiences* mother's touch, sound of voice, and smile *in a bodily way* and neurologically categorizes the experiential "concept" of nurturing long before baby can say or know the cognitive meaning of the word *mother*.) As new input from the environment is experienced somatically, the neuronal maps recategorize, integrating these new experiences with memory (reentrant mapping). Then, new maps are formed: these are categories of meaning which are verbally and cognitively expressed. The somatic concepts of primary consciousness are then *bootstrapped* (Edelman's term) into these new maps of higher order consciousness. *Metaphor* reflects the somatic–affective experience integrated with verbal consciousness. The bodily basis of primary consciousness and its preverbal meaning are the stuff on which unconscious latent wishes are made. The ego for Freud, we are reminded again, "is first and foremost a body-ego" (1923). The bootstrapping of that preverbal experience into verbal categorizations of higher order consciousness is the aim of dream interpretation. The meaning of the dream is in the dreamer, in the bodily registered experiences that have not yet been imbued with linguistic meaning. (The latent dream, Freud said, is given words only with the later dream work operation which he called "secondary revision.") Depending on the latent wish's valence for survival, the dreamer may disguise the dream's somatic meaning with verbal, cognitive distortion. In this light, metaphor, as Freud intuited one hundred years ago, is far more than metaphorical.

Edelman's book *Bright Air, Brilliant Fire* (1992) was dedicated to Freud and Darwin. In it, Edelman affirms the unconscious and the capacity of the individual to repress when input is negatively valenced. He states:

> Freud's notion of repression is consistent with the model of consciousness presented here.... Repression, the selective inability to recall, would be subject to recategorizations that are strongly value-laden. And given the socially constructed nature of higher-order consciousness, it would be evolutionarily advantageous to have mechanisms to repress those recategorizations that threaten the efficacy of self-concepts. Circuitry that interacts with value systems exist in the hippocampus and the basal ganglia [p. 145].

Thus Edelman agrees with Freud about the adaptive value of repression, specifying neurologically (in the functions of the hippocampus) at least one process of body–mind integration (a considerably more sophisticated resolution of dualism than the one Descartes had proposed in specifying the pineal gland as a spatial location in the brain where body and mind meet). Edelman's findings on those brain structures which provide for higher order consciousness also gave him cause to agree with Freud's insights about the unconscious: "My general conclusion, important for all theories of mind, is that given the existence of acts driven by the unconscious, conclusions reached by conscious introspection may be subject to grave error" (pp. 145–146).

Two metaphorical and not so metaphorical facts: Freud discovered the meaning of dreams while vacationing at Bellevue, in the hills outside Vienna. Edelman is a *violin virtuoso*. Edelman believes that there is another significant link to our understanding of unconscious and conscious integration: he believes that the *immune system* is a *somatic communication system* that is in constant conversation with the brain, on the level of primary consciousness. Ego defenses may well be shown to be the psychological elaboration of this immunoneurological intercourse.

If he is able to demonstrate this orchestration, this magnificent symphony of the soul, we believe that the nature of the dream as the disguised communication of latent wishes may be affirmed. And so too Freud's *belle vue,* his beautiful view, of the interpretation of dreams.

2

Basic Freudian Theory of Personality Development and Structure Relevant to Dreams and Dreaming

Most of the concepts of dream theory are part of such general concepts of psychoanalysis as the theory of personality structure, the theory of personality development, and the theory of symptom formation, a solid knowledge of which is needed to understand dream formation. These concepts will be discussed in terms of what is immediately relevant to dreams and dreaming and in terms of this book's intent to elaborate and clarify Freud's ideas.

FREUD'S DRIVE THEORY

1. Psychic life is energized by drives which impart motion and direction to all psychological processes. In psychoanalytic literature, the words *instinct* and *drive* are used interchangeably (Brenner, 1973), but the word *drive* is preferable because, after the first few weeks of life, what drives do for the human psyche differs from what instincts do in lower life forms. An instinct is an innate response to stimulations, a response characterized by a stereotyped behavior. This behavior may be, and usually is, more complex than a simple reflex response, but at least in life forms that have developed a nervous system, still comprises a stimulus carried through the peripheral sensory nervous system, a state of excitation in the central nervous system, and a motor response

carried through the peripheral motor nervous system and a muscle group. A drive is also innate, but its activation results in a much more complicated response. At the earlier id stages, the resulting behavior is as stereotypical and random as the one energized by instinct; but at the later id stages (when the primary process functions have developed), and increasingly as the ego develops, activation of drives in itself does not include a motor response but only the state of heightened central excitation. What will happen will depend on the id's primary process functions or the ego's secondary processes.

2. Freud first believed there were sexual and self-preservative drives, but he later postulated (1920) the existence of sexual and aggressive drives, the former energizing the loving, self-preservative, and sexual components of mental activities and behavior, the latter energizing the destructive components. The words *Eros* and *Thanatos* (for, respectively, the ancient Greek god of love and the ancient Greek personification of death) are used to represent, respectively, sexual and aggressive drives; the terms *Libido* and less commonly *Mortido* or *Destrudo* (Brenner, 1973, p. 21) represent, respectively, sexual and aggressive drives. The sexual drive, also, is sometimes said to be part of the life instinct, to indicate that for Freud, eros included not only sexual drives but all loving, self-preservative human behavior. Although this is a dualistic theory of drives, it is important to remember that, as Freud pointed out, with the possible exception of suicidal behavior, the two drives are always fused—the mixture may be prevalently erotic or prevalently aggressive; and in all observable instinctual discharges, both the sexual and aggressive drives participate: *and so do they in dreams.*

3. Drives are part of our reservoir of psychic energy and this reservoir is finite, not infinite.

4. Drives have a dynamic quality, a "force" wanting to be "discharged." They are discharged as "unconscious derivatives," which include psychological and psychosomatic symptoms and *dreams.*

5. Drives are discharged by being attached to "objects" in the interpersonal or in the intrapsychic world. Freud's word for this investment was *Besetzung;* in the psychoanalytic literature in English, the word used is *cathexis* from the Greek *Kathexis* and

Katechein, meaning to attach oneself, to hold onto, to have a hold of. When a drive can be attached to the desirable object, that drive is discharged, or gratified. The more intensely cathected an object is, the more important, the more "dear" is that object to the person cathecting it: that object is "overcathected." One can cathect an object with energies from eros, "love" that object, discharge and gratify one's erotic drives through that object; or one can cathect it with energies from *Thanatos,* "hate" that object, discharge and gratify one's aggressiveness through it. One can cathect an object directly through one's sensory and motor systems, by touching it, tasting it, smelling it, seeing it, hearing it; or by cathecting the mental representations and the memories of that object, the thoughts, the fantasies, the images about the object, *the dream* of that object.

When one has little or no interest in a given object, that object is "undercathected" or "decathected." Parts of one's body can be cathected (or decathected) with the energies of *eros* or *thanatos:* one has "a sense" of one's body, knows that one's hand is one's own hand even when that hand is behind the back, because the hand is cathected with psychic energy. When feelings and sensations about parts of one's body diminish or disappear (hysterical anesthesias) or increase (hysterical paresthesias), that part of the body has been under- or overcathected; that is, psychic energies from various drives have been under- or overinvested in that part of the body. In feelings of unreality or depersonalization, psychic energy is withdrawn from one's consciousness. In dreamless sleep, parts of the cerebral cortex are decathected and the body is largely decathected (hence one cannot act out one's dreams).

6. In conscious life, drives manifest themselves as "wishes." In discussing the characteristics common to all dreams, Freud pointed out that dreams occur during sleep, which is a state of suspension of interest in the external world, when object cathexes are deactivated. It is the time for mental recuperation, although it includes remnants of wakeful mental activity. The sleeping person becomes, if anything, self-cathecting, with the unconscious ego more open to stimulation from within. During sleep, both physical and psychological stimulations, exogenous and endogenous, are for the most part visually represented (for congenitally blind

persons such stimulations are represented by other sensory means), not through verbal representations or thoughts. Like daydreams, dreams are "wishes." This concept rendered Freud's dreams theory unacceptable to most of his contemporaries. This was before his theories on the id and the unconscious had become acceptable. Freud's psychoanalytic theory had been a truly Copernican revolution. By putting the id and the unconscious rather than the self and consciousness at the core of personality (as Copernicus had done by putting the sun rather than the earth at the center of the solar system), Freud had been as much a revolutionary as Copernicus. Also, most of his contemporaries took Freud's idea that "dreams are wishes" simply as a hedonistic theory, a naive wish-theory. To understand his dream theory in its complexity, one must see it within the entire context of psychoanalytic theory and especially within the wish–counterwish conflict theory (the theory of the neurotic conflict).

7. Drives can be modified, that is, they are capable of "vicissitudes," capable of displacement as they attach themselves to various objects and express themselves through various aims. This is true in waking life: id drives may show themselves through (a) behavior which the ego finds acceptable and consonant with one's conscious philosophy of life (i.e., "ego syntonic behavior"); (b) behaviors which the ego finds unacceptable and dissonant from one's conscious philosophy of life (i.e., ego alien or "ego dystonic behavior"); or (c) more or less defended unconscious derivatives. That drives can be modified is true in dreams, where id drives (the "dream thoughts") will attach themselves, through condensation and displacements to a variety of unconscious objects and preconscious "day residues."

8. Last and most relevant to symptom formation and dream formation, drive theory sees mental life and behavior psychodynamically; that is, as a continuous interplay of urging and checking forces, of drives and counterdrives (defenses), of cathexes and countercathexes, each of the opposing forces endowed with more or with less of the finite psychic energy available to the person.

FREUD'S TOPOGRAPHIC THEORY

In 1915 Freud described the topographic theory, postulating that psychological processes may occur at any of three levels of awareness: unconscious, preconscious, or conscious. The theory concerns these three levels or "layers," hence the word *topographic.* Even though the existence of a "subconscious" had been hypothesized before him, Freud was the first to emphasize the qualitative differences between the two kinds of nonconsciousness, the unconscious and the preconscious. He pointed out a psychodynamically qualitative difference, which has little to do with when a conscious experience becomes unconscious or preconscious, and has instead to do with whether that experience had been a conflictual or a nonconflictual one; that is, whether the experience had or had not been accompanied by anxiety, guilt, shame, or disgust.

The following points are immediately relevant to Freudian dream theory:

1. Experiences that have become unconscious, such as unconscious memories, are not dead skeletons in our psychic closets, but memories that are endowed with the psychic energy of drives. These unconscious memories clamor for expression and press toward consciousness and the external world to be discharged as feelings, thoughts, actions, or dreams. Freud referred to this as the "dynamic" influence of the unconscious (1912b, p. 262; 1923, p. 15). These unconscious memories may gain expression as "irruptions of the id" (A. Freud, 1936, p. 11), or almost uncamouflaged derivatives in highly regressed psychotic states (for instance, hebephrenic schizophrenia). In a majority of cases, they gain expression as highly modified unconscious derivatives: as ego alien or ego syntonic symptoms, as fantasies and screen memories, and, as dreams. *The Psychopathology of Everyday Life* (1901b) gives fascinating examples of everyday occurrences that are generally taken for granted or dismissed as accidental and meaningless, but which are actually psychologically determined incidents, unconscious derivatives.

2. Psychological processes occurring at unconscious and conscious levels follow different ways of thinking and different

conceptual modes, such as nonlogical thinking at the unconscious level, logical thinking at the conscious level, a little of each at the hypnagogic and hypnapompic levels (the levels of consciousness before falling asleep and before being fully awake). Thus, at the level of dream formation (when the latent dream is formed and most of the dream work changes the latent dream into the manifest dream), "prelogic predicate thinking" dominates; at the level of "secondary revision," chronologically the last operation of the dream work, some of the characteristics of conscious thinking begin to appear; at the level at which the dream is remembered, recounted, or written down, the characteristics of conscious thinking prevail in full.

3. While there are fairly clear-cut, psychodynamic, *qualitative* differences between unconscious and preconscious, there also are *quantitative* differences in depth of nonconsciousness. There is a sharp difference between the clarity of high noon and the darkness of midnight; but also degrees of darkness and light as one proceeds from dawn to noon to dusk to midnight. Similarly, there are degrees of nonconsciousness. There is the deep nonconsciousness of coma; the nonconsciousness of never-to-be-recovered memories of experiences one had in infancy and before language development; the nonconsciousness of conflict-laden unconscious memories; the nonconsciousness of something which is on the tip of one's tongue. There are degrees between nonconsciousness and consciousness: the deep nonconsciousness of dreamless sleep, the lighter nonconsciousness of REM sleep, the cloudy consciousness of hypnapompic states, the semiconsciousness of hypnagogic states, the cloudy consciousness of a healthy meal accompanied by wine, the less sharp consciousness following a heavy meal, the crystal sharpness of full consciousness.

FREUD'S STRUCTURAL THEORY

In 1923 Freud described his structural theory in which he arranged the mind's functions into "constructs," each having specific characteristics and adaptive functions. He called these constructs id, ego, and superego. Although quite distinct, the three constructs are functionally related: in terms of a systems perspective, they are psychodynamically interdependent parts of a whole, the human mind. There is much in the structural theory that is immediately relevant to Freudian dream theory, especially the concepts having to do with the id and its primary process functions. The following five points are immediately relevant to Freud's dream theory:

The Mind as a Whole

The mind, that abstraction representing the psychological part of the whole a human being is, developed, philogenetically and ontogenetically, in order to better assure adaptation and survival.

At the beginning of philogenetic or ontogenetic life, one finds a most simple, undifferentiated and impersonal psyche (the word *mind* is too advanced for such a primitive system), essentially a storehouse of energy. Its sole function is to maintain constancy (homeostasis) whenever constancy is threatened by internal or external stimulations. It does so through instantaneous instinctual discharges. This earliest psychoplasm is so undifferentiated that Freud aptly called it *"Es"* (German for *it*). In English-language psychoanalytic literature we call it *id*, the neutral pronoun from the Latin. In nonpsychoanalytic English we would call it *it*, neither *he* nor *she*. The id is "a construct," that is, an abstraction, the collective name, the umbrella term for a number of psychological functions and processes having, among others, some of the following common characteristics: (1) the energy of these functions and processes is in a highly mobile state and therefore easily displaced from one object to another; (2) these functions and processes are not governed by reason, logic, ethics, or morality; (3) they want immediate and undelayed gratification according to a primordial principle of life that Freud called the "Pleasure Principle" (1911, pp. 213–226). The id fulfills its role through two functions: the *reflex functions* from the very beginning of life (the earliest id), and a little later in infancy, the *primary process functions*. The primary process functions are quite central to dream formation and will be discussed shortly.

Advanced as the primary process functions of the id are when compared to the id's reflex functions, they cannot provide for adaptation and survival except for brief periods of time. Thus, a more differentiated psychoplasm evolves, capable of guiding the young child to less impulsive types of behavior. This psyche is unique to each person, much more "personal"; it is called the ego, the better to connote its uniqueness and distinctiveness. The common denominator of all the psychological functions and processes going under the umbrella term of *ego* includes the capacity to consider whether a given response is realistic (responses are still oriented toward homeostasis and pleasure). Therefore, it includes the capacity to tolerate delays before the desired gratification is obtained. And it includes the capacity to function under the "Reality Principle" (1911, pp. 213–226). The ego fulfills its role through the *secondary process functions*, which are coordinated, planned, and increasingly reasoned responses to stimulations.

But ego-coordinated, realistic behavior is not sufficient for human beings, who live according to socialized and acculturated life norms. A further evolution of personality is necessary whereby personality functions develop, having the capacity to direct behavior according to one more assessment of the appropriateness of possible responses. The only question the id-directed psychoplasm asks is, Is this pleasurable? The ego-coordinated personality asks two questions, Is this pleasurable and is this realistic? A third question is, If I engage in this or that response, will I retain or will I lose my parent's love? This further evolution results in the development of personality functions imposing their judgment on the feasibility of a given response, superimposing it upon the judgment which had been rendered by the reality-oriented ego. Freud called this third construct the superego, to connote its capacity to overrule the ego's decisions, to impose its primacy over the ego, and to give advice and consent to the ego. The superego has this power, of course, because it is formed through the internalization of the child's parent and has therefore the same life and death power over the child that parents have. All three constructs, id, ego, and superego, participate in dream formation; but the id and especially the primary process functions of the later id are most immediately relevant to dreams and dreaming.

The Id and Its Primary Process Functions

The reflex functions of the earlier id provide adaptation and survival by the instantaneous gratification of instinctual drives through "reflexes." The id's reflex functions utilize the *sensory system* (the afferent, centripetal components of the peripheral nervous system, and the sensory cells of the central nervous system) and the *motor system* (the motor cells of the central nervous system, the efferent centrifugal components of the peripheral nervous system, and the muscles to which these elements are connected).

Through the reflex functions, the id provides for a wide range of adaptive responses to internal and external stimulations, such as all the vegetative nervous system's adaptations to internal or external physiochemical changes (sweating, flushing of skin, temperature adjustment, etc.); digestion of stomach contents, emptying of the bladder or intestine; and for such a variety of adaptive responses as the kicking off of a blanket if that blanket causes discomfort, the baby's turning of the head toward a sound, the contracting of the pupils if the light is painfully bright, crying when the infant is in a state of discomfort, sucking the breast when the breast stimulates the infant's lips and the infant is hungry. Through the reflex functions, the id provides the energy for a great number of adaptive, homeostatic responses (many of which may be highly interpersonal in context but still are, nevertheless, solely instinctual, automatic, unreasoned, and narcissistic).

The *primary process functions* of the later id provide for that which the id's reflex functions cannot provide. The id's reflex functions do make the infant cry when in a state of distress, and this may result in the infant's caretaker coming to the rescue; but the infant's cry, in and of itself, does not cause that to happen. The id's reflex functions do make babies signal mother that they need to be held and cooed at and crooned with, but that signal also will not, in and of itself, make that occur. The id's reflex functions do prompt infants to suck on the breast when the nipple is put in their mouth, but those functions, in and of themselves, will not produce the breast. Similarly, the id's reflex functions can adequately empty the stomach (throwing up) when the stomach is painfully full, but cannot produce food to fill it when it is painfully empty. The id's reflex functions can adequately relieve the heart (crying) when it is painfully full, but cannot fill it with love when it feels painfully lonely. But, as we shall see, the id's primary process functions do these things.

The id's primary process functions can be defined as those primitive but highly adaptive psychological functions that perceive (through many senses), record (i.e., remember), and form mental images (at the appropriate time) of those objects and object relations through which drives essential to our biological and psychological survival have been gratified. As the definition implies, the id's primary process functions, in addition to the motor and sensory systems utilized by the reflex functions, utilize the perceptual, memory, and sensory systems. These systems have the capacity to perceive those objects and object relations and transactions that had permitted a drive's discharges, the capacity to remember what had been perceived, and the capacity to reproduce it in one's imagination, to flash it to one's consciousness, when needed.

The Three Systems Utilized in Primary Process Functions

The Perceptual System

In the state of awareness that accompanies most emergencies, all the infant's senses are at peak receptivity. If the baby is lucky and a loving caretaker hears the crying, something does happen and the emergency is over: if, for instance, the emergency is need of food and love, the infant is lovingly fed. When this happens, the infant's perception will record having been lovingly fed and record it through many senses: the sight and smell of the caretaker, the taste of what is put in the mouth, the fullness of the milk flowing into oneself. This is the beginning of *one* primary process of being lovingly fed.

Primary process perception is a *primitive* perception, one based on prelogic–predicate thinking, rather than logical thinking. The adaptive advantages of the development of perception, primitive though this perception might be, are enormous. "Perception is the mental representation of an object" (Hall, 1979, p. 24). It may also be the mental representation of a happening, for instance, being fed. Now the baby "knows" what has to happen when the emergency strikes, what has to be perceived for the emergency to be over; now the baby begins to "know" that for different kinds of emergencies, different "happenings" need to occur. Were it not for primary process functions, a person could satisfy his needs only through aimless trial-and-error behavior (Hall, 1979, p. 26).

The Memory System

But besides "knowing" what has to happen and has to be perceived for a given emergency to be over, the baby has also developed the capacity to remember what has happened and what was perceived, which gives the baby the feeling of having a measure of understanding and control over its fate and the mysterious happenings of existence. Now the infant "knows" that when hunger for food and love strikes, he or she must again see her (mother, the caretaker), hear her, smell her, taste her, fill up with her, exactly as it had happened the previous time. "A memory image is the mental representation of a perception. . . . The process which produces a memory image of an object that is needed to reduce a tension . . . is the primary process" (Hall, 1979, p. 25).

The Imaging System

Having developed the capacity to perceive and remember, infants also discover the capacity to reproduce in their imagination what they had perceived and remembered. They have now come a long way in mastering frustrations and deprivation, at least for a brief period of time. Thanks to prelogic–predicate thinking, both characteristics of id and primary process functions, *imagined gratification* (the image of the object, i.e., the image of milk in their minds), and *real gratification* (the actual object, i.e., actual milk in their mouths) are one and the same. Freud called this "perceptual identity" (1900, p. 566).

Prelogic–Predicate Thinking

Prelogic–predicate thinking is so called because in the infant's and child's cognitive development, it antedates logical thinking. In logical thinking, identical objects are identical and different objects are different. In prelogic–predicate thinking, identities between different objects are established "magically," that is, simply because we wish it to be so when the "predicates" of different objects are identical. In prelogic–predicate thinking, breast and thumb, thumb and lollipop are perceived as identical, because one wishes them to be so, and because they share one common predicate: they can all be sucked. In primitive perception, furthermore, objects or persons are perceived not in terms of their intrinsic, objective, inherent attributes but in terms of how one is changed by those objects or persons. Thus milk is perceived not as something intrinsically liquid, white, and sweet, but as one's own tongue covered with milk, as one's own mouth full of milk; a hostile, abusive parent is perceived not as a hostile abusive parent per se, but as oneself abused and victimized by that parent. All this and the resulting perceptual identity are very important in both symptom formation and dream formation.

Prelogic–predicate thinking is both the fabric, the internal grammar of (1) delusional thinking; (2) the thinking underlying young children's playing behavior; (3) the "logic" of prejudice; (4) the thinking behind the displacement of instinctual objects in normal development; and (5) the thinking behind the displacement of instinctual objects in symptom formation. A brief discussion of these will be helpful in order to better understand prelogic–predicate thinking in dream formation.

1. *Delusional Thinking.* In logical thinking, A = A, and B = B. In the prelogic–predicate thinking found in schizophrenics, A = B if A and B have one predicate or attribute in common. Thus A (i.e., Freud) is a psychoanalyst ("psychoanalyst" being a predicate of Freud), B (i.e., Dr. X) is a psychoanalyst ("psychoanalyst" being a predicate of Dr. X). Then A and B, Freud and Dr. X, have one predicate in common, that of being psychoanalysts. Ergo, delusional thinking will conclude: B = A, Dr. X is Freud.

2. *The Thinking Underlying Young Children's Playing Behavior.* A child is flapping her arms the way a bird flaps its wings. Now the child has created a predicate in common with B, the motion of flapping. Ergo, "I am a bird," the child playfully concludes.

3. *The Thinking Underlying Prejudice.* The color of fire is red. Both fire and the man's hair have in common the attribute of redness. Ergo, that man's character is fiery; all red-haired persons have a fiery temper.

4. *The Displacement of Instinctual Objects in Normal Development:* Breasts, thumbs, and lollipops have one predicate in common, all three can be sucked on. Therefore, in being weaned, the infant can move from breast to thumbsucking, and later from thumbsucking to sucking lollipops.

5. *Displacement of Instinctual Objects in Symptom Formation:* A male patient, a homosexual hairdresser, was unconsciously enraged at women. One of his fantasies was that he had several penises with which he wished to hit and strangle his clients (i.e., his preoedipal mother). He periodically suffered with a severe rash of his fingers, a conversion symptom. The internal grammar of the symptom was: the penis, when angry and erect, gets red and swollen. The fingers, when he had the rash, are red and swollen. A = B: "My swollen and red fingers are my erect and angry penises and I am hitting and strangling women with them."

A Summary of Primary Process Functions

Primary process functions are the first fantasy or daydream (good or bad) of infants, when awake; their first dream or nightmare, when asleep. It is good or bad: a beautiful daydream or a nightmare, depending upon how lovingly or unlovingly the infant had been ministered to. The primary process is the multisensory image of the *previous* gratification of a drive: a good gratification making the infant experience a "Nirvana" of pleasure or a turbulent gratification that satisfies basic biological requirements but is not very pleasurable. Respectively and correspondingly, the primary process is an ecstatic, pleasant image, daydream, or dream or a turbulent, unpleasant, nightmarish image, daydream, or dream.

Primary process is the imagined, or dreamed, gratification of a frustrated, ungratified drive. Since, through prelogic–predicate thinking, the image of the object and the object itself are the same, when engaging in primary process functions, babies flash to consciousness the image of the previous gratifications of that drive whose gratification is now being frustrated. If the current frustration and deprivation concern hunger for milk and mother, babies when awake flash to their consciousness the memory images of when they had been fed before, imagine and hallucinate those remembered images; when asleep, babies flash those images to the special consciousness of REM sleep and dream of being fed. The imagined or dreamed feeding is as good, at least for a period of time, as the actual feeding. Through the imaging components of the primary process functions, the sounds, taste, smell (and in dreams predominantly the sight) of being fed are reproduced as faithfully as the id's primitive perceptual, memory, and imaging capacities permit: and the baby is temporarily at peace. This is one way that the id is, or can imagine itself to be, "omnipotent." It can have anything it wants; it can have it when it wants it; it can have it, in lucky circumstances, realistically; it can have it, in bad times, illusorily, through primary process functions.

There are as many primary processes of needs and wishes as there are needs and wishes to gratify. The infant needs and wishes to be fed, to have his or her diapers changed, to be held, to be made to feel physically and emotionally warm and secure, to be relieved of all sorts of mysterious physical pains and discomforts. For each of these needs and wishes, there is a corresponding primary process. But within each drive, need, and wish and its corresponding primary process, there are qualitative differences in the actual gratification and, consequently and correspondingly, in its reimagined gratification; that is, in its primary process reproduction. This makes an important difference between "good" (pleasurable, satisfactory) and "bad" experiences and their corresponding primary processes; between "good" and "bad" daydreams and fantasies of *past* gratifications; between "good" (hopeful and optimistic) and "bad" daydreams and fantasies of *anticipated*, hoped for gratifications, between good dreams and nightmares.

Primary process functions are an important development in the growth of personality and in the evolution of the id. They significantly improve the still primitive adaptive capacities of the id's reflex functions (with its motor and sensory systems) through the important addition of perception, memory, and imagination systems. Primary process functions add significant new tools to the infant's adaptive equipment giving infants a measure of control over their fate, a measure of understanding of their world, and a sense of knowing what it is they must look for to obtain relief. They give the infant the capacity temporarily to obtain relief by imagining it or dreaming it. Because of all this, primary process functions are central to dream formation.

Primary processes play a central role in such psychological and psychobiological phenomena as daydreams and fantasies, hallucinations, and sensory privation. This will be discussed in the Appendix, to further clarify the role of primary process functions in dream formation.

3

The Theory of the Neurotic Conflict: Basic Freudian Theory of Symptom Formation

In *The Psychoanalytic Theory of Neurosis,* Fenichel says, "There are many ways to treat neuroses but only one way to understand them" (1945, p. 554). The theory of the neurotic conflict brings together operationally and clinically the three concepts (drive, topographic theory, and structural theory) discussed in chapter 2. It will be discussed only in terms of symptom formation; and symptom formation only in terms of what is immediately relevant to dream formation, and in terms of the parallels between symptom formation and dream formation. The basic references for this chapter are Freud (1926a) and Fenichel (1945, pp. 129–142).

WHAT THE NEUROTIC CONFLICT IS

In waking life, drives can be discharged into feelings, thoughts, and images or into actions, behavior, and the interpersonal world. The latter three kinds of discharges are not possible in the state of sleep, because, except for the ocular muscles and the small muscles of mouth, lips, and extremities, the body is decathected. Thus, in the state of sleep, drives can be discharged only onto preconscious day's residues and unconscious mental contents. According to Freudian theory, when this happens a dream is born.

Before the development of the ego and superego, the discharge of the id's drives will occur freely, without impediment or conflict, through reflex or primary process functions. After the ego and superego have developed, only those id drives in waking life can be "freely" discharged that have undergone processes of displacement and sublimation. This renders the discharge acceptable to ego and superego. In the state of sleep only those id drives can be discharged that have undergone the processes of transformation promoted by the dream work.

What is the neurotic conflict? "The neurotic conflict, by definition, is one between a tendency striving for discharge and another tendency that tries to prevent this discharge" (Fenichel, 1945, p. 129). In terms of topographic theory, the neurotic conflict is strictly unconscious. In terms of structural theory, the neurotic conflict is a conflict between a drive from the id and a defense from the unconscious ego, with the superego playing a role on either side of the fence. According to Fenichel:

> The conflict *ego vs. id* would in some neuroses more correctly be written *ego + superego vs. id,* and in others *ego vs. id + superego* . . . . The warding-off ego acts under the command of the superego, and wherever it is not simple anxiety but guilt feelings that motivate the defense, the formulation *ego + superego vs. id* is correct.
>
> On the other hand, in many neuroses (especially in compulsion neuroses and, to an extreme degree, in depressions) the ego defends itself against guilt feelings . . . . In such cases, the ego develops a double countercathexis, one against the instincts and another one against the superego . . . .
>
> Again we may summarize: The superego may participate on either side of the neurotic conflict, but the formulation remains valid: the neurotic conflict takes place between the ego and the id [1945, p. 132].

The discharge sought by the drive can be into imagination, feelings, and thoughts or into action, behavior, and the interpersonal world. In waking life, both kinds of discharges may be impeded, as is the case, for instance, in neurotic conflicts in which the patient is sexually impotent and unable to experience sexual feelings, think sexual thoughts, or produce sexual images. Or, only the discharge into action, behavior, and the interpersonal world is impeded, as for instance in neurotic conflicts where the patient, while still unable to have an erection, is capable of having sexual thoughts and of having some sexual feelings and images. In sleep, since there is no possible discharge into action, behavior, and the interpersonal world (the body is decathected), only discharges onto mental contents can be impeded: dreamless sleep, what Fenichel refers to as "sleep phobia" (1945, p. 190), although psychodynamically, it would be more accurate to refer to this as "dream phobia."

Although every person has a neurotic conflict, not everybody will suffer from all the psychological, psychosomatic, or mental dysfunctions of his or her neurotic conflict.

WHY THERE IS A NEUROTIC CONFLICT

There are general reasons, in part philosophical, and specific reasons, largely psychological, which account for a neurotic conflict, which is, in effect, a situation of a "house divided." Parts of the self are arrayed against other parts of the self in an internecine war within the personality—seemingly a paradoxical state of affairs. But, in reality, it is not paradoxical because with personality, as, indeed, with nature in general, "united we stand" may not be as adaptive as "divided we stand." The question, however, is still legitimate: Why does this situation of a house divided unto itself take place and why are parts of the self in conflict with other parts of the same self?

In nature there are "natural" contradictions, conflicts, a dialectical state of affairs; it is part of the natural order of things, part of the physical, biological, and social world. There are opposing positive and negative particles in atoms and molecules; opposing positive and negative forces in the world of physics (matter and antimatter), in the biological world (antigens and antibodies), in society (forces to change and forces that support the status quo), in the psychological world (drives and counterdrives). In this context, therefore, the neurotic conflict is one of the prices exacted by civilization, the psychodynamic bases for some of its discontents.

Animistic interpretations also lead the ego to be in conflict with the id drives and to "fear" the id. And there are actual and practical reasons for the ego to fear the id, because of the countless times behavior, energized by the irrational, instant gratification–bound, pleasure principle–oriented id, led to all kinds of painful outcomes for the young child. The ego may have been, at that early age, too weak, too immature, and undeveloped to oppose the id's power and to forestall its dangerous results, but not too young to record those results in its memory and prepare itself to handle matters in a different way at a later time.

But more important for symptom formation, there are specific reasons *why* there is, and indeed there must be, a neurotic conflict: specific occurrences within which and because of which the infant experiences powerful feelings of anxiety, guilt, disgust, or shame.

Before presenting my conceptualization of the psychodynamics of the neurotic conflict, a brief summary of Fenichel's conceptualization and especially his "triple stratification" concept (1945, pp. 132–140) is in order. While Fenichel's views on symptom formation are in full agreement with the substance of Freud's view, they elucidate and enlarge them.

Fenichel identifies four unpleasant basic feelings: "primary anxiety," "primary guilt," "primary shame," and "primary disgust." They are basic because they are experienced early in infancy and are the forerunners of later feelings. He relates these feelings to four corresponding psychological events: primary anxiety is related to the experience of unmastered tension; primary guilt, to the experience of frustrated hunger and annihilation; primary shame, to frustrated exhibitionistic or voyeuristic experiences; primary disgust, to the occurrence of something nonedible having entered the digestive tract. He then conceptualizes anxiety, guilt, shame, and disgust as being on three tiers, the earliest tier being *trauma;* the next, later tier, *danger;* the final tier, *panic.* This is the *triple stratification concept.*

On the trauma level, the infant experiences the primary feelings of anxiety, guilt, shame, disgust; these feelings are intense, occur automatically, and are experienced by the ego passively. On the danger level, the child experiences the second tier feelings of anxiety, guilt, shame, or disgust; these feelings are mild (*tamed,* is Fenichel's word), and are in the service of the ego. They are experienced actively, created by anticipation, and controlled and used by the ego as warning signals. On the panic level, the ego's anticipatory and controlling functions have failed and the child (or adult) experiences the third tier feelings of anxiety, guilt, shame, or disgust. These feelings are intense and overwhelming, are experienced passively, and are a return to the primary feelings. These are the clinical situations of the anxiety spells of anxiety hysteria, the annihilation spells of melancholia, the feelings of shame (a specialized form of castration anxiety) in paranoia, the feelings of disgust in anorexia.

Fenichel explores possible reasons for the neurotic conflict:

> Do any innate tendencies exist to suppress or inhibit sexual or aggressive impulses, besides externally aroused feelings of anxiety, guilt, shame, and disgust, tendencies that might operate even without frustrating experiences? Perhaps the helplessness of the human infant, which necessarily brings about traumatic states, suffices to create a primary hostility of the ego to the instincts? Perhaps a taboo on incestuous love, which is so drastically expressed in many primitive societies, may be something innate, and a main cause for the forces against the Oedipus complex?
>
> Ideas of this kind do not seem to be warranted . . . . Whenever we analyze neurotics . . . we find that *experiences* are responsible for the anxieties and guilt feelings, and that they are the motivating forces for their repression [1945, p. 140; emphasis added].

Fenichel, thus, believes that the neurotic conflict is inevitable because there are drives, and drives are part of life, and there are inevitable frustrations and counterforces which are just as much part of life: thus, drives cannot always be discharged with impunity. There will always be *externally* aroused painful feelings, frustrating experiences that originate externally, which will make the ego fear the id and fear its drives.

THE PSYCHODYNAMICS OF THE NEUROTIC CONFLICT

It is my belief that empirical observation already shows that parents discipline their children and socialize their drives by making children experience the four basic feelings of anxiety, guilt, shame, and disgust: "If you don't stop doing that, your penis will fall off!" (anxiety); "After all I have done for you, now you do this to me?!" (guilt); "You ought to be ashamed of yourself!" (shame); "How disgusting, what are you doing!" (disgust). But, in addition, there are specific, almost prototypic interpersonal encounters in which these feelings are experienced, either by themselves or in any combination.

I prefer to think of Fenichel's three tiers in terms of chronological and developmental states; of primary, secondary, and tertiary anxiety, guilt, shame, and disgust in clinical terms; of secondary anxiety, guilt, shame, and disgust as "motives of defense"; and of the tertiary states of anxiety, guilt, shame, and disgust as "the breakdown." What follows is in part a rephrasing of Fenichel's statements about the neurotic conflict and an elaboration of my own views.

All four primary feelings have the following characteristics in common: (1) They are experienced first, the earliest in life. (2) They are of great intensity. Primary *anxiety* "floods" the infant, makes the infant cry and shout in panic and terror; primary *guilt* makes the child feel abandoned and about to be annihilated; primary *shame* makes the infant want to disappear from the face of the earth; primary *disgust* causes nausea and gagging, makes the infant grimace with revulsion, and ends in spitting or vomiting. (3) They are experienced passively. The infant feels that these feelings come from a place "outside" about which the infant knows nothing. As indicated before, everyone has a neurotic conflict, because everyone has experienced primary feelings of anxiety, guilt, shame, and disgust in infancy. *But not everybody suffers from the emotional, psychosomatic, or mental results of his or her neurotic conflict.*

All four secondary feelings have the following characteristics in common: (1) They are experienced later than the primary feelings, after and because the primary feelings have already been experienced, and are experienced only after there has been some development of ego functions. (2) They are not intense or strong: secondary anxiety consists of twinges of nervousness, intimations of fear, mild tension; secondary guilt consists of hints of remorse, mild self-reproach, and moderate feelings of regret; secondary shame only makes the child coyly timid and a bit retiring; secondary disgust may be just a physical sensation of bitterness on one's tongue, a hint of nausea, some hypersalivation, just a suggestion of wanting to gag. (3) They are experienced "actively." Secondary feelings are "motives of defense": they "*motivate*" the unconscious ego to set up *mechanisms* of defense against the id's drives.

All four tertiary feelings ("the breakdown") consist of the pathological results of the neurotic conflict and constitute the painful fabric of the psychoneuroses and psychoses afflicting mankind. They have the following characteristics in common: (1) They are experienced last if they are experienced at all. While everybody has lived through the primary and secondary feelings in childhood, *not everybody will have a breakdown.* (2) They are intense: tertiary anxiety is the free-floating anxiety making patients who are having a phobic or panic attack believe that a disaster is about to occur (a heart attack, insanity, losing control). Tertiary guilt is the all-pervasive dejection of involutional melancholia, of a depressive psychosis, of agitated depression, strong enough to drive some to suicide. Tertiary shame is the intense shame of patients suffering with acute paranoid feelings, desperately wanting to hide from the persons about whom they hallucinate, a shame making them want to crawl into a deep hole. Tertiary disgust is the chronic nausea of patients suffering from anorexia nervosa, making them vomit at the mere sight of food. (3) They are experienced passively: patients experience these feelings as ego alien and as flooding them from the external world, even though they are often secondarily rationalized as being caused by internal problems and past misdeeds. The tertiary feelings, thus, are identical to the primary feelings, except that they are experienced, if at all, later in life.

Let us now examine the specific events causing the infant or child to experience any of the four primary feelings.

1. *Primary anxiety* is experienced, most typically, in situations in which the infant's mainly erotic drives have become overcathected either because of internal dynamics or because of an external stimulus, and need to be discharged; but the objects needed for the discharge, the objects those drives need to cathect, are not present ("unmastered tension" in Fenichel's terms).

This is typically seen in the *eighth month anxiety*[1] or with infants who have a seductive-rejecting parent who overstimulates the infant with excessive fondling and then disappears, just when the infant is frantically wanting to be soothed.

---

[1] It is usually about the eighth month of age that infants peacefully in the arms of the primary caretaker become frantic, intensely anxious if a stranger comes and interacts with the caretaker. It is believed that these infants perceive the stranger as coming in between the caretaker and themselves, effectively separating them from the caretaker, and therefore creating a situation of objectlessness, of uncathectable objects, of "unmastered tension."

2. *Primary guilt* is experienced, most typically, in situations in which the infant's oral–aggressive drives have become overcathected, again either because of internal or external circumstances, and need to be discharged. But the object needed for the discharge, the object those drives need to cathect to (for instance, the parent at whom the child is enraged), make the child experience a feeling of loss of love for discharging their angry hunger. This is typically seen in infants whose parents are unable to tolerate the infant's normal expressions not only of angry hunger but also of autonomy, independence, or "temper."

3. *Primary shame* is experienced, most typically, in situations in which the infant's exhibitionistic drives have become overcathected, again because of exogenous or endogenous factors, and the cathected object, usually a parent, responds not with loving appreciation but by ridiculing the child.

4. *Primary disgust* is experienced, most typically, in situations in which the infant's oral drives have become overcathected, and the cathected object is an inedible object that the infant identifies with food because of predicate thinking (i.e., the unsupervised infant swallowing chips of paint peeled from the crib), in which case a self protective hypersecretion of gastric juice will provoke nausea and throwing up. More often, the cathected object is edible in a physical sense but is "wrong" in a psychological sense (mother is "sour" because of the hostile, destructive way she is nursing the infant), in which case the entire transaction is as "disgusting" as if the object itself, the milk, were sour: the infant will experience nausea and will throw up.

The secondary anxiety, guilt, shame, and disgust (Freud's "signal anxiety" [1926a] and Fenichel's "tamed anxiety" [1945]) are "motives of defense," functions of the unconscious ego "motivating" the ego to set up mechanisms of defense against the id's drives. The neurotic conflict can now be seen as a three-component system: *the id's drives, the ego's defense motives, and the ego's defense mechanisms.* The following formula may help to conceptualize symptom formation: The unconscious ego's secondary feelings (for instance, secondary anxiety) motivate the ego to set up defense mechanisms (for instance, repression) against those drives (for instance, incestuous libidinal drives) whose discharge had previously resulted in the painful experience of a primary feeling (for instance, primary anxiety). When the unconscious ego's motives of defenses and defense mechanisms fail in their defense functions, the person experiences the corresponding tertiary feeling (for instance, the panic of anxiety hysteria). In concrete and anthropomorphic language, it is as if, in fulfilling its adaptive, defensive functions, the unconscious ego carried on this extensive dialogue with itself:

> I feel the stirring of a familiar drive whose discharge, at previous times, caused me to feel the awful pain of a primary feeling. At that time, I was too weak to do anything about that but I recorded what happened and remember it. Now it can happen again and I am afraid; but now I can do something about it. I must ward off that drive, and to make sure I succeed in doing so, I will give myself a signal to ward off that discharge: I will make myself feel a small amount of that awful primary feeling, I will make myself feel a secondary feeling which will motivate me to ward off that troublesome drive. Or, I have failed, I have not succeeded in doing that, I feel again that awful primary feeling, there has been a breakdown (i.e., the defenses against that problematic, problem-creating drive have broken down), and I am flooded with the tertiary feeling.

THE DYNAMIC EQUILIBRIUM OF THE NEUROTIC CONFLICT AND SYMPTOM FORMATION

The neurotic conflict is always in a state of dynamic equilibrium, as finely and delicately tuned as the biological processes of the body (opening and closing of valves in heart and gastrointestinal tract, fluid and oxygen exchanges between cells, enzymatic reactions within the tissues, and so on). This equilibrium is as continuously monitored as is the equilibrium of our biological processes. Just as the biological processes mentioned above do not stop when we are asleep, the psychological processes maintaining the equilibrium of the neurotic conflict do not stop when we are asleep but dreaming. This equilibrium is the result of never-ceasing adjustments between stimulations and responses. It is comparable to the equilibrium of the biological processes within the body which is the result of never-ceasing adjustments between physiochemical stimulations (e.g., the presence of partly digested food in the stomach) and physioanatomic responses (e.g., the opening of the pyloric valve and the progression of food into the duodenum). The *general* purpose of the dynamic equilibrium of the neurotic conflict is, of course, adaptation. The *specific* purpose is the fulfillment of the neurotic conflict's function; that is, the protection of the socialized, moralized, idealized conscious ego from too direct and immediate an experience of the raw, primitive id and superego. The specific purpose of the dynamic equilibrium of the neurotic conflict is to oppose the discharge of those overcathected drives whose previous discharges had caused the person to experience the painful feelings of primary anxiety, guilt, shame, or disgust.

From the moment we are born, we are plunged into an ocean of stimulations, physical and psychological, exogenous and endogenous, simple and complex, stimulations simultaneously touching our conscious and our unconscious mind, overcathecting and undercathecting parts of our ego, id, and superego. Every time a conflicted drive (i.e., one that has become part of that person's neurotic conflict) has been overcathected by a stimulus, there will at once be a compensatory overcathecting of ego defenses (motives of defense and mechanisms of defense). Conversely, every time a conflicted drive has become undercathected because of a direct or indirect discharge, there will be a compensatory undercathecting of ego defenses. As we know, the ego's functions include the examination of all stimulations entering the mind from outside or from within, to monitor, with the superego's "advice and consent," all changes in psychic energies and cathexes within the system, and to administer all responses. The healthy ego, as a good administrator or strategist, effects all needed adjustments in the neurotic conflict by displacing and apportioning energies on this defense motive here or on that defense mechanism there, whenever and wherever these adjustments are most needed. The overriding purpose of this activity is to maintain the dynamic equilibrium of the neurotic conflict, and to fulfill the neurotic conflict's adaptive function.

The amount and variety of stimulations capable of touching our mind in significant ways, the quantity and quality of stimulations capable of resonating with conflicted unconscious drives, capable of plucking our inner psychological chords, is staggering. If we add to that the human capacity to interpret and respond to the present in the light of the past (transference), our receptivity and vulnerability to all sorts of external stimulations will be multiplied even further. This is true for seemingly trivial interpersonal occurrences amplified and distorted because of transference; when we are stimulated by powerful, intimate interpersonal encounters; when we are touched by a powerful, deeply symbolic play, film, book, poem, lecture, or painting. In more ways than one can ever know consciously, unconscious processes are continuously being twanged, like a guitar's strings, by the sensory, intellectual, and emotional kaleidoscope of the world experiences. A tabloid describing a street accident or a murder with sensational words and photographs unavoidably touches the sadistic and voyeuristic drives locked in a person's heart. To see a couple on a bench kissing each other, unavoidably touches the unconscious, libidinal drives locked in a person's neurotic conflict. A film, explicitly depicting "kinky" sexuality or incest or sexual abuse or homosexuality or cannibalism (in tasteful, artistic films no less than in common, ordinary pornography) unavoidably touches corresponding chords in our neurotic conflict. Even a passage in the Old Testament or a deeply metaphoric poem that may well challenge the conscious comprehension of the reader will touch her or his unconscious mind in deep, powerful ways.

If all human beings are touched in mysterious ways by the everyday experiences of human intercourse, the unconscious and the neurotic conflicts of psychiatrists, psychotherapists, and psychoanalysts are even more exposed to stimulations, particularly powerful and potentially harmful, stimulations originating from their patients' conscious problems and unconscious processes. Without a previous personal analysis and without scrupulous and rigorous continuous self-analysis (i.e., analysis of one's countertransference), psychotherapists would soon display dysfunctional mental symptoms.

THE PROCESS OF SYMPTOM FORMATION

Symptom formation can best be understood through the following five interrelated concepts, the basis for which has been laid down in the preceding pages:

1. In order to maintain the dynamic equilibrium of the neurotic conflict, if and when life circumstances *overcathect* problematic drives, there must be a corresponding *overcathecting* of

defenses. (Since we are discussing symptom formation, not symptom relief, we don't need to discuss the *undercathecting* of problematic drives.)

2. The neurotic conflict can be seen as consisting of two halves, the *drive half* and the *defense half*, the latter including motives of defense and mechanisms of defense. The *dynamic equilibrium principle* requires that if and when the drive half of the neurotic conflict has been overcathected, more energy will have to be displaced and apportioned to the defense half, so that the defense half will be slightly more heavily cathected than the drive half. Thus the dynamic equilibrium of the neurotic conflict is maintained, and the adaptive function of the neurotic conflict is fulfilled.

3. Psychic energy is finite not infinite, and the energy available to the ego for both its defensive functions and its reality-oriented functions is equally finite. This is a crucial concept if one is to understand the progression of symptom development from neurotic to psychoneurotic to psychotic states.

4. As the overcathecting of problematic drives continues, the overcathecting of those defenses impeding their discharge proceeds at the same pace. There will come a time when defense motives and defense mechanisms are so overcathected that, while the discharge of the conflicted drives is still impeded (and, therefore, the "breakdown" is still prevented), the overcathected defense motives and defense mechanisms will begin to "spill over" into consciousness and behavior, that is, into the person's subjective feelings, affective experiences, and ways of acting and being. There are three immediate and direct results of an overloaded neurotic conflict: (a) the spilling over of overcathected defense motives; (b) the spilling over of overcathected defense mechanisms; and (c) the "dammed-up state." There can be, therefore, three groups of direct symptoms of the neurotic conflict.

a. The anxiety neuroses, guilt neuroses, shame neuroses, and disgust neuroses are all caused by the spillover of the corresponding overcathected defense motives. Since the motives of defense (the secondary feelings) are, by definition, not very intense, these neurotic states are tolerable, only mildly unpleasant conditions, sometimes as transient as the overcathecting of the corresponding conflicted drives had been, easily ignored or rationalized ("It must be the weather"; "I must have a virus"; "I have been working too hard"; "It must be something I have eaten").

b. The inhibition neuroses are related to the spillover of overcathected defense mechanisms. These can be conditions subjectively more troublesome. They are directly caused by the inhibition of those drives whose discharge the mechanisms of defense are effectively impeding. These conditions include inhibitions of oral, anal, phallic, and genital drives (anorexia, constipation, timidity, impotence, and frigidity, and so on); inhibitions of "sexualized" or "aggressivized" ego functions, that is, inhibitions of any ego functions upon which the id's drives had been displaced (inhibitions of reading, writing, seeing, hearing); inhibitions of partial instincts; inhibitions of feelings (inability to feel love or anger); and so on. These states, too, can be as transient as the overcathecting of the inhibited drive had been, not too painful and easily rationalized. Or they may be chronic and quite troublesome.

c. Conditions whose major symptom is a state of chronic fatigue. They are related to what Fenichel calls "a state of relative insufficiency of the ego" and the "dammed-up" state. These conditions are caused by the enormous amount of energy consumed by the ego in the defensive task. The ego is so occupied in keeping the door locked to the overcathected drives pushing onward, that it is left with little energy for its extrapsychic functioning and its realistic tasks. Hence, "neurasthenia," literally, nervous fatigue, nervous tiredness, nervous lassitude.

It must be stressed that the direct symptoms of the neurotic conflict, the neurotic states, *consist only of the defense half of the neurotic* conflict: the drive half is not part of the symptoms.

As the case may be, the overcathecting of problematic drives may continue. When this is so, psychic energy being finite, there will come a time when the overtaxed ego has no more energy left to overcathect already heavily taxed defenses against still surging drives. In other words, the administrator has no more resources, the strategist has no troops left to oppose the invasion of the socialized, moralized, idealized conscious ego by the barbaric id and the superego. A compromise is reached and a compromise product, *partaking of both drive and defense,* is formed and becomes part of the person's subjective feelings, affective experiences, and ways of acting and being: psychoneurotic or psychotic symptoms make their appearance. A breakdown of "dams" and defenses has occurred. It is a breakdown with varying degrees of severity on a continuum of lesser or greater maladaptiveness. The defense half of the neurotic conflict still monitors, to an extent, the drive half. The ego's defenses still distort, to a degree, the conflicted drives that have invaded the territory of the conscious ego. And that is the essence of the compromise, that the problematic drives enter the patient's conscious ego still under disguises determined by the ego; the ego's basic adaptive function (to protect the person's socialized, moralized, idealized consciousness from too direct an experience of the raw and primitive drives) is, to a measure, maintained.

From a psychodynamic perspective, and in terms of the theory of the neurotic conflict, it is precisely the degree and the extent to which the defenses still monitor the drives (the degree and extent to which the ego is still capable of distorting and disguising those drives), that make important differences between psychoneurosis and psychosis. In both psychoneurotic and psychotic symptoms, both drives and defenses are part of the symptom (unlike neurotic symptoms, where only the defense half of the neurotic conflict appears). But in psychoneurotic symptoms the drive is better defended; in psychotic symptoms, less so. The defense components of the neurotic conflict appear as tertiary anxiety, guilt, shame, or disgust, the drive components appear as symbolized, distorted, disguised, ego alien derivatives of the drives. Predicate thinking, again, will be found to be very important in the process through which the offending drives are symbolized and disguised. This is particularly relevant to dream formation, where the "dream wishes" of the latent dream are symbolized and disguised largely through predicate thinking.

CASE EXAMPLES

1. Before beginning therapy, a young male patient had suffered for years with anxiety neurosis: mild nervousness (the spillover of secondary anxiety, a motive of defense), lack of sexual enthusiasm and assertiveness, a tendency to blame others, and a

propensity for excessive meekness and docility (the spillover of such defense mechanisms as repression, projection, and reaction formation, defenses whose function was to inhibit or otherwise distort his incestuous erotic and aggressive drives). He also experienced tiredness and chronic fatigue, from the dammed-up state. But when he entered therapy with anxiety hysteria, a psychoneurosis, both the defense and drive components of his conflict showed through. He experienced panic attacks (tertiary anxiety), premature ejaculation (repression of fuller potency and symbolization of unconscious hostility through regression to a sexuality that "soiled" and "defiled" his girl friend), and a number of functional "anxiety equivalents" such as tachycardia, sweating, trembling, and midriasis representing the acting out of the forbidden sexual and aggressive drives through predicate thinking. When one is being sexual and aggressive, one's heart rate is faster, one may sweat or tremble, one's pupils are dilated.

2. Another patient, a young man in his midthirties who had been physically abused by his father in his childhood, had suffered for two to three years with guilt neurosis (neurotic depression): mild sadness (secondary guilt, a motive of defense), and the inability to express even justified anger (the defense mechanism of repression against his unconscious oral sadism). Again, only the defense components of his neurotic conflict showed in his consciousness and behavior. When his unconscious rage became overcathected by the abuses and mistreatment of a tyrannical father-in-law, he developed psychoneurotic depression and entered treatment. Now both the defense and the drive components of his neurotic conflict showed through. He experienced severe depression (tertiary guilt); extreme submissiveness to his father-in-law (this was transferential: transference itself is based on at least one defense, displacement; this also reflected repression and denial, both defenses of the unconscious rage at his own father); and he repeated, in very dramatically expressed statements, that he wished to be dead. This last symptom, which effectively terrified his father-in-law and wife, was the "compromise product" partaking of both drives and defenses. The unconscious rage at the father who had abused him in his childhood and the mother who had not protected him from father, were expressed cryptically and through transferential displacement against the

father-in-law who had tyrannized and mistreated him for the previous two to three years, and against the wife who much too often
had taken her father's side against him. But the drive was still
fairly well defended. Had he developed psychotic depression, and
attempted to commit suicide, that would have been an example
of a less well-defended drive (suicide can be the ultimate act of
anger).

3. A third young patient, a red-haired woman with a very
fair complexion, had suffered with shame neurosis since puberty.
While in a neurotic state, the direct symptoms of her neurotic
conflict had included a great facility to feel embarrassed (secondary shame, the motive of defense), timidity, and a retiring, unos-
tentatious and reserved way of being (the defense mechanism of
repression against unconscious exhibitionistic drives). She had
entered a semicloistered religious order as an unconscious adaptation (aimed at avoiding any possibility for even appropriate self-
displays), and left it when the order changed from its monastic
habit into regular clothes. "Living in the world" inevitably overcathected her exhibitionistic conflicts and she had been feeling
increasingly tense and anxious. The evening before the day her
psychoneurotic symptoms broke through, she had given a lecture
at the library where she worked, had made a couple of "very
embarrassing slips of the tongue," had stammered a few times,
and had felt she had made "a total fool of herself." The day
after, she developed *erythrophobia* and a skin rash over breasts and
abdomen. Now both the defense and the drive components of
her neurotic conflict showed: intense shame about blushing in
public and about her skin rash (tertiary shame but also tertiary
guilt because she consciously believed that she herself had caused
the rash through "inappropriate" sexual behavior). She was totally unaware of any exhibitionistic desires (repression and denial
of exhibitionistic drives toward her father, who in her early and
late childhood had stimulated her exhibitionism and then ridiculed and shamed her for it). But the conflicted drive was also
part of the symptom. By blushing (because of her complexion,
her blushing was quite visible), she attracted people's attention,
she was "seducing" father into looking at her; in going to a male
dermatologist for her rash, she was "exhibiting" her breasts and

abdomen. But the drive was still well defended: there was complete lack of awareness of any exhibitionistic wishes on her part and the price she was paying in tertiary shame and guilt was very high.

4. A young woman born and raised in a rural hamlet on a Mediterranean island had suffered for years with a disgust neurosis which had probably started with primary disgust while being breast-fed by a psychotic mother. Through the years that preceded the final overcathecting of her conflicted hunger, she had suffered with an ego syntonic lack of appetite (for food and for life, the defense of repression against her angry hunger) and frequent mild nausea which was a spillover of secondary disgust. The overcathecting of her unconscious hunger for "the wrong food" occurred when she married a man who preferred fellatio to genital intercourse. In her psychoneurotic state she developed severe anorexia and protracted vomiting (tertiary disgust). Through predicate thinking, her husband's penis was the same to her unconscious and to her superego, as her mother's breast: to fellate her husband was the symbolic, distorted expression of the forbidden drive.

SUMMARY AND CONCLUSIONS

According to Freud and also Fenichel, the neurotic conflict is a conflict between id drives whose discharge had previously caused the person to experience the painful primary affects of anxiety, guilt, shame, and disgust, and ego defenses warding off those drives to prevent the reexperience of those painful affects. The superego participates on either side of the conflict. The unconscious ego keeps the neurotic conflict *in a state of dynamic equilibrium* by overcathecting or undercathecting defenses according to whether the conflicted drives had been overcathected or undercathected by internal or external circumstances.

Neurotic states (the direct symptoms of the neurotic conflict) develop when the overcathected defenses still manage to ward off the overcathected conflicted drives but spill over into the person's consciousness or behavior. As a result, the person experiences various degrees of subjective discomfort, his or her ways of being and acting are inhibited to varying degrees, and behavior is more or less severely dysfunctional.

Psychoneurotic and psychotic symptoms occur when the depleted ego can no longer overcathect defenses to ward off the discharge of overcathected drives; a compromise product is formed that partakes of both drive and defenses, a product that allows the discharge of the conflicted drive, thus giving it the needed outlet and alleviating the defensive task of the ego, but a discharge still under the requirements of the defensive ego. The psychoneurotic and psychotic symptoms appear in the person's consciousness or behavior in more or less disguised form: more disguised, better defended in psychoneuroses, less so in psychoses. The painful *primary* feelings (now called "tertiary") appear in the patient's consciousness and subjective experience as intense and painful feelings of anxiety, guilt, shame, and/or disgust.

The process of dream formation parallels in many ways quite faithfully the process of symptom formation according to the theory of the neurotic conflict. Symptom formation and the theory of the neurotic conflict have been discussed in detail precisely because of this parallelism.

Part II

DREAM FORMATION

4

Dream Formation, 1

DREAM FORMATION IN TERMS OF THE THEORY OF THE NEUROTIC CONFLICT

As discussed in the previous chapter, some drives whose discharge has *not* caused the person to experience painful feelings of anxiety, guilt, shame, and disgust, undergo displacement and sublimation and become part of the ego. But those drives, whose discharge did cause the person to experience those painful affects, remain unconscious, become part of that person's neurotic conflict, and are in a state of dynamic equilibrium with an array of ego defenses that prevent their discharge. These unconscious drives are not dead skeletons in our psychic closet; they constantly try to surge forth. The nature of the struggle and its outcome are different in the state of wakefulness and in the state of sleep.

When we are awake, the conflicted drives emerge as various kinds of unconscious derivatives, such as transferential likes and dislikes, screen memories and screen fantasies, slips of the tongue, of the hand, "irruptions of the id" (A. Freud, 1936), and as psychoneurotic and psychotic symptoms. When we are asleep, they emerge as dreams. Thus, dreams are born as all other unconscious derivatives are born.

Dreams are the counterpart, in the state of sleep, of the psychoneurotic and psychotic states that may exist when we are awake. Dreams too, as psychoneurotic and psychotic symptoms, are compromise products, products partaking of both drives and defenses. So much are dreams the equivalent of psychoneurotic

69

or psychotic symptoms that when there are no dreams between yesterday's overcathecting of drives and the day after, no dreams as an "in-between" product between yesterday and today, a psychoneurosis or psychosis will develop. But let us go back to the theory of the neurotic conflict and examine possibilities in which, because of differences in the psychodynamic equilibrium of the respective neurotic conflicts, different clinical scenarios emerged.

Will There Be a Dream or Not?

A first scenario is illustrated by a patient whose neurotic conflict, before beginning therapy, had been in an overcathected state for months, his defenses close to being overwhelmed by powerful, surging, conflicted drives. His overcathected defenses were still managing to ward off the overcathected drives but had already begun to spill over into his consciousness and behavior; he had been experiencing Fenichel's "direct clinical symptoms of the neurotic conflict" (1945, p. 168).

In his first session, he spoke of a "terrible night" he had recently had. The preceding day had been difficult, a day filled with experiences resonating with and further overcathecting his already overcathected, unconscious drives. He wanted to sleep both to forget the difficult day and because he felt exhausted; that is, he was in what Fenichel called the "neurasthenic state" (1945, p. 185). But, agitated and disturbed as he was with tension, he could not fall asleep; the day's events intruded on his consciousness and effectively countered the attempts to sleep. The day's events were screen memories, representations of repressed happenings going back to childhood, which the day's events had overcathected. He finally fell asleep, but woke up with a jolt after a few minutes. Against his wishes, he found himself thinking about all the unpleasant events which had occurred during the day: a dangerous-looking man in the subway who had frightened him; a supervisor who had made him feel guilty; a story someone had recounted which he had found disgusting. These events resonated with unconscious drives. In his dozing consciousness, he tormented himself with all sorts of demons, until he fell asleep for a moment or two before abruptly waking up startled. This continued until morning; Fenichel called this "sleep phobia" (1945, p. 190), but I prefer to call it "dream phobia."

If this patient's unconscious ego and superego had allowed him to fall asleep, he would undoubtedly have had a dream, a compromise product including the overcathected drives, which would have become his latent dream, and the defenses, which would have modified the latent dream into the manifest dream. But since he feared what he unconsciously wished (which is the psychodynamic essence of phobic phenomena; and which is why I prefer the term *dream phobia*), he could not dream, his unconscious ego and superego awoke him just as a dream was about to be conceived. The result was NREM sleep, that is, sleep without dreaming, the equivalent of a neurotic state (defense, but no drive). Next morning he rose from bed feeling more exhausted than he had the evening before. There had been no dream to lighten his overcathected state, to serve as an outlet for the overcathected drives, to undercathect his neurotic conflict, to make the defensive task of the ego less strenuous. The day following the night when he had not dreamed, he felt more intensely anxious. An attack of free-floating anxiety, a psychoneurotic symptom, brought him into therapy a few days later.

A similar scenario is illustrated by what happened to the young woman discussed above who had spent an agitated night before awakening with a rash and the erythrophobia. She had kept reviewing the events of the evening before with disturbing feelings of anxiety and shame, slept only fitfully, and could not dream.

A third scenario, conversely, is one in which the patient's psychodynamic state, the state of his neurotic conflict and its dynamic equilibrium, the kind of ego, superego, and "stabilized personality" (Hall, 1982, pp. 116–122) this patient had, were all such that a dream did occur. This patient was in a neurotic state similar to the one just described—ego's defenses close to depletion, overcathected defenses barely managing to ward off the overcathected drives. But his ego and superego still allowed a dream, symbolically acting out the dangerously overcathected drives. This patient did not "need" to produce further symptoms to act out the overcathected drives.

Will the Dream Be Beautiful or a Nightmare?

Just as with psychoneurotic symptoms, drives are better disguised and better defended by a still supple ego than they are in psychotic symptoms; in dreams too drives can be better disguised and defended ("beautiful dreams") or less well so (nightmares). To Freud, anxiety dreams were those in which "dream wishes" (i.e., the id drives) were not sufficiently disguised. There is a definite correlation between ego strength and "quality" of dreams. At one end, one finds persons with an ego capable of disguising all sorts of primitive drives into manifest dreams which will be highly pleasing from any realistic, moral, ethical, or esthetic standpoint, in other words "beautiful dreams"; and at the other end, are those with a very depleted ego who therefore have nightmares. A person with a depleted ego may have horrible but mercifully brief dreams from which they awaken brusquely and abruptly. Their ego still has enough strength to resort to one last defense against the drives, the defense of self-awakening. Others with an even weaker ego cannot invoke that ultimate defense: their nightmares are endless dreams of horror-filled visions provoking intense tertiary anxiety, guilt, shame, and disgust. Let us examine, again, a number of possible scenarios.

If the young woman with erythrophobia had dreamed on the night before she broke down with her symptoms, she might not have developed those symptoms. Her dream might have been this: "I was giving a lecture at the library. Everybody found the lecture very good." This would have been a well-defended dream, a "beautiful dream." The conflicted drive (exhibitionism) is gratified, but the ego defenses disguise it so well that it appears in the manifest dream in a very innocuous and innocent form. She is "giving a lecture": thus it is her mind that she is exhibiting, not her body (displacement and sublimation); and she is displaying her knowledge to "everybody," not to her father; and "everybody found the lecture very good" (father is appreciative of her, rather than mocking and ridiculing her as had been his habit, thus she is turning the dream into the opposite of reality). A "beautiful dream" indeed.

Another hypothetical "beautiful dream" might have been: "A friend of mine was wearing a beautiful red dress. I liked it very much." The conflicted drive is, again, very well disguised. The skin, reddened by the excitement of exhibitionistic behavior, becomes "a beautiful red dress"; and it is not the dreamer displaying it, but a friend of hers (displacement and projection).

A third, hypothetical scenario: "I was naked to the waist at Grand Central Station. Nobody was noticing it, but I felt extremely embarrassed. I could have crawled into a hole." The drive is still defended: the wish to expose the lower part of her body is repressed, she is only "naked to the waist"; father is displaced onto "nobody" and father's "noticing" it is repressed so that, in the manifest dream, "Nobody was noticing it." But the drive is much less defended than in the two previous dreams: she is naked, and in a public place, Grand Central Station. The dreamer is experiencing tertiary shame (she "could have crawled into a hole"). This would not have been a beautiful dream, it would have been a nightmare.

"Beautiful Meadow"

This was the first dream of J, the patient to be discussed at length in chapter 7, a young man whose neurotic conflicts included rage at his father.

> I was walking in the plaza of a college campus. The campus was not hard cement, but a beautiful meadow, and the scene was positively heavenly, brilliantly green grass, flowers, blue skies, chirping birds, actually like the campus upstate where I went to college. I was walking with an elderly gentleman, white-haired, clean shaven, I don't know who he was, but he was not my father. I was carrying some heavy textbooks and suddenly I stumbled on a rock and the books fell on the man's foot, but he wasn't hurt. He joked with me about it, even bent down to pick up the books for me. He complimented me for being such a good graduate student.

A very well-defended dream, a "beautiful dream." Its length, the profusion of beautiful words and alluring adjectives (soft meadows, beautiful flowers, chirping birds, even a blue sky) tag it for a resistance dream (in Freudian theory long dreams are resistance dreams) with much "secondary revision," one of the major defensive operations of the dream work (see chapter 5). And the dream's latent content is extremely well camouflaged through a plenitude of defenses. To mention just some: the cruel, abusive, definitely nongentle father of his childhood is rendered as "an elderly gentleman" (displacement; that the elderly man was indeed the dreamer's father is further suggested by the volunteered denial: "I don't know who he was but he was not my father"[1]; the more lethal objects with which he wished to hit his father become "books" (displacement and sublimation); and he wanted to strike father on other parts of father's body, not on the feet (displacement again). Still the drive shows through: the books do strike father. Seven years later the same patient, a white man, dreamed this dream.

"Back Alley"

> I was walking in some back alley with a black man. I was carrying a heavy baseball bat. I stumbled and the bat fell off my hands. But I picked it up and, I don't know what came over me, bashed and smashed the head of the man with it many times, it was awful, blood splattering all over, I felt awful, I woke up bathed in sweat. Boy was I glad it was only a dream. I guess I am becoming aware of how angry I am.

The drives are still somewhat defended: father is represented as "a black man" (displacement). Before hitting father, the dreamer "stumbled" and "the bat fell off" his hand (countercathexes, counterdrives); the ego has still enough energy to produce a secondary revision ("I don't know what came over me") and to wake up the dreamer relatively soon. Nevertheless, the conflicting aggressive drives are discharged much more manifestly and the dreamer is experiencing tertiary guilt ("I felt awful") and tertiary anxiety ("I woke up bathed in sweat"). This was not a beautiful dream, this was a nightmare.

DREAM FORMATION IN TERMS OF THE SOURCES AND THE CONTENT OF DREAMS

The Source of Dreams

As indicated in discussing dream formation in terms of the theory of neurotic conflict, a person conceives a dream (or any other

---

[1] A volunteered denial is an unmistakable indication of denial. No one asked him if the elderly gentleman might have been his father, but he needed to volunteer it. It is like

unconscious derivatives, including neurotic, psychoneurotic, and psychotic symptoms) whenever the drives which are part of that person's intrapsychic world have been excessively overcathected by intrapsychic or extrapsychic processes.

Strictly speaking, a dream needs no external sources to be conceived and produced. Drives can be overcathected by internal psychobiological processes alone, in the absence of external psychological stimulations. One can become more hungry, more thirsty, more in need of love and nurture without any stimulations from sight, sound, smell, of food, water, or the nurturing person. This, however, is a moot question since, from the moment a living organism is conceived, that organism is in an environment that is always stimulating it and its intrapsychic processes. Furthermore, external psychological stimulations can overcathect the person's internal drives and thereby contribute to the gestation and birth, if not the conception, of dreams. As we shall see in a moment, Freud emphasized the importance, in dream formation, of the "day's residues," the preconscious experiences from the day of the dream; the "day's residues" are, indeed, extrapsychic experiences.

Freud listed the sources of dreams (1900, p. 163) as follows: (1) "Recent and Indifferent Material," consisting of psychological, extrapsychic, conscious processes going back to recent events in the dreamer's life; (2) "Infantile Material," which includes psychological, intrapsychic, unconscious processes going back to the dreamer's childhood and infancy; (3) "Somatic Sources," consisting of processes occurring in the dreamer's body.

"Recent and Indifferent Material in Dreams" (pp. 165–188)

Concerning this group of dreams, Freud wrote: "If I examine my own experience on the subject of the origin of the elements included in the content of dreams, I must begin with an assertion that in every dream it is possible to find a point of contact with the experiences of the previous day. This view is confirmed by every dream that I look into, whether my own or anyone else's"

---

someone prefacing a hostile statement by volunteering, "I don't mean to be nasty, but . . . ."

(p. 165). Several pages later, he listed four possible "recent sources":

> The source of a dream may be either—(a) a recent and physically signifi-
> cant experience which is represented in the dream directly, or (b) several
> recent and significant experiences which are combined into a single unity
> by the dream, or (c) one or more recent and significant experiences
> which are represented in the content of the dream by a mention of a
> contemporary but indifferent experience, or (d) an internal significant
> experience (e.g. a memory or a train of thought), which is in that case
> *invariably* represented in the dream by a mention of a recent but indiffer-
> ent impression [1900, p. 180].

Freud noted that this latter source (e.g., a train of thought or a memory) need not always be a "recent" source, but may be connected, through displacement of instinctual objects and of time, to recent impressions by "more or less numerous links" (p. 180). He added, "In interpreting dreams we find one condition always fulfilled: one component of the content of the dream is a repetition of a recent impression of the previous day" (p. 180). In other places, he referred to these "recent impressions of the previous day" variously as "remnants of trivial experiences" (p. 177), as "day's residues" (p. 228), and as "preconscious residues of the previous day" (p. 555).

"Infantile Material as the Source of Dreams" (pp. 189–219)

As one reads Freud, it becomes obvious that he gave this source an increasingly important role. He said, "I have pointed out as a third peculiarity of the content of dreams that it may include impressions which date back to earliest childhood, and which seem not to be accessible to waking memory" (p. 189). A few lines later he noted, "[W]e find to our astonishment that experiences from childhood also play a part in dreams whose content would never have led one to suppose it" (pp. 190–191). At the end of the same page he added, "[*W*]*e find the child and the child's impulses still living on in the dream*" (p. 191). Several pages later, he commented, "The deeper one carries the analysis of a dream, the more often one comes upon the track of experiences in child-hood which have played a part among the sources of that dream's

latent content" (p. 198). And in concluding his address of infantile sources of dreams, he stated: "Dreams frequently seem to
have more than one meaning. Not only . . . may they include several wish-fulfilments one alongside the other; but a succession of
meanings or wish-fulfilments may be superimposed on one another, the bottom one being the fulfilment of a wish dating from
earliest childhood. And here again the question arises whether it
might not be more correct to assert that this occurs 'invariably'
rather than 'frequently' " (p. 219).

"Somatic Sources" (pp. 220–240)

Writers preceding Freud believed that dreams were the sleeper's
reactions to sensory stimulations from without (auditory, olfactory, or tactile sensations) and bodily stimulations (arising from
sexual, digestive, or other excretory functions). "Nervous" and
"bodily" stimuli were considered the anatomic sources of
dreams, along with disturbed digestion, accidental positions of
the body, or physical happenings occurring during sleep. Indeed,
according to some writers, these were actually the sole and exclu-
sive source of dreams. Freud, however, believed that dreams were
primarily a psychological phenomenon, that somatic stimulations
were the least important factor in the conception and birth of
dreams, that it was "impossible to attribute the wealth of ide-
ational material in dreams to external nervous stimuli alone" (p.
221). He also believed that when somatic processes contribute to
the creation of a dream, those processes become part of "the
whole" that the dream is; this, according to the psychological
principles of censorship, is dream work and dream as wish-fulfillment. He wrote:

> [T]he dream-work is under the necessity of combining into a unity all
> instigations to dreaming which are active simultaneously. We found that,
> when two or more experiences capable of creating an impression are left
> over from the previous day, the wishes derived from them are combined
> in a single dream, and similarly that the psychically significant impression
> and the indifferent experiences from the previous day are brought to-
> gether in the dream-material, provided always that it is possible to set up
> communicating ideas between them. Thus a dream appears to be a reac-
> tion to everything that is simultaneously present in the sleeping mind
> as currently active material. . . . We can foresee, then without any great

difficulty, what will happen if fresh material in the form of sensations is added during sleep to these currently active memories. It is once again owing to the fact of their being currently active that these sensory excitations are of importance for the dream; they are united with the other currently active psychical material to furnish what is used for the construction of the dream [p. 228].

A little later Freud stated, "The essential nature of the dream is not altered by the fact of somatic materials being added to its psychic sources: a dream remains the fulfilment of a wish . . . " (p. 228).

As we shall soon see in discussing the wish to sleep: when sleep is disturbed by sensory stimulations, inner organs' excitations, or bodily stimulations which are strong and persistent enough to overcome sleep, the sleeper will awake without having dreamed. But if sleep is disturbed by sensory stimulations, whether interior or exterior, and by overcathected drives from the sleeper's intrapsychic world, a dream will be produced. To summarize: all three major sources of dreams are important, but of the three (recent material, infantile material, somatic sources), the infantile material is the major stimulus in the conception, if not in the gestation and birth of a dream, and therefore, it is the dream's major source.

The Content of Dreams

The sources of a dream and that dream's content are closely interrelated. An event capable of becoming the source of a dream (i.e., capable of producing a dream), can become part of the content of that dream. As we have seen, the discussion of the sources of dreams indicated that, according to Freud, the content of dreams can be expected to include memories of psychic experiences going back to both the recent and the remote past. Similarly, the content of dreams includes both the "yesteryear" and the "yesterday."

The "Yesteryear"

The content includes unconscious memories of repressed events going back to infancy and prelatency childhood. These are events that have been repressed according to the psychodynamics of the neurotic conflict and defended according to the principles and requirements of the dynamic equilibrium of the neurotic conflict. These unconscious memories become the source of a dream (and can become part of the content of that dream) when and because they are overcathected, that is "heavy" with psychic energy needing to be discharged. The unconscious memories of these repressed events are, in dreams, further overcathected by recent life events (i.e., events experienced in the day or days preceding the dream). This reciprocal overcathecting—I call this *the mirror relationship*—occurs when repressed events and recent life events bear similarities with each other (based on prelogic–predicate thinking) and, because of these similarities, resonate with each other. What I call the "yesteryear," Freud referred to as the unconscious leg of the dream (1900, pp. 552, 562). This material, as it is flashed to the special consciousness of REM sleep, constitutes the latent content of the dream.

The "Yesterday"

The content includes preconscious memories of events going back to the day or days preceding the dream, that is, memories of recent life events. These memories are stored in the preconscious as "day's residues" or "psychic remnants of daily experiences." As indicated above, the "day's residues" are overcathected by the unconscious leg of the dream, which the day's residues in turn overcathect when the contents of the unconscious leg of the dream bear similarities (based on prelogic–predicate thinking) with those day's residues and, because of these similarities, resonate with them. What I call "the yesterday" is what Freud referred to as the preconscious leg of the dream (1900, pp. 552, 562; 1913, pp. 273–275). This material, as it is flashed to the special "consciousness" of REM sleep, constitutes the manifest content of the dream.

The day's residues are, most commonly, from the day immediately preceding the night of the dream. In patients suffering with severe insomnia or dream phobia, I have seen dreams which contained life events experienced two to four days before. (If a dream including those day's residues had been dreamed earlier on, that dream had not been remembered.) This is also the case with patients seen once or twice weekly. Events experienced two or three days before the session, had had a particularly sharp resonance with unconscious memories that were pertinent to what these patients were working on at the time. Subject to the vicissitudes of transference and resistance, including such invariably ambivalent wishes as the wish to work on their problems with the analyst and the wish to please the analyst with the gift of a dream, and subject to the requirements of the dynamic equilibrium of the neurotic conflict, those events may have remained preserved in the preconscious as particularly vivid day's residues ("currently active psychical material," Freud would say) until the night preceding the day of their session, at which point the day's residues finally become part of the dream.

An illustration: P was a single woman in her midthirties, whose father had been cold and undemonstrative, always hard to please, and avaricious with affirmation of his daughter. Her mother had died when P was 16 months old; her father had never remarried, and she had been raised by father's two unmarried sisters. At the time of the dream, which occurred early in therapy, P had a fairly strong therapeutic alliance and was experiencing the beginning of a strong, positive idealized parental transference. She saw me as a benign, caring, and accepting parent figure, the father (and on a deeper level, the mother) she had never had. At the time I was seeing her twice a week, on Mondays and Thursdays. She reported the dream during the Monday session; it had been dreamed the night before, Sunday.

"A Glorious Feeling"

P started the session in a happy mood and told me the dream at the very beginning of the hour. She was very happy about it.

> It was a glorious feeling. I was in session with you, but you did not look like you . . . no beard, and besides you were completely bald, your head looked like an egg! But you told me that you were very pleased with me, the way I cooperated with you, the progress I was making . . . it felt very, very good.

Right after the dream she told me that on the preceding Thursday, right after our therapy session, she had watched a film in which Carl Rogers interviews a patient by the name of Gloria (at that time, P was studying for a doctorate in counseling). This is a film I know well, having myself shown it a few times to my social work students. At the end of the film Gloria tells Rogers that she wished he had been her father; Rogers is clean shaven and completely bald, so I conjectured that I looked like Rogers, and was, in the dream, to begin with at least, Carl Rogers or a Carl Rogers figure. P told me that the next day after seeing the film, a woman supervisor at work had warmly praised and complimented her. She told me all that, clearly not realizing, consciously, the connections between the patient's name in the film, Gloria, and the "glorious feeling" of the dream, or between the supervisor's praising and complimenting her at work, and my being pleased with her in the dream. But the point here is that the day's residues of a dream dreamed on a Sunday night did go back to the previous Friday and Thursday.

Not all of a dream's unconscious memories go back to childhood. One also finds in dreams, materials which belong both to "yesteryear" and "yesterday," psychical material experienced in the day or days preceding the dream but immediately repressed into the unconscious because of strong connections to unconscious material repressed in childhood.

On the session preceding the dream, L, a neurologist, a rigid, formal, and austere patient, at the end of what had been, for him, a difficult session—in which, for the first time, he had expressed some anger, surprised me (and himself) immensely by saying, "Okay, *donkey*, see you tomorrow." He quickly apologized, and mumbled, "I am sorry, ehm, . . . I mean, I will see you tomorrow, Doctor. . . ." That night he dreamed.

"Patting a Donkey"

> A very strange dream . . . I was in one of the stables of my grandfather's farm in Italy . . . patting one of the donkeys.

L spoke briefly of his grandfather, a harsh and authoritarian man and the fact that his grandfather had died of a stroke. That he used the word *stroke* was telling. It would have been more in keeping with his usually very formal speech if he had used the term *cerebrovascular accident.* He did not refer to having called me donkey the week before, and, as I later found out, he had no recollection of that slip of the tongue, which related to a recent life event that bore similarities (based on predicate thinking) to material from a much earlier time.

The Mirror Relationship

There is a mirror or reciprocal relationship between the yesteryear and the yesterday, between the unconscious and preconscious legs of the dream.

From the Unconscious to the Preconscious

The unconscious ego, in order to build the manifest dream's facade and camouflage and distort the latent dream, takes over and overcathects those preconscious contents (those day's residues) which are psychodynamically appropriate, namely those preconscious components, those day's residues which have prelogic–predicate thinking similarities to corresponding unconscious contents. In other words, to distort the latent dream, the unconscious ego overcathects those day's residues best corresponding, in terms of prelogic–predicate thinking similarities, to the unconscious contents being discharged in and through the latent dream. Those elements in the preconscious, which are best suited psychodynamically to be a cover for the unconscious drives which are part of the latent dream, become the manifest dream. In this unconscious to preconscious direction, the unconscious ego is, indeed, like a clever and skillful casting director and makeup artist; it is similar to using a naturally portly actor, a Charles Laughton or an Orson Welles, to represent a Falstaff or a Pantagruel, or a naturally thin actor to portray a starved, emaciated character.

In effect, in the hours or days preceding the dream, the dreamer may have experienced, in the extrapsychic world, a great number of persons and situations (recent life experiences, the yesterday, the preconscious leg), among which might be, for example, an abusive father-in-law, a coldly punitive meter maid, a police officer accidentally dropping his club, a critical female

supervisor, a woman in a subway train, drugged, nodding dream-
ily, and so on. In the hours or days preceding the dream, the
dreamer's neurotic conflict may include a problematic unconscious complex which is overcathected, and therefore clamoring
for discharge, an unconscious complex going back to childhood
(infantile experiences, the yesteryear, the unconscious leg). Depending upon which unconscious complex most needed a discharge, that preconscious day's residue will be appropriated
which is psychodynamically appropriate: the abusive father-in-law,
if the unconscious complex needing to be dreamed about is anger
at the abusive father of one's childhood; the abusive meter maid,
if the unconscious thought is about anger at the castrating mother
of one's oedipal years; the police officer dropping his stick, if the
complex is about the wish to castrate father; the critical woman
supervisor if the unconscious complex is about anger at a critical
preoedipal mother; the woman in the train "under the influence," if the unconscious wish is to see mother reaching a sexual
climax. In other words, those preconscious contents and day's
residues are selected by the casting director, the unconscious ego,
which are best suited to represent and impersonate, on the stage
of the manifest dream, the characters, thoughts, and feelings of
the latent dream which are waiting in the wings of the unconscious and clamoring to burst onto the stage.

From the Preconscious to the Unconscious

As we examine the reciprocal relationship between the yesterday
and the yesteryear from the opposite direction, from the preconscious to the unconscious, we find a mirrorlike similarity to the
process just described.

In the hours or days preceding a dream, each person has
indeed experienced, consciously, hundreds of life events, some
of which have been experienced, consciously, with joy, some with
pain, some with indifference. Some of them, those truly unimportant, consciously and unconsciously, will eventually be forgotten. Most of them will be stored in the person's preconscious.
Of the hundreds of life events, persons, situations each dreamer
experiences in the hours or days preceding a dream (the father-
in-law, the meter maid, the police officer dropping his club, the

supervisor, the woman in the subway train, and so forth), some are unconsciously experienced with a special weight and feel, and stand out, unconsciously, from the whole because they are connected with corresponding unconscious contents, connected because of prelogic–predicate thinking similarities and identities. It is *only* these preconscious contents that will overcathect the corresponding unconscious contents.

If, in the hours or days preceding the dream, the problematic complex in the dreamer's unconscious, which happening to be overcathected, is clamoring for a discharge, has to do with anger at the abusive father of the dreamer's childhood, then the experience with the abusive father-in-law will be the day's residue which will have a special weight and feel, stand out from the whole, and be the overcathecting one. If, in the hours or days preceding the dream, the overcathected problematic complex needing discharge has to do with anger at the oedipal castrating mother, then the experience with the meter maid will be the day's residue which will have the special weight and feel, will stand out from the whole, and be the overcathecting one. Similarly, the police officer dropping his club, or the critical supervisor, will become the overcathecting experience if and when the problematic complex needing to be dreamed about, had been, respectively, the wish to castrate father, or anger at the preoedipal mother.

Day's Residues and the Mirror Relationship

Earlier we said that in the Freudian theory of dreams, the yesteryear is of paramount importance; but the yesterday is of importance too. The mirror relationship between the two highlights the important psychodynamic role of the day's residues as overcathecters of the infantile sources of the dream.

The day's residues are of great importance also clinically. Although they are only triggers for the infantile sources of dreams, which they overcathect, or facades for those sources, which overcathect them, the day's residues, as they appear in the patient's manifest dream, tell the analyst which present-day events, situations, persons, experienced consciously and stored preconsciously, have been invested with transferential energy. The day's residues tell which elements have been overcathected by the dreamer's unconscious, and therefore, have been connected with the primary experiences, stored in the unconscious, which are the roots of the patient's neurosis or pain. The yesterday, as it appears in the patient's manifest dream, enables the analyst to understand the patient's present-day realities, tensions, problems, and pains psychodynamically, with the third ear, as they are connected with and psychodynamically caused by past primary experiences. The yesterday, as it appears in the dream, enables the analyst to know who, in the patient's present (perhaps a spouse, the analyst, a friend, a teacher) has become transferentially someone from the distant past (father, mother, older brother, or sister). The day's residues are paths taking the analyst toward greater knowledge of their patient's unconscious; as such, they are essential in the early stages of therapy, when we should only make "interpretations on the level of defense," in the later stages of therapy (the working through stages), and whenever we need to make interpretations within the context of the transference.

In the "Glorious Feeling" dream, P had dreamed of me but I did not look like myself, had no beard, was completely bald, my head looked like an egg. In one of her associations to the dream, she had told me of the film in which Rogers interviewed Gloria, who had seen Rogers as a good parental figure, while Rogers had praised her as a "pretty nice daughter." Another association was about a woman supervisor who also had praised her, and in the manifest dream, I, who did not look like myself, had also praised her. It was her associations, all day's residues, all belonging to the yesterday, that indicated that P had invested in me feelings belonging to the past. It was the yesterday that confirmed that she had developed a positive parental transference toward me, that suggested that she saw me as the father she did not have. It suggested also that she saw me as mother—making me clean-shaven was less a castration than it was making me motherlike; besides, my head "looked like an egg," and eggs are female, not male.

With L's dream too, the day's residue of a slip of the tongue from the previous session overcathected and was overcathected by an old memory going back to his childhood. But in the reciprocal relationship between the yesterday and the yesteryear, it was the yesterday that tipped me off to the beginning of a transference onto me of positive and negative feelings he had experienced decades before toward his father and grandfather.

"Sicilian Bamboo"

M was a single woman in her late thirties, toward the end of her fourth year of therapy. She had been coming three times a week, and using the couch, for about three years before the dream.

> I dreamed of the phony plant at the foot of the couch here in the office, you once said it's a reproduction of a Sicilian bamboo. But the plant, in the dream, was real, not artificial . . . and it was dry, very dry, almost dying. Only two buds were still alive. I watered it.

The plant being dreamed about (indeed an artificial reproduction of Sicilian bamboo) had been at the foot of the couch and, therefore, in her full view. But only at this point in her analysis, and for the first time, had the plant become part of the manifest content of one of her dreams. Significant unconscious feelings included anger at the ungiving and hypocritical mother of her childhood and the wish to kill and revive her. Transference was a largely negative maternal transference through the lens of which she saw me as ungiving and hypocritical, a phony plant indeed. These feelings were being overcathected, at that point in analysis, by the fact that she was dating a man who, as were so many men she had dated through her adult life, was unnurturing and "phony" (she had recently "discovered" he was married), another mother figure. But only at this point in analysis had the "phony" plant at the foot of the couch (a preconscious mental content, a yesterday content) become the psychodynamically most "appropriate" day's residue, a psychodynamically "perfect" symbol for the unnurturing ("dry, very dry"), hypocritical ("phony") boyfriend-analyst-mother. And only at that point in her therapy had the artificial plant indeed become something I could use to lead her toward further knowledge of her unconscious: insofar as the day's residue was connected with me (it was in my office, at the foot of my couch, as Sicilian as I am, and as "phony" as she was seeing me at that time), I could use it for an "interpretation within the context of the transference."

DREAM FORMATION: THE WISH TO SLEEP

One of the basic purposes of dreaming is to preserve sleep; there is a wish to sleep. "[*T*]*he wish to sleep (which the conscious ego is concentrated upon, and which, together with the dream-censorship and the 'secondary revision'.* . . *constitute the conscious ego's share in dreaming) must in every case be reckoned as one of the motives for the formation of dreams, and every successful dream is a fulfillment of that wish*" (Freud, 1900, p. 234).

In order to sleep, which is biologically essential for rest and recuperation, one tries to create or recreate a condition of relatively high and undisturbed homeostasis, by decathecting consciousness and shutting off stimulations coming from the external world and, to an extent, from one's own body. This is attained through neurophysiological processes of inhibition and deafferentiation of specific areas of the cerebral cortex responsible for the psychological phenomenon of "consciousness."

When we are deeply asleep *and not dreaming,* we do not generally smell or taste, do not feel the weight of the sheets or the touch of a hand on our body, do not hear or see. Our eyes can be gently pried open without waking us up, and there will be no recollection of the event afterward. Our muscular system too is largely decathected, which is why most of us need a horizontal or reclining position to sleep well; if we fall asleep sitting up, we'll wake up the moment the muscular system needs to be recathected to prevent slipping or falling onto the floor.

Everything else being equal—how tired one is, how long it has been since one has last slept, the strength and persistence of sensory stimulations—the depth of one's sleep and the accompanying degree of neurophysiological inhibition and deafferentiation (and, therefore, the "wakeability" of the sleeper) will vary in accordance with the intensity of the wish to sleep. The quality of the sensory stimulations (in addition to, or even regardless of their strength) will also determine whether a given stimulus does or does not "awaken" those parts of the cerebral cortex that are "asleep." A nursing mother deeply asleep *and not dreaming* may hear the whimpering of the infant sleeping in the next room sooner than the loud ring of a telephone or banging on the door. The picture changes considerably when we are asleep *and dreaming*: cortical vigilance operations are less decathected; and sensory stimulations may and may not trigger a dream; but if a dream is dreamed, those stimulations become regularly part of the dream. In this state of neurophysiological separation from the external world, the only stimulations that can enter the system and disturb homeostasis are:

1. Sensory stimulations from the external world;
2. Bodily stimuli from within one's body, that is, bodily sensations from the body's organs and the body's sexual, digestive, and excretory functions;
3. Psychological stimuli from within one's preconscious, that is, experiences from the day or days preceding sleep, the day's residues;
4. Psychological stimuli from within one's unconscious, that is, overcathected drives from the intrapsychic world.

The following are some possible outcomes:

Sleep is disturbed by the sensory stimulations from the external world, or by bodily stimuli from within, stimuli strong enough and persistent enough to overcome sleep. *Outcome: the sleeper will awake without having dreamed.*

Sleep is disturbed by the psychological stimuli from highly overcathected day's residues from within the sleeper's preconscious. *Outcome: agitated sleep, no dream sleep, dream phobia.*

Sleep is disturbed by (1), (2), and (3), but also by (4), psychological stimuli from overcathected drives from within the sleeper's unconscious. *Outcome: a dream, a compromise product between intrapsychic drives and defenses, and also, between stimuli from without and from within and the wish to sleep.*

5

Dream Formation, 2

In 1910, Freud published the five lectures he had delivered at Clark University, Worcester, Massachusetts, in 1909. In one of those lectures he said: "Small children always dream of the fulfilments of wishes that were aroused in them the day before but not satisfied" (1910a, p. 34). In *The Interpretation of Dreams* he published many children's dreams, including his daughter's, age 8½, his son's, just over 5, and the famous "strawberry dream" dreamed by Anna Freud at 19 months of age. He wrote: "The dreams of young children are pure wish fulfilments and for that reason quite uninteresting compared with the dreams of adults" (1900, p. 127). At that point, Freud believed that children's dreams were undistorted and uncensored and that their latent and manifest contents were identical. But in the 1911 edition of the *The Interpretation of Dreams* he modified the above sequence to read: "The dreams of young children are frequently pure wish-fulfilments and in that case quite uninteresting compared with the dreams of adults" (1900, p. 127, n 1, 2). In a footnote added in 1911, Freud wrote: "The fact should be mentioned that children soon begin to have more complicated and less transparent dreams" (1900, p. 131); and in the third edition, that footnote reads: "It should be mentioned that young children often have more complex and obscure dreams." In a still later edition, he noted that "Experience has shown that distorted dreams, which stand in need of interpretation, are already found in children of four or five" (Freud, 1900, p. 127, n 1). These changes signal

Freud's movement away from the belief that children's dreams are undistorted and uncensored.

Probably only infants' dreams, the primary-process-based dreams of being fed, are totally undistorted. After that, all dreams, including children's dreams and need dreams related to the need to eat, drink, urinate, and defecate, orgasmic sexual dreams, the need to wake up, and so on, are never totally undistorted and uncensored. As indicated in the previous chapter, if a physiological or sensory stimulus is strong and persistent enough, and we are in a state of normal sleep, that stimulus will wake us up. If a biological need triggers a dream, that is because it has further overcathected already overcathected internal drives, and those drives producing the dream will undergo a degree of distortion according to the dynamics of the neurotic conflict. (This will be discussed and illustrated with dream examples in chapter 8, in connection with simple dreams.) Thus, most dreams, adults' and children's alike, are distorted and censored.[1]

Dream formation consists in the process of distortion and censorship, processes changing dreams from latent to manifest through the psychological operations of the dream work.

> The psychical process underlying [dreams] might originally have been expressed in words quite differently. You must distinguish the *manifest content of the dream,* as you vaguely recollect it in the morning and laboriously (and, as it seems, arbitrarily) clothe it in words, and the *latent dream-thoughts,* which you must suppose were present in the unconscious. . . . The manifest content of the dream is the distorted substitute for the unconscious dream-thoughts and this distortion is the work of the ego's forces of defense—of resistances. In waking life, these resistances altogether prevent the repressed wishes of the unconscious from entering consciousness; and during the lowered state of sleep they are at least strong enough to oblige them to adopt a veil of disguise [Freud, 1910a, p. 35].

A few lines later, he continued: "The manifest dream, which you know from your memory when you wake up, can therefore

---

[1]Dreams dreamed in conjunction with severe psychic crises, decompensation, severe psychoses, or highly regressed states may be only minimally distorted and censored. Paraphrasing Frieda Fromm-Reichman who believed that schizophrenics speak with the unconscious tip of their tongue (1948), in the above conditions, the unconscious is on the tip of the dream.

only be described as a disguised fulfillment of repressed wishes" (1910a, pp. 35–36).

Latent and manifest dreams are conflicted unconscious wishes expressed, so to speak, in two different languages: the latent dream in the language and with the requirements of the unconscious, the manifest dream in the language and with the requirements of consciousness. The manifest dream is the translation of the latent dream into the language of the conscious ego. In the process of translation, the ego modifies it to make it adhere to the requirements of ego and superego: it thus camouflages and distorts it into the latent dream. Freud described this process of distortion and camouflage as the product of "censorship" (1900, p. 142).

The word *censorship* as used by Freud refers to the ego's defensive operations adaptively protecting the conscious, socialized, and moralized ego from too direct an experience of the primitive unconscious drives of id and superego, according to the dynamics of the neurotic conflict. Censorship works day and night or whenever our psyche is functioning. When we are awake, censorship censors our unconscious processes through the psychological operations of the ego's mechanisms of defense, which allow into consciousness only derivatives of the unconscious. When we are asleep and dreaming, censorship censors our psychic processes through the psychological operations of the dream work, which include condensation, displacement, dramatization, secondary revision, and symbolism, and any of the ego's defense mechanisms which are part of the dreamer's personality. Therefore, censorship while we are asleep is not different from when we are awake, the sole difference being that it is the sleeping rather than the waking mind that is censored. When we are asleep, at the dream formation stage, censorship distorts the latent dream into the manifest dream; when we are awake, at the dream interpretation stage, censorship resists the retranslation of the manifest dream into its latent antecedent. While censorship is to be identified with the unconscious ego and the superego, it is not to be thought of as an anthropomorphic entity.

According to Freud, the psychological operations of the dream work are condensation, displacement, dramatization, secondary revision, and symbolism. Let us now examine in detail the dream work and its defensive operations.

CONDENSATION

Empirical observation alone already suggests that the manifest dream is a highly condensed rendition of the latent dream. "The first thing that becomes clear to anyone who compares the dream-content with the dream-thoughts is that a work of *condensation* on a large scale has been carried out" (Freud, 1900, p. 279). Condensation consists of the compression of many latent dream thoughts into one element of the manifest dream. In condensation, "one recognizable idea or memory stands in fact for a number of previously unrecognizable, far more important and apparently unrelated ideas and memories" (Stafford-Clark, 1965, p. 74). Condensation may also "compress" into one word (sometimes a neologism) feelings and thoughts belonging to another context, time, and place. It is not possible to know the full extent of condensation in any one dream, that is, to know how many latent dream-thoughts have been compressed into one manifest dream component: "It is in fact never possible to be sure that a dream has been completely interpreted" (Freud, 1900, p. 289).

In addressing the what (i.e., the *object* of condensation, what latent dream-thoughts have been condensed into the manifest dream) and the "how" of condensation (i.e., the *process* of condensation, the factors determining the selection of the dream-thoughts being condensed), Freud pointed out that "Associative paths lead from one element of the dream to several dream-thoughts, and from one dream-thought to several elements of the dream." He continued to demonstrate "that the whole mass of dream-thoughts [are] submitted to a sort of manipulative process in which those elements which have the most numerous and strongest supports acquire the right of entry into the dream content" (Freud, 1900, p. 284). In other words, those dream-thoughts "acquire entry" that are the most heavily overcathected and that have common elements or features (in predicate thinking terms). In a rather felicitous analogy, Ella Freeman Sharpe compared the condensing work of the defensive ego to the working of a magnet that, from hundreds of particles strewn over a surface, only attracts particles made of metal (Sharpe, 1978, p. 25).

In Freud's own dream about Irma (1900, p. 107), thoughts, feelings, and memories about at least seven persons were condensed into Irma, the central element of the manifest dream.

These include Irma herself, another patient Freud would have gladly exchanged for Irma in that July of 1895, Freud's oldest daughter, another patient by the same name who had died from poisoning, a child Freud had examined in the neurological department of a children's hospital, another woman patient to whom Freud had once given a physical examination, and his own wife. In the same dream, Dr. M stood for at least three persons: Dr. M himself, Freud's eldest brother, and his father. The night after reading an article on a physiological discovery by a fellow psychiatrist in Vienna, Freud had a one sentence dream: *"It's written in a positively norekdal style"* (1900, p. 296). Freud had thought the discovery was grossly overestimated and the paper written much too emotionally. In free associating about the dream, he thought that the neologism *norekdal* was "a parody of the [German] superlatives '*kolossal*' and '*pyramidal.*' " Reflecting upon his associations, he continued: "At last I saw that the monstrosity was composed of the two names 'Nora' and 'Ekdal'—characters in two well-known plays of Ibsen's [*A Doll's House* and *The Wild Duck*]. Some time before, I had read a newspaper article on Ibsen by the same author whose latest work I was criticizing in the dream" (1900, p. 296). And in an example of condensation in a dream of a patient of mine, the word *reserpine* was a condensation of "reserved penis" (see chapter 7).

One can again see parallels between dream formation and symptom formation, dream work defenses and the ego's defense mechanisms. Overdetermination operates both in condensation and in symptom formation, and in the form which various unconscious derivatives take when they slip into consciousness in the wakeful state. Condensation can reinforce the ego defenses utilized as part of the selective thinking employed in symptom formation. For instance, a young boy may reinforce his castration anxiety by selectively focusing on, and overcathecting such experiences as the falling of his baby teeth, the cutting of his hair, the trimming of his fingernails, his tonsillectomy operation, the mutilation of a man's limb in a car accident whose sensational photograph he saw in a tabloid newspaper. He will condense all these experiences to support his belief in the likelihood of castration, ignoring and leaving undercathected the fact that a new tooth grew to replace the deciduous one, and that his hair grew, and so did his nails, and that most people are not mutilated in car accidents.

DISPLACEMENT

Freud noted that in some dreams it can be seen that "the elements which stand out as the principal components of the manifest content of the dream are far from playing the same part in the dream-thoughts. And, as a corollary, the converse of this assertion can be affirmed: what is clearly the essence of the dream-thoughts need not be represented in the dream at all. The dream is, as it were, differently centred from the dream-thoughts—its content has different elements as its central point" (1900, p. 305).

There is in displacement a shifting of emphasis, focus, intensity, attention, importance, and feelingfulness from one element in the latent dream to another in the manifest, or vice versa. Through displacement, what is central and crucial in the latent dream is peripheral and trivial in the manifest, or vice versa. One element is highly charged in the latent dream, minimally so in the manifest, or vice versa. Because of displacement, feelings about this or that dream's element in the manifest dream can be "overreactions" or "underreactions" when compared to the corresponding feelings about this or that dream's element in the latent dream. That about which the displacement occurs can be a person, an action, an inanimate object, a body part, a location in space, a place.

In the manifest content of Freud's dream about Irma's injection, Freud (1900, p. 107) was examining Irma's oral cavity; in the latent dream, he may have been examining her vagina. His friends Otto and Leopold were examining her chest; in the latent dream, they might have been examining her pelvis (both examples of "displacement upward"). In another of Freud's dreams (1900, pp. 136–145) the centerpiece in the manifest dream was Freud's uncle's beard; it represented Freud's ambition in the latent dream. For one of my patients, the pharingeal bleeding she dreamed about in the manifest dream was a displacement upward from vaginal bleeding (menstruation) in the latent dream; and while she was "totally unconcerned" about the bleeding in the manifest dream, she was concerned about it in the latent dream and that too was a displacement. Again, similarities and parallels with the psychological processes of growth and development and symptom formation in waking life are obvious.

To begin with, displacement, of course, is a basic process in the development and vicissitudes of instinctual energy. Drives have a source, an aim, an impetus, *and an object.* A drive's object is the most variable feature of a drive, since the psychic energy of the drive can be *displaced* from one object to another. The process of rechanneling the psychic energy of a drive from object A to object B, the process of cathecting object B if object A is not available, is indeed the process of displacement.

Displacements are an essential process in the psychogenesis of symptoms and an essential element in their "fabric." Most hysterical symptoms are displacements. Inhibitions caused by the *sexualization* of ego functions are displacements. Transferential phenomena are based on displacements. Overreactions (profuse weeping, sentimentality, and so on) in watching a love scene, or a death, or some other meaningful event at a movie usually coupled with underreactions when those events had occurred in the person's real life—are based, among other processes, on displacement.

Similarities and identities because of predicate and prelogical thinking are important in the choice of objects onto which unconscious processes displace themselves. In dreams, these similarities and identities and the censorship's demands for optimum disguise and distortion play an equal role in the selection.

DRAMATIZATION OR CONCRETE PICTORIAL REPRESENTATION

Condensed and displaced, the overcathected unconscious drives of the id, the unconscious thoughts and feelings that will become the latent dream, will be "represented" in the manifest dream through dramatization, yet another psychological operation of the dream work. Dramatization serves a dual purpose: (1) it permits the representation of the overcathected thoughts and feelings, their "dreamability," so to speak; and (2) by representing these thoughts in a special form (concrete and pictorial rather than verbal and abstract), it completes, furthers, and perfects their distortion. Since the essence of this psychological operation is the representation of thoughts and feelings as concrete images, dramatization can also be called "concrete pictorial representation." As the next pages will show, this wording reflects Freud's thinking better than *dramatization,* which was the term, Freud tells us (1900, p. 50), used by Spitta, one of his contemporaries who theorized about dreams (Spitta, 1882, p. 145).

Concrete pictorial representation is a psychological operation of the greatest importance. Freud was clear about the importance of the distorting function of this operation. Similarly, he expanded on its role in representing conjunctions, logical connections, and causal relations in dreams (1900, pp. 310–338).

Some basic concepts first: extrapsychic reality, the world outside of us, its people and artifacts, nature and all man-made objects, can be represented in our minds *abstractly and verbally* as words; or *concretely and sensorially* as sensations and perceptions. A bird can be represented abstractly and verbally by the word *bird* or sensorially and concretely by the visual image, or the drawing, of a bird. One's father can be represented abstractly by his name or by the word *father* or sensorially by flashing to one's mind the way he looks or sounds when he speaks. One's mother can be represented by the word *mother* or by the way she looks, sounds, tastes, smells, or feels to one's hand.

Early in life, children represent reality concretely and sensorially, and think in highly concrete terms. One of my children, when asked by her mother to make a drawing of what I did when I went to work in the morning, proudly produced a piece of paper covered with circles. Asked to explain how that represented what I did at work, she said, "Why, when Daddy leaves in the morning, he says he is going to the hospital to make rounds." Also early in our philogenetic development, language was more concrete, words were more "sensorial" (pictograms, hieroglyphics).

As we grow, we learn to represent reality abstractly and verbally. Verbal representations of reality have two great advantages over sensorial representations: time-economy and a high degree of abstraction and generalization. When we represent the object *chair* by its name, we do that in a fraction of a second and the word *chair* "generalizes" enough to include all kinds, styles, and models of chairs. But to represent a chair sensorially one has to take the time to visualize one; and to reach a degree of generalization, one has to recall the sights of many kinds of chairs: kitchen chairs, reclining chairs, garden chairs, beach chairs, Chippendale chairs, and so on. The advantages of verbal over sensorial representations are even greater when abstract rather than concrete objects have to be represented. The difficulty of representing a concrete object, a chair, sensorially is multiplied many times when one has to represent sensorially such abstract concepts as *loyalty* or *ownership* or *possession*. To represent loyalty sensorially, for instance, one may have to go through the cumbersome process of visualizing a Boy Scout standing in front of a flag, one hand on his heart, reciting the Pledge of Allegiance. To represent sensorially, again visually, ownership or possession, one has to go through the equally ponderous procedure of imaging someone sitting or squatting on what is being owned or possessed.

When we are mentally ill, or tired and dozing, or in the process of falling asleep, we regress to varying extents to sensorial thinking (1900, p. 535). Elsewhere, also in *The Interpretation of Dreams*, Freud gives examples of "hypnagogic thinking" and "hypnagogic hallucinations" (1900, pp. 344–345) occurring in the process of falling asleep.

In dreams we revert to representing the psychic world of thoughts, feelings, and memories by concrete and sensorial means to a much larger extent than we do in waking life or did in childhood. Thus, concrete pictorial representation is a *regression* from the more mature and developed, abstract and verbal model of thinking to the more primitive and undeveloped, concrete and sensorial model. In dreams, the overcathected unconscious drives, the condensed and displaced thoughts, feelings, and memories of our unconscious, and all abstract representations of previous psychological experiences, are given a concrete, sensorial, and predominantly visual form. Even when he calls this operation "dramatization," Freud clearly sees its sensorial aspect: "The transformation of ideas into hallucinations is not the only respect in which dreams differ from corresponding thoughts in waking life. Dreams construct a *situation* out of these images; they represent an event which is actually happening; as Spitta (1882, p. 145) puts it, they " 'dramatize' an idea" (Freud, 1900, p. 50).

Freud saw dramatization not only as a regression but also as a *displacement* to the earlier, more primitive model of thinking.

> We have not yet referred to any other sort of displacement. Analyses show us, however, that another sort exists and that it reveals itself in a change in the *verbal expression* of the thoughts concerned. In both cases there is a displacement along a chain of associations; but a process of such a kind as occur in various psychical spheres, and the outcome of the displacement may in one case be that one element is replaced by another, while the outcome in another case may be that a single element has its *verbal form* replaced by another. . . .
>
> The direction taken by the displacement usually results in a colourless and abstract expression in the dream-thought being exchanged for a pictorial and concrete one. The advantage, and accordingly the purpose, of such a change jumps to the eyes. A thing that is pictorial is, from the point of view of the dream, a thing that is *capable of being represented*: it can be introduced into a situation in which abstract expressions offer the same kind of difficulties to representation in dreams as a political leading article in a newspaper would offer to an illustrator. . . . A dream-thought is unusable so long as it is expressed in an abstract form; but when once it has been transformed into pictorial language, contrasts and identifications of the kind which the dream-work requires, and which it creates if they are not already present, can be established more easily than before between the new form of expression and the remainder of the material underlying the dream [1900, pp. 339–340].

Now the dream-thought becomes usable for representation. Earlier in *The Interpretation of Dreams* in what was, in effect, a parenthesis in his introduction to the concept of the dream work, Freud had written:

> The dream-content, on the other hand, is expressed as it were in a pictographic script, the characters of which have to be transposed individually into the language of the dream-thoughts. . . . Suppose I have a picture-puzzle, a rebus, in front of me. It depicts a house with a boat on its roof, a single letter of the alphabet, the figure of a running man whose head has been conjured away, and so on. Now I might be misled into raising objections and declaring that the picture as a whole and its component parts are nonsensical. . . . But obviously, we can only form a proper judgment of the rebus if we put aside criticisms such as these of the whole composition and its parts and if, instead, we try to replace each separate element by a syllable or word that can be represented by that element in some way or other. The words which are put together in this way are no longer nonsensical but may form a poetical phrase of the greatest beauty

and significance. A dream is a picture-puzzle of this sort [1900, pp. 277–278].

In "On Dreams," Freud referred to "condensation, displacement and pictorial arrangement of psychic material" as three operations of dream work (1901a, p. 666). And to further support this use of *concrete pictorial representation,* the reader's attention is called to some of the words in the quotations above. "The transformation of ideas into *hallucinations*" (Freud, 1900, p. 50; emphasis added), hallucination is obviously a sensorial phenomenon. "The direction taken by the displacement usually results in a colourless and abstract expression in the dream-thought being exchanged for a *pictorial and concrete* one" (p. 339; emphasis added). "The dream-content, on the other hand, is expressed as it were in a *pictographic* script"; and "A dream is a *picture* puzzle of this sort" (pp. 277–278; emphasis added). Freud referred to "condensation, displacement, and *pictorial* arrangement of the psychic material" (1901a, p. 666; emphasis added). The italicized words justify my contention that to refer to "dramatization" as "concrete pictorial representation" does no violence to Freud's thinking about it. And, in fact, the word *dramatize,* again, was not, originally, Freud's, but Spitta's (Freud, 1900, p. 50).

In terms of dream work and dream work's distortion, the essence of concrete pictorial representation is that something abstract in the latent dream is rendered as something concrete in the manifest dream. If this abstract-to-concrete transformation has not occurred, we are not witnessing concrete pictorial representation.

"Possession" (an abstraction) in the latent dream becomes "sitting on something" (a concretization) in the manifest dream. Sexual excitement, reaching a climax, or experiencing a nonsexual feeling of ecstasy, of joy, of "feeling high" in the latent dream (all abstractions) becomes seeing oneself on top of a skyscraper (a concretization) in the manifest dream. The thought and attendant feelings of sexual ejaculation in the latent dream, which are abstractions, become a "leaking pen" (a concretization) in the manifest dream. The latent thought of male sexual potency (an abstraction) becomes a gun shooting straight bullets in the manifest dream (a concretization). The abstract thought of male sexual impotence in the latent content becomes, in the manifest dream, the concrete image of a gun shooting bullets that limply fall on the ground as soon as they leave the barrel. The abstraction of erection in the latent dream becomes, in the manifest dream, the concrete image of an elevator going up at great speed or of an airplane taking off. The latent content idea of erection followed by vaginal intercourse becomes, in the manifest dream, an elevator going up and down an elevator shaft. The latent thought of an angry erection becomes, in the manifest content, an elevator going up and through the roof (when one is angry, one "hits the ceiling"). Again, if the abstract-to-concrete transformation is not present, we are not dealing with concrete pictorial representation.

Hypnagogic phenomena are helpful in illustrating concrete pictorial representations. They are an intermediate psychic product between, on the one hand, the more mature and developed, abstract and verbal model of thinking, and on the other hand, the more primitive and undeveloped, concrete and sensorial model. Freud first mentioned these phenomena in discussing sensory excitations in dreams: "The chief evidence in favour of the power of subjective sensory excitations to instigate dreams is provided by what are known as 'hypnagogic hallucinations', or, to use Johannes Müller's term (1826), 'imaginative visual phenomena' " (1900, p. 31). What happens in hypnagogic phenomena is that, in the process of falling asleep, but while still fully awake and alert, we find ourselves reviewing the day's events, we do so using words and thoughts in our mind. As we begin to fall asleep, we begin to alternate between verbal and abstract forms of representation and concrete and sensorial (mainly visual) forms. As we approach sleep, we shift more and more toward the concrete and sensorial models; and shift entirely to concrete and sensorial means as we fall asleep and dream. Something similar happens when we think about an intellectual, philosophical, or mathematical problem while tired, with a definite shift from abstract and verbal to concrete and sensorial means of representation. In Freud's words:

> Herbert Silberer (1909) has pointed out a good way of directly observing the transformation of thoughts into pictures in the process of forming dreams and so of studying this one factor of dream-work in isolation. If,

when he was in a fatigued and sleepy condition, he set himself some intellectual task, he found that it often happened that the thought escaped him and that in its place a picture appeared, which he was then able to recognize as a substitute for the thought [1900, p. 344].

Elsewhere, Freud cited Silberer's examples of hypnagogic phenomena to illuminate the shift toward concrete pictorial representation while falling asleep. In one example, Silberer (1909) was thinking of revising an uneven passage in an essay: as he dozed off, he saw himself planing a piece of wood (Freud, 1900, p. 304). In another example, Silberer (1909) was trying to compare the views of Kant and Schopenhauer about the concept of time; as he was feeling more and more drowsy, a concrete and plastic symbol, as though it were a dream picture, came to him, a visual image that captured sensorially the abstract thoughts he was trying in vain to conceptualize (Freud, 1900, pp. 503–504).

Let us direct our attention to Freud's use of the word *plastic.* While he quotes Silberer's use of the phrase "a concrete and plastic symbol," he elaborates its meaning extensively. The terms *dramatization* and *concrete pictorial representation* are sometimes referred to as "plastic representation" (Freud, 1932, p. 190). Freud used the word *plastic* in its original sense, capable of being molded and receiving form. He used it as related to "the plastic arts," sculpture and painting. In that sense, therefore, and applied to dream formation, the choice of the word is felicitous. In the first of his chapter subsections on means of representation in dreams, writing about the problem of representing conjunctions, logical connections, and causal relations, he said: "The incapacity of dreams to express these things must lie in the nature of the psychical material out of which dreams are made. The plastic arts of painting and sculpture labour, indeed, under a similar limitation as compared with poetry, which can make use of speech" (1900, p. 312).

As indicated throughout this section, converting the abstract thoughts of the latent dream into the concrete images of the manifest dream, thus making the dream thoughts dreamable, is the most important function of concrete pictorial representation. But concrete pictorial representation's role also includes representing in dreams various logical aspects of the dream thoughts.

It is not altogether clear, and of greater importance to the neurophysiologist and neuroscientist than to the psychoanalyst, how a person's extrapsychic experiences are preserved and stored in the mind as memories, either preconscious or unconscious; or how the logical aspects of those experiences are preserved and stored. Freudian psychoanalysis holds that the logic of the unconscious differs from the logic of consciousness and that concepts of time (e.g., before, during, after, and so forth) and space (e.g., above, below, side by side), also differ from their counterparts in consciousness and Aristotelian logic. Freud believed that dream-thoughts "usually emerge as a complex of thoughts and memories of the most intricate possible structure" (1900, pp. 311–312). He posed the question of how these complex thoughts retain their logical connectedness in the dream: how are conjunctions (e.g., if, because, although, either, or) represented in dreams? He answered: "For the most part dreams disregard all these conjunctions, and it is only the substantive content of the dream-thoughts that they take over and manipulate. The restoration of the connections which the dream-work has destroyed is a task which has to be performed by the interpretative process" (1900, p. 312).

Logical connections, connections between dream-thoughts, causal relations, and commonly shared attributes can be reproduced in the dream, Freud believed, by specific means of representation. *Logical connections* are represented through simultaneity in time. He said "Here they [dreams] are acting like the painter who, in a picture of the School of Athens or of Parnassus, represents in one group all the philosophers or all the poets. It is true that they were never in fact assembled in a single hall or on a single mountain-top; but they certainly form a group in the conceptual sense" (1900, p. 314).

Intimate connections between two dream-thoughts, for instance dream-thought A and dream-thought B, are represented through contiguity between the elements in the manifest dream representing those dream-thoughts. Freud said, "In the same way, in our system of writing, '*ab*' means that the two letters are to be pronounced in a single syllable. If a gap is left between the '*a*' and the '*b*,' it means that the '*a*' is the last letter of one word and the '*b*' is the first of the next one" (1900, p. 314).

Causal relations are represented by two procedures. Freud explained that "the commoner method of representation would be to introduce the dependent clause as an introductory dream and to add the principal clause as the main dream" (1900, p. 315). The second means of representation of causal relations "consists in one image in the dream, whether of a person or thing, being transformed into another" (1900, p. 316).

Commonly shared similarities and attributes can be represented by a process of unification. "Similarity, consonance, the possession of common attributes—all these are represented in dreams by unification, which may either be present already in the material of the dream-thoughts or may be freshly constructed. The first of these possibilities may be described as 'identification' and the second as 'composition' " (Freud, 1900, p. 320). In *identification*, which is heavily dependent on predicate thinking, the latent dream could be about overcathected feelings concerning person A. Person A has predicates or attributes in common with person B, about whom the dreamer has psychodynamically neutral feelings. Only B appears in the manifest dream; A, the psychodynamically significant person, will only appear, if at all, through free associations. This is a case where the dream work operates as *concrete pictorial representation* in that feelings (an abstraction) about a person are rendered by imaging a person (a concretization); and operates as *displacement* in that feelings about A are shifted into feelings about B. In *composition*, an image is constructed, made out of elements belonging to several persons: but of all the persons so condensed into one composite image, and of all the elements condensed into that composite image, only one person, or only one element, is psychodynamically significant but remains effectively camouflaged by the masquerade of the composition. In one case where composition was at work, the latent dream was about overcathected wishes by a son to see his father as effeminate and at the same time as a powerful and brutal muscle man. The manifest dream "composed" the image of a heavily muscled and bearded man, dressed in a ballerina's tutu made of lacy tulle, holding a dainty little parasol high over the head while executing a very feminine and delicate dance step. Here too, the dream work utilized condensation as well as concrete pictorial representation. Composition frequently makes the manifest dream amusing and humorous, which furthers the distortion and makes the forbidden, latent thoughts even less identifiable.

All these examples show how concrete pictorial representation not only makes the dream dreamable by converting the dream-thoughts into images, but at the same time fulfills the requirement of censorship by effectively distorting the latent dream—this distortion being the major role and function of the dream work.

SYMBOLISM

To fulfill the requirements of censorship, the dream-thoughts, the overcathected unconscious drives that are being made into a dream, are not only condensed, displaced, and represented through concrete pictorial means, but also rendered symbolically. Freud (1900) recognized the importance of symbolism early in his work on dreams. Referring to a dream which he had earlier called "The Language of Flowers" (p. 315), he elaborated it in its entirety to evidence the use made of symbolic elements by the dream. "The analysis of this last, biographical, dream is clear evidence that I recognized the presence of symbolism in dreams from the very beginning. But it was only by degrees and as my experience increased that I arrived at a full appreciation of its extent and significance . . ." (p. 350).

He observed that some elements of the manifest dream lend themselves poorly to free associations and, when associations are given they seem more intellectualized connections than true free associations: "As a rule the technique of interpreting according to the dreamer's free associations leaves us in the lurch when we come to the symbolic elements in the dream-content" (1900, p. 353).

Some elements of the manifest dream may indeed be connected to their latent antecedents symbolically, and it may be possible to interpret them by "translating the symbols." Freud was explicit about the importance of symbolism in dreams and the possibility of interpreting dreams through a knowledge of symbols. But he was equally explicit about the need for caution in doing so and about the possibility of misinterpreting dreams only through a knowledge of symbols. In *The Interpretation of Dreams* he noted that "the presence of symbols in dreams not only facilitates their interpretation, but also makes it more difficult" (p. 353). Fifteen years later, in his *Introductory Lectures on Psychoanalysis*, he said of dreams:

> They allow us in certain circumstances to interpret a dream without questioning the dreamer.... If we are acquainted with the ordinary dream symbols, and in addition with the dreamer's personality, the circumstances in which he lives and the impressions which preceded the occurrence of the dream, we are often in a position to interpret a dream straightaway.... [However] interpretation based on a knowledge of symbols is not a technique which can replace or compete with the associative one. It forms a supplement to the latter ... [1916b, p. 151].

And he was most explicit in the importance of the "associative method" in "On Dreams" (1901a):

> It would, incidentally, be a mistake to expect that if we had a still profounder knowledge of dream-symbolism (of the "language of dreams") we could do without asking the dreamer for his associations to the dream and go back entirely to the technique of dream-interpretation of antiquity. Quite apart from individual symbols and oscillations in the use of universal ones, one can never tell whether any particular element in the content of the dream is to be interpreted symbolically or in its proper sense, and one can be certain that the *whole* content of a dream is not to be interpreted symbolically. A knowledge of dream-symbolism will never do more than enable us to translate certain constituents of the dream-content, and will not relieve us of the necessity for applying the [associative] technical rules which I gave earlier [p. 684].

In this context Freud differed significantly from Wilhelm Stekel (1911), whose theories and techniques concerning dreams he viewed with only faint praise and severe criticism. On the one hand, Freud, speaking of symbolism, noted "I arrived at a full appreciation of its extent and significance, and I did so under the influence of the contributions of Wilhelm Stekel (1911)" (1900, p. 350). Nonetheless, he referred to Stekel as a writer "who has perhaps damaged psycho-analysis as much as he has benefited it" (1900, p. 350). And again: "Stekel arrived at his interpretations of symbols by way of intuition, thanks to a peculiar gift for the direct understanding of them. But the existence of such a gift cannot be counted upon generally, . . . its findings have no claim to credibility" (1900, p. 350). Yet again: "Regard for scientific criticism forbids our returning to the arbitrary judgement of the dream-interpreter, as it was employed in ancient times and seems to have been revived in the reckless interpretations of Stekel" (1900, p. 353). And Freud's strongest indictment of Stekel: "[T]his author's lack of a critical faculty and his tendency to generalization at all costs throw doubts upon others of his interpretations or render them unusable" (1900, p. 357).

Freud knew that symbolism "is not peculiar to dreams, but is characteristic of unconscious ideation . . . and it is to be found in folklore and in popular myths, legends, linguistic idioms, proverbial wisdom and current jokes, to a more complete extent than in dreams" (1900, p. 351). He discerned that we come to know the meaning of symbols "from very different sources—from fairy tales and myths, from buffoonery and jokes, from folklore (that is from knowledge about popular manners and customs, sayings and songs) and from poetic and colloquial linguistic usage" (1916b, pp. 158–159). He explored the nature of the symbolic relationship, the connection between *what is being symbolized* (which is in the unconscious, in the latent dream, and in the latent content of myths, legends, proverbs) and *what symbolizes it,* namely, *the symbol,* which is in the manifest dream and in the manifest content of myths, legends, and proverbs. He wrote:

> In a number of cases the element in common between a symbol and what it represents is obvious; in others it is concealed and the choice of the symbol seems puzzling. It is precisely these latter cases which must be able to throw light upon the ultimate meaning of the symbolic relation, and they indicate that it is of a genetic character. Things that are symbolically connected today were probably united in prehistoric times by conceptual and linguistic identity. The symbolic relation seems to be a relic and a mark of former identity [1900, p. 352].

In a footnote added in 1925, he wrote: "This view would be powerfully supported by a theory put forward by Dr. Hans Sperber (1912). He is of the opinion that all primal words referred to sexual things but afterwards lost their sexual meaning through being applied to other things and activities which were compared with the sexual ones" (1900, p. 352).

I believe that both phylogenetic and psychological factors explain symbolic relations, that there are both conceptual and sensorial connections, mainly auditory but also visual, between the symbol and what the symbol represents, that there are both conceptual and sensorial links (mainly auditory) between the symbol and its meaning. Sensorial connections are more obvious in the ontogenetic development of language. The child develops language onomatopoeically. The sounds accompanying physiologically and psychosexually important activities (for instance, urination and defecation), become *phoneticized* and become the words for those activities. But this may have been true also in the philogenetic development of language: the sounds accompanying physiologically and psychosexually important activities could have become the words for those activities. These words later became extended to natural events having sensorial (mainly visual and auditory) similarities to those activities. The sound of urination became the word for urination and for rain; and later, rain, similar in sound and appearance to urination, became the symbol for urination. The sound of defecation became the word for defecation and for thunder; and later, thunder, similar in sound to defecation, became the symbol for defecation. Sperber's theory would confirm this (1912, cited by Freud, 1900, p. 352).

Also, sounds, soon to become words, initially accompanied pleasurable sexual activities. Later those sounds and words could have been used to accompany nonsexual activities (work, for instance), to transfer to work the psychic energy and pleasure-filled interest previously attached to the pleasurable sexual activity. Still later these sound-words lost their primitive sexual significance and only connoted nonsexual matters. In contemporary Sicilian songs, for example, the fishermen's words, accompanying the pulling of fishing nets, the spearing of fish, and so forth, are highly sexualized words or semitransparent sexual symbols.

But there is also a conceptual connection because of conceptual similarities between the symbol and what the symbol represents. Thus, a sword may symbolize a penis because they both enter and penetrate flesh. A bag may symbolize a vagina because they both may be penetrated and can hold and contain. The Queen of England may symbolize mother because they are both important. An airplane may symbolize an erect penis because they both defy gravity. But whether the connecting link is phonetic or conceptual, the common denominator between the symbol and what the symbol represents is always based on predicate thinking. Swords and penises, bags and vaginas, Queens and mothers, airplanes and erect penises have at least one predicate, one attribute, in common and that makes each pair prelogically identical. That predicate thinking is at the basis of all symbolic connections also explains the fact that new symbols are continually being coined. Rockets and intercontinental ballistic missiles are today frequent symbols of male genitals. One of my patients represented her overprotective ("hovering") mother as a hovercraft. Only time can tell whether these are simply displacements or whether they will become symbols.

Following, are some examples of symbolism in dreams from Freud's major section on symbolization in *The Interpretation of Dreams* (1900, pp. 353–359) and from references to symbolizations scattered throughout his writings.

Parents: Kings, queens, emperors, empresses, the president or prime minister of a country, an important historical figure, a prominent person, the "father of our country," one's country of origin (fatherland or motherland); the CEO of a company, the dean or president of a school or university, a Pope, a police officer, a meter maid (for castrated father); and so on (1900, p. 353; 1916b, p. 153; 1939, p. 12).
Children: Princes and princesses, little animals (e.g., the American slang term, *kids*), insects, bugs (especially for unconsciously hated younger siblings), vermin, and so on (1900, p. 358; 1916b, p. 153).
Women: Houses, homes, towns, citadels, fortresses, tables, tables laid out for a meal, ships, and so forth (1900, p. 355; 1916b, pp. 156, 162).
Female genitals: Boxes, cases, chests, bags; pits, caves, hollows; cupboards, ovens, sinks; hollow objects; doors, gates; garages; treasure boxes, jewelry boxes, honey jars, bottles of perfume; pill boxes; blossoms, flowers, bushes, pollen; the mouth, or ear, or eye, and so on (1900, pp. 359, 365–366; 1916b, pp. 156–157).
Male genitals: Elongated objects, sticks, tree trunks, umbrellas, canes, watering cans, faucets, springs, pencils, pens, clubs, baseball bats, hockey sticks, golf clubs, sharp weapons, knives, daggers,

pikes, revolvers, pistols, rifles, cannons, hammers, plows, air-planes, missiles, a nail file, one's "little brother," a relative, the hand, the foot, the nose, a finger, the number 3 (1900, pp. 358, 360, 380; 1916a, p. 337; 1916b, pp. 154–155, 163–164).

Genital organs: Landscapes, wooded hills, maps, machinery; all beasts used as genital symbols in mythology and folklore, such as fish, snails, cats, mice, and snakes (1900, pp. 356–357, 366; 1914, p. 12).

Female genitals and anus: Two rooms which were originally one or a familiar room divided into two in the dream (1900, p. 354). A child understands female genitals and anus as one single area, the infantile "cloaca theory" to which Freud referred in *Three Essays on the Theory of Sexuality* (1905b, pp. 187n, 196, 199).

Male masturbation: Beating, rubbing, playing with a child, playing on the organ, the number 5 (the five fingers of the hand), and so on (1900, pp. 357, 365; 1916b, pp. 156–157, 164–165).

Female masturbation: Playing the piano, the organ; typewriting, knitting, playing with one's fingers, playing with one's rings, and so on (1916b, p. 156).

Brothel, harem: A suite of rooms (1900, p. 354; 1916b, pp. 197–198).

Castration: Baldness, hair cutting, shaving of beard and/or mus-tache, falling of teeth, decapitation, any kind of bodily mutilation, and so on (1900, p. 357; 1916b, pp. 156–157).

Warding-off castration: Any symbol of the penis multiplied many times, lizards or other life forms known for regenerating capacit-ies (1900, pp. 357, 412; 1919, p. 235; 1922, p. 273).

Sexual acts, mainly coitus: Steps, ladders, walking up and down, dancing, rhythmic activities (1900, p. 355n; 1916b, pp. 157–158).

Sexuality: Getting into the water (1900, pp. 399–400).

Parent's body: Smooth walls, facades of homes, representing the baby's memory of climbing over parent's or nurse's body (1900, p. 355).

Right and left: Right and wrong. (Freud credits Stekel [1911] with having put forward this meaning which he affirms [1900, pp. 357, 380].)

Birth: Water, in ontogenetic memory of amniotic fluid and in phylogenetic memory of evolution from amphibious reptilian life forms; also, the myth of birth by a storm, a water bird, the myth of heroes, the myth of Venus as born from the waters (1900, p. 400; 1916b, pp. 153, 160; 1939, p. 12).

Death: Traveling; also, poetic references to "death as travel," Avernus as the country from which no *traveler* returns, colloquialisms of death as "the last *journey*," or references to dying as "passing away," and the dead as "the departed" (1900, p. 385; 1916b, pp. 153, 161). However,

Orgasm: Can be symbolically represented as death, a reference to the suspension of full consciousness at the climactic moments of genital orgasm; a French slang term for climax is "*la petite morte*," the little death.

This list of symbols must be taken with reservations, qualifications, provisos, and exceptions. It must not be taken as the final word as to which actual latent content of dream-thought is being represented by the symbols found in the dream's manifest content. The reader must heed Freud's repeated warnings on the limitations of interpretations of dreams based on knowledge of symbols, and must be wisely respectful of the craftiness and resourcefulness of the defensive ego and of censorship. This list is a valuable guide to deciphering of symbols in dreams, nothing more and nothing less. It is of some help in telling the analyst what the patient's dream says but of very little help in telling the analyst what to tell the patient about the dream.[2]

It is important to remember that, among the various symbols the unconscious ego may choose, that symbol is selected that is most appropriate to the dreamer's life-style and character. To symbolize a penis, a militaristic, aggressive person may choose a gun; an intellectual or literate person, a pen; a workman, a pick, a shovel, a tool, or a utensil. Also, the symbol is selected that is most appropriate to the person's psychodynamics and most helpful in terms of aiding the other operations of the dream work; for instance, the operations of condensation. Thus, to represent

---

[2]Listings under the word *symbol* in the "General Index" of *The Interpretation of Dreams* (1900, pp. 747–748) and the entire "Index of Symbols" in the *Index and Bibliographies* volume of the *Standard Edition* (pp. 173–176) offer some indication of how many other symbols Freud discovered and described from the analysis of his own and his patients' dreams. Additionally, in the "General Subject Index" (pp. 223–404), there are countless other references for things symbolized.

sexuality and aggressiveness, a gun will be selected to represent the male sexual organ; but a leaking pen will be chosen to symbolize in a condensed fashion the wish to penetrate and to smear or the wish to penetrate and impregnate.

The unconscious uses symbols in symptom formation as it does in dream formation; for instance, in conversion symptoms, symbolically "masculine" organs (nose, tongue, hands, feet, all "penetrating" body parts) or symbolically "feminine" organs (throat, stomach, anus—all "receptive") are utilized to represent symbolically masculine or feminine orientations or conflicts.

SECONDARY REVISION

Secondary revision is the process described by Freud by which the dream work gives the dream its final touches and constructs its final form. "[A] psychical force is at work in dreams which creates this [the dream's] apparent connectedness, which, that is to say, submits the material produced by the dream work to a 'secondary revision' " (1900, p. 449). Secondary revision is the product and result of that force. It is a psychological process which "is concerned to fuse together elements in a dream which are of disparate origin into a whole which shall make sense and be without contradiction" (1900, p. 459). "Its function would then consist in arranging the constituents of the dream in such a way that they form an approximately connected whole, a dream-composition. In this way the dream is given a kind of facade . . . " (1901a, p. 666).

The term *secondary revision* "has previously been given the somewhat misleading English rendering of 'secondary elaboration' " (editor's note, Freud, 1900, p. 488). While secondary revision is not the least important psychodynamically, it is chronologically the last psychological operation of the dream work. This is so because, as Freud explained, "*it only comes into operation* AFTER *the dream-content has already been constructed*" (1901a, p. 666). This is so because it is administered by an ego which is in the process of awakening, the ego of the twilight state which precedes waking up; and because it continues revising the dream hours after the dream has been dreamed, as the dreamer recollects the dream, writes it down, or recounts it to a friend or to the analyst. It is not the least operation of the dream work psycho-dynamically, that is, in terms of fulfilling the requirements of censorship, because, in the very process of revising the dream further, it further distorts its latent content. Strachey informs us in his introduction that Freud's "first hint at the process of 'secondary revision' seems to be given in a letter [to Fliess] of July 7, 1897 (Letter 66)" (Freud, 1900, p. xix). In *The Interpretation of Dreams*, Freud discussed secondary revision at length and considered it an important operation of the dream work.

Some examples of secondary revision include the following: adding, here and there, prepositions, conjunctions, and pronouns; interjecting adjectives, other qualifying words, temporal and spatial adverbs; explaining, elaborating, clarifying; giving the material a "logical" sequence and arranging the dream thoughts in a progression that makes sense. It also includes interpolating intermediate and connecting words, strategically linking two portions of the dream, or cleverly building a bridge between two parts of the manifest content. Additions and amplifications but also editions and omissions may occur as in dreams where secondary revision deletes the most significant passages. A patient of mine dreamed that "someone gave me a piece of paper with a short but most important message. . . but the words were smudged and could not be made out." Another patient reported: "This man was telling me something in a loud and clear voice. . . but when it came to the most important part of what he was trying to tell me, his words became slurred and his voice became practically inaudible." Finally, secondary revision may manifest itself by the addition, at the conclusion of the dream, of the face-saving line, "It's only a dream," which is especially common in anxiety dreams. The closing line attempts to reduce the psychodynamic importance of what had been dreamed and had, in part, escaped censorship.

The secondary revisions of the dream, chronologically the last to modify and distort the dream, are the first to vanish. Referring to the interpolations (prepositions, conjunctions, connecting words, intermediate words) that form the "shreds and patches" of secondary revision, Freud said: "They are less easily retained in the memory than genuine derivatives of the material of the dream-thoughts; if the dream is to be forgotten they are the first part of it to disappear, and I have a strong suspicion that the common complaint of having dreamt a lot, but of having forgotten most of it and of having only retained fragments, . . . is based upon the rapid disappearance precisely of these connecting thoughts" (1900, pp. 489–490).

As already indicated, secondary revision continues to revise the dream long after the dream had been dreamed and up to the time the dream is recounted. When the dream is told during the analytic hour, these eleventh hour revisions can be precious: they may reveal more than they conceal. The long-winded explanations patients may give as they introduce or try to clarify the dream they are about to tell or have just recounted are still secondary revisions, and as such they are parts of the dream and may be helpful. In a dream that will be presented in its entirety in chapter 6 ("Avenue M, in Flatbush"), one patient began to recount a dream that had opened with his taking a subway train to an undisclosed location in Manhattan. Then, instead of continuing with the dream, he spoke about the fact that as a child he had lived in Flatbush, an area of Brooklyn, New York, and went on and on talking about Brooklyn and Flatbush. But the word *Flatbush* was the key to the interpretation of the dream he finally told. Flatbush stood for "flat bush" and represented, through symbolization, displacement, and concrete pictorial representation, his mother's pubic hair and genital organs, her undemonstrative, apathetic, emotionally "flat" personality, and "flat" (i.e., avaricious and unnurturing) breasts.

Secondary revision revises the dream still further when the dream is written down or told a second or third time. Telling the dream to anyone before telling one's analyst, and writing down dreams are resistances; the best way to work on a dream psychoanalytically is to suggest to the patient to forget all about the dream until the dream comes to mind during the analytic hour. The secondary revisions occurring when a dream is told to the analyst twice during the session also distort the dream further. As the dream is repeated the second time, the patient's resistances increase and censorship is alerted to impose more secondary revisions to the dream. This may be especially true if, the first time the patient tells us the dream, we thought we had not heard it or understood it well enough and we had asked the patient to tell us the dream a second time. But these eleventh hour revisions of the dream as first told in the session may actually turn out to help the analysis of the dream. As Freud put it (1900):

> If the first account given me by a patient of a dream is too hard to follow I ask him to repeat it. In doing so he rarely uses the same words. But the parts of the dream which he describes in different terms are by that fact revealed to me as the weak spot in the dream's disguise. . . . That is the point at which the interpretation of the dream can be started. My request to the patient to repeat his account of the dream has warned him that I was proposing to take special pains in solving it; under the pressure of the resistance, therefore, he hastily covers the weak spots in the dream's disguise by replacing any expressions that threaten to betray its meaning by other less revealing ones. In this way, he draws my attention to the expression which he has dropped out [p. 515].

In a session during which a dream is told, everything in the session (whether told to the analyst before or after the dream) is either an association to the dream or, through secondary revision, is part of the dream. To keep this in mind can be of great help in understanding or even in interpreting dreams, especially with obsessional patients. Obsessional characters make a rigid distinction between what they tell us from the couch (that is "work," "therapy") and what they tell us on the way to the couch from the waiting room or the office door (for them, this is not "work"; this is "conversation," "pleasantries," "amenities"). What they tell us from the couch, therefore, is more guarded and better censored, while what they tell us on the way to the couch is less guarded and may give us clues to the dream that is to come. A patient greeted me in the waiting room with an exuberance which was highly uncharacteristic for his usually somber and austere demeanor, and said, "I had a real whopper of a dream . . . can't wait to tell you." He was totally unaware, of course, that he had tipped me off as to the fact that the main character in his dream was likely to be me ("whopper," an allusion to "wop," i.e., Italian, my nationality by birth). Another patient told me he had dreamed of "going down a chute to a basement of some sort." Secondary revision impelled him to spell the word *chute* twice, which alerted me to the possibility that another, similarly sounding word was involved, *shoot.* The manifest dream had indeed used *chute* to disguise the wish to *shoot* his father. Secondary revision, by "overdoing it," so to speak, undid the distortion.

The distortion produced by secondary revision, as the distortions produced by condensation, displacement, concrete pictorial representation, and symbolization, has the same target: the dream-thoughts, the overcathected drives of the neurotic conflict which have become the dream. It has the same adaptive purpose, to protect the conscious ego from too direct an experience of the primitive id and superego. It yields the same result: a compromised product, the manifest dream. As discussed previously, censorship while we are asleep operates in essentially the same way as when we are awake. It uses the same defensive operations at both levels of consciousness and against the very same unconscious processes. Nevertheless, conscious and unconscious ego, consciousness and the unconscious, *are* and *do have* different psychological and psychodynamic traits and characteristics. The distortion produced by secondary revision is a distortion regulated by an ego and a censorship with psychological and psychodynamic traits and characteristics shared by both consciousness and the conscious ego and the unconscious and the unconscious ego. In Freud's words: "not everything contained in a dream is derived from the dream-thoughts, but . . . contributions to its content may be made by a psychical function which is indistinguishable from our waking thoughts" (1900, p. 489). He also said:

> [T]he psychical function which carries out what we have described as the secondary revision of the content of dreams is to be identified with the activity of our waking thought. Our waking (preconscious) thinking behaves towards any perceptual material with which it meets in just the same way in which the function [of secondary revision] we are considering behaves towards the content of dreams. It is the nature of our waking thought to establish order in material of that kind, to set up relations in it and to make it conform to our expectations of an intelligible whole [p. 499].

It will be helpful to remember that levels of consciousness and corresponding levels of thinking belong, descriptively and psychodynamically, *on a continuum.* Thinking while asleep (i.e., dreaming) and thinking while awake (Freud's "waking thought" and "waking thinking") are on a continuum. Somewhere in the middle of this continuum is the level of thinking found during secondary revision, whose thinking is regulated by an ego having the psychological and psychodynamic traits of both thinking while asleep and thinking while awake. In the discussion of the topographic theory, I pointed out that, descriptively if not psychodynamically, nonconsciousness and consciousness should also be conceptualized as being on a continuum. Between the deep darkness of a moonless, starless night at midnight and the crystal clear luminosity of a bright sunny day at high noon, there are the intermediate states of increasing light (dawn) and increasing darkness (dusk). Similarly, between the deep nonconsciousness of coma and the sharp and vivid consciousness of a healthy mind at peak levels of alertness, there are intermediate states of decreasing nonconsciousness and increasing consciousness at one extreme of the continuum, and decreasing consciousness and increasing nonconsciousness at the other extreme.

Thus at one pole of the continuum one finds dreamless sleep, REM sleep, hypnapompic states, the twilight states of just before getting up, the not quite full consciousness preceding the first cup of coffee or the taking of a shower or exercising or practicing yoga, and the clearer consciousness following whatever are one's morning "waking up" rituals. At the other pole of the continuum one finds the decreasing consciousness of tiredness and fatigue, the decreased consciousness following a heavy meal, the decreasing consciousness following whatever are one's evening "unwinding" rituals, the increasing nonconsciousness of drowsiness, dozing, and slumbering, hypnagogic states, REM sleep, dreamless sleep. The psychological and psychodynamic traits of the ego are on the same continuum, as they too oscillate from, to, and between prelogic and magic features and capacities at one extreme of the continuum and logical and cognitive features and capacities at the other extreme. It is therefore useful to think of a continuum along which one finds a totally nonconscious ego, the ego of REM sleep, the awakening ego, and the fully awake, conscious ego.

The fully awake ego and, to a degree, the awakening ego, because of this continuum principle, proceed by Aristotelian logic, and thereby need to put perceptual and sensorial material in order, in their proper frame of reference. In this context, Freud, in a passage added to *The Interpretation of Dreams* in 1914 (p. 501n), reminded us of the words of Havelock Ellis (1911): "Sleeping consciousness we may even imagine as saying to itself in effect: 'Here comes our master, Waking Consciousness, who attaches such mighty importance to reason and logic and so forth. Quick! gather things up, put them in order—any order will do—before he enters to take possession' " (1900, p. 501). The fully awake ego has Aristotelian requirements that go even farther, screening out that which is not coherent, logical, and relevant. This too has important implications concerning the censorship, applied through secondary revision, which is administered by the awakening ego. The fully awake ego and, to a significant degree, the awakening ego abet cognitive consonance and abhor cognitive dissonance. This also fulfills the requirements of censorship insofar as it facilitates or outrightly produces distortion. Secondary revision, in Freud's words, "fills up the gaps in the dream-structure with shreds and patches. As a result of its efforts, the dream loses its appearance of absurdity and disconnectedness and approximates to the model of an intelligible experience" (1900, p. 490). As the dream's manifest content becomes more and more intelligible, its latent meaning becomes less and less so: the awakening ego's requirement to make intelligible patterns of the dream-thoughts distorts them further.

Discussing the fully awake ego's characteristic of screening out that which does not make logical cognitive sense (1900), Freud said:

> In our efforts at making an intelligible pattern of the sense-impressions that are offered to us, we often fall into the strangest errors or even falsify the truth about the material before us. . . . In our reading we pass over misprints which destroy the sense, and have the illusion that what we are reading is correct. The editor of a popular French periodical is said to have made a bet that he would have the words "in front" or "behind" inserted by the printer in every sentence of a long article without a single one of his readers noticing it. He won his bet [pp. 499–500].

The last psychological operation of the dream work is indeed far from the least psychodynamically. Like condensation, displacement, concrete pictorial representation, and symbolization, secondary revision significantly obscures the latent dream just as it clarifies the manifest.

Condensation, displacement, concrete pictorial representation, symbolization, and secondary revision are the major defenses that censorship employs to distort the latent dream into its more acceptable manifest counterpart; the staples, so to speak, of the psychological operations of the ego when we are asleep. In addition, most of the ego's mechanisms of defense can be enlisted in the "beautification" process of the dream: projection, denial and undoing, regression, turning into the opposite, and reaction formation. Once the analyst has become acquainted with the dreamer's psychodynamics, "favorite" defenses, and defense clusters that the dreamer utilizes in the state of wakefulness, he or she will begin to recognize those same defenses in the dreamer's dreams and see how the dreamer uses them in the state of sleep.

OTHER PSYCHOLOGICAL OPERATIONS OF THE DREAM WORK

Ella Freeman Sharpe approached the defensive operations of the dream work from one more perspective. In the introduction to her work on *Dream Analysis,* Khan described her as "someone firmly established in her own discipline of literature and teaching" before she became a psychoanalyst (1978, p. 9). He noted that she was the "first person to recognize that the dream-work and the grammatical structure of language are of one and the same order" (p. 9). Sharpe, in her own words, proposed "to approach the subject of dream mechanisms through the avenue of the accepted characteristics of poetic diction" (1978, pp. 18–19). She went on to describe the laws of poetic diction: "These laws are inherent and intrinsic in the best verse and so may be regarded as being the product of the closest co-operation between preconscious and unconscious activity. 'I sing because the linnets may and pipe because I must.' The laws of poetic diction, evolved by the critics from great poetry and the laws of dream formation as discovered by Freud, spring from the same unconscious sources and have many mechanisms in common" (1978, p. 19). Sharpe specifically discussed the utilization by the unconscious ego and censorship of *simile, metaphor,* and *personal metaphor, metonimy, synecdoche,* and *onomatopoeia* (1978, pp. 19–30).

In *simile*, one equates different objects by means of a common attribute, the similarity being expressed by means of the words *as* or *like*; A = B because A and B have a common attribute (predicate thinking, one of the characteristics of the prelogic thinking of the id and the unconscious discussed previously). In dream distortion, similes are usually rendered as *metaphors*, the words *like* and *as* are omitted: the simile "the penis entered my body as a knife enters one's flesh" becomes the metaphor "the knife entered the body." The latent dream's wish for sexual intercourse becomes the manifest dream's metaphor of an attack by knives. In more conventional Freudian language, there is a displacement from penis to knife and the knife becomes the symbol for the penis.

In *personal metaphor*, human and personal feelings and attributes are transferred to nonhuman or impersonal objects. There is originally a simile: "the tree, moved by the wind, sounded like you when you sigh . . ."; then, through elimination of the words *like* and *as*, there is a metaphor: "a sighing tree." The manifest dreams might be: "I dreamed of a sighing oak" or "I dreamed of a pine or of a yew tree." The latent dream thought by the first dreamer was about his sturdy and severe father, unhappy ("sighing") about the dreamer's misbehavior. It became, through personal metaphor, the manifest dream of "a sighing oak." The latent dream by the second dreamer was about a longing ("pining") feeling toward his mother, transferentially represented by "*you*," the therapist. It became, through personal metaphor, the manifest dream of "a pine or, perhaps, a *yew* [i.e., you] tree." In more ordinary Freudian language, in these two dreams there were displacements (from parental figures to tree), projection (attributing human feelings to inanimate objects), and symbolization (an oak tree for sturdiness and severity).

In *metonymy*, the whole (i.e., A) stands for the part (i.e., B). When censorship uses metonymy to distort the dream, B, the part (the conflicted object in the latent dream), is rendered, in the manifest dream, as A, the whole (a more acceptable counterpart). The dreamer's latent dream could be about a particular lawyer, judge, priest, sailor about whom the dreamer has forbidden thoughts and feelings. Through metonymy, the manifest dream will be about a bar (i.e., the Bar, the legal profession), a bench, (i.e., the bench, in the sense of judges and courts of law), or the U.S. Navy and the Catholic Church, the institutions of which sailors and priests respectively are a part. In more conventional Freudian terms, there is, in metonimy, a displacement from the part (in the latent dream) to the whole (in the manifest dream).

In *synecdoche*, the part (i.e., B) stands for the whole (i.e., A). When censorship uses synecdoche to distort the dream, A, the whole (the forbidden object in the latent dream) is rendered, in the manifest dream, as B, the part (a more acceptable counterpart). One dreamer's latent dream might be about mother (the whole) and the manifest dream be about soft rounded hills, breasts (the part). Another dreamer's latent dream could be about father (the whole) and the manifest dream about tall and pointed mountain peaks, the penis (the part). In more ordinary Freudian language, in synecdoche, there is a displacement from the whole (in the latent dream) to the part (in the manifest dream) and symbolization (hills and mountain peaks as symbols of breast and penis).

In *onomatopoeia*, a word, representing A, is used because it echoes or resembles the sound of another word, which represents B. When censorship uses onomatopoeia to distort the dream, the word B, representing a forbidden object or activity in the latent dream is rendered, in the manifest dream, as the word A, representing a more acceptable or innocuous object or activity. An Italian-born patient had a dream whose latent content concerned feces ("cacca" in Italian). His manifest dream was about a chemical formula, KOH, which pronounced in Italian sounds like "cacca." A second patient, whose latent dream had to do with rivalry with his father (who was a college president) and included the grandiose wish of owning a college, had a laconic manifest dream about "Iona College" (i.e., I own a College). A very gifted psychoanalytic trainee reported a dream she herself had whose manifest content included two lions who were having intercourse. Secondary elaboration had this detail rendered as "fucking lions." She understood the dream through its onomatopoeia: the lions having intercourse stood for the dreamer having been told that she was "fucking lying." In more ordinary Freudian language, there is, in onomatopoeia, displacement from one word in the latent dream to another in the manifest dream and regression to one's early personal experiences with language, when sound was fused with meaning.

Part III
DREAM INTERPRETATION

6

Dream Interpretation, 1

Working with dreams is a broader concept than the more specific one of "interpreting dreams." Working with dreams in a Freudian fashion is to approach the royal road to a knowledge of the unconscious activities of the mind, to enter it, and to travel it as far as possible—as far as the patient needs to and can tolerate without harm.

THE ANALYST'S TASKS IN WORKING WITH DREAMS

When the patient tells the analyst a dream, the analyst has three tasks: *understanding the dream's session in which the patient tells the analyst the dream; understanding the session's dream; and responding to the dream.*

Understanding the Dream's Session

The first step in working with dreams, understanding the dream's session, consists of "hearing" the dream's session psychoanalytically, with the third ear. How and why this is done is part of the general technique of Freudian psychoanalysis, and the reader is referred to the many excellent books on the subject. (Suggested reading on general technique of Freudian psychoanalysis includes Greenson [1967] and Glover [1968].) But it is important to think about and listen to what the patient says during the dream's session as if the session itself were a dream, with its manifest and latent content. Examples of how to do this are presented at the end of this chapter.

Understanding the Session's Dream, Knowing What the Patient's Dream Says

The second step in working with dreams is to understand the dream, to know what the dream says. When the patient tells the analyst a dream, the analyst, listening to the patient with relaxed attention, should try to hear the dream with the third ear, that is, try to hear "in between the lines" of the communication, try to hear the patient's unconscious, try to hear the "less than fully manifest content" of the dream, the dream's "semimanifest" and "semilatent" content, and maybe, the dream's latent content.

Most commonly one talks of dreams as having a manifest and a latent content. I prefer to think of dreams as having a "manifest" content, a "semimanifest–semilatent" content, and a "latent" (or "truly latent") content. As indicated previously, there is a distinct difference between the sharp clarity of noon and the deep darkness of midnight, but there are many gradations of light and darkness as one proceeds from night to dawn and noon and from day to dusk and midnight. There are qualitative differences in the various levels of consciousness and nonconsciousness. Similarly, there is a sharp difference between the manifest dream and the latent dream, but in-between the two there are many gradations. The difference between these gradations are sometimes as imperceptible as the difference in light at certain hours around dawn and dusk, but are recognizable psychodynamically by the different degrees to which the dream wishes are increasingly defended and camouflaged as one moves from the latent dream to the semilatent, the semimanifest, and the manifest dream.

Listening to the patient with relaxed attention, analysts should try to hear with the third ear both what their patient is saying and what they themselves are thinking and feeling. They should be open to any associations that patient's material may bring to their mind, any kind of resonating between the patient's story and the analyst's own consciousness, try to be open to any thoughts and feelings emerging from their own preconscious and unconscious in response to what the patient is saying. I tell myself and my students to let all kinds of associations and memories bubble up to consciousness while listening to the patient's dreams. In so doing, analysts will engage their minds (*internally*) in a number of psychodynamic speculations, conjectures, fantasies, and hypotheses about the dream and its latent content, at least some of which will prove precious in capturing some portions of the semilatent or truly latent dream. I call this the analyst's *internal soliloquy*. While doing that, of course, analysts should also engage in self-analysis, that is analysis of countertransference. They should scrupulously question the source and nature of their associations, and discern whether these thoughts and feelings come from the patient, the analyst, the patient's past, or the analyst's past. Thus positioned and engaged, if the analyst is "good" with dreams, the analyst will *understand the dream*, will know what the patient's dream says, and will understand the dream's latent content.

Barring countertransferential problems, it is usually not difficult to understand the patient's dreams tentatively and speculatively, to know what the patient's dreams say, to interpret the dream (internally), provided, of course, the analyst "knows" the patient, clinically and psychodynamically. Exceptions, of course, abound, as is always the case with human beings. For instance, it may be difficult to understand, even tentatively and speculatively, dreams of very resistant patients, or terse dreams where an unusually high degree of condensation has occurred, or to decipher even tentatively and speculatively, the latent content of the so-called "simple" dreams.

Being conversant with dream formation and the psychological operations of the dream work is of paramount importance. As indicated in chapter 5, dream formation consists of a series of steps through which the latent dream is changed into the manifest dream, a series of steps (the psychological operations of the dream work: condensation, displacement, concrete pictorial representation, symbolism, and secondary revision) which distort the latent content into its manifest version. By being fully conversant with these steps, one can retrace them, travel them in reverse, so to speak. In doing so, one retransforms the manifest dream into its latent predecessor and one has, in effect, understood the dream, learned what the patient's dream is saying.

This second step of working with dreams does indeed flow directly from dream formation. Understanding the dream, this second step we are discussing, is the reverse process, the process in which the manifest dream is retransformed into the latent dream.

One sees again important parallels between, on the one hand, dream formation and on the other, symptom formation, between this step in understanding a dream's latent content and understanding the latent content of the patient's symptoms. The process of understanding the latent dream is indeed the same process as, or one parallel to, that of understanding symptoms and other derivatives of the unconscious as they appear in the patient's life and in the dream's session. The process of understanding symptoms and other derivatives of the unconscious, the process of understanding the dream work and its psychological operations, is indeed the same process as, or one parallel to, that of understanding defenses. In both dream formation and symptom formation, one sees in operation the adaptive steps taken by the psyche for the purpose of protecting the socialized conscious ego from too direct an experience of the unconscious, the primitive id and superego.

Case Example

On the day preceding his "Patting a Donkey" dream, L's neurotic conflict included unconscious, intense anger against his father and grandfather. <u>On the most latent level of dream formation,</u> the unconscious anger became the latent dream. The latent dream included such thoughts and feelings as, "I am striking my father and grandfather, I am telling them that they are animals, I am calling them asses, I am making them so angry that they are having a stroke." Through censorship and the psychological operations of the dream work, the latent dream becomes the semilatent dream: identical thoughts and feelings are now cathected on the transferential father and grandfather, that is, the analyst. Further censored and worked over by the psychological operations of the dream work, the semilatent dream becomes the manifest dream: L is lovingly stroking and patting a donkey. By knowing the steps through which censorship and the psychological operations of the dream work transform L's latent dream into its semilatent and manifest counterparts, and by retracing those steps, one understands the dream, one knows what L's dream says. On the most latent level of symptom formation, this anger was a pathogenic complex (pathogenic, i.e., generating *pathos*, pain). It probably included such thoughts and feelings as the wish to strike father and grandfather, to call them names, to make them so angry as to cause them a stroke. The pathogenic complex clamored for discharge, but was kept away from consciousness through censorship and the psychological operations of various mechanisms of defense. On a semilatent level, through the defense of displacement, and possibly projection, it became intense anger against the transferential father and grandfather, that is, the analyst. Further censored and worked over by the psychological operations of the mechanisms of defense, the anger was finally expressed against the analyst in a mild, subdued, derivative form. At the end of that session (the session preceding the dream's session), L's tongue slipped and he called me *donkey* instead of *doctor*. By knowing the steps through which censorship and the psychological operations of the mechanisms of defense transform L's latent pathogenic complex into his semilatent and manifest symptoms, by retracing those steps, one understands L's symptoms, one knows what L's symptoms say.

There are other parallels and similarities between dream formation and symptom formation, between dream analysis and psychoanalysis. In both dream analysis and psychoanalysis, in order to understand dreams and to understand symptoms, in order to understand the defenses of the dream work and understand the ego defenses of the wakeful patient, it is necessary to retrace those adaptive steps taken by the psyche in altering unconscious contents into either dreams or symptoms. In both dream analysis and psychoanalysis, resistance will oppose the process of retransforming manifest dream and manifest symptoms (both are derivatives of the unconscious) into latent dream and conflicted id drives, and oppose the retracing of the adaptive steps taken by the psyche to protect socialized consciousness from the unconscious.

Basic psychoanalytic theory describes the oral, anal, phallic, and oedipal fixations that are behind the person's disabilities and conscious pains. The analyst conversant with psychoanalytic theory knows which of several ego defenses the adaptive psyche is more likely to utilize at those fixation points in development, and thus knows when to retrace a regression, when to reverse a reaction formation or correct a projection, when to help with the unearthing of a repression, when to fill the gaps of a denial. Similarly, basic psychoanalytic dream theory teaches us about dream formation and dream work. The analyst conversant with the defenses of the adaptive psyche in converting the latent dream into the manifest dream, knows how to retranslate the manifest dream into the latent dream, how to understand the dream, and how to take this step of working with dreams.

This second step in working with dreams is part of what I call the *theory of technique* of dream interpretation. It consists of the theoretical roots and rules of the interpretation technique. It is, to a large extent, based on the theory of dream formation and it flows directly from this theory, being a way of deciphering dreams by retracing and reversing the steps of dream formation. It is, to an extent, a "science": it can be learned through books or in the classroom. The extent to which this step in working with dreams is *not* a science and cannot be learned in the classroom or through books is the extent to which it is based on one's capacity to listen to one's patients, and to oneself, with the third ear, a capacity that can only be developed through one's own personal psychoanalysis and psychoanalytically supervised psychotherapeutic practice.

Responding to the Dream, Knowing What to Say to the Patient about the Dream

The third step in working with dreams involves responding to the dream, knowing what to say to the patient about a dream. When Freud first began working with dreams, he would ask the patient to break the dream down to its parts and say anything that came to mind about it. Later he modified this technique and simply waited for patients to say whatever was coming to mind about any part of the dream or about anything at all.

Having taken the first two steps of working with dreams, having engaged in the *internal soliloquy*, having understood, conjecturally and speculatively, the dream's session and the session's dream, and having understood at least tentatively what the patient's latent dream says, the analyst has the choice of three types of responses: *silence, intervention,* or *interpretation.* Having understood at least conjecturally the dream's session, and especially, what has been going on in the patient's analysis up to this time, will be essential in guiding the analyst in choosing among these three responses. Generally speaking, the analyst should respond with a sensitive and expectant *silence,* and respond with interventions, or even interpretations, only toward the end of the session, if at all.

This third step in working with dreams is *not* based on theory to the same degree as the second step. It does *not* flow directly from the theory of dream formation. To the extent that it is not based on theory, it is *not* part of the theory of technique of dream interpretation, and to that extent it is more art than science. It cannot be learned in the classroom or through a book, it can be learned only through psychoanalytically supervised psychotherapeutic practice, and from dream analysis in one's own personal analysis. To the extent that this third step is based on theory, it is governed by the same general rules governing psychoanalytic technique (nondirectiveness, the fundamental rule of free association, listening with the third ear), and by the two basic principles to be discussed next. But even when based on theory and governed by technical rules and principles, the analyst's clinical skills will modify and temper theoretical principles and technical rules. Those clinical skills are a combination of technical sophistication and clinical experience, and a sixth sense, that intangible, unmeasurable, unquantifiable something that is part of the art of psychotherapy and dream interpretation. For instance, most Freudian analysts, including myself (since I am more "active" than not and less inclined to see psychoanalysis as an "obstetrical procedure"), follow the general rule in interpreting dreams. According to this general principle, the patient should only be guided to reach insights about their dreams, should first understand their dreams on their own. Therefore, according to this rule, analysts should respond with interventions, and especially interpretations, later rather than earlier.

But there will be specific instances when these analysts' clinical skills and sixth sense will make them feel that an intervention, or even an interpretation, will further the analytical work. When this is so, even these analysts, and certainly this author, will respond with interventions, and even interpretations, sooner rather than later. It is important to underline that, if the analyst chooses to respond to the dream with a response other than silence, the response need *not* include, as beginners in dream analysis think, an *interpretation* in the strict sense of the word, that is, a translation to the patient of the manifest content of the dream into the latent.

TWO BASIC THEORETICAL PRINCIPLES GOVERNING DREAM INTERPRETATION

There are two basic principles which govern dream interpretation: *ultimately, one must analyze the dream's latent content, not the manifest; second, one can respond to dreams on the level of the defenses or on the level of the drives, and on the level of the transference.*

First Principle: Ultimately, One Must Analyze the Latent Not the Manifest Content

A dream has not been fully analyzed until analysis has proceeded all the way to the latent wishes, which the dream is fulfilling under the cover of the manifest dream. The yesteryear, the infantile sources of dreams, has to be understood and responded to until the unconscious id drives have been understood and responded to. These unconscious id drives are part of the drive half of the patient's neurotic conflict, now condensed in the patient's latent dream. This principle applies to dream interpretation in psychoanalytic psychotherapy and psychoanalytically oriented psychotherapy. It is a basic principle; Sharpe called it "the cardinal rule of psychoanalysis." She said:

> This cardinal rule is that the meaning of a dream is ascertained by analysing the manifest content into its latent thoughts. The first impulse in connection with any dream is to try to interpret its meaning as it is given in the manifest content, and I believe this impulse has to be checked as much by the analyst in himself as in the patient [1978, p. 75].

Second Principle: One Can Respond to Dreams on the Level of the Defenses or on the Level of the Drives, and Whenever Possible on the Level of the Transference

To respond on the level of the defenses means to respond with interventions or interpretations concerning the dream's defenses, to respond to the psychological operations of the dream work (condensations, displacement, concrete pictorial representation, symbolism, and secondary elaboration, and any other ego defenses operating in the dream). It means to respond to the dream's manifest and semimanifest–semilatent contents.

The defenses to which the analyst is choosing to respond in working with a dream are part of the manifest dream or of its semimanifest–semilatent antecedent. The manifest dream, and its semimanifest–semilatent counterpart are, by definition, the defended dream, or a better defended dream than its latent predecessor. All their parts are disguises obtained through the psychological operations of the dream work, disguises (distortions) of counterparts hidden in the latent dream. What specific defenses are part of the manifest (and semimanifest–semilatent) content of a given dream will be revealed or suggested by: (1) the material offered by the patient in the dream itself; (2) the material offered by the patient in the dream's session (*in a session in which a dream is told, everything the patient says in that session, before or after the telling of the dream, can be an association to the dream* and can be used to understand what defenses are part of that manifest content or semimanifest–semilatent dream); (3) the material offered by the patient in the sessions preceding the dream session.

If the analyst has opted for a response on the level of defenses, such a response would consist of interventions or interpretations about any of the defenses. Since we are talking of the defenses occurring in dreams, interventions or interpretations might be made about any of the defensive operations of the dream work. All the components of the manifest and semimanifest–semilatent dream are disguises of and defenses against corresponding parts hidden in the latent dream. Since they are a result of the dream work, all these manifest components are condensations, displacements, concrete pictorial representations, symbolizations, and secondary revisions of corresponding elements in the latent dream. Thus:

1. Positive or negative feelings in the manifest dream may correspond to equally positive or negative feelings in the latent dream. However, in the manifest dream, these feelings may be attached to mental representations totally different from those to which they are attached in the latent dream. Feelings in the

latent dream may be displaced or condensed to totally different objects, feelings, or events in the manifest dream.

2. Lack of feelings in the manifest dream may correspond to
powerful positive or negative feelings in the latent dream. The
latent dream's feelingfulness has been distorted into the manifest dream's feelinglessness through repression, denial, isolation, or other operations of the dream work.

3. Finally, any mental representation, person, situation, place,
plot, or storyline in the manifest dream is a distortion of various counterparts in the latent dream, distortions which have
been obtained through any or all of the psychological operations of the dream work.

Therefore, responses on the level of the defenses could consist of interventions or interpretations touching on any part of
the manifest (or semimanifest–semilatent) dream or of the associations to the dream. The touching may consist of questions, or
of requests for more associations, about those parts of the session's dream or the dream's session which are defenses. Or it may
take the form of echoing, rephrasing, underlining, and emphasizing this or that defense component of what the patient has been
saying in the dream's session or in previous sessions, if what he
or she has been saying is connected logically or prelogically with
the dream. Again, and this cannot be emphasized enough, *how*
the touching is done and *what* will be touched upon (which of all
defenses contained in the manifest and semimanifest–semilatent
dream) are to a very large extent part of the art of dream interpretation. It is governed by many factors, most important among
which is the analyst's clinical sense as to what, in all the material
the dreamer has shared with the analyst in the dream's session
and in preceding sessions, would be particularly helpful as an
entryway to the royal road to the unconscious.

To respond on the level of the drives means to respond with interventions or interpretations to the dream-thoughts, the dream's
unconscious id wishes, the dream's drives which are part of the
drive half of the patient's neurotic conflict. The drives to which
one is responding are in the latent dream. To respond to dreams
on the level of the drives is to respond to the dream's latent
contents; it is tantamount to following the first principle, that is,

to follow the cardinal rule. To respond to dreams on the level of the drives is to enter and travel through the royal road to the unconscious.

To respond with interpretations on the level of the drives is a powerful response. It should be used only after a deliberate and informed choice. It can be a potentially traumatic response so it should be used only when the following conditions are present:

1. A high degree of certainty about knowing what the latent dream is about, that is, certainty about having successfully taken the first two steps in working with dreams, understanding the dream's session and the session's dream;
2. A high degree of assurance that the patient has the ego strength and capacity to absorb, tolerate, and utilize a response at this level;
3. The patient has been seen by the analyst for a long enough period so that the therapeutic alliance is sufficiently solid to warrant a response at this level;
4. None of the clinical exceptions to the applications of the cardinal rule exist.

The drives on the level of which the analyst chooses to respond are part of the latent dream. Just as the manifest dream is, by definition, the defended dream, so the latent dream is, by definition, the undefended dream, the undisguised dream, the undistorted dream, the locus of the raw id wishes of the yesteryear. The unconscious id wishes are part of both the dream and of the drive half of the dreamer's neurotic conflict. Which specific drives are condensed within a particular dream's latent content will be suggested by: (1) the material offered by the patient in the dream itself; (2) the material offered by the patient in the dream's session; (3) the material offered by the patient in the sessions preceding the dream session. All this material is understood and deciphered by the analyst internally through one's knowledge of dream work and through listening with the third ear, one's intuition, being in touch with the patient's unconscious, and with one's own unconscious.

If the analyst has opted to respond, not with silence and not on the level of the defenses, but rather, with a response on the level of the drives, such a response would consist of interventions or interpretations about any of the drives thus identified. These interventions or interpretations will consist of touching on any of the drives that are part of the dream's latent content. The touching may consist of questions, of requests for more associations. Or, it may take the form of echoing, rephrasing, underlining, and emphasizing this or that drive component of what the patient has been saying in the dream, in the dream's session, or in previous sessions, if the material the patient has offered connects with the dream. Again, how the touching is done and what will be touched upon, which drives of all those condensed in the latent dream will be touched upon, is to a large extent part of the art of dream interpretation. This is governed by the analyst's clinical sense as to what kind and content of intervention and interpretation will constitute the best approach.

To respond to a dream on the level of the transferences means that the interventions or interpretations the analyst makes, whether on the level of the drives or on the level of the defenses, should *not* be about the figures and occurrences in the patient's latent dream (semimanifest–semilatent), should *not* be about figures and occurrences going back to the yesteryear. The analyst's responses to the dream should be about the transferential counterparts, the transferential masks of those figures and occurrences. The transferential counterparts with which the analyst should choose to work in responding to dreams within the context of the transference, will be suggested by: (1) the psychic material in the dream itself; (2) the material offered by the patient in the dream session (in a session in which a dream is told, everything the patient says, before or after the telling of the dream, can be an association to the dream, and can be crucially helpful in suggesting the transferential counterparts to work with); (3) the material offered by the patient in the sessions preceding the dream session, when this material is psychodynamically connected with the dream in question. All this material is deciphered, by the analyst, in transferential terms, that is, is heard by the analyst with the third ear, as the analyst listens both to the patient and to him- or herself. The analyst's capacity to do so is based, of course, on clinical and psychodynamic familiarity with the patient, but even more so on the analyst's competence and freedom from countertransferentially induced mental blocks. It is indeed a condition sine qua non for effective and helpful psychoanalytic psychotherapy.

Responses within the context of the transference will be about figures and occurrences within the patient's current extrapsychic world that the analyst has recognized as being the transferential counterparts of corresponding figures and occurrences in the patient's intrapsychic world. This means that the analyst will *not* tell patients, neither indirectly through interventions nor directly through interpretations, that their latent dream is about oedipal or preoedipal love or anger at father or mother (responses on the level of the drives). Nor will the analyst tell them that the manifest of semimanifest–semilatent dream is about anxiety, guilt, disgust, or shame about father or mother (responses on the level of the defenses). The analyst will, rather, suggest to patients, indirectly through an intervention or directly through an interpretation, that their dream is about love or anger (drives); or about anxiety, guilt, disgust, and shame (defenses) concerning someone in the patient's current world (analyst, spouse, significant friend, teacher, supervisor, authority figure, and so on) who has been invested with transferential energy belonging to and displaced from father, mother, and the past. This is crucial if the analyst is not to make of dream interventions and interpretations, at best a sterile intellectual exercise, in which the patient is informed that he or she is really dreaming about mommy and daddy, or at worst a process that will cause the patient's resistances to increase many times, or the patient to experience enough panic to terminate therapy precipitously.

Responses within the context of the transference will consist, again, of touching on any part or parts of the dream itself, the dream's session, and the sessions preceding the dream which would be helpful to the interpretation of the dream at the level of the transference. This may consist of questions, requests for more associations about any of the figures or occurrences in the manifest dream, or in the manifest content of the psychic material presented in the dream's session or in the sessions preceding the dream. It may take the form of echoing, rephrasing, underlining, emphasizing this or that figure or occurrences in the patient's current world. How the touching is done and what will be touched upon, that is, which of the figures and occurrences in the patient's current world will be touched upon, is again part of the art of interpretation of the transference. This is governed, mainly, by the analyst's clinical sense as to what would be most helpful toward the deepening of the analytical work.

Interdependence of the Two Principles: Applying and Not Applying the Cardinal Rule

The two principles of dream interpretation have been discussed. The analyst must analyze the dream's latent content, not the manifest; and the analyst must respond to dreams on the level of the drives or on the level of defenses, and on the level of the transference. These two principles do not contradict, but rather complement each other. The first principle is a *theoretical* rule. In emphasizing that ultimately one must analyze the latent content, it states that one must apply the cardinal rule of dream analysis. The second principle is a *clinical* rule. It indicates that the analyst has three choices in working with dreams and that one of these choices is to respond to dreams on the level of the defenses, that is, on the level of the semimanifest–semilatent dream; thus, *not* to apply the cardinal rule.

The reader's attention is called again to the words *ultimately* and *appropriately*, the two words which I used in the formulation and discussion of the first principle. One applies the cardinal rule at the right time, and appropriately in terms of clinical considerations. These may indeed move the analyst temporarily to ignore the latent content, suspend the cardinal rule, and choose to respond to the semimanifest–semilatent dream and on the level of the defenses.

The cardinal rule emphasized the importance of the latent content and the unconscious wishes. The latent content must never be emphasized at the expense of the manifest content or at the expense of the day's residues. Chapter 4 showed that the day's residues may only be triggers for the unconscious drives which they overcathect, and facades for those same unconscious drives. Those drives, in turn, can overcathect and use those facades for camouflage. However, when it comes to responding to dreams on the level of the transference, it is the day's residues that show, in terms of *today's* realities, which *present day* figures and occurrences, preconsciously stored and now part of the manifest dream, are invested with transferential energy. It is the day's residues that reveal in terms of *today's* tensions and problems, how *present day* figures and occurrences, preconsciously stored and now part of the manifest dream, are connected with childhood events and with the primary experiences which are the root of the dreamer's neurosis. The day's residues are indeed essential for the interpretations at the level of transference. The "Sicilian Bamboo" dream (chapter 3) is a good illustration of the fact that the yesterday (the plant at the foot of the couch: the analyst) and the present day's realities, tensions, and problems (the unnurturing married man M was dating at the time) had been invested with transferential energy and were connected with primary experiences going back to the unnurturing mother of M's childhood. Only by referring to the plant and to myself could I understand the patient's unconscious latent wishes which were, through the chain of their derivatives, producing painful and disabling conscious feelings, thoughts, and behavior.

As we have said, there is a *theory of dream formation*, a body of knowledge about what dreams are and what goes into their conception, gestation, birth, and development. There is a *theory of technique of dream interpretation*, a body of knowledge about the theoretical sources and rules concerning techniques of interpretation. And there is a *technique of dream interpretation*. And we have been saying that technique of dream interpretation is more art than science. Even though it is based on a theory of dream formation and a theory of technique of dream interpretation, even though it is governed by rules and principles, it must, even more, be ruled and guided by the analyst's clinical skills, which must always modify and temper theoretical principles and technical rules. Therefore, the cardinal rule of dream analysis will have well-defined clinical exceptions that can be taught and learned. But also, there will be less well-defined clinical exceptions, and only a sixth sense will guide the analyst to recognize these exceptions and be sensitive to those times when the cardinal rule should not be applied.

The major exceptions to the cardinal rule of dream interpretation, exceptions that are more clearly defined and definable, which can be taught in books and learned in a classroom, are: (1) first dreams, and dreams dreamed in the early stages of psychoanalytic psychotherapy; (2) dreams dreamed at times of severe psychic crises; (3) dreams used for diagnostic or prognostic purposes; (4) the special purpose dreams. Definite and clear as these exceptions may seem, they will at times occur in dubious clinical situations. For instance, how early must an early stage of therapy be to qualify as an exception to the cardinal rule? How severe must a severe psychic crisis be? It is here that the analyst's clinical skills and sixth sense will have to make the difference.

In one instance the cardinal rule can be applied, because none of the clinical exceptions exist, and the analyst's clinical skills and sixth sense tell him or her that the rule can indeed be safely applied. Thus, the rule should be applied and the analyst applies it, knowingly and deliberately; analysis progresses.

In another instance, the cardinal rule cannot be applied, because at least one of the clinical exceptions exists and the analyst's clinical sense tells him or her that the rule cannot be safely applied and should be broken. But the analyst, because of inexperience or countertransference, does apply it, and analyzes the dream's latent content—Freud called this "wild psychoanalysis" (1910b, pp. 221–227). When this is the case, the patient's psyche is being violated, defenses are harmed, resistances will increase, decompensation may ensue.

In a third case, the cardinal rule cannot be applied, because at least one of the clinical exceptions exists or because the analyst's clinical skills and sixth sense tell him or her that the rule cannot be safely applied. Thus, the rule should be broken. The analyst breaks it, knowingly, deliberately. When this is the case, no harm is being done to the analytical process; analysis continues to progress, the cardinal rule will be applied when, at some future time, it will be safe and appropriate to do so.

In a fourth case, the cardinal rule could have been safely applied. None of the clinical exceptions existed and the analyst's clinical skills and sixth sense should have told him or her that this was so. But the analyst does not apply it, the cardinal rule is being broken, unnecessarily and unknowingly. The analyst breaks the rule without realizing that he or she is doing so. As a result, the dream is analyzed incompletely, because the analyst mistakenly assumes that he or she has analyzed the latent dream, while only the semimanifest–semilatent dream has been analyzed. In this instance, the analyst has led himself or herself astray.

The cardinal rule may be broken unknowingly and unnecessarily because of inexperience or because of unconscious countertransferential needs that cause analysts to understand a dream only in terms of its manifest or semimanifest–semilatent content. In these instances, analysts fail to apply the cardinal rule without realizing that they are doing so. In positive transference dreams, the patient may need to take the dream at its manifest face value and try to seduce the analyst into also taking the dream at that level. If the positive content of the patient's dream is narcissistically pleasing to the analyst, he or she may be countertransferentially vulnerable to that seduction, and unknowingly and unnecessarily break the cardinal rule by colluding with the patient's wish to have the dream understood only on its manifest or semimanifest–semilatent level. The patient's wish is part of the patient's resistance; the analyst's collusion with that wish is a counterresistance.

In the so-called *simple* dreams (see chapter 8), the dream is simple only on its manifest level. The patient may need to have the dream taken as a truly simple dream because, again, of unconscious resistances. Analysts may be seduced by the dream's manifest simpleness, and unknowingly and unnecessarily break the cardinal rule by colluding with the patient's need to have the dream taken on that level. (Again, this is a resistance on the patient's part, a countertransference and a counterresistance on the analyst's part.) "Beautiful dreams" (chapter 4) also are "beautiful" only on the manifest level, and analysts may unknowingly and unnecessarily break the cardinal rule if they also see these dreams only at that level.

THE ANALYST'S TASKS IN WORKING WITH DREAMS: ILLUSTRATIONS

"Avenue M in Flatbush"

About the Patient, T

T, a patient of a student of mine, was 31 years old, male, Jewish, recently separated from his wife, whom he labeled "a typical

WASP." He had been married for about one year. Therapy had
started six weeks before. T came to therapy once a week, sat up
(i.e., did not use the couch), had always been on time; he maintained continuous eye contact with the therapist which made the
therapist slightly uncomfortable. T's symptoms included loneliness, depression, feeling alienated from his father who appeared
to prefer T's four-year younger brother. He was not too verbal,
but had been relating to the therapist. Major affects included
depression and anger. His basic character structure was obsessional. The dream was told during the seventh session.

About the Therapist

She was Jewish, in her midthirties, a first-year psychoanalytic student. She had conducted the initial interview with T who stated
that he wanted to be assigned to a woman therapist and preferably
to her.

About the Six Sessions Preceding the Dream's Session

First Session. T opened the session by saying that the therapist
reminded him of his guilt-provoking mother. For the rest of the
session, T talked mostly about his father, who put him down constantly, especially about T's skills in playing baseball.
Second Session. T said he does not understand why his ex-wife left
him. With her, as with most women, he feels like "a babe in the
woods." Since the separation, he had only had "one-night
stands" (this was some years before the advent of AIDS).
Third Session. T talked about his "roommate," a psychiatrist, who
previously lived with a woman he "kicked out" to make room for
T. T and "roommate" enjoy each other, have "rap sessions" that
go into the night. Mild homosexual anxiety was verbalized, rather
intellectually.
Fourth Session. Paying his therapy fees weekly makes T feel as if he
were "going to a hooker."
Fifth Session. T talks again about his father: "I was born too early
in his marriage, spoiled all his fun. Maybe that's why he hates
and resents me."
Sixth Session. T presented mostly preconscious material about his
brother, whom he professes to hate.

About the Dream's Session (Seventh Session)

T first spoke about having visited his father the day before the night of the dream. He told his father he had been playing softball in a league and that he had been doing very well. Father ridiculed him, "You are just bragging, I bet you struck out every time." His brother and a friend of brother's had come to visit T in T's apartment the day before. Throughout the visit, T felt restless, "Maybe I was angry . . . I surely wanted to throw them out." He then spoke of how much, in contrast, he enjoys the company of his psychiatrist roommate. Then: "I had a dream last night." (He then engaged in a detailed description of where he lives: Brooklyn, and Avenue M, Flatbush stood out "louder"[1] in my mind as I was listening to my student.) T then recounted the dream:

"Avenue M in Flatbush"

> I buy a token. I go upstairs to catch a train. It's an El station. A few feet ahead of me are two black guys. I follow them. One of them turns and throws a rock at me. I catch it, I felt they were holding me back, so I turned and left.

T showed no interest in the dream. In the rest of the session, he talked about having felt very lonely lately and of wanting to meet women. His friend offered to introduce him to some nurses in the hospital where he was taking his residency. T refused, "I want to do it by myself." Having heard the dream, let us now see how the analyst could carry out the three tasks we have specified in working with dreams.

The First Task: Understanding the Dream's Session and the Sessions Preceding It. The Internal Soliloquy.

As we engage in the internal soliloquy, as we try to hear the dream's session and the preceding sessions with the third ear, as

---

[1] Patients may talk in an even voice, and yet some words or phrases are heard as if they were "louder." I exhort myself and my students and supervisees to pay attention to this. It could be a signal "from within oneself" that the patient's louder word or phrases, possibly from her or his unconscious, have struck a chord of psychodynamic significance, which can add precious understanding of the latent meaning of a dream or other unconscious derivatives.

we try to listen to the dream's session and the preceding sessions as if the sessions themselves were a dream, with a manifest, semi-manifest, and semilatent and latent content, as we try to be open to any associations T's material brings to our own mind, as we try to hear any resonances between T's story and our own conscious-ness, as we try to let all kinds of thoughts and feelings "bubble up" to our consciousness while listening to T's words—as we do that, what does come to mind?

Sessions Preceding the Dream's Session, Semimanifest Content

"I am a suspicious little boy, nobody loves me, everybody is out to harm me, to strike me out, to throw me out of the ballgame, to throw me out of the game of life. No wonder I never lose eye contact, over-analyze, am always on guard. I have to be ready and protect myself from the barbs my father and brother and all peo-ple may throw at me." And: "Nobody loves me . . . my father hated me even before I was born, I was born too soon, I intruded into his fun too early, he has never let me forget it, always puts me down, prefers my brother to me." And: "My mother, for now I can only tell you that she is a guilt-provoking woman, I can't tell you how I really feel about her, that's why I have hardly talked about her." And: "My ex-wife was a mystery to me, all women are a mystery to me, with women I am like a babe in the woods. I don't even know why she left me, I cannot yet tell you why my wife left me, maybe it has something to do with my mother, my wife was a WASP, what's a little Jewish boy doing with a WASP. Maybe that's why I married her, being a WASP, she was sure to be very different from my guilt-provoking mother." And: "At least I have this male friend, and he seems to like me, and he is a lot better than my father, that's why I like him, he is a giving person, he even threw out his girl friend for me, he raps with me, but even this is problematic, could I be homosexual?"

Sessions Preceding the Dream's Session, Semilatent and Latent Contents

"I married a WASP, or did I marry a . . . wasp, a woman who stings like my mother did? Maybe I married her because she was like my mother, so I could have a second chance with mother . . .

and she abandoned me, just like my mother did. Did my mother abandon me because I was bad, because I was angry?" And: "I am afraid to tell you yet, woman therapist, how I really feel about my mother. . . can I trust you? I have to pay, every time I come to see you, it makes me feel like I am coming to a hooker. Are you a hooker, an exploiter of men, an exploiter of little babes in the wood such as me?" And: "I am a very angry little boy (girl?!?), that's why everybody hates me, that's why my father ridicules me and puts me down. I hate everyone who hates me . . . I hate, I hate, I hate." And: "I am much more frightened of my feelings about my roommate than I have let you know. He is a doctor, maybe I should marry him, shouldn't a little Jewish girl marry a doctor? My God, what am I thinking, am I homosexual?!"

Dream's Session, Semimanifest Content

"As I have been saying, my father always puts me down. I tell him that I play baseball well, that I am a regular guy, that I can hit, that I am a mensch, and he tells me that I am a schmuck, that I only strike out. I am angry at him." And, "I am angry at my brother too, so intrusive of him and his stupid friend to come and visit me."

Dream's Session, Semilatent and Latent Contents

"I am not just angry at my father, I am furious at him, I want to kill him, but he is the big man, so I better obey him and be a schmuck and strike out in baseball, and strike out with girls, no matter how lonely that makes me feel." And: "I am furious at my brother too, I want to kill him too." And: "My father prefers my brother to me, I wish to throw my brother out at home plate, strike him out. He came to visit me, the SOB, not that, the word *bitch* is not a reference to my mother, I am not ready to tell you yet, female therapist, how I feel about my mother. He came to visit me, the son of a gun, and I felt restless and anxious with rage. I did throw him out of the house, but I wanted to kill him." And: "I don't care how small I am and how big my father is, my anger is so big, it makes me big. I want to kill him."

The Second Task: Understanding the Session's Dream. More of the Internal Soliloquy.

As we again let all kinds of thoughts and feelings "bubble up" to consciousness as we listen to T's dream, what do we hear, what does come up from within ourselves?

Session's Dream, Semimanifest Content

"I want to tell you, in great detail (after all, I am kind of obsessive), where I live so that you will know exactly where I am, how I feel: Brooklyn, Avenue M, Flatbush." And: "I am getting out of where I am, I am getting out from under my father and brother, I am coming upstairs, into the air, onto the El, onto a more elevated station in life, the elevated place where my brother is, my brother, always a few feet ahead of me, the son of a gun, on the same elevated place where my father also stands." And: "I am going to catch a train, the train taking me to you, therapist." And: "Of course I have to buy a token, I have to pay for everything in life, this is my destiny, being such a schmuck." And: "And there, ahead of me, two men, two black men, my father and brother, ahead of me, as always? I will follow them, follow in their footsteps, maybe they will teach me the secrets of life, they will teach me how to make it with girls, how not to strike out." And: "But father is no help, he is contemptuous and disdainful, he is angry at me, he throws a rock at me, a hard rock, a hard ball, not a soft catchable ball, a hard ball on which I can only strike out." And: "But I catch the rock, take the injustice, swallow, once more, the hard ball, the hard injustice." And: "I better stay away from them, I better withdraw."

Session's Dream, Semilatent and Latent Contents

"Yes, I want to tell you, in detail, where I live, so you will know exactly how I feel, deep down. I live on Avenue M, that's "M" for "Mother," and Flatbush, that is, a flat place, a desert, only flat bushes, no luxuriant vegetation here, no nurture, an emotional desert." And: "Yes, I do live, internally, on my father and brother (and mother?). I am, angrily and hungrily, dependent on them (and her?), but this bush is flat, these testicles (my father's and

brother's) are flat, give little sustenance . . . about my mother's
flat, unnurturing breast, I cannot talk to you about that yet." And:
"My wish is to go up, so I go up, I am up, I am going to feel up,
I am going to feel high, I am having an erection." And: "I only
make a token payment, I am so great, really, deep inside, that I
only make 'token' payments." And: "There are my father and
brother, as bad and sexual as black men are supposed to be. No,
I am the two black men, with two or four black, dirty, powerful
testicles." And: "Father is no help, he does not want me to be
up, to feel up, to feel high, to have an erection, to go to Manhattan where I can meet girls, to go to Manhattan where I can meet
my therapist (who, who knows, might free me, might be a better
mother to me than my mother was). My father does not want me
to meet women, to meet my new mother, to meet my mother."
And: "My father throws me a hard ball, not a softball, not the
soft testicle or breast I wish for. The SOB throws me nothing I
can feed on, or chew on with anger or hit back at him." And: "I
will only *appear* to withdraw. . . in the magic reality of my dream,
I go back downstairs, to my unconscious, where all kinds of beautiful, wicked, forbidden wishes lurk." And: "It's me throwing the
hard rock at my father and brother, it's me killing them . . . then
I can go, then I do go to beautiful, wicked Manhattan, and be
sexual like black men are, be sexual like father and brother are,
and perhaps, meet a real woman (and, perhaps, meet mother,
although my real feelings and thoughts about mother are still too
deep and frightening and I can't yet tell you about them)." And:
"*I am* having sex with my father, not he with me, angry sex, loving
sex, better a soft testicle than no breast, than nothing at all. My
father will be my mother." And: "*I have* thrown the hard rock at
father and brother, *it's I* who is contemptuous and disdainful of
them, not they of me, it's I who is ahead of them, not they of me,
with my hard testicles, my hard penis, I have hit father and
brother, I have killed them. I have won, I am going to Manhattan,
where the bushes are not flat."

Some of the psychological operations of the dream work,
some of the dream's defenses were:

Concrete pictorial representation: subway token for admission price,
payments, symbolic payments; *elevated train* for elevated station in

life, feeling "high," erection; *train* for analysis, movement, progress; *rock* for father's hardness of character, hardships in life, hard words from father and brother; *flatbush* for lack of nurturing, desolation.

Displacement: rock for testicle; *two black guys* for father and brother.
Condensation: rock for projectile, food, testicle, breast; *father* for father and mother.
Synecdoche: M for mother; *bush* for pubic hair, whole person (mother or father).
Secondary Elaboration: the details given before the dream.
Projection: In the latent dream, it is T throwing the stone, being ahead of father and brother, etc. These activities are projected onto father and brother.

The Third Task: Responding to the Dream

Silence, interventions, interpretations? Interventions or interpretations on the level of the defenses, of the drives, within the context of the transference? What clinical and psychodynamic judgments should guide the analyst in terms of how to respond to the dream?

With first dreams, the general rule or formula is: Not much can be said (we hardly know the patient), not much should be said (it could increase resistance, would contaminate the transference, and could hardly be accurate: again, we do not really know the patient), and just enough might have to be said (i.e., with patients who have already announced that they do not believe in dreams, or who have said they never remember their dreams, and with very resistant patients).

T had not said that he never remembered his dreams, had not protested disbelief in dreams. After only six sessions of therapy he had already remembered a "good" dream (a terse and concise dream, not a long-winded and highly detailed dream, as resistance dreams often are; and a dream not too highly defended). He had not shown any conscious interest in his dream, and had asked no explanations about it. To say nothing to him about his dream would have been appropriate. Also, this being a first dream, the cardinal rule of dream interpretation was to be suspended. If a response at all were to be given, it should be a response about the semimanifest dream, on the level of the defenses, definitely not a response about the latent, or even the semilatent dream, not a response on the level of the drives. So, should there have been a response at all? And, if so, should the response have been within the context of transference?

T's transference seemed to be developing well. There was evidence of some positive transference. T had been coming on time, had not missed sessions or payments, had already remembered a dream; but there was evidence of some negative transference. The therapist did remind him of his guilt-provoking mother and made him think of a prostitute, hence the relentless eye contact. Again, should there have been a response, on the level of the defenses, and within the context of the transference, or would silence have been the best response of all?

Speaking hypothetically, if responses about the semimanifest dream, on the level of the defenses, had been chosen, such responses as the following would have been appropriate. One might ask for associations about the manifest dream in general; ask for associations, more specifically, about subway trips; ask for more thoughts and feelings about where T lived currently and where he lived as a child.

Still hypothetically, if T had dreamed this dream several years later and responses about the semilatent and latent dream on the level of the drives (within the context of the transference or not) had been indicated, such responses as the following would have been appropriate. One might ask for associations about black men and their sexuality; ask for associations about throwing rocks, about anger, about being held back, about people being ahead of him. Or, more boldly, one might ask whether T might have wanted to be ahead of someone else, the therapist, maybe; or ask if he were angry and wanted to throw rocks at someone else, the therapist again.

The dream's latent content suggested, mainly, anger at father and, possibly, oedipal issues. There were, however, hints that the core of the neurosis could have been about anger at mother and about preoedipal, oral issues, such as depression. There is also the fact that T spoke very little of his mother, as if anger at father was less fearsome, and less defended than anger at mother. And there were the references to mother as "guilt-provoking" and "hooker"; and the Flatbush/flat-bush onomatopoeia. Since nothing in the manifest dream referred to mother, and since these hints were quite indirect, it is difficult to imagine what could have been said to T on the level of the drives, having to do with thoughts and feelings about his mother.

I told my student that if T had been my patient, I might have said:

> I think the dream is a positive dream. It suggests that a part of you wants to get better, feel better, be "upstairs," up in the open fresh air where the El trains are, on a more elevated way of feeling; that a part of you wants to move, to go places, to move in life. You have expressed some reservations about me, I do remind you of your guilt-provoking mother, but I do really believe that, mostly, you like to come to therapy, believe in therapy. You remember your dreams, haven't been late once, haven't canceled any session . . . I wonder whether in the dream you are coming to your therapy session.

It would have been a response entirely on the level of the defenses, a response about the semimanifest content of the dream, and an intervention on the level of the defenses within the context of the transference. It would have been a statement about his conscious feelings about therapy, a statement about the positive side of his ambivalent feelings about it. It was meant to strengthen and nurture a therapeutic alliance that had barely begun to develop, that was still, understandably, very tentative, fragile, and ambivalent. This kind of response might have helped him continue to remember his dreams.

The therapist told me that she did use this kind of response with T in their next session and that it helped. Two years later, this student became my analytical supervisee. We did not work with T, but she was still seeing him. He was coming three times a week, had become an analytical patient, and did much work with his dreams. Preoedipal issues of some importance had begun to emerge, and depression had become a prominent symptom. But the strong therapeutic alliance permitted him to withstand the depression and to continue to work on it. T's therapist indeed felt that the oedipal issues had been in large part a cover for strong feelings of abandonment by, and anger at, mother.

"White Poodle" and "Going North, Vaguely"

Freud thought of dreams as a highly individual product, and therefore believed that they cannot be analyzed in a vacuum, without knowing the patient and without the patient's associations. To understand and respond to dreams, we must know the dreamers historically and understand them psychodynamically. Yet, the following illustration consists of the response[2] given by me to two dreams, "White Poodle" and "Going North, Vaguely" dreamed by a patient completely unknown to me. Not even the dreamer's gender was known by me, all I knew was that the dreamer was in his or her "late life"; no information was available on the dream's session or on the session or sessions preceding the dream. The dreamer may not even have been in psychotherapy.

This is what I call "playing with a dream." In playing with a dream, the response, of course, may be inaccurate, and, in some cases, as in this instance, there may be no way of verifying it later on. Playing with a dream consists of engaging in an internal response strictly within one's own mind; that is exactly what we should do and all we can do with most of our own patients' dreams when they are communicated to us in the first session or in an initial interview. As with these two dreams, we know very little about the dreamer initially. This is why playing with a dream is a perfectly respectable and potentially very useful enterprise.

"White Poodle"

(dreamed early in the week)

> A playful white poodle runs away from its owner on the street and runs toward a grassy curb. The owner who is in her twenties, seems worried. I catch the dog and leash it for her. She was dressed in a coat, bobbed hair style, good features, intelligent face; seems preoccupied. Although she had seemed worried when the dog had run out on her, I am not certain, nor is she, that my help was desired or necessary.

My response to the research inquiry, based on my soliloquy, included these thoughts. (Italicized words were part of the dream's

---

[2]It was a response to a clinical research project, "Dreams by Late-Life Dreamers" (Ephron, 1972, Personal communication).

manifest content.) I shall assume the dreamer is a Caucasian woman in late life. On the semimanifest and semilatent levels, I hear her saying, "I am myself as I am now, in late life, and I am also myself as I was in my twenties, and I am myself also as a *white poodle*. I am *worried* and *preoccupied* about my wishes and desires: they are *white*, good and clean and pure, and they are also animal-like, like a *poodle's*, like a dog's, bad and unclean and not so pure. I am ambivalent about my wishes and desires, a part of me wants them to *run away* from me, and a part of me is worried about them running away from me, a part of me wants these wishes and desires to go to the *grass*, that is, to softness, and self-indulgence and Dolce Vita, and a part of me wants them to be *curbed*, a part of me wants them to be *caught* and *leashed*, and a part of me feels this is neither *desired nor necessary*."

"I am ambivalent about myself, too: in part I want to hide these animal-like wishes and desires, hide them within my chest, under *a coat* that will render them invisible, in part I don't want to hide them. In part I want to be dressed decorously, with *a coat*, in part I want to be dressed youthfully, my hair *bobbed*. I am feeling my wishes and desires of me *in my twenties* and I am feeling them now that I am in late life." On the latent level I hear her saying: "I am letting myself *get away* from a superego that wants to *curb* and *leash* my wishes and desires. I want to have no defenses against them, no *coat* disguising them. Yes, of course my wishes and desires are animal-like, like a *poodle's*, but they are good, that is, *white*."

Less in terms of resonances within me and on a more theoretical plane, I think the dreamer is preoccupied with drives and their control, uncertain as to whether these drives are safe, to be gratified and enjoyed, or bad, to be curbed and leashed. This ambivalence, this existential and psychodynamic uncertainty, shows in several of the dream's manifest elements. Such elements as grass, playfulness, poodle, whiteness, help being neither "desired" nor "necessary": these suggest life, abandon, vibrancy, self-confidence, joie de vivre, a Dionysian Weltanschauung. On the other hand, such elements as catching and leashing the dog, a curb, seeming preoccupied and worried, these suggest self-control, austerity, abnegation, abstinence, an Apollonian philosophy of life.

Furthermore, dogs go to curbs to urinate and defecate; the dreamer could be interested in, respectively, urethral–anal and oral–genital gratifications; the wish-fear to lose control voluntarily over urinary and anal sphincters, the wish-fear to lose control voluntarily over pleasurable preoedipal and oedipal drives; the wish-fear to exhibit publicly all kinds of primitive, animal-like behavior. There is finally, the counterpoint of age: the dreamer is, in reality, in her late life; she is in her twenties when personified by the dog's owner; and is in her childhood when represented by a dog, who, frisky and playful, seems indeed to be a puppy. Thus, the wish–fear of losing control go back to memories of having lost control over drives in infancy, and also to more current wishes and fears of losing control over impulses in general. Considering the realistic late-life age of the dreamer, the wish *voluntarily* to lose control over sphincters, may be poignantly compounded by urinary and anal incontinence, the fear of losing sphincter control *involuntarily*.[3]

"Going North Vaguely"

(dreamed later in the week)

I am pushing my way through traffic on 42nd Street, by the Times Building, going north toward 43rd Street. It's vague, first I'm on foot, then in a car, then in a subway train heading uptown. I am with Ike, my friend, who respects me. Ike decides we should get off the train to get something for his son, or, it's vague, it's my little brother, who is a chubby 4-year-old shaped like a ball. He decides we will get the next train and crosses to the west side of 7th Avenue. I and the chubby one wait on the east side. The chubby one wanders off eastward to look at a newsstand display. I go to him, fearing traffic might hurt him. I see Ike coming back: he is slender, 5 foot 10 inches, dressed in a vaguely pale yellow suit, like the uniform of an Army officer. The chubby one is wearing the same colors. We are now heading north, to Westchester. We arrive at Ike's house as arrangements are being made for a wedding reception. I arrive at an upper

---

[3]In "playing with dreams," more than one semimanifest, semilatent, and latent scenario will "bubble up" to the analyst's mind. Resonances between the dream and the analyst's conscious and unconscious mind will be as numerous as the analyst's creativity and imagination (and superego) will permit. The semimanifest, semilatent, and latent scenarios given above were those that I found most likely. With one's own patient, as one gets to know the patient, one can rule out or confirm the scenarios one had hypothetically constructed earlier on. With this patient, not my own patient, this, of course, was not possible and the correctness of the scenarios presented could not be verified.

entrance. At the stairs-landing, a young couple is kissing. I pass them by.
Ike's wife greets me, warmly as usual, but hurriedly, because of the wedding preparations, guests arriving, etc., half-squirmy, a little perfunctory
in her embrace . . . worse, her face and body are covered with black pim-
ples, hard, like bumps on a prickly pear, it's difficult to hug her, annoying,
hampering, like a hair shirt.

My response to the research inquiry, based on my internal
soliloquy, included these thoughts (italicized words are part of
the dream's manifest content). This is the same dreamer of the
previous dream: thus I am still assuming the dreamer is a Caucasian woman in her late life. On the semimanifest and semilatent
levels, I hear her saying: "I am afraid of what this dream stands
for, that's why the manifest dream is so long and detailed, and
that's why so much is *vague* about the dream. I am afraid of something concerning Ike and Chubby, that's why I dress them in
yellow, the color of fear. Life continues to be difficult for me; as
time (the *Times Building*) keeps ticking on, I have to *push my way*
through all kinds of difficulties and pains. This dream is about
when I was *4 years old*, Chubby's age, about when my brother
Chubby was born, it was painful for me to have this rival in Ike's
affection. Yes, the years between 4 (*42nd, 43rd Street*) and 7 (*7th
Avenue*) were painful years for me, they were the years I had to
push myself through all the *traffic*, the crowdedness that Chubby's
arrival caused. This dream is about all kinds of pain in my psychic
interiors, that's why I told Dr. Ephron, who is conducting this
research on dreams, that my abdomen is painful. This dream is
about all sorts of psychic pressures inside of me, that's why I told
him I felt bladder pressure when I woke up."

"Ike is not just a friend, Ike is my father, that's why I call
him *Ike*, that's why I give him the nickname of one of the Fathers
of our country, Dwight *"Ike"* Eisenhower. Of course he is my
father, that's why his son is my brother. I had thought that Ike,
my dad, was my friend, and that he really *respected* me, but he
likes Chubby so much that he *gets us off the train to get him something*.
He likes Chubby so much that he doesn't mind abandoning me
at the subway stop, abandoning me, who needs him just as much
as Chubby needs him. Here I am, baby-sitting Chubby, even having to protect him from his voyeurism and get him back as he
wanders off. I am afraid, *yellow*-afraid, of my feelings of sibling

rivalry against my chubby brother, I am afraid of my feelings about Ike's liking Chubby so much, I am so afraid of these feelings that in the manifest dream I am going *North*, which stands for head, reason, intellect, rather than South, which stands for guts, passion, feelings. How much I love my father, when he comes back to me, look how handsome he is, dressed indeed like Ike when Ike was a General."

"We are in Westchester now, in Ike's house, my dad's and mom's house. Crowds again, if it's not Chubby crowding me, interfering with my pleasure, it is something else, like *receptions* and *wedding preparations*. I still have to *push* my way *through traffic*, no peaceful, serene place just for me. My mom kisses me, *warmly* but *hurriedly*, does she really want to kiss me? Does she really love me? She kisses me *perfunctorily*, even *squirms* in *kissing* me. It's hard to hug her, when she is as *prickly* as that, her *pear*-shaped breasts are prickly, it's hard to get good milk from such a breast; why is she so prickly?"

And on the latent level I hear her saying: "I am *pushing my way* through a crowd of feelings, a crowd of defenses. I am going South, not North, South to my unconscious, to my psychic guts, where there are all kinds of beautiful, angry feelings stored. I am angry at father and brother, I am 'pissed' at both of them, that's why I told Dr. Ephron that my bladder was bursting when I woke up. I am angry at them, I want to poison both of them with my intestinal gas, that's why I told Dr. Ephron I woke up with a sense of flatulence. I am angry at Chubby for being born, look at the monster, *shaped like a ball*, that's why I have him, in the manifest dream, *wandering off eastwardly*, where *traffic might hurt him*. I want traffic to hurt him. I am angry at my father, whom I love so much, angry at him for favoring Chubby. I am now in my parents' house, and I am an important person, as important as Chubby is to my dad, that's why I place myself, in the manifest dream, at *an upper entrance*. Mother neglects me again, I am angry at her too. I want to *annoy* her, *hamper* her, *prick* her. I am the *prickly pear*" (see note 3, above).

Again, less in terms of resonances and on a more theoretical plane, there is much "movement" in this dream: from South to North, eastwardly (Chubby and the dreamer), westwardly (Ike).

This physical, geographic movement suggests a whirlwind of psychological movement in the dreamer's inner life. The dreamer is in pain, physically and psychologically, in psychological and existential disharmony. The physical pains (dental pains, abdominal cramps, bladder pressure) resonate with the psychological pains, the painful conflict between pleasure and abnegation: seeking the pleasure of Westchester (as bucolic and serene as the dreamer wishes it to be), and enduring the abnegation of that pleasure (no, Westchester will be as crowded and bustling as Times Square). There is also the painful conflict between guilt over self-indulgence (i.e., indulging one's death wishes against Chubby) and the frustration over self-denial (i.e., rescuing the *wandering Chubby* from the *dangers of traffic*). Only toward the end of the dream is some harmony momentarily attained. Chubby has disappeared, the dreamer makes a grand entrance into the parental home, dreamer, mother, and father are reunited—but the harmony is momentary, the serenity ephemeral; the house is split level (*upper* and *lower entrances*), mother is busy with guests, her embrace is *hurried* and *perfunctory, hairshirts* and *prickliness annoy* and *hamper* any expressions of love.

7

Dream Interpretation, 2

In this chapter, we shall illustrate the application of the clinical tasks and technical principles, and my *internal soliloquy* technique, described in chapter 6, by discussing specific dreams in depth. The soliloquy technique illustrates my internal thinking in working with dreams. In almost all these dreams the cardinal rule of dream interpretation—analyzing the latent content, responding to the dream on the level of the drives—was applied. As stated in the previous chapter, this response is indeed a powerful one, to be used only when the analyst is confident about having correctly understood the dream's latent meanings, assured that the patient is able to tolerate and utilize this kind of response, and believes, not because of countertransference, that the patient and the therapeutic alliance are strong enough. Needless to say, none of the clinical exceptions to the application of the cardinal rule was extant.

The dreams selected for this chapter were dreamed by three of my patients. Each of the three patients, of course, had many more dreams in the course of his analysis. The dreams selected for inclusion here were chosen because of their thematic and psychodynamic similarities. The dreams occurred at various stages of psychoanalytic psychotherapy; consequently, in some of them the cardinal rule was applied only to a degree, in accordance with the characteristics and requirements of the stage of therapy at which the dream had been dreamed or because of clinical or psychodynamic considerations present at the time.

(Again, this reflects the art more than the science of dream interpretation.)

L's DREAMS: "PATTING A DONKEY," "GUINEA PIG," "SUCCESSFUL INTERCOURSE," AND "EGGSHELLS"

Let us start by discussing four dreams dreamed by L, the austere
neurologist mentioned earlier. These dreams are being discussed
together, not only because of thematic and psychodynamic similarities, but also because they show how the "line of therapy"
progressed from oedipal and father-centered (the first two
dreams), to preoedipal and mother-centered (the last two
dreams). The work done with these four dreams will show, step
by step, how the analyst carries out the three tasks in working
with dreams discussed in chapter 6.

L started psychoanalysis at 35. He had been born into an
upper middle class family in central Italy; he was an only son. His
mother was an exacting, demanding, ebullient, fiery woman, a
mixture of narcissistic, compulsive, and hysterical characteristics,
probably a borderline character. L consciously loved her, had
been a respectful, obedient, and devoted son, and was unconsciously enraged at her. L's father had died in his late fifties, when
L was 22. He was an elegant, mild, kindly, amiable, melancholic,
passive man, a physician who did not practice medicine and administered his father-in-law's vast land holdings. He was dominated by his wife, whom he loved and admired, and who bemused
and slightly frightened him with her fierce temperament. He
loved L in a remote, intellectual, distracted fashion, more senti-
mental than concretely demonstrative. L liked his kindness, consciously loved him in a distant and lukewarm fashion,
unconsciously was angry at him for not protecting him from his
mother. Truly oedipal anger at father was more complex because
L's libidinal wishes toward mother were more complex. Both on
the preoedipal and oedipal level, mother was at once desirable
and fearsome.

L came to the United States with his widowed mother at 23,
shortly after graduating from medical school. He was single, a
successful neurologist, had lived with his mother until her death,

which occurred when he was 30. He was sexually impotent, had strong obsessional tendencies, and the classical defenses of the obsessional character (repression, regression, denial, undoing, reaction formation, and intellectualization). He was an elegant, serious, somber, glum, frowning man, not truly cold, not truly distant or remote, likable in spite of his grave demeanor. While his manners were stern, brusque (never harsh), he was, interpersonally, unfailingly courteous.

"Patting a Donkey"

> A very strange dream. . . . I was in one of the stables of my grandfather's farms in Italy . . . patting one of the donkeys.

This dream had been dreamed after about eighteen months of therapy. L had been coming three times a week for about a year and was using the couch. The dream (see chapter 4) had been dreamed the night after a session in which L had, for the first time, expressed mild anger at me, and at the end of which he surprised himself by a slip of the tongue. As he left, he said, "Okay, *donkey*"—instead of "doctor"—"see you next week." He mumbled a quick apology and left, red-faced. I said, "See you next week." I made no comments about the slip of the tongue.

In the dream's session, after telling me the dream, he told me that he spent all the summers of his childhood, from late June to late August, at his maternal grandfather's villa on a large farm estate; that his father had a small office there for his bookkeeping work for grandfather; that he spent hours in grandfather's "immense" library, with father reading to him from books of poetry and Ariosto's epics on the deeds of Orlando and Rinaldo. He said that he found the time spent with father "both boring and interesting"; that grandfather was gruff, harsh, authoritarian but not unloving, and he both feared and loved him. Grandfather and father frequently took him to the stables to see the farm animals, and grandfather died of a stroke when L was 12. He added at that point, "Incidentally, my father also died of a stroke."

The first two tasks at this point were to understand the dream's session and the sessions before it, and to understand the session's dream; that is, to know what the dream says. As I engaged in my internal soliloquy of conjectures and speculations about the session's dream and the dream's session, my soliloquy included these thoughts. L had talked about his father and grandfather almost as one person. Yes, the two men were very different, but father's office and grandfather's library were adjacent, both men took him to see the animals in the stables, both men had died of a stroke. He himself had joined the two men together, by telling me that his grandfather had died of a stroke, "and so did my father, incidentally." The word *incidentally* made me think of the word *accidentally*; the fact that he used the word *stroke*, rather than *cerebrovascular accident*, which would have been more consistent with his usually formal manner of speaking, was probably a clue to the meaning of the latent dream. The word *stroke* has to do with striking, hitting, injuring someone with a blow, and with stroking, caressing, soothing, rubbing gently. I also thought, in my internal soliloquy, that time with his father was "boring," when and because L was repressing anger at father for being distant, remote, intellectual, undemonstrative, and inferior to grandfather (father had a small office, while grandfather had a huge house, an "immense" library). Yet, time with father was also "interesting," because when father read Ariosto's tales to L, the boy could think of his father as the great Orlando and of himself as the almost heroic Rinaldo. He did not refer to the slip of the tongue from the previous session the week before. And I noted that he had not said a word about his mother. I tentatively concluded that the dream was about drives of both anger and love toward grandfather, father, and analyst. Through condensation, L saw the three of us as donkeys; he unconsciously wished to "stroke" us. Patting us was a condensation of the wish (latent dream) to strike at us angrily, to give us a "stroke," to make us die "accidentally," not "incidentally"; and the wish to stroke us lovingly.

The third task was to respond to the dream, to know what to say to the patient about the dream. I had now to decide whether the dream should be handled with silence or with a response, and, if a response was warranted, whether it should be an intervention or an interpretation on the level of the defenses,

or the level of the drives and within the context of the transference.

We were still in the early–middle phase of therapy. The
cardinal rule was not to be followed, an intervention on the level
of the drives was not appropriate. But the therapeutic alliance
was fairly strong, and so was the patient's ego. Thus, the patient
could tolerate some movement down the royal road to his unconscious, the "stable" of his "animal"-like drives. Having to select
that which seemed most useful to progress down that road, and
that would help to bring repressed material into consciousness,
I elected to ask him for more associations about his grandfather's
animals on the farm. He mentioned grandfather's bulls, cattle,
horses, rabbits, and yes, donkeys. I thought that his associations
about bulls could eventually lead us to thoughts and feelings coming from the "bull" within him, lead us to his bullish, obstinate,
anally regressed anger at me, grandfather, father. I hoped that
they would lead us, ultimately, way down the royal road, to
mother, and would also lead us to his bull-like libidinal drives. I
thought and hoped that associations about rabbits would eventually lead us to thoughts and feelings about his timid, rabbit-like
father and to thoughts and feelings about me, a "Conigliaro"
(rabbit is *coniglio* in Italian). I thought that associations about
donkeys might lead him to recollect the slip of the tongue of the
previous session and thus lead us to further progress in the analysis of the transference. (I did not refer to the slip of the tongue,
except obliquely: I did ask him for associations to the various
animals in his grandfather's farm, but I did not specifically mention donkeys; he did.) At the end of the session, I said:

> I wonder how you really feel about those donkeys in the dream, whatever
> they may represent. . . . I wonder what 'patting' them really means.

It was a response on the level of the defenses, since "donkeys" (manifest dream) was the result of the dream work's defenses camouflaging, through displacement, father and me
(latent dream). "Patting" (manifest dream) was the product of
the dream work defenses disguising, through condensation, the

drives to strike and stroke (latent dream). There was, in my response, a tactful[1] allusion to the transference, since I did mention
donkeys, and the word had appeared in his slip of the tongue
toward me, the transferential father, in the previous session.
There was in my response also an indirect exhortation to think
and reflect more on what he was really doing with those donkeys,
and who those donkeys represented. The associations I asked for,
and the response I gave to L's dream, were motivated by an internal agenda: to make further progress down the royal road to L's
unconscious, and to bring repressed material into consciousness.
More specifically, to bring into consciousness the mild anger at
grandfather for being harsh and gruff, and the strong anger at
father for being, with L, so distant, remote, intellectual, and undemonstrative, for not being as "grand" as grandfather, or as heroic
as Orlando. This anger was reached in the second of the four
dreams.

Theoretical Appendix: Some of the Dream Work Defenses

From the dream's manifest content:

Very strange: secondary elaboration and an allusion to the need
(defense) to distance himself from the dream's content, to render
it as ego alien, "strange" (extraneous) as possible.
Dream: secondary elaboration, and again the defensive attempt to
distance himself from the dream's latent wishes, "It's only a
dream."
Patting: concrete pictorial representation of the ambivalent wishes
to strike, injure, hit, stroke, caress, soothe, and a condensation
of those wishes.
Donkey: displacement from father, grandfather, and analyst; condensation of father, grandfather, and analyst; concrete pictorial
representation of donkey's attributes: stupidity, stubbornness,
and so on.

From associations—one listens to the dream's session as if it were
a dream:

---

[1]Tact may be a requirement in psychoanalysis; even skirmishes with the unconscious can
be frightening.

Grandfather died of a stroke: onomatopoeia for striking.
Father died of a stroke: onomatopoeia for striking.
Incidentally: onomatopoeia for accidentally (the wish was of accidentally striking father and grandfather).
Donkey, in the slip of the tongue: onomatopoeia for doctor.

"Guinea Pig"

L dreamed this dream, the second of his quartet of dreams, about one year and a half after the "Patting a Donkey" dream. Although many other dreams had occurred during those eighteen months, "Guinea Pig" and "Patting a Donkey" both showed movement toward anger, oedipal or otherwise, at father. Much had happened in the eighteen months or so between the dreams. L had continued to come three times a week and he had now been in analysis a total of about three years. He still had a serious, austere, and severe demeanor, but was slightly less somber and slightly less of a frowning, glum person. He tended to be polite, brusque, and curt with men, respectful with women. Now 38, handsome, elegant, of impeccable manners, the women in his professional circle (nurses, administrators, and colleagues in the hospital with which he was associated) saw him as quite a catch, but probably an inveterate bachelor. His interpersonal life was slightly improved; he dated occasionally, had had brief, entirely platonic relationships. He had become fairly potent in masturbation, but had not tested his sexual potency with women. The last time he had attempted intercourse had been in Italy, in the last year of medical school—he had told me this in his first or second session of analysis, but, significantly, repeated it to me in the dream's session.

In the eighteen months between the two dreams, L spoke little about his mother, some more about his maternal grandfather, and a great deal about his father. More incidents were related concerning his father's remoteness, his distance and passivity, his melancholic and low-spirited disposition, his being vibrant and fully alive only when talking of a new play or a new book, his being close to L and interested in L only in regard to L's grades in school, the books L was reading, films L had seen. But, "he never asked me how I was doing, or how I was doing with women." At these times in analysis, L's voice would become harsh, acrid, sharp, just short of agitated and excited, his affect more intense, and at the same time, taut, controlled, restrained. One could hear the unconscious anger underneath.

It was during this period of therapy that L told me more about his father's death. The death had been sudden; his father had died of a massive brain hemorrhage at 59. L was then 22 and in the fifth year of medical school, which in Italy requires six years. L had grieved over his father for several months, "more internally than visibly," remembering how gentle and kindly father had been. He did not feel any feelings of guilt at the time, but now he thought that "maybe subconsciously I did. As I am talking about my father now, I wonder whether then I felt I could have been more appreciative of his good qualities and more forgiving of his quirks." Throughout this eighteen month period, in the sessions in which he was talking about his father's death, L would only speak of his father's "good qualities" and his affect was considerably more mellow. After a few sessions during which he had not referred to father's death, he would resume talking about his father's "quirks" and again become harsh, acrid, and intense (and tense, taut, and reined in). L did not say anything new about his grandfather but elaborated some more on his summers at the farm estate. Grandfather took him on long rides in his horse and carriage, took him to visit the animals in their various stables and enclosures, taught him to play chess. Grandfather was cordial and protective of L's father. Grandfather's death was very painful to L. He spoke little of his mother, only saying that she fought incessantly with her father, L's grandfather. He remembered about one dream a week; there had been several dreams whose latent content was anger at father, and four or five with oedipal and preoedipal content concerning mother.

With me, L was different from what he was like outside of therapy. We were now in the middle phase of therapy, and there had occurred some splitting between observing ego and irrational ego. In "easy" sessions, he could be considerably more genuine and could relate to me in a more open, even friendly, fashion. He was now addressing me by my first name (at the time of the "Patting a Donkey" dream, I had been, strictly and only, Dr. Conigliaro). In "hard" sessions, he could be less guarded about being harsh, could observe himself as sounding harsh (or taut, reined in), would comment about that, and would wonder out loud if he really felt the way he sounded. In sessions during which his unconscious demons pressed toward consciousness less urgently, the "easy" sessions, he could be jocular, or express his anger at me through facetious, civilized derivatives of the unconscious. For instance, two or three times he referred to me, jokingly and gingerly, as "Doc" (a civilized way of castrating me: he only mutilated my professional title!). Half-turned toward me from the couch, he said, "Don't get excited, I said 'Doc,' not 'donkey.' " (A few sessions after the "Patting a Donkey" dream, he had remembered the *donkey* slip of the tongue.) And at least once, also during an "easy" period, he made a playful reference, carefully and cautiously, to my last name and wondered out loud ("I am only joking, of course," he interjected) whether there was, after all, a *coniglio*, a timid rabbit, under my confident exterior. In sessions in which his unconscious drives were pushing against his defenses with greater energy, the "hard" sessions, he could be very angry at me. In spite of the many changes in his attitudes and demeanor within therapy, as opposed to outside of therapy, his basic anal-retentive characterology had not changed very much.

For a period of about six months toward the end of this period, up to about two to three weeks before the dream's session, L had been more angry at me. Throughout this period, he experienced me as intellectual and scholarly, "just a university prof, not a feeling person," accused me of not really caring about him, of preferring teaching to helping patients, of being cold and unrelated, of exhibiting no interest in his sexual dysfunction or in his difficulties in striking up friendships with women. There usually are books or magazines I am reading on the floor around my chair; on "good" days, L would tease me about them; on "bad" days, he angrily referred to them as evidence of my lack of interest in my work with patients. Throughout this period, the observing ego was not working too well for him and he had no conscious idea that he was really experiencing, transferentially, his father.

Then a "lull" occurred, the "doldrums," a periodic occurrence in psychoanalysis after periods of intense work and activation of the transference; it lasted about two to three weeks, up to the time of the dream's session. During this lull, L reverted to being his usual self: relatively open, moderately friendly, occasionally droll, basically constricted and cautious, controlled and vigilant against himself, anal-retentive. It was during the middle of this lull, about one to two weeks before the dream's session, that a curious incident occurred. L, who had never done so before, arrived with a container of coffee from the luncheonette around the corner and asked if he could sit up for a few minutes to drink from it. He told me he had not yet "touched it" and offered to pour some of it into a cup for me. Before I could accept or decline, he said, "But, I already put in some artificial sweetener, you are so health-conscious, you will think artificial sweeteners are poison."

On the day of the dream's session, L seemed both more subdued and more guarded than he had been over the last two or three weeks. He lay on the couch and launched right away into the dream.

"Guinea Pig"

> I was back in medical school, my sixth year, doing my internship in microbiology. I had to inject some germs into a guinea pig, it was part of some research the head of the Institute was doing. I refused to, it could have killed him, I mean the guinea pig. It was a funny looking guinea pig, the usual size, but with big, floppy ears.

L was silent for a while (so was I, already engaged in my internal soliloquy). When I asked him what he was thinking about, he said that his mind was blank, then began to talk of what I felt were inconsequential subjects. He became silent again and after a few minutes I asked him to try and think out loud. Interspersed amid matters about which I heard no resonances from within myself, what I heard "louder" was his telling me that his last year of medical school had been a difficult year; that he had enjoyed his internship in microbiology; that he had experienced the head of the Institute as a grandfatherly old man; that his own father having died the year before and his grandfather having been dead for almost ten years, this man was like "some kind of a father figure." He also said that a friend of his, a male pediatrician he liked, had called in sick with hepatitis the week before; that this friend reminded him of a physical education instructor he had had in high school, a man L didn't like at all. L had needed help to improve his form in the high hurdles races and this man could not care less. He added that it was in that "difficult year" that he had almost fallen in love with a senior resident at the Institute, an older woman in her forties, had gone to bed with her, and had been impotent.

The first two tasks at this point were to understand the dream's session and sessions before it, and to understand the session's dream; that is, to know what the dream says. My soliloquy included the following thoughts. In talking of the grandfatherly head of the Institute of Microbiology, he was also talking, unconsciously, through condensation, of his grandfather, his father, and myself. The friend pediatrician (i.e., a person who works with children) was, again via condensation, father and myself; the physical education teacher, the man who could not care less for L and his form in the high hurdles race, was also a condensation of the father who "never asked how I was doing with women," the analyst who "did not really care about" him, and father and the analyst who did not help him overcome the hurdles of life. I also thought that the guinea pig with big, floppy ears could have been a rabbit; that he had assigned a gender to the guinea pig, by saying (manifest dream) that the injection could have killed *him.* Both the session's dream and the dream's session were full of germs, diseases, death, and death wishes. Unconsciously, one or two weeks before the dream's session, he had wished to kill me with the poisonous artificial sweetener in the coffee. The wish to kill, in the dream, was represented in the form of an injection, a phallic representation. There was only one, subtle reference to mother, the older woman with whom he had been impotent in his last year in medical school. I finally thought that in the eighteen months preceding the dream, the sessions had concentrated primarily on father and grandfather and minimally and only peripherally on mother. Throughout those eighteen months, the transference had been, primarily, a paternal transference. The session's dream and the dream's session too were primarily about men (the head of the Microbiology Institute, father and grandfather, the male pediatrician, the male physical education teacher, a male guinea pig), that is, about the father in his unconscious; and only minimally, and only peripherally, about women (the female resident), that is, about the mother in his unconscious.

My internal soliloquy completed for the moment, I tentatively concluded that the dream was a dream of "para-oedipal"[2] and oedipal rage at father, and transferentially, at father-in-the-analyst. The dream was about the para-oedipal rage directed at the father who had been a poor role model, had been distant and remote, intellectual and undemonstrative, had not helped L with women. It was about the rage directed at the father who had not protected him from mother, had not helped L's fear of mother, paradoxically had not helped L to be a more conventionally oedipal child who covets a mother who is desirable and not fearsome, a conventionally oedipal child who "simply" fears father's wrath for these desires. (L's oedipal complex was indeed more complicated than that: his mother was desirable, as most mothers are to the oedipal child, but she was also very fearsome. L's oedipal feelings had been complicated by very stormy preoedipal experiences with a borderline mother.) The dream, at a deeper, more unconscious level, was about conventionally oedipal rage at the father who had thwarted L's oedipal desires.

I also believed that the latent dream's para-oedipal rage was not too distorted, and since it had already made its appearance in therapy (L's overt rage at me and covert rage at father through most of the eighteen months of therapy that preceded the dream), it could be worked on with interventions or interpretations. The latent dream's oedipal feelings, on the contrary, were more distorted and could only be inferred by his mentioning the older woman in the dream's session and his mentioning again, at that juncture, that he had been impotent.[3] This level of rage, the oedipal rage, had not yet clearly appeared in therapy and

---

[2]"Para-oedipal," that is, nearly oedipal, not quite oedipal, and or course, derivative of truly oedipal happenings.

[3]Even when one's father is a weak and unsubstantial man—and L's father, although dominated and intimidated by his wife, was not weak and unsubstantial—the oedipal father, made even bigger by the oedipal child's projection of rage and competitiveness, is always awesome and frightening and will cause the child to suppress his oedipal strivings. Hence, L's impotence with the older woman at the Institute (the woman "belonging" to the head of the Institute, father's woman), was, primarily, caused by his preoedipal conflicts with his borderline mother.

could not be worked on. I concluded that the semilatent dream was about death wishes against father and assorted father figures (analyst, head of the Microbiology Institute, male pediatrician, physical education instructor), that is, wishes to kill us all for para-oedipal reasons. The fact that the killing was done through a syringe injecting poison was par for the course for an obsessive–compulsive character, which L was. The obsessive–compulsive defends himself against expulsive oedipal–phallic strivings (expulsion of sexual energies, of semen) through regressions to anal-retentive strivings. Thus the syringe, a penetrating instrument injecting germs, was an apt representation for a phallus injecting the oedipal father not with semen, but with poison, that is, feces.

The third task was to respond to the dream, to know what to say to the patient about the dream. I had to decide if the dream should be responded to with silence or interventions; and if interventions were warranted, whether they should be on the level of the drives, the defenses, and within the context of the transference.

First of all, I had to decide whether to respond with silence or an intervention. L had not expressed any interest in his dream. We were well into the middle phase of therapy, the therapeutic alliance was strong, so was L's ego. If I opted for an intervention, it might have been possible to follow the cardinal rule; an intervention on the level of the drives, some drives, might be appropriate. The para-oedipal rage at the father-in-the-analyst was close to the surface, the oedipal rage was deeper and well defended. Thus, I could interpret the para-oedipal rage, but I would want to be circumspect about the oedipal rage. To respond with silence would not have been wrong. L had said nothing to indicate that he wanted to work on the meaning of his dream, had been working well through most of the previous eighteen months. The doldrums that had preceded the dream had only lasted two to three weeks; he did not seem "stuck." Since it was entirely conceivable that the dream would induce him to resume work at the level he had reached before this last lull, the "obstetrical procedure" referred to previously could have been followed.

I decided in favor of an interpretation. I also felt (not countertransferentially, I still believe) that a substantial, and if necessary, lengthy interpretation was appropriate. Having so elected, the task was to select from the whole of my soliloquy, and from all the patient had said and done in the last several months, up to and including the dream's session, what seemed most likely to promote further progress, and seemed most useful to bring repressed material into consciousness. Also I was convinced that L's frightening preoedipal feelings about his mother were defended against through para-oedipal feelings which had been expressed, in the preceding eighteen months, through a florid and fairly undefended negative paternal transference. Thus, the obvious choice of intervention was to work with this last, most proximate and least defended layer and to make L's unconscious para-oedipal death wishes against father come alive through the analysis of the transference. I first asked for more associations to the dream's manifest content, always a safe procedure, whether one has elected to respond with silence or with interventions. Not much more was produced (after all, he was an anal-retentive person). But he did say that the head of the Institute was nice but remote because of his high rank; and he mentioned that the guinea pig with the big floppy ears made him think of the donkey of the slip of the tongue of almost two years previously. I said:

> I think that the guinea pig with floppy ears is a rabbit, a "guinea" rabbit, an Italian rabbit, at best a timid "*Conigli*-aro," at worst, a nasty one. Over the last six months or so, you have often felt I was a "bad rabbit," a bad "*Conigli*-aro," a bad father, intellectual and scholarly, just a "university prof" (by the way, were you cutting *me* down, by cutting the word *professor* to *prof*?), one who prefers teaching to helping his patients, one more interested in books and magazines than in you, someone who doesn't truly care, and has no interest in your sexual problems or difficulties with women. You do remember having said all that of me, don't you? And so much of what you said about me, you have also said about your father. You have been very angry at me. In the dream, I am the guinea pig, and a *part* of you wants to kill me.... Look, the thought of poisoning me even came up a couple of weeks ago, when you thought the artificial sweetener you had put in the coffee you offered me, would be poison for me. By the way, in the dream I am represented by the guinea pig, but also by the head of the Institute, remote like your father, but whom you did not dislike; and in your associations to the dream, I am represented also by the physical education instructor, whom you disliked, but also by your friend the pediatrician, whom you like.

It was an interpretation on the level of the drives, but not on the level of the deeper, more deeply unconscious, better defended drives. It was an interpretation on the level of the death wishes against the para-oedipal father, but not on the level of the death wishes against the oedipal father. It was an interpretation within the context of the transference. It was an interpretation that afforded us some further progress down the royal road to the unconscious, toward the analysis of oedipal feelings, and, I hoped, toward the powerful and frightening preoedipal feelings about his mother (which, by the way, appeared in the two dreams to be discussed next). In my interpretation, I went on at some length about the thoughts and feelings he had verbalized against me in the previous six months, wanting to prevent a late surge of resistance, through denial and repression, against those very same thoughts and feelings. Although I did not interpret the oedipal anger at the father-in-me, I prepared the ground for its later analysis by alluding to his castratory wishes through my reference to his cutting the word *professor* down to *prof* (the reader will remember that he had done that before by cutting the word *doctor* down to *doc*). Remarking that only "a *part*" of him wanted to kill me, that I had been represented also by the head of the Microbiology Institute, whom he did not dislike, and his pediatrician friend, whom he liked, was consciously intended, by me, to prevent too much superego guilt over his death wishes.

Theoretical Appendix: Some of the Dream Work Defenses

From the dream's manifest content:

Back in medical school: displacement from back into the childhood years which analysis deals with.
Medical school: displacement from another "learning" environment, therapy.
Sixth year: displacement from early years in life (6 and younger).
Inject: symbolism for any kind of bodily penetration (genital, anal, oral, cutaneous).
Germs: concrete pictorial representation of anything noxious and infectious; displacement from "dirty" semen or feces.
Guinea: onomatopoeia for "guinea," Italian.

Guinea pig: displacement from head of the Microbiology Institute, therapist, father; condensation of all these.

Pig: symbolism for therapist's "piggish" traits; concrete pictorial representation of pig's attributes; projection of his own piglike characteristics.

I refused: denial.

Funny looking: secondary elaboration.

Funny-looking guinea pig: displacement from rabbit-like therapist.

With big floppy ears: like a rabbit, a *coniglio;* i.e., a displacement from and onomatopoeia for therapist, Conigliaro.

From associations—one listens to the dream's session as if it were a dream:

Head of the Institute as grandfatherly: displacement from grandfather and a "grand" father, a father more substantial than his own father was in reality.

Male pediatrician: displacement from father (fathers deal with children too) and therapist (therapist is a physician too).

Physical education instructor who did not help him with his form in jumping the high hurdles: displacement from father and therapist who did not help him with his problems with women.

High hurdles: concrete pictorial representation of difficult problems in life.

"Successful Intercourse"

The third of L's four dreams was dreamed about one year after the "Guinea Pig" dream. Through this year, L had continued to come three times a week. By the time of this dream, he had now been in analysis about four years. During this year of therapy, L spoke about his father and of his father's feelings about mother; about his mother, much more than he had ever done before; and some, about his maternal grandmother. Talking about his father, he told me that in his teen years, he, L, had been lukewarmly and covertly appreciative of his father's scholarliness and intellectual interests ("I guess I did not want to demonstrate my appreciation openly . . . he did not demonstrate his affection openly"). At the same time he had been contemptuous, not too covertly, of his father, his political sympathies, his life-style. He had felt some guilt for this lack of appreciation and contemptuousness; he had felt grateful to his father for his financial generosity; and he began to see that father could not help acting as he did. I believed that in talking as he did about his father, L was continuing to work on his feelings about the para-oedipal father; that the positive feelings he had been expressing about his father were, in part, genuine. He was truly trying to look at father more objectively, to accept father's "quirks," truly trying to forgive him on the para-oedipal level. On the other hand, these feelings were also a reaction formation to powerful feelings about the oedipal father. What he was saying about his father was often ambivalent (he tempered his gratitude over his father's financial generosity by saying, "Of course it wasn't his money, it was mother's and grand-father's money"). The guilt over the contemptuousness was also a screen for oedipal contemptuousness which, in turn, was a reac-tion formation to oedipal awe, envy, and fear.

L first spoke about his mother by telling me how his father felt about her. Father was intimidated and bemused by mother, fearful of her unpredictability, erratic manners, volatility, ebul-lient and fiery temperament; resentful of her dictatorial, de-manding, exacting paroxysms; amused, almost entertained, by her mercurial, sprightly manners. Father both enjoyed and ad-mired mother's wit and liveliness, was indulgent about her sauci-ness, impertinence, and capriciousness, was in awe of mother's physical beauty; that all in all, father loved mother very much, and L was sure, "enjoyed her tremendously in bed." He then began to speak at some length about how he himself felt about his mother. He told me that he was often frightened by her excit-ability; that she fluctuated between bursts of exactingness on the one hand and fits of temper on the other; that she could be a charming "fairy lady" one moment and a "witch on the broom" in another; that his feelings about her probably were the same as the feelings his father had about her, that is, "mixed." I believed that in talking as he did about his father's and his own feelings about mother, L was beginning to work on his oedipal feelings. But he was continuing to work on his feelings about the para-oedipal father: guilt over these feelings was diminishing. Our work on these feelings was beginning to overcathect feelings about the oedipal father. He had practically admitted oedipal feelings toward mother by saying that his feelings about mother duplicated his father's feelings. I believed, therefore, that more work on the oedipal feelings would soon become possible and that work on the powerful feelings about the preoedipal mother would also begin in the near future.

L did not say much that he had not said before about his maternal grandfather, primarily reiterating that he had admired, loved, and feared him. But in the session immediately preceding the dream's session, he told me more about his mother by way of talking about his grandfather. He told me that his grandfather and mother fought often, "big, loud, screaming fights"; that grandfather loved her very much, was not afraid of her, "told her off a couple of times when she had been too harsh on me"; that his mother ("she was not afraid of anyone") was afraid of her father; that summer vacations on the farm estate had not been quite the same after grandfather's death, which occurred when L was 12.

By this time, L's sexual dysfunction had become a little less severe. He dated a little more frequently; about three months after the "Guinea Pig" dream, his relationships with women had become sexual, and around the time of the "Successful Intercourse" dream, he had been going out with the same woman, a nurse, for four months, a record for him. He was consistently potent in masturbation, more so than before the "Guinea Pig" dream. He masturbated about two to three times a week. His masturbatory fantasies had acquired a more and more aggressive and sometimes even sadistic flavor. They usually revolved around powerful, successful women whom L would awe with extraordinarily potent sexual performances, or humiliate with curt, "cutting" remarks, or frustrate by refusing to engage in foreplay and, thus, hurt them vaginally by penetrating them before they were ready. In sexual intercourse, he was somewhat potent almost every other time—but potent only in a strictly physiological, "phallic" fashion, not in a truly psychological, "genital" way. His penis would have an erection, but he did not enjoy the sexual act as much as he enjoyed masturbation, and was frequently distracted by performance anxiety. He was mostly attracted to accomplished, slightly hysterical women, although the nurse he was dating at the time of the dream was neither. L continued to remember and bring into analysis about one dream a week. There had been several dreams whose latent content included both erotic and angry drives toward mother.

With me, L, in his courtly, polished, and polite fashion was more genuine, open, friendly, occasionally jovial. He was still basically constricted, cautious, and vigilant against himself, but a little less than before. The rage at me (i.e., at the para-oedipal and oedipal father-in-me) that had prevailed before the "Guinea Pig" dream, had been replaced by mild feelings of guilt over having been so "difficult" with me the months before. These feelings toward me paralleled the conscious feelings of guilt and regret he had been expressing about having been unappreciative of his father. We were not in the doldrums, however; he was working in the analysis and providing abundant material concerning his mother. He obviously needed to distance himself from these feelings and did so by sometimes talking about her through his father's and grandfather's experiences with her. When he did talk of his mother more directly, his tone of voice or fidgeting on the couch indicated unmistakable feelings of anxiety. I believed that the previously negative paternal transference had gone back to being largely positive. He needed this positive paternal transference to be able to verbalize negative feelings about his mother as he was doing. This paralleled his need to talk about mother through the intermediation of father and grandfather. The currently positive paternal transference and our work on his super-ego guilt over the previously negative, para-oedipal, paternal transference accounted in part for the slight improvement in his sexual functions. I also felt that a truly oedipal, negative, paternal transference would not develop until he no longer needed father's and grandfather's protection from mother, from his negative feelings about her, and his fear of her. While the negative maternal transference toward me had not developed, it was operative in his masturbatory fantasies, and in the type of women he was attracted to (accomplished and hysterical, mother figures). The negative maternal transference was also operative in his impotence with this type of woman.

The dream's session started in the usual manner. L greeted me in what was by now his customary fashion, politely jovial and

slightly controlled, but his demeanor was more serious and composed than it had been lately. He lay down and proceeded to tell
me the dream.

"Successful Intercourse"

> I had intercourse with Ms. X. It was successful, very successful. I was very
> hard, hard as a rock.

He added: "a very natural dream . . . . Ms. X is a very difficult
woman, but I find her attractive and sexy. I fantasize about her
when I fondle myself. But I would be frightened to have sex with
her, she is one of the hospital's most powerful administrators; but
I do have sex with her, in the dream, I must be getting better,
the dream forecasts improvement, improvement in my '*bête noir*,'
my sexuality." Notwithstanding L's conscious feelings which, even
now, four years into psychoanalysis, were only infrequently accompanied by a very expressive outer mimicry, one could not help
being struck by the contrast between the positive and optimistic
thoughts being expressed and the somber tone and dark countenance with which he expressed them. He then spoke about another woman, Ms. Y, a patient of his, a "really difficult patient"
whose condition was proving refractory to treatment.

As the session continued, L drifted into talking of women
and girls he had dated while in medical school and as an adolescent, adding, "But you know how it is with Italian girls 'of good
family,' they can be difficult, they don't let you go very far. . . ."
He drifted further into preadolescence and spoke about a teacher
who taught him Latin in high school, a Ms. Z, adding that Latin
had always been "difficult" for him, and that Ms. Z had been a
very "difficult" woman. I felt tempted to say, "Another '*bête
noir*'?"; after all, in the two dreams previously described, he had
depicted his father as an animal, why would his mother be an
exception? I virtuously restrained myself. He then spoke about
the summers in grandfather's country home. At that point, the
regressive drift[4] stopped and he went back to talk about Ms. X.

---

[4]In a session without undue resistance, patients "drift" from the present into the recent
and then more and more remote (but not unconscious) past, and drift further and further
into earlier and earlier preconscious memories. Then the drift suddenly stops and patients

Yes, he finds her attractive, but she is a "hard woman, a difficult woman." Recently, she had "dressed him down" about an insurance problem with a patient. He had felt angry at her, "I felt like throwing the book at her, I mean, literally. I was carrying a heavy book and felt like hitting her over the head with it, which of course I wouldn't dream of doing." But still, he repeated, he finds her desirable; "And in the dream . . . we do it . . . this is a very good dream, I'm getting better."

Although, in terms of conscious positive feelings L had lately mellowed toward me, he was not usually inclined to praise me, nor was he characterologically predisposed to be lavishly laudatory. This, and his somber demeanor in telling me that he was getting better and that the dream forecasted improvement, made it easier for me to resist the countertransferential temptation to accept the rare compliment and to resist believing his interpretation of the dream.

The first two tasks at this point were to understand the dream's session and sessions before it, and to understand the session's dream, that is, to know what the dream says. My internal soliloquy included the following thoughts. He had used the word *difficult* concerning women several times. A few times, in the past, he had used that word as a euphemism to describe his seductive and rejecting mother. Ms. X, the powerful hospital administrator, Ms. Y, the patient refractory to treatment, Ms. Z, the teacher who had tried to teach him Latin, the Italian girls "of good family," all "difficult" women: these were all condensations and screens for his mother. His comments that "Latin had been a difficult subject" for him, and that "Italian girls of good family don't let a young man go very far," were fairly transparent disguises of his feeling that all the women in his experience, starting with his mother and ending with Ms. X, had been "difficult" for him and had not let him go very far.

His choice of words about Ms. X's rebuke, "she *dressed* me *down*," made me think of a mother literally undressing a child of his pants and underpants to beat him, and of a mother figuratively

---

catapult themselves into the present. When this happens, it often means that the last, just recollected, preconscious memory is a screen memory of an unconscious event which the patient is still not ready to recollect, often an event at which some important fixations had occurred.

undressing a child, baring not his body but his mind, reading his thoughts and feelings, making the child feel naked and vulnerable. I also thought that several of his masturbatory fantasies concerning Ms. X had a subtly sadistic semimanifest flavor; that his sexuality was indeed a *bête noir* when focused on his mother, a fearsome, awesome woman, beast-like, in her unpredictability and angry outbursts, "black" in her witch-on-the-broom modes, black as sexually voracious African-American women are imagined to be. His very insistence about the dream being only sexual in nature was highly suspect. And his saying, "I wouldn't even dream of doing that" (i.e., hitting her over the head with the heavy hardcover book) was a volunteered denial tipping me that the dream was precisely that, a dream of hitting someone over the head, or on her lower body parts (displacement). But, most important, a preconscious memory that he had shared with me several months before "bubbled up" to my consciousness and helped me understand, albeit tentatively, the latent content of L's dream.

The memory had been of being at grandfather's villa in the country, at maybe 9 or 10 years of age. There was a small pond in the garden with a statue in the middle, "a sculpture, a cheap imitation of Botticelli's painting, 'The Birth of Venus.' " L was seated on the edge of the pond, absent-mindedly throwing pebbles in the water. His mother suddenly came out of the house, yelling, telling him not to throw stones at the statue (did she unconsciously know what he, unconsciously, was up to—not a preposterous possibility). He burst into tears and told her he was not throwing stones at the statue, just at the goldfish in the pond, and, and anyway, he was not throwing "stones," just small pebbles. He had felt unjustly accused and felt miserable for hours. He told me the story in a gravelly tone of voice (pun intended), and with a controlled but clearly angry affect. My soliloquy now included the thought that his latent dream was about hitting mother with rocks or something as hard as rocks.

My internal soliloquy of resonances, conjectures, and speculations completed for the moment, I did, albeit tentatively, conclude that the dream indeed had nothing to do with unconscious, oedipal, libidinal drives, nothing to do with unconscious wishes to make love to Ms. X, or to his mother, the Venus of his oedipal childhood. The dream, rather, had to do with unconscious, pre-oedipal anger, the wish to break Ms. X's (i.e., mother's) head, or genitals, with his hard-as-a-rock penis, or feces. My tentative conclusion was speculative but highly consistent with (1) the clinical and psychodynamic picture; (2) my reading of the manifest, semilatent, and latent meaning of the session's dream and the dream's session; and (3) the preconscious memory about him at the pond which he had shared with me months before. His impotence, sexual as well as nonsexual, was, as impotence often is, part of a system of interrelated conflictual feelings. There was fear of unconscious anger at Ms.'s X, Y, Z (i.e., mother); fear of the unconscious wish to mutilate and disfigure them; fear of the unconscious wish to throw hard rocks at them (not just stones or pebbles); projection onto them of those unconscious wishes; fear of retaliatory abandonment; fear of retaliatory mutilation and castration by the powerful Ms.'s X, Y, and Z, the powerful, unpredictable mother, all women powerful in their own right, and even more powerful and castrating because of having been invested with L's projections.

The third task was to respond to the dream, to know what to say to the patient about the dream. What was I going to do this time? We were now in the later–middle phase of therapy. The therapeutic alliance and L's ego continued to be solid. L's anger at his mother was still very well defended; he still needed to distance himself from it by talking about it indirectly, through his father's and grandfather's experiences with her. Anger at the accomplished and powerful women in his life, most notably anger at the redoubtable Ms. X, that is, the secondary negative maternal transference[5] had become a little more obvious. Even he recognized the "slightly" sadistic content of his masturbatory fantasies about Ms. X. His anger at the mother-in-me, the transferential mother, his primary negative maternal transference, had not truly developed. Considering all this, I felt that it was too soon to apply the cardinal rule fully, and that an interpretation fully on the level of the primary drives, the preoedipal rage at mother, would

---

[5]I think of the transference experienced toward and with the analyst as a primary transference; and of the transference experienced toward and with other significant persons in the patient's life as secondary transferences.

have been premature. I also thought that since the primary negative transference had not developed, and since there had been
no obvious transferential incidents in the analytic situation (as
there had been at the time of the "Guinea Pig" dream, when he
offered me coffee that he thought I would think was poisonous),
I had no transferential incidents through which I could have used
myself to analyze the rage he felt toward his mother-in-me. Therefore, an interpretation of the rage within the context of the primary transference was neither possible nor indicated. Since free
association, both toward women in the past and in the present,
had been plentiful, I thought I would not ask about any more
associations and would use, for my intervention, the thoughts he
had already expressed about Ms. X. I said:

> Whatever you were doing in the dream with Ms. X, you are furious at her.

To have added, "When she humiliated you, you were so furious at her, you wanted to hit her, not with the hardcover book
you were carrying, but with your hard penis," would have been
true but too close to his still unconscious wish of wanting to throw
rocks at his real, flesh-and-blood mother, not just at mother as
represented by the Venus sculpture. It was more of an intervention than an interpretation because I said nothing about what I
thought he was doing with Ms. X in the dream. It was an intervention on the level of the drives experienced within the secondary
transference, toward Ms. X. It was *not* an interpretation on the
level of the primary drives experienced toward mother. The intervention, nevertheless, moved us deeper on the royal road and
closer to where, in his unconscious, those primary preoedipal
drives were still ensconced. My saying "*whatever* you were doing
with Ms. X," raised L's consciousness about the possibility that
what he *was* doing with Ms. X in the dream was, indeed, not just
sexual in nature.

The "Guinea Pig" dream and dream's session had revealed
L's latent para-oedipal rage at secondary father figures (i.e., the
male pediatrician, the physical education instructor, the head of
the Institute of Microbiology). That dream and dream's session
had, through the paternal negative transference, revealed his
para-oedipal rage at the primary father figure, the analyst. But

that dream and dream's session had only hinted at his oedipal rage at father. This dream, the "Successful Intercourse" dream and dream's session revealed L's preoedipal rage at secondary mother figures (i.e., Ms.'s X, Y, and Z). Since the maternal negative transference had not developed, neither dream nor dream's session had revealed the preoedipal rage at the primary mother figure, the analyst. And this dream and dream's session only hinted at his preoedipal rage at mother. In the next therapy period, which culminated with the last of L's quartet of dreams, the "Eggshells" dream, the primary maternal negative transference developed and it became possible to work on L's preoedipal rage at mother.

Theoretical Appendix: Some of the Dream Work Defenses

From the dream's manifest content:

Ms. X, Ms. Y, Ms. Z, the Italian girls of good family: displacements from mother.
Ms. X, Ms. Y, Ms. Z, the Italian girls of good family: *mother*, condensations.
(Sexual) intercourse: displacement from any kind of exchange or transaction, sexual, aggressive, social interchange.
(Penis) hard: displacement from the excitement of anger to sexual excitement.

From associations—one listens to the dream's session as if it were a dream:

(Penis) hard: displacement from the pebbles he had thrown, and the rocks he had wished to throw, at the Venus statue, that is, at mother.
I must be getting better, the dream forecasts improvement: secondary elaboration and denial of the dream's real meaning.
Bête noir: displacement from mother, a "black beast" in his unconscious; also, projection of his own animal-like angry and libidinal drives.
Ms. X dressed him down: displacement from mother scolding him and metaphor for mother taking off his pants to spank him.

"Eggshells"

L dreamed the fourth and last of this group of dreams about two years after the "Successful Intercourse" dream. During this period, L had continued to come three times a week; by the time of this dream, he had been in analysis a total of six years. In this period, he spoke a great deal about his mother and about women in his life who, as was becoming more and more clear to him, too, were all mother figures.

Concerning his mother, L repeated at greater length, what he had told me about her volatile and fiery character, her demanding, exacting personality, her erratic, changeable manners. He told me that she was beautiful, elegant, and fastidious about her appearance, "vain, a true peacock"; that she was "charming and delightful" in her good moments, "adorable" when something had pained her, then she was tearful, soft, and vulnerable. But she was "frightening and dreadful" when she lost her temper, and yelled and shrieked. When that happened, she would lose her breath, or choke, or wheeze, and later on he had wondered whether she might have had asthma. When she wheezed and lost her breath, he would watch her, horrified and terrified by the thought that she could actually choke and die. When, as a small child, he would accidentally spill water at the breakfast table or make crumbs in dunking bread in his cup of milk, his mother would sometimes ignore his behavior, at other times have a fit of rage and send him to his room, and sometimes reassure and comfort him. Because of her unpredictability, he often felt "dangling" where she and he were concerned, never knowing how she would react to him. A significant memory was of being 3 or 4 years old and knocking down the soft-boiled egg he was forced to have for breakfast every morning. The egg fell off the marble kitchen table at which he was eating, and the "bright yellow yolk splashed all over the floor, it was fascinating, and mother was furious." He hated eating soft boiled eggs every morning, the runny white made him gag. Another significant memory was of a tantrum he had at 4: "I remember stamping and stomping on the floor. . . I even remember the shoes I was wearing, some stupid, slippery, dressy, black shoes," and mother spanked him hard, and "I was furious at her, and very frightened." Mother could be demonstrative and cuddle him, but more often was distracted, or angry, or "in a mood." When talking about his mother he no longer needed to distance himself from what he was saying, by talking first of his father or grandfather's experiences with her.

Ms. X was still the chief administrator in the hospital with which L was affiliated. L had lunch with her in the hospital's dining room once or twice a week. They had become "friends of a sort"; he still found her both attractive and formidable; she had "gorgeous breasts" and her breasts made him think of "large, ripe, juicy tomatoes" (I interjected: "Italian tomatoes?" He responded with a cross between a chuckle and a snort.) Once he found himself staring at her breasts and she noticed it, and "in her typical, arch way," she seemed amused, but he felt uncomfortable and embarrassed. He had continued to date the woman he had begun to see a little over two years before. He told me that she was of Italian extraction and in her late twenties; that she was sweet and accommodating; that he enjoyed "making love to her." She seemed to like him very much, and wanted some sign of commitment on his part, but he was not ready "to tie the knot and be roped in." He never told me her name and referred to her, consistently, as "my young nurse." He also told me that he realized, now, that many women in the hospital found him attractive and "a good catch"; that this pleased him, but again, he "was not interested in being roped in." L's sexuality was not very different from what it had been in the previous period of therapy. He was more consistently potent with his "young nurse"; had not tried sexual intercourse with anyone else. His sexuality in intercourse was still more masturbation of his penis by the woman's vagina than a truly "genital" object relation (he enjoyed "making love *to*" rather than *with* his young nurse). He still masturbated two to three times a week, and his masturbatory fantasies continued to be angry and aggressive. There had been, during this two-year period, more and more dreams with erotic, but especially, angry feelings about his mother on the latent level and about various mother figures on the semimanifest level.

With me, there had occurred a definite change in attitude and demeanor. The primary, negative maternal transference had developed. On "easy" days, the controlled friendliness and vigilant joviality of the previous period of therapy had been replaced

by a curt and snappish manner. On "bad" days, both his anger
at mother and his anger at me, the transferential mother, were
expressed in a clipped, curt, brusque, staccato fashion, a bitter
and cold anger. The reader may remember that, in the period
of therapy that had culminated with the "Guinea Pig" dream,
the para-oedipal anger at father and at me had been expressed
in a harsh, sharp, acrimonious way. The less overt way in which
he was now expressing his rage at mother, suggested that he was
more afraid of his anger at mother, and mother's retaliatory
anger at him, than he had been of his anger at his father. We
were now late into the middle phase of therapy and there was a
good degree of splitting between observing and irrational ego. In
sessions in which the splitting was in action, it operated in a different fashion from previously. The observing ego, in a snappish,
clipped, angry, and cross manner, would comment on how snappish, clipped, angry, and cross he had been. In sessions in which
the primary, negative, maternal transference was more acute and
the splitting of the ego was not working too well, he would experience me (to some degree, at least, after all, L was not psychotic)
just as if I were acting as his mother had acted or could have
acted; and he would be feeling quite miserable.

For about four months before the "Eggshells" dream, he
had been more intensely angry at me. He told me that he believed
that under my controlled demeanor, I was very angry inside. After
all, once, while sitting in the waiting room, he had heard me
yelling at a patient; he believed therefore that given some provo-
cation, and probably I did not need much of one, I too would
explode, just like his mother. I was an "unnurturing" therapist;
I was a demanding and exacting person, as shown by the fuss I
had made, the month before, when he had been just a few days
late with his monthly payment. I was obviously vain and narcissistic
about my attire, and maybe even foppish, as witness my medal-
lions and bracelets and the kerchiefs or foulards I wore around
my neck. (I interjected: "Maybe I am a peacock, too?"—a not
very veiled reference to his mother.) In the month or so that
preceded the "Eggshells" dream, two memories were recounted,
and two incidents occurred in therapy, which I used later on in
my interpretation of the dream.

One memory was of being, again, 3 or 4 (preoedipal age), L and his father had gone to an area near a large pond ·on grandfather's estate, where grandfather raised ducks, geese, and swans. There were also two or three peacocks. L remembered how majestic and beautiful the swans had seemed as they glided, seemingly without effort on the water, and how magnificent the peacocks had looked when they displayed their tails. Father accidentally stepped on one egg that was lying on the ground. L remembered (again, as he had, a few weeks before, remembered knocking his soft-boiled egg off the breakfast table) the bright yellow yolk, mixed with fragments of eggshells, on the stones on the ground. Father laughingly said, "Well, the goose that laid that egg won't like that!" L had felt the impulse to step on some of the eggs himself. "It'd have been real fun to do that and see the yellow yolk splashing all over"; but he controlled himself. The following session, L had been particularly angry at me. In his coldest, most contemptuous tone he again accused me of being vain and narcissistic about my appearance. I said, "Vain and narcissistic, just like a peacock"—a reference, again, to the transference. Toward the end of the session, in a gruff fashion, but with a tone that was half fearful and half pleased with himself, he said, "Well I was quite a ball-breaker with you today." And I said, "Is it my balls, you wanted to break, or my eggs? Only yesterday, you remembered the time your father accidentally stepped on a goose's egg and you wanted to do the same." This was the first of the two memories and of the two incidents.

The second memory was of being in the kitchen, watching a maid cleaning some freshly killed chickens that she was going to roast for dinner. He remembered watching her with a mixture of horror, curiosity, and squeamishness and remembered being particularly fascinated "with the many little yellow round globes in the chicken's interiors, I guess the mother hen's eggs in the ovaries." The second therapy incident occurred one or two sessions later. He had been, again, very angry at me. Toward the end of the session (I was, then, a pipe smoker) I accidentally inhaled some tobacco juice[6] and for twenty or thirty seconds,

---

[6]Was I choking from trying to "swallow" the rage he was "spitting out" at me? A cigar—or a pipe—is never just a cigar!

coughed rather convulsively. L became alarmed and in a gruff, but also fearful tone, asked me if I was all right. As I regained my composure, I said, rather gently, "Did you think I was going to choke to death?"

On the day of the dream's session, L seemed tense, preoccupied, distracted, unhappy. He mentioned right away having had a dream the night before, but for the first fifteen to twenty minutes talked about various incidents in the hospital that had "aggravated and agitated him." He spoke about a patient of his, Sister Q, a Catholic nun, ill with multiple sclerosis, unappreciative of the improvements he had achieved with her, "a very angry woman, she never smiles; and so snotty, a Madame of the Sacred Heart, you know the aristocratic order that runs the Female Academy of the Sacred Heart, the school on Fifth Avenue where all the wealthy Catholic families send their daughters to" (his mother in Italy had gone to a school run by that congregation). He spoke of a woman social worker who always gives him problems with home plans for patients he is discharging. He characterized her as hysterical, belligerent, thoroughly unpleasant, and that morning he had felt like "kicking her." The day before had been a difficult day too, all kinds of people, mostly women, making unreasonable demands on him, complaining to him, not being pleased with him. His girl friend, the night before, had gone to visit her parents and he had not been able to see her and he was angry at her too. He then told me the dream.

"Eggshells"

> I was climbing a steep mountain, a very narrow path, with a woman, no one I recognize. She was ahead, I was behind, connected to her through a long rope, like people use when they go rock-climbing. It was difficult, my boots were slippery, the footing underneath was treacherous and slippery because it was covered with eggshells. I yelled something at her about some difficulties ahead, she lost her concentration and slid and fell down the escarpment. I braced myself by grabbing a tree, or she would have carried me down too and we would both have slid down the mountain. The rope got wrapped around another tree, and she was dangling from it, and the rope got wound tight around her waist and she had difficulty breathing.

After telling me the dream, L was silent for two or three minutes. He then proceeded to give me some more details about the dream: how narrow and steep the path was up the mountain, how "barren the mountain was, except for a few, straggling, but not scrawny trees on one side of the path," how difficult it was to "progress" up the mountain, both because of the eggshells strewn all over the path and because his boots were slippery. He told me that he felt he was to blame for the woman's fall, if he had not yelled at her, she would not have fallen off the mountain; that the fact that he did not recognize her must have meant that she represented all the women who had been the bane of his existence, beginning with his mother and ending with Sister Q; that yes, he was angry at his mother and those other women, "but not to the point of wanting them dead, of course"; that the rope made him think of all the "strings attached" to getting anything from his mother, for instance, having to behave perfectly. All this was said in a wooden, tense voice and with a glum, tense, intense, taut, and controlled affect. Then, quite unusual for him, he asked me what I thought the dream meant. Based on the conclusions I had reached through my internal soliloquy, I decided to answer; but first, let me describe the soliloquy.

The first two tasks at this point were to understand the dream session and the sessions before it, and to understand the session's dream; that is, to know what the dream says. My soliloquy included thoughts and "resonations" around various themes. I thought that the dream was about mother and mother figures. Associations to mother and mother figures had been produced even before he had told me the dream (in a session with a dream, everything the patient says, before or after the dream, should be regarded as an association to the dream). These associations included what he had said about Sister Q, a woman as difficult and hard to please as his mother, a woman belonging to the same religious order operating the schools his mother had attended in Italy; what he had said about the hysterical social worker he had felt "like kicking"; and what he had said about all the women who "had been making unreasonable demands" on him. I also thought that the steep pitch of the mountain and the difficulty of the "progress" up the narrow and slippery path were transparent

representations of the difficulties he was experiencing in uncov-
ering powerful and frightening feelings about mother and various
mother figures, and a representation of his difficulties in making
"progress" in therapy. In yelling at the woman about "difficulties
ahead," he was telling me, the analyst, about the difficult times
soon to come in therapy, and yelling at the mother-in-me about
it. The path was "treacherous" because his superego saw complaining against his mother as treachery. To proceed on that path
was fraught with the peril of falling off a mountain. Anything
concerning mother was perilous; thus the mountain itself, barren
and hard to climb, and the path, slippery and hard to negotiate,
were a good representation of his "difficult" mother. The "straggling, not too scrawny, trees on only one side of the mountain"
were also a perfect representation of a mother who could be
nurturing ("not scrawny"), but was ambivalent about nurturing
("trees only on one side of the mountain"). The unidentified
woman also was his mother, as he himself had said in the free
associations after the dream; "yelling" at one in the manifest
dream represented anger at the other in the latent dream. He
was now conscious at least in part, of his responsibility in causing
the woman to fall. He did say that she fell because he had yelled
at her, but qualified the degree to which he was responsible for
her fall, that is, the magnitude of his rage, by adding, "but not
to the point of wanting them dead, of course."

I also thought of the following connections: that he had slippery boots in the dream, and slippery shoes at the time of his
tantrum at the age of 4; that the woman in the dream was left
"dangling," and, because of his mother's unpredictability, he often had felt he had been left "dangling"; that the woman in the
dream dangling from a tree, the rope wound tight around her
waist, had difficulty breathing, and his mother had difficulty
breathing when she lost control over her temper. When I had
coughed from inhaling tobacco juice a few sessions before the
dream's session, he thought I was about to choke to death. The
rope connecting the dream's two protagonists represented not
only the "strings attached" to any transactions he had had with
mother when she had been alive, but represented, also, his still
ambivalent dependency on all mother figures in his external

world: Ms. X, his "young nurse" who wanted some sign of commitment on his part (but he was "not ready to tie the knot and
be roped"), and the many women in the hospital who found him
attractive and "a good catch."

I also thought that in the dream he was stepping on eggshells
strewn on the mountain path, and at the time of the tantrum,
enraged at his mother, he had stamped and stomped on the floor.
The theme of stepping, destructively, on anything had come up
in the memory of his father stepping on a goose's egg and L's
wishing to do the same. Eggshells breaking and egg yolk splashing
had figured prominently in the memory of the time he had "accidentally" knocked off the table the soft-boiled egg he was forced
to eat at breakfast every morning. Thus, ideas of stepping on eggs
and seeing their contents splash were within a context of anger,
resentment, and self-defense. Eggs had figured prominently also
in the memory verbalized shortly before the dream's session:
seeing eggs inside a freshly killed "*mother* hen" whose entrails the
maid was cleaning. Everything L was saying and remembering
about eggs, eggshells, egg yolk, and egg albumen were all screens
of thoughts and feelings about his mother. The connection between mother and the memory of father stepping on the egg was
made more evident by the details included in the recounting of
that memory (the details having to do with beautiful swans and
beautiful peacocks, all transparent symbols of his beautiful and
vain mother).

I concluded that the unidentified woman in the manifest
dream was indeed his mother, as he himself had surmised, and
a condensation of all the women who had been "the bane of his
existence." The semimanifest dream had to do with the "difficulties ahead," the difficult task of talking about and against
mother. The semilatent dream was a dream of generalized nonspecific anger at mother, anger still partly distorted, or at least
qualified, reduced in magnitude, and a dream of fear and guilt
over that anger. The latent dream was a dream of preoedipal rage
at mother; its latent drives being wishes to kick, step, stomp, and
stamp on mother's abdomen, vulva, eggs; the wish to make
mother dangle as she had made him dangle; the wish to smother
mother as she had smothered him; the wish to cause her to choke
and to be short of breath. The dream also included ambivalent

feelings about wanting and not wanting to be connected with, tied up to, being a "catch" for mother and the various mother figures in his world, including Ms. X, his "young nurse," and the woman in the hospital.

The third task was to respond to the dream, to know what to say to the patient about the dream. I decided I would make an interpretation on the level of the drives and within the context of the transference. I thought the following facts justified my decision. The therapeutic alliance was solid and L's ego solid enough and strong enough to have allowed him to attack me the way he had been attacking me in all the previous months. There already was a good degree of insight on his part about his anger at mother and, certainly, at various mother figures, even though he had qualified his rage by saying, "I am angry at my mother and those other women, but not to the point of wanting them dead, of course"; in the process of doing so, he admitted being angry. There had been two incidents (wanting to "break my eggs" and thinking I was choking on tobacco juice) that would allow me to use myself to demonstrate to him the rage he felt toward the mother-in-me, that is, allow me to make an interpretation which would make his still partly unconscious rage at his mother come alive in the transference.

He had asked me about the meaning of the dream. I first asked him for some more associations about eggshells and the woman in the dream losing her breath. I was not really counting on him giving me new material in those two areas, nor did I need him to; I had enough to make my interpretation meaningful to him. I only wanted to refresh his memory on what he had already told me, the better to help him accept the interpretation. L repeated what he had said to me many times before about his mother's losing her breath when she "went off"; and, "I told you about those two times I saw eggs crushed." I said:

> You want to step and stomp and stamp on me, and break my eggs, and see my inside stuff come out and splash all over—you want to have a tantrum right here—you want to choke me and see me lose my breath—you want to dangle me and have me hang by a tree down the mountain.

It was an interpretation on the level of the drives, but entirely within the context of the transference. Not once did I refer to his mother directly, I only went further down the royal road to his unconscious where his deepest feelings about her lay. I left it up to him, whenever he was ready, to tell me more about his preoedipal rage at her and his preoedipal and oedipal love for her.

L listened to my interpretation, body tense, hands clenched. Within minutes, he relaxed and said, "Yes, I have been angry at you. I am not sure you deserve it all. Mind you, I am not getting you off the hook" (I interjected, "Or off the rope?"). "I still think you have a vile temper, inside—but it's my mother I am basically upset about." Many months later he told me that when I had been coughing convulsively, months before, and he thought I was choking, in part he was enjoying my discomfort but in part he was genuinely concerned. "With my mother too, when I saw her getting short of breath and heard her wheezing and coughing, in part I was enjoying it, maybe I wanted her to die, but in part I was genuinely concerned for her—I didn't really want her to die."

Theoretical Appendix: Some of the Dream Work Defenses

From the dream's manifest content:

Steep, narrow: concrete pictorial representation of "difficult."
Mountain: displacement from mother, symbolism of mother.
Woman: displacement from mother and condensation of all women he had been talking about.
No one I recognize: denial.
Ahead, behind: concrete pictorial representation of mother's superiority over him.
Rope: concrete pictorial representation of dependency on and connectedness to mother.
Rock climbing: concrete pictorial representation of difficulty in conquering mother.
Rock: concrete pictorial representation of mother's hardness and imperviousness.

Slippery boots: concrete pictorial representation of not having a sure footing where mother is concerned.

Egg: displacement from and symbolism of mother.

Eggshells: displacement from and symbolism of mother's exterior that he wishes to crack.

Yelled: concrete pictorial representation of anger.

Difficulties ahead: displacement from difficulties ahead in therapy and difficulties with the internalized mother.

Sliding down the mountain: concrete pictorial representation of depression, disasters, etc.

Rope around her waist: concrete pictorial representation of the wish to tie, to bind, to choke mother.

From associations—one listens to the dream's session as if it were a dream:

Sister Q, hospital social worker, his girl friend: displacements from mother.

Barren: concrete pictorial representation of mother's emotional sterility.

Straggling trees: concrete pictorial representation of how infrequent and discontinuous nurturing from mother was.

Not too scrawny: concrete pictorial representation of fact that mother could be nurturing.

Progress up the mountain: concrete pictorial representation of progress in therapy and progress with the internalized mother.

Postscript

L terminated our work together four years later at the age of 45; he had been in psychoanalysis three times a week (except for the first six months) for about ten years.

The two years immediately following the "Eggshells" dream were difficult and painful. For a period of about six months right after the dream, L was depressed. The glum, frowning, somber public persona of the first year or two of therapy had returned fully, but with an important difference. Now L knew his glumness and somberness were an expression of depression. Before, he believed he was a truly cold, contemptuous, and distancing individual. The glum and somber facade was only for outsiders: with me, or with his woman friend, he was either openly depressed or openly nasty. During this period, L became almost completely sexually impotent but, to his surprise, he enjoyed immensely cuddling up to his girl friend, holding her and, especially, being held by her.

Then the depression lifted and L alternated between expressing positive and negative feelings about me. The maternal transference had developed more fully. There were times when L admired me for the way I dressed or spoke, commented appreciatively about my taste in this or that, expressed feelings of care and interest that seemed sincere. There were times when he heard me as harsh and critical, fantasized, fearfully, about my "Sicilian temper" and what might happen to him "if a bee got into my bonnet" or expressed, angrily or contemptuously, negative feelings about my "foppish attire" or "affected way of speaking." And there were times when he would think I looked sickly and would inquire about my health with what in part was sincere solicitousness. But more and more often he remembered having experienced similar feelings about his mother, remembered how much he had admired her beauty, delighted in her elegance, feared her explosions, despised her for her vanity, worried over her health, and fearfully held his own breath as she was losing hers.

Not infrequently, L would connect, all by himself, the disparate feelings he would be experiencing about me with his memories about his mother. But there were times when I had to help him along. For instance, when he referred to "a bee in my bonnet," I would say, "Am I a woman? Wearing bonnets? Whom are you really speaking about?" But throughout this two-year period, the splitting between observing ego and irrational ego was operating most of the time; there were instances when he would stop in the middle of an angry tirade and say: "Listen to me, I am breaking your balls [I would interject, "Or is it eggs?"] about something last week I was complimenting you about!" Or, "What am I doing, talking about your *affected* speech? When you speak Italian, you have a Sicilian intonation; my mother had an *affected* Northern Italian speech!" Earlier on during these two years we worked primarily on his negative preoedipal feelings *against* his mother (anger, fear, etc.). Later on, more and more, we worked on his preoedipal and oedipal positive feelings *for* her: his love and admiration for her, and his understanding that it had been difficult for her being the daughter of an attractive, authoritarian, and very strong father. More and more he would conclude his perorations by saying, "Well, I guess I should forgive her, she was a victim too." He was indeed making peace with his mother. About two years after the "Eggshells" dream, he and his girl friend started living together, and he began seriously considering marrying her. He had become consistently potent sexually.

In the last two years of L's analysis we continued working through his feelings about his mother and, predictably, he resumed talking about his father; but the oedipal feelings concerning his father which I had anticipated, never materialized. Anger at father (and rather mild, at that) took mainly the form of regret that his father had not been "more of a man, like grandfather." "I could have been more of a little Oedipus toward my mother, if he had been stronger with her." I could still have been right in presuming, at the time of the "Successful Intercourse" dream, that a full oedipal transference (as opposed to para-oedipal) would not appear until the negative maternal transference had developed and had been resolved; that is, until he no longer needed his father's (and grandfather's) protection from his mother. Still this did not happen because, possibly, L lost interest as the symptoms that brought him into therapy abated. He may have feared opening up the oedipal area and paying for it with a symptomatic relapse. If termination was, in part, a flight into health, after ten years of hard work, L was entitled to it.

L married his "young nurse" the year after terminating therapy. About a year after that I received a card announcing the birth of a son. There was a short but warm note attached to the card, starting with "How are you, *Doc*?" (*Doc* was underlined three times.) It was a reference to when, long after the doctor–donkey slip of the tongue, he would call me "Doc" and jokingly say, "I said 'Doc,' I didn't say 'donkey'. . . . ' Was he castrating me, once again? Was that his way of saying he had not fully worked through his oedipal rage? I don't think so. A cigar may never be "just a cigar," but I feel that in calling me "Doc," there was more warm affection than cold anger, more a cozy, homey humor than a hostile, sarcastic rejoinder.

J's DREAMS: "BEAUTIFUL MEADOW" AND "BACK ALLEY"

These two dreams were briefly discussed in chapter 4 from the point of view of dream formation and to illustrate the difference between "beautiful dreams" and nightmares. They are being discussed now from the point of view of dream interpretation and are presented together because they are, again, thematically and psychodynamically related in a special way. Having been dreamed seven years apart, they show how identical latent drives can be represented, in the manifest dream, in two very different versions. Also, they illustrate how the cardinal rule, seven years earlier and seven years later, was applied in two very different ways.

When he began therapy, J was an affable, jovial, "soft" 25-year-old man. "Softness" was a distinguishing characteristic (characterologic, as we shall soon see). He spoke softly and usually had a smiling, friendly, open, soft countenance. Severely myopic, he wore thick glasses through which his sparkling blue eyes smiled engagingly. Neither fat nor thin, he was not athletic, and his porcelain-white arms and legs (he often wore medium-length shorts) had a babyishly soft look. He was not particularly good looking but made a pleasing first impression because of his rosy, accepting face. Also, he was always perfectly neat and clean. He usually sat in a passive, receptive fashion: slumped back on the chair, his legs apart, and stretched out straight in front of him, heels resting on the floor. But at least through the first three to four years of therapy, I often had the feeling that beyond this facade, there was an impenetrable barrier behind which hid another J; when his face smiled, but not his eyes, I felt again that behind the eyes, lay another J. Inner tension was often betrayed by his fingers drumming on the arms of the chair or by the swinging of his knees, back and forth, in and out, in what seemed to be more a release of energy than a classic masturbation equivalent.

J began therapy because he was "dissatisfied with life." A coworker of his at the city's Department of Social Services was going to the Fordham Graduate School of Social Services and was

taking my course in clinical psychiatry (he had referred J to me).
This man had told him that he was probably obsessive–compulsive
and could benefit from therapy. In the first session, speaking of
himself, he told me that he was "not great looking but not very
ugly either," so why couldn't he get a girl friend? He thought he
was a nice person, and that people generally liked him, so why
was it that in his social groups, at work or at play, he was always
peripheral, never central, nobody's "best" friend, not truly "important" to anyone, man or woman? He believed that he was not
stupid, so why had school always been so difficult for him? Was
he obsessive–compulsive, could he benefit from therapy? And he
believed there was more to life than he had experienced so far.

"Beautiful Meadow"

"Beautiful Meadow" was J's first dream and he told it to me
during his sixth session. He had been coming once a week and
was not using the couch. In the first five sessions, besides telling
me why he was seeking therapy, he had told me that he had been
born and raised in Brooklyn, New York, a third-generation Irish
Catholic; that he was the middle of three children (he had a
brother, four years older, and a sister, five years younger); that
his father, a plumber, was fanatically religious, and a chronic
alcoholic who drank every night and to the point of drunkenness
on weekends. When his father was "only slightly drunk," he
would tease him and his brother, and when "very drunk," he
would "sometimes" beat them up and then go into psychotic-
like religious monologues and litanies. Father stopped beating
them when his brother was 16 and he, 11. Father ignored his
daughter and was never abusive with her and was verbally but
never physically abusive with his wife. His mother came from a
middle-class family and had been a schoolteacher before marrying father.

    J also told me that he had gone to Catholic parochial schools.
He was liked by teachers and most peers because of his good will,
agreeableness, and helpfulness. He worked very hard at school,
but never achieved good grades because of difficulties with concentration and memory. He was never left behind, but had to
struggle to be promoted to the next class. Until college, he had

been very religious, and had even considered becoming a priest. At puberty for two to three years he had become scrupulous about "sins," sexual sins, sins of anger, and sins of imperfection; for instance, having made an "imperfect confession." In his late adolescence, he had become "a liberated Catholic," had decided that masturbation was not a sin after all, and masturbated frequently. He liked girls, had sexual desires toward them, but was timid with them and "respected them." Many young women liked him, but "like a brother." He also said that he had gone to a state college upstate and had graduated seven years later, at 24; that attaining passing grades had been difficult in college too; that he had majored in sociology and obtained a bachelor's degree in social work. As soon as he had found his current job as a caseworker with the city's Department of Social Services, he had moved away from home and was now living, with a roommate, in a small apartment in Brooklyn. Only two or three years later did I learn that when his father was "only sightly drunk" he truly delighted sadistically in teasing the two boys; and when he was "very drunk," he beat them up regularly, not just "sometimes," and very brutally.

Diagnostically, I thought that J was not only unconsciously angry and an obsessive character neurotic, but *almost* a person with a pervasive developmental retardation, if not arrest. There may have been an undiagnosed learning disability more subtle and complex than simple dyslexia, maybe even a chronic attention disorder. At any rate, the task of warding off a great amount of unconscious anger seemed to distract him, to distance him from life, and to prevent him from achieving even a small degree of success in age-appropriate work or play activities. I believed that his basically obsessional characterology showed not only in his compulsive masturbation, but also in the way he studied, thought, and lived. There was a great deal of unresolved, unintegrated rage within, as made evident by his reactive gentleness, agreeableness, and "sweetness." It would be two to three years before he would begin to acknowledge, and at first only in a highly intellectualized fashion, that he was angry at his father. He had to appear "soft" to hide the feared and wished-for "hardness" within; beneath the obsessional characterology and the veneer of reactive "sweetness," there was a subclinical depression.

In the fifth session of therapy, the session before the dream's session, J spoke about his wish "to put his act together" so that he could go back to school and get a master's degree in social work "without too much of a hassle and without too many difficulties in learning and in doing the reading." He spoke some more about his father, telling me that father had never showed interest in his schooling during grammar school and high school, had never appeared disturbed by his poor grades, and had been against his going to college. His father would say, "Look at me, I didn't even finish high school and I have made a good living for you kids and your mother all your fucking life." His father would refer to him, J, as "college hot shit" and would gloat over J's difficulties with finishing college. All this was said with the same equanimity, serenity, and detachment with which he had spoken to me throughout our first five sessions together. In the sixth session, he came in glowing and proudly announced he had had a dream, a "beautiful dream."

"Beautiful Meadow"

> I was walking in the plaza at Fordham's Lincoln Center campus. The college was not hard cement, but a beautiful meadow, and the scene was positively heavenly, brilliantly green grass, flowers, blue skies, chirping birds, actually like the campus upstate where I went to college. I was walking with an elderly gentleman, white-haired, clean-shaven, I don't know who he was, but he was not my father. I was carrying some heavy books, and suddenly I stumbled on a rock and the books fell on the man's foot, but he wasn't hurt. He joked with me about it, even bent down to pick up the books for me. He complimented me for being such a good graduate student.

J had smiled in his usual sunny way while telling me the dream and looked at me expectantly when he had finished. I smiled back and told him to tell me whatever came to his mind. He told me that he really wished to go to graduate school, maybe to Fordham, where his friend was going, and that, in terms of that wish, the dream seemed a good omen; the dream seemed such a good omen also because everything was so beautiful in it, the green meadow, the flowers, the chirping birds, the blue skies. The detail of the old man also was encouraging, the old man must have been a professor and how delightful that a professor should have been so nice to him, especially after he had been so clumsy with his heavy books. He then told me that he sometimes wondered whether his father, in his heart of hearts, actually regretted not having finished high school. His father had had a truly difficult childhood, being one of seven children, "smack right in the middle, just like I am," and from a very poor family. Father's father had been a "real terror." He told me again that his major "conscious heartache" in life was not being truly "important" to anyone; that he wished to be "central" to someone; that the fact that he was not was a sign of some inferiority on his part, was his fault, no one else's. He was humorous but not truly witty and hilarious; not stupid, but not really bright or brilliant; agreeable and cooperative, and a follower, not one who ever initiated anything. No wonder his friends liked and accepted him but were not "wild" about him. He then added, "It does not irritate me that they prefer and choose each other, it's my fault."

The first two tasks at this point were to understand the dream's session and the sessions before it, and to understand the session's dream; that is, to know what the dream says. As J was talking, I was listening and at the same time was engaged in my usual internal soliloquy of hypotheses, conjectures, and resonances. My soliloquy included these thoughts. Because of its length, copiousness of adjectives, partiality for symbols, and for images of beauty, grace, and loveliness, the dream was a highly defended dream, as one would expect in the sixth session of therapy with a highly defended, nonpsychotic patient. Highly defended as the dream was, I still felt encouraged by the fact that it had been remembered and shared. The ice had been broken, albeit infinitesimally, a door to the royal road to the unconscious had opened. I also thought that the volunteered denial, "he was *not* my father," strongly suggested that the elderly gentleman indeed was his father. The manifest dream, indeed, was full of denials: the elderly gentleman was *not* hurt, was joking with him, hence was *not* angry at him; was complimenting him, hence was *not* critical of him; the Fordham Lincoln Center plaza was *not* cement, was a meadow, therefore was *not* hard, was soft. That denial occurred also in his associations to the dream: it did *not* irritate him that his friends preferred and chose each other rather than him, it was *not* anyone else's fault that he was not truly important to anyone. I felt that the transference had already begun to develop: the "elderly gentleman" in the manifest dream, the "professor," was his father but also me—I also teach at the Fordham Lincoln Center Campus. The transference too was appropriately highly defended. In reality I was not (not at that time anyway) white-haired, and I did, at that time too, have a beard. Therefore, depicting me, in the dream's manifest content, as white-haired and clean-shaven, had the defensive purpose of both disguising me and condensing me with his father, who was white-haired and clean-shaven.

I thought, therefore, that the dream had to do with father, and specifically, with anger at father; this was also suggested by his referring, in the fifth session, to his father's feelings about education and J going to college. He had spoken, also in the fifth session, of his wish to go back to school and be able to learn "without too much of a hassle and without too many difficulties in learning and doing the reading," and by that probably he was unconsciously referring to his father "hassling" him about education. His learning difficulties, possibly, were not related only to brain dysfunctions but also to an unconscious need to under-achieve in order not to antagonize his father. Telling me about his father's miserable childhood and unconscious wish to have continued schooling, while possibly true, was also a manifestation of superego defenses. I also believed that "*smack*" (his father, he had told me, "one of seven children, was smack right in the middle") was an onomatopoeia for the beatings his father rou-tinely gave him. Reminding me that he, J, also was "right in the middle," suggested some identification with father and was one more expression of the superego defenses that are usually so prominent in the first stages of therapy.

My internal soliloquy momentarily completed, I tentatively concluded that the semimanifest dream had to do with J's wish to resume his education, and to resume it at Fordham with me, the transferential father, a new father, who would perhaps be more benign than his own father, a new father who thought he was a good graduate student rather than a "college hot shit." The semilatent dream had to do with fear and guilt over wanting to attack father with heavy, possibly lethal objects. The latent dream had to do with anger at the father who hassled him about education, teased him, called him names, and beat him up. Thus, I opined, dropping the heavy books on the older man's foot represented hitting father, and me, on some other part of our body, probably a body part having predicate thinking similarities with another, equally protruding body part (i.e., a penis). The book, something *high*-minded and superior, stood for an object or weapon much more base, *low*, lethal. These thoughts and feelings came from the "*down*" parts of him, his hard unconscious drives, his guts. He sanitized them by changing the Fordham New York City campus to an "*up*state" campus (*up*: intellect, reason, head, intellectualization). These thoughts and feelings were so frightening and "ugly," that he needed to beautify and cosmeticize them by filling the manifest dream with beauty and beautiful images.

The third task was to respond to the dream, and to know what to say to the patient about the dream. What would I do? This was a first dream, and with first dreams, *not much can be said, not much should be said, just enough might have to be said.* Therapy had just begun, the patient was highly defended, and so was his dream. I thought I had learned a great deal about J from his dream, but felt that "not much could be said and not much should be said." I did not truly know J, all I thought was hypothetical and conjectural. The cardinal rule, obviously, could not be applied, and interpretations on the level of the drives were, of course, contraindicated. But I believed that something, "just enough," ought to be said: J had not asked for the meaning of the dream; on the other hand, he had seemed proud of the dream, had looked at me expectantly after telling it to me, had seemed to want to be praised for having had it and having remembered it. One of his associations had included how sad he felt for not being truly important to anyone. Also, it was J's first dream and I wanted to help him continue remembering dreams. He wanted to be "important" to someone and be praised by someone and I wanted to be sensitive to that need and gratify it to a degree. I wanted to say "just enough" to help us with the therapeutic alliance and the fledgling transference, but not too much. To say too much would be seductive, would contaminate the transference, and gratify his dependency too much. I said:

I too am glad you remembered this dream; dreams can help us a great
deal in understanding you, your 'conscious heartaches,' as you call them,
and what may bother you deep inside.

   Through my response, I was trying to tell him that I appreciated his remembering his dream and bringing it to therapy, that
is, that I appreciated him; and I was telling him that it would be
helpful if he continued to remember dreams. By saying to him
that there was more to his plight than his "conscious heartaches,"
that there were matters and concerns bothering him deep inside,
I was gently knocking on doors to the royal road to his unconscious, thus aiming at promoting the analytical process and the
progress down that road. By using the same words he had used
earlier in the session, "conscious heartaches," I was telling him
that he was being heard, that he was not talking to a wall, I was
trying to foster the therapeutic alliance, the joint endeavor that
therapy must become if it is to be successful. I was trying to
strengthen that alliance also by using the pronoun *us* ("dreams
can help *us* a great deal").

Theoretical Appendix: Some of the Dream Work Defenses

From the dream's manifest content:

Walking: concrete pictorial representation of movement in
therapy.
Fordham's Lincoln Center Campus: displacement from therapist's
office.
Not hard cement: denial—this place (therapy, unconscious memories, childhood) is far from soft.
*Beautiful Meadow, positively heavenly scene, brilliantly green grass, blue
skies, chirping birds*: secondary elaborations and turning into the
opposite of a much harsher and uglier psychic landscape.
Upstate: displacement from downstate (therapist office).
Upstate (i.e., North): displacement from South, feelings, genitals,
passions, gut feelings; symbolism for intellectualizations, head,
thoughts, ideas, reason.
Elderly gentleman: displacement from father and therapist.
Gentleman: denial and turning into the opposite (father was not
a gentle man).

Was not my father: volunteered denial.

Carrying: concrete pictorial representation of the feeling of being burdened, weighed down.

Heavy books: displacement from heavy weapons. Also *books:* concrete pictorial representation of ideas, symbolism and displacement from base, "low" feelings to "high"-minded ideas and thoughts.

Stumbled: concrete pictorial representation of hesitancy, indecision, conflict.

Rock: concrete pictorial representation of a hard, uncaring, unprotective mother or of the hard, brutal father.

Books fell on elderly gentleman's foot: concrete pictorial representation of something happening accidentally; distortion of latent dream's wish to do something (not accidentally!) to elderly gentleman's foot.

Elderly gentleman's foot: displacement downward from a higher part in one's anatomy.

Not hurt, joked with me, complimented me: denials; in latent dream, father is seriously wounded by J's attack; in real life, father never joked, never complimented him about his studies, teased him, mocked him, and called him foul names.

From associations—one listens to the dream's session as if it were a dream:

Smiling in a sunny way: denial of turbulent feelings within.

Wish to go to school: displacement from wishing to learn more about himself.

Wish to go to Fordham School of Social Service: wish to be near transferential father, the analyst.

The nice professor: displacement from therapist.

Smack in the middle: onomatopoeia for "smacks" (blows) he got from father.

Does not irritate me: denial.

"Back Alley"

As I just said, "Beautiful Meadow," tentatively as it could only be at this early point, had taught me a great deal about J. Much happened in the seven years between "Beautiful Meadow" and "Back Alley." What follows, about those seven years, is only what is relevant to a discussion of J's dream and to the stated intent of this section of this chapter, namely, to show how, seven years apart, identical latent drives can be represented, in the manifest dream, in two very different versions, and to illustrate how the cardinal rule, seven years earlier and seven years later, can be applied in two very different ways.

J had started coming twice a week in the second year of therapy and three times a week from the third year on. In the first two to three years after "Beautiful Meadow," I learned that J's childhood and early adolescence had been a true nightmare, much more painful and violent than he had let me know early on. His father was a violent man, physically and verbally abusive. When "very drunk," which was every Friday and Saturday, he beat M (J's older brother) and J repeatedly and violently—never in their faces, though, so that no tale-telling marks were visible when the children went to school. When only "slightly drunk," he would still beat them up, maybe less violently, or would threaten to beat them up. There was no evidence, either historical or clinical, that he had ever abused the children sexually, but a large part of his "teasing them," consisted of telling them, in graphic and explicit ways, about what he would do to their "pretty little mouths," or their "pretty little asses" with his large, hard penis (he would occasionally unzip his pants and show them his organ). An invasive and intrusive man, there were no boundaries between him and his two sons that he did not consistently violate. As J would put it, dramatically (and accurately) toward the end of analysis, father was "ALWAYS THERE," a presence bigger than life, a multisensory (visual, auditory, tactile, and olfactory) presence even when not fully "present" physically. When deep in his drunken sleep, he would snore so loud that the entire small railroad flat resonated with the sound and its four other occupants, awake or asleep, knew exactly where the fury came from. When too drunk to beat the boys up, he was still very much present through his lewd psychotic reveries and booming religious litanies. He also gave forth a strong, unpleasant, body odor.

J's father drank to excess only on Friday and Saturday nights; he only drank at home. He rarely missed work because of his alcoholism. There was a degree of peace in the family only when father was out. J's mother was a timid, repressed, ineffectual, submissive person, totally dominated by her husband. J's father had been, in his youth, a strikingly handsome man. J's mother may not have been in love with him, but she married him when she was a few months pregnant with M. She was not totally uncaring toward her children, but was undemonstrative, and when her husband was physically abusive to her sons, she would run into the bathroom sobbing hysterically. She never intervened to protect the boys from him. The physical violence against the boys stopped when M, "a very big boy at 16," in the middle of a beating grabbed a baseball bat, knocked father half-unconscious on the floor and told him that he would kill him if he laid so much as a finger on him or on J—this was in J's presence; J was then 12. (J told me the story with emotion about four years into therapy, referred to it in passing several times after that, and then, again, also with much feeling, a few sessions before the "Back Alley" dream.)

J grew up as a timid and quiet boy. At home, he was always on guard, trying to be out of his father's reach, to avoid being beaten, staying out in the street as late as possible when father was at home (but this did not always work: father could beat him up for coming home too late). Outside of home, he was generally sweet and engaging. He idolized his brother, who was consistently protective of him outside the home and, when he could (and did, after the episode at 12) inside the home. Significantly, only the extent of his father's physical and verbal violence (and of his fear of his father), and the extent of his mother's extreme passivity about her husband's violence and her sons' fears, had been omitted in the history that J had given me in the five sessions preceding his first dream. Except for more details, in the years following "Beautiful Meadow," J did not say anything about his postlatency life that he had not told me before. No important memories concerning prelatency years were ever remembered.

By the time of "Back Alley," J, now 31, had been coming to therapy for about seven years, and three times a week for about four and a half years. His appearance had changed. He wore more "adult" clothes more appropriate to his age and status in life (for instance, he rarely, now, wore shorts). He no longer looked "babyish," he wore contact lenses. He still had a basically friendly and open countenance, but did not smile as consistently, was not as persistently engaging and as insistently ingratiating as before. Besides, he could now be angry and when angry, he did not look friendly and did not smile. He was still working with the Department of Social Services and was a supervisor. He felt that people at work, peers, superiors, and supervisees, not only liked and accepted him, which was not a new experience for him, but appreciated and respected him, and this was something he had never experienced before and about which he felt "very happy." He still intended "eventually" to go to a school of social service to get a master's degree. (He did, after he had terminated analysis, although he did not go to Fordham.) Still unmarried, he had been dating a young woman for about one year. The relationship was fully sexual and moderately intense; they did not live together but saw each other frequently. He was "very happy" about the fact that, for the first time in his life, a woman did not treat him, "like a brother," happy about "being sexual," and about the fact that, also for the first time in his life, he seemed to be fairly "important," "central," to someone. I frequently had the feeling that J was "very happy" more about the "result" of his social and personal experiences than with the experience itself; that there was a "distance," or a barrier of a sort, between his "happy" experiences and his conscious self.

The biggest change with J was in having become able to be angry at his father and in his relationship with me. His capacity to express anger at his father, of course, grew slowly. The first two to three years after "Beautiful Meadow," he expressed anger in restrained or disguised forms: jocularly or laughingly; or intellectually and in a self-distancing, semi-detached fashion: "I must have been angry at him when he did that," "I am sure I was angry." In the two to three years which preceded "Back Alley," it was expressed in a more feelingful and genuine way. And a year or so before "Back Alley," he spoke of the way his father had treated him with more intense and immediate feelings. As he recounted his father's physical and nonphysical abuses, tears of sorrow and rage would come to his eyes, and he would even sob. The memories of his father's verbal abuses evoked pain and rage too.

J's overall way of being and behaving in therapy had also gradually changed. Now, when not angry, he would lie on the couch more tranquilly (less drumming of fingers, less spasmodic opening and closing of thighs). When angry he would sit up and stomp his feet on the floor, or punch the pillow on the couch, or even get up and take a few steps around the room. At these times, I might say, "Whom are you really punching? Who is on that pillow? On whom are you stomping your feet?" He had also become able (this too occurred in a gradual, slow progression) to be angry at me, to accuse me of not helping him enough. Why was he still so tormented by what his father had done to him, after all these years in therapy? Why couldn't he leave those memories behind? Did disinterest, maybe contempt, maybe even anger, hide behind my "analytical silence"? The year or so before "Back Alley," he would storm at me, loud and hysterically, would again get up from the couch and punch the pillow (once he threw it on the floor, not in my direction). I might again say, "Whom are you punching? Maybe you wanted to throw the pillow in my direction?" The therapeutic alliance, of course, had in the meantime become very solid. He had strong, positive "real feelings" toward me, liked, and trusted me and that helped him considerably in his growing capacity to express anger at his father and at me. And yet, even when he gave in to these bursts of intense anger and pain at father and analyst, loud and dramatically, in a sincere, nonintellectual, genuine fashion, even then I felt that there was more anger within, more tears behind the eyes, more sorrow and rage behind a not-yet-penetrated (impenetrable?) barrier. Several dreams, maybe five to ten a month, were remembered and shared in this period, dreams whose latent content indicated that there was indeed more rage at his father than was being expressed and that the negative transference toward me was both toward the abusive father and the neglectful mother. J's ups and downs with anger, guilt over the anger, and fears of retaliation, were accompanied by ups and downs of conscious depression (sadness, conscious feelings of guilt toward me or other parental figures) or unconscious depression (guilt equivalents: minor accident proneness, mildly self-destructive behavior).

A few times, in the years preceding "Back Alley," J had recounted the time M had hit father with the baseball bat. The first or second time he did so, it was done in a slightly detached, self-distancing fashion. He might joke about father's stunned expression at M's rebelling against him and attacking him. "He looked like a big black bear astonished at seeing a bear bigger than him," he had said once. Subsequent times, he recounted it with more feelings of glee, rage, guilt, and fear. And a few sessions before "Back Alley," that episode was brought up again and again, and father was likened, again but without laughter this time, to a *black* bear. Conscious guilt over the conscious delight were the two prevalent emotions. The last three sessions before the dream were characterized by intense anger: at me and at his father. Then, there came the dream's session.

J arrived a few minutes late (unusual and uncharacteristic for him), mumbled a few words about having been detained in the office by a telephone call from an abusive, difficult client. He seemed shaky. He lay on the couch and said: "What a dream last night!" In a rather tremulous voice he told me the dream.

"Back Alley"

> I was walking in some back alley with a black man. I was carrying a heavy baseball bat. I stumbled and the bat fell off my hands. But I picked it up and, I don't know what came over me, I bashed and smashed the head of the man with it, many times, it was awful, blood splattering all over, I felt awful, I woke up bathed in sweat. Boy, was I glad it was only a dream. I guess I am becoming aware of how angry I am.

J was silent for several minutes, and so was I. He broke the silence by repeating, "What a dream!" and adding, "Am I that angry? Am I truly a violent person?" In my internal soliloquy, I had already connected the dream to the time M had attacked father with the baseball bat and had concluded that the latent dream had to do with J's wish to do the same. J went on talking of how he felt about the dream's gory details, and what a relief it had been to be able to wake up and realize "it was only a dream." He asked, "Aren't you going to say anything? It was quite a dream, wasn't it?" I said, "What do you mean, 'quite a dream'?" He said, "Oh shit! The analytical shit, again, the analytical 'stance,' the books call it—here I am, spilling my guts, and he is silent." I said, " 'He'? Who?" He yelled, "You, of course, it's you

I am talking about!" He sat up, looking rather agitated, looked at me, seemed reassured by what I felt was a calm, accepting countenance on my face, lay down again, and said, "I have been very angry, lately, at you, at my father, that's no news to you, or to me, but *this* angry? *so much* angry? I marvel, sometimes, and I guess at some level it reassures me, how well you tolerate it, and I guess you have helped me, I am freer with my feelings, but I do wish you would talk more, say more. I think I would progress faster if you did, you are slowing down my progress, damn it!" I said, "What comes to mind, as you are thinking of your dream?" After a few minutes of silence, lying rather calmly on the couch, he spoke about two male professors in college who "irritated him mildly." I said: "Mildly? Lately you have been able to be much more in touch with your feelings of anger. Maybe it was not just 'irritation'?—maybe it was not just 'mild'?" He said, "Maybe, but in those days I was scared shitless of my anger, and I guess I am today too, because of the dream." He then spoke of the client who had telephoned him just as he was about to come and see me, what a difficult person this man is, and that it was because of him that he had been late. In the rest of the session, up to my intervention, he fluctuated between expressing, again, anger at me for my silence, and appreciation of the progress we had made so far, between awe about the intensity of the dream's anger and relief that he could tell me about it.

The first two tasks at this point were to understand the dream's session and the sessions before it, and to understand the session's dream; that is, to know what the dream says. All along, I had been engaged in my internal soliloquy. He was obviously angry, both at me and at his father, both in the dream's session and the sessions before it, and in the session's dream. The session's dream was a transparent dream of murderous rage at his real father and at his transferential father, a nightmare, an anxiety-and-guilt dream exactly because the latent content was so poorly disguised. The black man was his father, "the black bear" of recent associations, and myself, the transferential black-bad father. In the back of his mind, the back alleys of his mind, he wanted to kill me and father, using the same weapon, the baseball bat that M had used twenty years before when J was 12. I found myself thinking of his father threatening to sodomize J anally and orally with his penis, of his father threatening to bash and smash little J's small mouth and anus with his large penis, and I thought that the baseball bat was not only a displacement from the bat M had used in reality, but also a displacement from, and a symbolism for, J's penis. In other words, I wondered whether, tit-for-tat, or rather penis for penis, J wanted to do to his father what his father had threatened to do to him, to sodomize father, to bash and smash father's anus or mouth. I also asked myself whether there was a measure of horrified enjoyment, on his part, in repeating, again, the manifest dream's details. I thought about the fact that, when he had first told me the dream, and, again, when he went over its gory details a second time, I had felt tempted to say, but restrained myself, "I once quoted Plato to you, 'Bad people do what good people dream about,' " an intellectualization I had used years before right after his first dream of anger at father and me. I thought to have quoted Plato might have been appropriate years before, but my need to reassure him now was motivated by countertransference. I must have felt the same feelings J's father had felt when M had attacked him. In reassuring him, I was reassuring myself, I was telling the both of us that J was no killer, that he only dreamed what "bad" people do. I also thought that the association of anger at the angry, difficult client who had made him late for his session, was not only consistent with the dream's anger but was also a reference to me. I too "retarded" him, I also slowed down his progress with my "analytical stance." The association to the two professors at whom he had been "mildly irritated" in college, also was consistent with the dream's meaning, and an association that connected the dream more clearly to me and to the dream of seven years before. I also am a professor, and, in the previous dream, it was a professor on whose foot he had "accidentally" dropped the heavy books he was carrying. But there were many other connections and similarities between the two dreams; more about this later.

The third task was to respond to the dream, and to know what to say to the patient about the dream. My soliloquy concluded for the moment, it was now time to decide how to respond to the dream. Should I respond with silence or with an intervention? I decided a response was warranted for several reasons, and specifically, a response in the nature of an interpretation on the level of the drives and within the context of the transference. Among these reasons: first, generally speaking, a response was warranted because J's ego was strong, the therapeutic alliance was solid, I did know J (we had been working together for close to seven years), and I did understand the session's dream and the dream's session. The cardinal rule could be safely applied. More specifically, this kind of response was warranted because the anger against real and transferential father, which was a prominent part of the dream, was *almost* manifest, manifest enough, poorly distorted enough, to cause the dreamer to experience anxiety and guilt. But it was not totally manifest, not totally undistorted: for instance, J had not even made the connection between the dream's baseball bat and M's baseball bat, had not even made the connection between this dream and the dream of seven years previously. If I was right with my conjectures about his unconscious wish ("penis for penis") to sodomize father, J had not made the connection between the baseball bat and his penis. Thus, an interpretation was called for to promote further progress on the royal road to the unconscious. Also, it was "quite a dream," as J had put it, and it deserved a response. J had been courageous and trusting in remembering and sharing the dream, he was anxious and distressed about the dream. He was entitled to a response; a terse and relevant interpretation was not necessarily a seductive or otherwise countertransferentially induced action. I decided that the response would follow the cardinal rule, it would be a response on the level of the drives and within the context of the transference. I said:

> Yes, obviously, you are very angry. A part of you, a part of you in the back of your head, a part of you in a back alley of your head, wants to kill me. Yet, also obviously, another part of you does not want to kill me and is afraid of killing me and feels guilty for wanting to kill me.

J was silent for a while and then said, "Yes, a part of me wants to kill you, but only a part of me, not all of me, not even a very large part of me. And I have the feeling I have dreamed this dream before, but I cannot think of when." I did not want to tell him, not then anyway, of the dream seven years before. I felt it would have been bragging, and there was no urgent need why I could not have waited for him to remember that one dream on his own. So, I only said,

> In the back of your mind, you have been angry at me before you con-
> sciously knew you were; and, of course, there have been many dreams
> similar to this in the past but not as courageously undisguised.

But I felt that he was very close to being able to make the seemingly safe connection between the dream's bat and M's bat, and I felt it was important to help him make that connection if we were to go further down the royal road to his connecting murderous bats with what I hypothesized to be sodomizing penises. So I said, "But why a bat, why a baseball bat?"

To my surprise, he said, "Well, that's elementary, my dear Watson: that's the weapon M almost killed my father with twenty years ago. So my dream is about my father, more than about you. And this is both a relief and very, very frightening."

Theoretical Appendix: Some of the Dream Work Defenses

From the dream's manifest content:

Walking: concrete pictorial representation of movement in therapy.
Back alley: displacement from "back-of-the-mind"; concrete picto-rial representation of unconscious.
Black man: displacement from therapist and father (father had looked like a "black bear" at the time M had attacked him with the baseball bat); concrete pictorial representation of badness and danger.
Heavy: concrete pictorial representation of intensity of feelings.
Stumbled: concrete pictorial representation of hesitancy, indeci-sion, conflict.
Bat fell off: concrete pictorial representation of impotence, of pe-nis limpness.
Don't know what came over me: secondary elaboration and denial.
Bashed and smashed: undisguised representation of aggression; but also metaphors for the other forms of aggressive acts he wished to perform against father.

The man: displacement from therapist and father.
It was awful: direct, undisguised representation of tertiary feelings.

From associations—óne listens to the dream session as if it were a dream:

It was quite a dream: secondary elaboration, "It's only a dream!"
Spilling my guts: displacement from anal component of his anger.
He is silent: displacement from father.
Two male professors: displacement from therapist and father.
The client who had abused his lateness for session: displacement from therapist and father, who also had retarded his development.

Also on a theoretical plane: "Back Alley" was a typical "anxiety dream," from which J woke up in a state of tertiary anxiety and guilt because the latent content was not sufficiently well disguised and distorted. In "Back Alley," the ego's dream work's defenses distorted and disguised the dream's drives poorly, *not* because the ego was depleted by pathology, but because, after seven years of therapy, the ego was stronger and better able to tolerate anxiety. The id drives behind the dream's latent wishes had been, in part, analyzed, and to the extent that they had been analyzed, had undergone processes of displacement and sublimation, and the superego was weaker.

As indicated at the beginning of this section, these two dreams were selected because, having a similar thematic content but having been dreamed seven years apart, they are an excellent teaching tool to demonstrate how identical latent drives will be represented in the manifest dreams in two very different ways because of psychodynamic changes within the dreamer. To begin with, in the "Beautiful Meadow," dream, the id drives were stronger and a stronger superego demanded a more radical censure of them; and a more defended and fearful ego complied. Thus one can see the ego's dream work's defenses distort, disguise, and sanitize the dream's "ugly" latent content into a "beautiful" manifest content in "Beautiful Meadow"; not so at all in "Back Alley." Similarly, the dark, dangerous recesses of the "back of the mind" (the unconscious), where all kinds of primitive, unsocialized, raw, explosive, libidinal, and aggressive drives lie lurking, are beautified into a serene and bucolic university campus in the first dream; not so at all in the second dream, where they are represented as a dangerous back alley. The powerful, dangerous, abusive father, the black bear of J's past, is cosmeticized into an elderly, gentlemanly college professor in one dream, presented as a black man in the other. The instrument through which J "dreams out" his aggression is presented, in the first dream, as a genteel, intellectual, and scholarly symbol, a set of (arguably heavy!) books; as a lethal baseball bat in the second dream. In "Beautiful Meadow," the books "accidentally" fell on the man's foot, no harm was done, the man was not hurt, he joked with J about it, even bent down to pick up the books himself. In "Back Alley," the tool of aggression, now a baseball bat, is used to bash and smash the man's head (or other anatomically vulnerable body parts), and blood splatters all over. In the first dream, the grass is brilliantly green, the skies are blue, the birds are chirping, the scene is heavenly, and J is feeling marvelous. In the second dream, the alley is dark, the scene is awful, J feels horror-filled, and wakes up bathed in sweat.

Postscript

J terminated therapy two years later, at the age of 33; he had been in therapy for a total of nine years, one year once a week, one year twice a week, and the remaining seven years three times a week. He had changed considerably. He was much less "soft," had continued to wear contact lenses, and was always dressed appropriately. He was still working with the Department of Social Services, was liked and also much respected for his clinical and administrative skills as a social worker and supervisor, for his talent in running workshops, seminars, and in-service training sessions within the department, and for his literate interests and erudition. He had become an avid reader of quality fiction and psychological and psychoanalytical books. He was teased about this and called "the shrink" or "the professor," but he knew the teasing was friendly and admiring. The department was going to send him for graduate training the following year, he was going to a school other than Fordham. He was still a friendly and cheerful young man of a smiling and open countenance, affable and amiable; but, at the same time, he was, and could be, more serious, his joviality and cordiality were more appropriate, he could be firm, assertive, angry, and displeased, could stand up for his rights, could disagree with supervisors or figures in authority. The underlying depressiveness had diminished considerably, but there were still periods of mild sadness, and he could periodically be remorseful about having been "too assertive," regretful about having been "too selfish," full of compunctions about having been "fresh and disrespectful." He still had some difficulties with recent memory, retention, and recall but had developed "gimmicks" (note taking, mnemonic devices, etc.) to cope. He was now living with the young woman he had been dating for the last three years and was seriously contemplating marriage. Anger at father had gradually abated, and so had his anger at me. In the last two years of therapy we had worked through the transference neurosis and the superego defenses that still made him occasionally punctilious and scrupulous, and had worked on helping him better differentiate between anger and assertiveness.

In summary, there had been much symptom relief and much characterological and psychodynamic change. Nevertheless, his occasional bouts of sadness and scrupulosity indicated the degree to which his superego could still be harsh and demanding. His not wanting to go to Fordham, where I teach, while probably a wise decision, also suggested that the transference neurosis had not been fully worked through. His voracious interest in psychological and psychoanalytical books, although an indication of a healthy identification with me, also suggested the degree to which the oral and mother-related components of this neurosis had not been worked through.

But, possibly more significant than these three points, I often had the sense with J, that beyond the facade, there was a barrier behind which hid another J. When he had begun to improve socially and interpersonally, I frequently felt that he was more happy with the "results" of a "good" social or personal experience than with the experience itself. I often had the experience, with J, that there was a "distance," a barrier of a sort, between "good" experiences and J's self. All this occurred less and less frequently, but had not disappeared entirely; and, why did he still have problems with memory? To this day, many years after J stopped working with me, I ask myself: After nine years of therapy, had the veil of amnesia about the physical abuse suffered in childhood not been *fully* penetrated? If so, was it because of reasons other than technical mistakes on my part? Had the rage at his father not been *fully* relived in the transference or not fully actively remembered? If so, again, aside from errors on my part, why? Why had the "barrier of impenetrability," of the "distance" between his "good" experiences and his conscious self, not fully disappeared? Of course, one can ask oneself forever, obsessively and perfectionistically, how "full" is a "full" analysis of anything our patients suffer with. But to this day I wonder whether J's infancy and early childhood were even more awful than he let me (and himself?) know. I wonder whether J after all had been sexually abused. I wonder whether, while all of J's clinical and psychological problems were clearly related to obvious and understandable psychodynamics, whether he also suffered from some subtle neurological impairment, the kind of right hemisphere brain dysfunction often associated with Attention Deficit Disorder, and whether this neurological dysfunction could, *in part*, account for both his difficulties with recent memory, retention, and recall, and his difficulty in remembering more fully the psychodynamically potent events of his troubled past.

C's DREAMS: "BROWN-REDDISH URINE," "ON THE LAKE," "THE TRANQUILIZER," AND "ON THE 'SIN' OF AN ACCIDENT"

C's dreams also are grouped together because of thematic and psychodynamic similarities, the major similarities being the leit motif of ambivalent libidinal and aggressive oedipal and preoedipal drives, and the ambivalent dependence on and the feeling of "obligatory" obedience to the oedipal and preoedipal mother typical of men suffering with premature ejaculation.

"Brown-Reddish Urine"

C started analysis at the age of 35. He was a good looking, personable, and likable young man with a successful practice in general psychiatry (no electroconvulsive therapy). He had been born and raised in Italy and had come to the United States at the age of 18 with his mother and his younger sister. In the United States he took required premedical courses, went to medical school, graduated (at 24), and became board certified in psychiatry (at 29). His mother did not adjust well to life here and returned to Italy when C was 29. C's younger sister married during C's psychiatric residency and lives in a nearby state.

C came from an upper middle-class family. His father died of a massive heart attack at the age of 44 when C was 6. He was a successful businessman, and 14 years older than C's mother. At the beginning of therapy, C had only a few, vague memories of him. He remembered his father as energetic, assertive, personable, handsome, elegant, humorous, and loving. His mother told him that his father "adored him." On many Saturday mornings father would take him to his plant, C "loved it" and enjoyed the fuss his father's employees and workers made over him. When they took trips on the lake in their cabin cruiser, father would have him sit on his lap and have C "steering" the wheel of the boat. C remembered missing his father but did not remember "crying a lot or carrying on." His mother, however, told him that for a few weeks after father's death he had been morose, grouchy, and uncharacteristically cantankerous; that he had had trouble sleeping; he would either wake up and ask to sleep with mother or sleepwalk into his mother's bed. Mother would let him fall asleep next to her. C remembered nothing of this. His mother had married when she was only 18; she had just attained an undergraduate degree from an Italian university. She was "stunningly beautiful." C once showed me her photograph as a young bride: she was indeed beautiful. Early on, C often referred to his mother's "breathless" way of talking. She spoke exquisite Italian, softly and gently, usually in ecstatic, breathless, and enthusiastic tones, all the while smiling "seraphically." She rarely raised her voice; there was indeed a "breathless" quality to the way she spoke, carried herself, and "glided through life." It was clear, however, that she was a strong woman, "mother was not a piece of fluff." She was rigorous and demanding (of herself and her children). She loved her husband, and their marriage appears to have been a happy one. When he died, she, only 30, grieved and missed him very much, never remarried, and apparently never dated or showed interest in marrying again. After her husband's death she did go back to school for advanced studies, and taught in a prestigious private high school for girls in her city until she left for the United States at 42 with C and her youngest daughter. C was the third child: he had two sisters, five and four years older, and a younger sister, four years younger.

C began therapy because of "dissatisfaction with life." He elaborated, "I have a good practice, live in a nice apartment, people like me and think well of me. It looks like I am having a great time. I go skiing, play tennis like a mean son of a gun, travel, have friends, have had girl friends, but something is missing." He related well, was open and quite spontaneous, pleasant and affable. Although he was eager to please, to make a good impression, to be "a good, cooperative patient," there was nothing ingratiating or deferential about him. He could and would tease me about the diplomas on my wall ("your Boy Scout badges," he called them) or my occasionally formal way of dressing. He would needle me about the art work in my office (my own work), would tease me about "being Freudian," but always in a good-natured fashion, never acidly or nastily.

In the six sessions preceding his first dream, C gave me the family history outlined above and described his life-style a little further, his being what he called "compulsively compulsive from Monday to Friday and compulsively noncompulsive Saturdays and Sundays." He described himself as "a tight ass" about money and rules of behavior, but at times "very loose" in spending or "very lax in small aspects of conduct or morality." In the fifteen years he had been in the United States, he had had no serious love affairs, only three "liaisons" (his words) of two to three weeks duration each, and several "one-night affairs," usually during his skiing trips. C was a tall (6'1" or 6'2"), well built, good-looking man, well bred, cultured, well read (he enjoyed good fiction and history books). He spoke English fairly well and with practically no Italian accent. He frequently slipped into Italian, which he spoke incredibly well. His Italian was rich, elegant, refined. This occasionally caused me to be countertransferentially tempted to just sit back and enjoy his verbal pyrotechnics. He rarely remembered his dreams. He had read very little Freud and some Adler,

Jung, and a few of the contemporary psychoanalysts, had no interest in analytic training, was slightly mocking, in his amiable and charming manner, of Freud's "emphasis on sexuality." He lived alone. During his sixth session (the one preceding his first dream), he told me that he suffered "with a mild case of premature ejaculation."

The psychodynamic picture was that of an oedipal fixation defensively handled through regression to anality. The clinical picture was one of an obsessive–compulsive character neurosis moderate in severity. He was the son of a very young mother who was beautiful, loving, and deliberately or inadvertently seductive; and the son of an equally attractive, loving, and tender father. He had suffered the trauma of a sibling entering his life at the height of the anal stage. Mainly because of these two facts (love for the "stunning" mother and anger at her for betraying little Oedipus by loving her husband and giving birth to another child; love for the glamorous father and anger at him), an otherwise commonplace oedipal fixation had become particularly intense.

"Brown Reddish Urine"

> I was in bed with this woman. I suddenly urinated brown-reddish urine on the floor, dirtying it all up. I was not upset, indifferent might be the right word.

The dream was told in the seventh session of therapy and was C's first dream. C had been coming once a week and was not using the couch yet. He told me the dream at the very beginning of the session. "Well, well, well, Sigismondo" (i.e., Freud), "I had my first dream, but nothing to get excited about." He told me the dream, then told me that he was suffering with a minor bladder infection, and one of the symptoms had been some blood in the urine, so it was a "very simple, obvious dream, nothing to get very excited about." (Thus, twice in five minutes he told me that there was nothing to get "excited" about.) He asked me no questions about the dream, did not refer to the dream again for the remainder of the session and neither did I.

The first two tasks, at this point, were to understand the dream's session and sessions before it, and to understand the session's dream, that is, to know what the dream says. My soliloquy included the following. Telling me twice that there was nothing about his dream to get excited about suggested that the reverse might be true, that something very exciting was happening in the dream, that some parts of C (his id? his superego?) were very "excited." Similarly, that he told me twice that the dream was very simple alerted me to the fact that the dream, of course, was not simple at all. I also thought that the urine in the manifest dream was brown, not just red, and brown is the color of feces, not of blood. "Floor" in the manifest dream could represent the lower parts of a woman's body, the pelvic region of the woman he was in bed with; and that "dirtying it all up" could be the concrete pictorial representation of the wish to do exactly that, to dirty, soil, and defile that woman. He was not, in the manifest dream, "upset" ("indifferent might be the right word," he had said), which suggested that the opposite might be true in the latent dream. This correlated with my thoughts about the double protestation that there was "nothing to get very excited about" concerning his dream. From the little I knew at the time about his mother ("stunningly beautiful," a strong woman, rigorous and demanding, "not a piece of fluff"), I conjectured that the woman in the dream could indeed be mother. I tentatively opined that the dream's latent wishes were phallic, anal, and urethral drives toward the mother of his preoedipal and oedipal years. I hypothesized that he wished to ejaculate prematurely ("suddenly") not semen, but urine: fecal ("brown") and angry ("reddish") urine onto mother's lower body parts ("floor"). I also thought that the dream's content correlated well with the psychodynamics of his presenting symptom, premature ejaculation: the abruptness of the urination (manifest dream) dovetailed with the precipitousness of his premature ejaculations. The manifest content represented the premature ejaculator's unconscious feeling that mother must not be denied, must be given in to, must be instantaneously pleased by immediate compliance, and, simultaneously, frustrated by ejaculating prematurely. The displacement of "loving" semen to "dirty" urine paralleled the premature ejaculator's regression from loving phallic drives to aggressive and defiling anal and urethral drives.

The third task was to respond to the dream, and to know what to say to the patient about the dream. Having tentatively understood what C's dream said, I had to decide what to say to C about his dream, if anything, and whether to respond to the dream with an intervention or an interpretation. Again, this being a first dream, the application of the cardinal rule was out of the question. I felt C was a cooperative, motivated patient who would most probably continue telling me dreams: silence would be appropriate (besides, he had asked no questions about the dream and had not referred to it during the rest of the session). I decided to say nothing; but I felt and thought that it was a dream to file and remember because it was C's first dream, and first dreams often have a way of encapsulating the core of the patient's neurosis.

"On the Lake"

"On the Lake" was dreamed about four years after "Brown-Reddish Urine," C had been in analysis a little over four years. Through the first year of therapy, C had been coming once, then twice a week; during the three years which preceded this dream he had been coming three times a week.

In this therapy period, C told me that his father was indeed an energetic, assertive man, a "Type A personality," handsome and elegant, loving and humorous. He was a very large man, unusually tall for an Italian (he had been a basketball player at school). He owned a very profitable factory on the outskirts of the city and much real estate in town, was fairly cultured and well read. C remembered little on his own about the fact that his father had been very loving of him, but first-hand memories about it began to emerge as we went on. In speaking of his mother, C told me again numerous times that she was very beautiful; that in her breathless, ecstatic, seemingly undemanding way, she was quite strong and got what she wanted both from the children and from her husband, and "got it pronto because she was everybody's beloved and because she was what she was: a very determined and headstrong woman." His father adored her and she adored father; father and mother were very affectionate toward

each other in front of the children, "appropriately so, never indecently or exhibitionistically." At home, in private, she was not
very careful about being fully dressed, "not that I ever saw her in
her birthday suit, never, but, you know, her house robe might
not be fully closed, or her pajama top would be partly unbut-
toned." When father died, mother suffered terribly and maybe
"she let me and my baby sister sleep with her more than she
would have otherwise because she missed Dad an awful lot." He
told me that he remembered vividly his sister's birth (he was 4
years old). He did not like her much at first; for a few months
he wet the bed at night, "but both father and mother were very
good about it."

C also told me that his older sisters had been "ordinarily
loving and protective." He had had a happy and essentially un-
eventful life both in Italy and later in the United States. He was
a very good student, likable, athletic, popular. Later on in this
therapy period, however, I learned that he had had a period of
excessive religiosity and obsessive scrupulousness around puberty.
Also once, at 16, he had had a fairly severe anxiety attack which
had not been recognized as such at the time. In this attack, upon
awakening one morning, he developed shortness of breath, began
to hyperventilate, and felt very dizzy; he thought he was going to
have a heart attack, "like Dad" and felt very fearful. He attributed
the anxiety to his belief that he was about to die. When the symptoms abated a few hours later, he concluded that they had been
caused by the exertion of a swimming competition the day before
in which he had placed second. (Later, I learned that the night
before the attack, he had had his first sexual experience with a
prostitute, had ejaculated almost immediately, and the woman
had gently teased him.) He also told me that he had had two
anxiety attacks in the first months after his arrival in the United
States; that during the two years when he was getting acclimated
to life in this country and taking premedical courses in college,
his obsessiveness in studying "for the first time ever" almost got
in the way of achieving his usual high grades and "mother was
very disturbed about it."

During this therapy period, C was still successfully practicing
general psychiatry and was ostensibly happy and well adjusted.
About three years into therapy (one year before the "On the

Lake" dream) he had started a relationship with a woman about ten years younger (29). She was a lawyer, born in the United States of Italian parents, and an attractive, affirming, elegant, affectionate woman. C seemed genuinely fond of her and she of him. She had never been married before and they did not live together, "she values her independence as much as I do," but traveled together for skiing trips and once went to Italy together. The relationship was sexual, C was frequently premature in his ejaculation. It was during this therapy period that I also learned that C masturbated almost daily and frequently felt dizzy afterward. In therapy, C continued being eager to please me, wanting to be a good patient, wishing to make a good impression, but, again, without being deferential or obsequious. He would still occasionally tease me about this or that, but not in an obnoxious fashion. He rarely missed sessions and was compulsively punctual with time and payments. He brought in a dream about every three or four sessions. The therapeutic alliance was strong, transference toward me was primarily a paternal transference, and it included both fairly strong positive dimensions and subtle, not strong, negative ones. There were positive and negative maternal transferential dimensions toward Mary, his woman friend.

In the two to three months preceding the dream, C's transferential feelings had become stronger. The positive dimensions of the paternal transference included the feeling that I liked, respected, and admired him; while I did like and respect him, he aggrandized my feelings somewhat. The negative dimensions of the father transference, stronger than before but still subtle and mostly covert, manifested themselves in his teasing me more frequently. Just a few sessions before the dream, I had dressed more formally for a special occasion and he needled me in a slightly more biting way about my attire. Concerning the mother transference, while he and Mary continued to like and enjoy each other, there had been some acting out of unconscious feelings on his part. Just a few weeks before the dream, he had forgotten her birthday (C was not a man to forget anniversaries), and a number of times had acted toward her thoughtlessly and impulsively, which, again, was not C's characteristic or characterologic style. Three or four times, in describing his interactions with Mary, he used, to describe his behavior, the expressions "half-cocked" and "cockamamie," without the slightest awareness of the implications of those words; and premature ejaculation had been more frequent and more severe.

In the session preceding the dream, a Thursday, C told me that his mother, "just 63, and still stunningly beautiful," had just written to him. She had met a widower, a wealthy businessman more or less her age, and was going to go out with him. He added: "Can you imagine it, your 'old lady' dating? Dating a man, for the first time since Dad died, 33 years ago—well, the first time as far as I know, unless I have been asleep all these years." He reminisced about the summer home on the lake, which the family still owned, and the family's old boat, which had long been sold off, and added, "She did not write that to me, of course, but maybe this old goat is a sailor too, like Dad was—I wonder if they will go out sailing."

The dream's session was on the following Monday. C was uncharacteristically somber and serious. He told me the dream almost immediately.

"On the Lake"

> A huge, big, really big man, running recklessly, like a chicken without a head—ludicrous, because he was all dressed up, businessman "uniform," so to speak: a pin-striped, three-piece suit, watch-and-chain, brief case—a grown man, not a kid, running toward this boat and jumping into it with both feet, again like a little child would. The boat tilted dangerously. I woke up feeling dizzy.

For a few minutes after telling me the dream he was silent. He then told me that he and Mary had watched *An American Tragedy* on TV that weekend, and that the male protagonist, out on a boat on a lake with his fiancée, tipped the boat to drown her. Next he remembered being 8 or 9. It was summertime and he, his mother, and his favorite uncle, his father's younger brother, were leisurely riding in the motor boat on the lake where the family's summer home was. He remembered he had just eaten. As he was falling asleep, he caught sight of his mother dozing on a chaise lounge, "a seraphic smile on her lips." He carried on and on about the stupidity of the businessman of the dream, the way he jumped with both feet into the boat, "rocking the boat," acting like a kid, "What did he think he was, a kid of 5?" and about the incongruity of someone fully dressed "in the businessman's uniform" acting like that, and in a boat too. He added that that night, he had been "awfully premature" in making love and when he tried to make love again, he could not have an erection. He also said, "How strange, that I felt dizzy when I awoke." He then asked me what I thought the dream was all about.

The first two tasks at this point were to understand the dream session and sessions before it, and to understand the session's dream; that is, to know what the dream says. In response to the session's dream, my soliloquy included the following thoughts. The "huge, big, really big man" stood for myself, for the businessman he had told me about in the session before the dream's session, and ultimately, for his father (father was tall, an amateur basketball player, a "big man" realistically and of course psychologically: the oedipal father, even if a dwarf physically, is always a giant psychodynamically). The "huge, big man" also stood for C himself, the grandiose oedipal child; "running recklessly" represented the energy, recklessness, and impulsivity of instinctual feelings; "chicken without a head" denoted the unreasoning, feeling-based nature of drives and impulses and also represented (condensation, again) castration, the punishment for the acting out of such drives and impulses; "chicken without a head" together with "ludicrous" expressed his hostility against the three of us (father, businessman, and myself). I also thought that the manifest dream's detail about the businessman's "uniform" was a reference to me whom he had recently needled for my formal attire. His describing the businessman as "not a kid," and the businessman's jumping into the boat "like a little child would," indicated that the businessman was, indeed, not only the businessman himself, father, and me, but also "a kid," that is C. "Jumping (into the boat) with both feet" portrayed decisiveness, lack of ambivalence. The fact that "the boat tilted dangerously" was a way of saying that the latent action of the dream was indeed powerful, pleasurable, and conflictual enough to "rock" the (psychic) boat, his mind, and to deserve indeed, the punishment of castration. My soliloquy also included the thought that his mother's letter, about which he had told me the previous Thursday, and over which he had had time to think and feel a great deal on all levels of consciousness for an entire weekend, had indeed had a powerful effect. The dream seemed connected with and could have been triggered by mother's letter and the news that she was going to go out with the businessman.

In response to the dream's sessions, my soliloquy included the following thoughts. The fact that the major association to the dream was the memory of a boat trip when he was 8 or 9, suggested that something psychodynamically important might have occurred on a boat trip at an earlier time, when C was younger than 8 or 9 (all dreams have an "infantile source"). Since the memory was a voyeuristic memory, "catching sight of mother dozing on the chaise lounge with a seraphic smile on her lips," then the psychodynamically important incident which had occurred on the earlier boat trip had probably included a voyeuristic incident. Therefore, the memory of the experience at 8 or 9 had to be a screen memory of another, repressed, and therefore more intense experience which had occurred earlier on, probably when he was 5. He had said of the businessman acting like a kid, "What did he think he was, a kid of 5?" His going on and on after the dream about the "businessman's uniform" was, again, connected with his teasing me about my formal attire on a recent occasion. Having watched *An American Tragedy* the night before the dream had overcathected unconscious feelings against the oedipal mother who had betrayed him with father, and now with this "old goat." Mother's letter had overcathected unconscious erotic feelings toward the beautiful and stunning oedipal mother. No wonder the night before the dream he had been more impotent, sexually, than usual: *An American Tragedy* and mother's letter had touched enough unconscious chords to worsen his sexual disability.

In response to the session before the dream, my internal soliloquy included the following thoughts. He needed to remind me, once more, that mother even at 63 years of age, was still "stunningly beautiful." His saying, "Maybe I have been asleep all these years," could have meant that he was suddenly doubtful of his mother's "virtue" in not having dated anyone in the 33 years that had passed since his father's death, and, at the same time, was a subtle reference to all that he had repressed, concerning mother, over the last 33 years. His likening this man to father ("Maybe this old goat is a sailor too, like Dad was") confirmed my belief that the manifest dream's businessman was C's father in the latent dream; that his calling this man "an old goat" was a transparent representation of his anger at this man and at the oedipal father.

In response to all the sessions before the dream's session in the therapy period being considered here, my internal soliloquy included everything that I found myself *selectively* remembering and *selectively* resonating with. His father was a tall, large, big man, big on the basketball court (big "balls" for mother's beautiful "basket"), big in terms of financial and business success, that is, a very "potent" man, potent sexually and nonsexually, a man by whom the competitive oedipal child could easily feel defeated, a man vis-à-vis whom the emulous oedipal child could easily feel *second.* I thought that his anxiety attack, at 16, had come the day after the morning in which he arrived *second* in a swimming race, the day after the night he had been impotent, that is, *"second"* with a prostitute. In his anxiety attack he had felt dizzy, and he felt dizzy consistently after he masturbated, and he had awakened from the dream feeling dizzy. His father and mother were "very affectionate toward each other in front of the children," and this may have made little Oedipus feel mad (dizzy?) with desire and jealousy. In saying that to me, he had added, "they were appropriately affectionate, never indecently or exhibitionistically," which suggested unconscious voyeuristic fantasies which he needed to deny.

In response to all the sessions before the dream's session in the several years of this therapy period, I further thought that competitiveness against father, at least in the intellectual arena (C was a physician; father had "only" achieved the equivalent of a bachelor's degree), had been suggested by C's saying that his father "was *fairly* cultured" (emphasis added). Unconscious guilt both over his unconscious aggressive competitiveness with father and over father's premature death (unconscious death wishes) was suggested by C's feeling, during the anxiety attack at 16, that he was about to have a heart attack and die, "like Dad." This was further suggested by his behavior (sullen and surly, morose and cantankerous) for several weeks after his death. Concerning C's mother, I found myself *selectively* remembering and resonating with the fact that he had continued to remind me of how beautiful his mother was; that she "was not very careful about being fully dressed," that is, that she had overcathected his voyeuristic impulses. His adding, "not that I ever saw her in her birthday suit, never" was a double denial suggesting strong, unconscious desires to indeed see her in her "birthday suit." The fact that his mother got from her children and her husband what she wanted pronto, correlated with a personality characteristic fairly common in mothers of men suffering with premature ejaculation. I finally thought that in his interactions with Mary, the major maternal transferential figure in his life, he was still experiencing sexual difficulties; that his expressions concerning his behavior (or misbehavior) with her, showed that he felt, with her, inferior to father ("half-cocked," only half a sexual male), and strongly connected with mother ("cockamamie").

My soliloquy temporarily concluded, I tentatively assumed that the dream's latent content was about C's oedipal libidinal and aggressive drives toward his mother and aggressive drives toward his father; that these drives went back to age 5 and included a strong voyeuristic component, that is, the drive to watch something libidinal and aggressive concerning mother. Whatever he had wished to do or had actually done, had been done recklessly and unambivalently, "with both feet." These drives were powerful enough to rock his psychic boat or, in their enactment, the boat itself. I also tentatively decided that, if what he remembered having happened when he was 8 or 9 indeed was, as I believed, a screen memory for something that had happened when he was 5, the dream offered one more opening onto the royal road to where, in C's unconscious, lay the still repressed memory of what happened when he was 5.

The third task was to respond to the dream, and to know what to say to the patient about the dream. I had now to decide if the dream should be responded to with silence, interventions, or interpretations: and, if interpretations were warranted, whether they should be on the level of the drives, on the level of the defenses, and within the context of the transference. My internal thinking included the following thoughts. He had asked me what the dream was about. The therapeutic alliance was very solid and so was C's ego, but the transference was only fairly developed. In the last two to three months before the dream, the positive dimensions of the paternal transference had become stronger, but the negative dimensions were still subtle and mostly covert. This, to an extent, militated against a full application of the cardinal rule.

But what I thought and felt most intensely was that C was ready to remember something psychodynamically more important than what he had actually remembered in the dream's session, something which had happened earlier than when he was 8 or 9, something which had happened when he was 5, something that was "pathogenic," and contributed to his pain, to his neurosis. I thought and felt that the dream, and the associations to it, were an invitation to venture further onto the royal road to the unconscious, an invitation not to be refused. C was asking to be helped to remember more, was asking to be helped to make the unconscious conscious, which is, after all, a central task of psychoanalytic psychotherapy. "[T]he task of psycho-analytic treatment can be expressed in this formula: its task is to make conscious everything that is pathogenically unconscious" (Freud, 1916b, p. 282). Thus, I decided that I would only hint, indirectly, at the latent meaning of the dream, and use the dream mainly to help him remember that which was still "pathogenic." I said:

> My hunch is that the dream, and the boat memory of when you were 8 or 9, are about something pleasurable that you wished to do, or see, when you were a kid, something that you might be able, now, to remember; something pleasurable and, you thought, reckless; something so pleasurable and, you thought, so reckless, that just the thought of it made you dizzy, dizzy as you feel when you masturbate.

It was an "intervention," in that it aimed at helping him to move further on the royal road to the unconscious; and it was an "interpretation" only in that it alluded to latent wishes behind the manifest dream. It was a response on the level of the drives and not within the context of the transference. I tried scrupulously to "measure" each and every word in the response for maximum positive effect and minimum negative impact. Thus, I referred to my thoughts about the dream as a "hunch" in order

to weaken their impact on him in the event I was countertransferentially mistaken about his readiness to hear those thoughts. In
referring to the "recklessness" of the dream's latent wish, I repeated, twice, "you thought," in order to suggest, again, "just in
case," that his behavior was not as reckless as he felt it to be.
Because of the fact that the negative dimensions of the paternal
transference, as they were being acted out with me in therapy,
were still subtle and mostly covert, I chose not to use the dream
to work on his hostile and competitive feelings about his father;
but I did use the word *kid* because he had referred to the businessman (i.e., his father and myself) as "the old goat" (a kid is a
young goat), in order to prepare the ground for when I could
help him see, at some later time, that he, the kid, the "young
goat," was indeed competing with us old goats. Because of the
fact that the negative dimensions of his maternal transference (as
they were being acted out with Mary) were still too indirect, I
chose not to refer to his associations about *An American Tragedy*;
and I did not use the greatest majority of the thoughts and feelings I had had in my internal soliloquy. But I did clearly refer to
the boat memory of age 8 to 9 as a starting point to recover
memories going back to age 5. I directly touched on the voyeuristic components of the earlier experience ("something pleasurable you wished to do, or see"). I unambiguously connected his
dizziness after masturbation and his dizziness in the dream to
whatever had happened when he was 5, as this was the incident
the repressed memory of which was, I believed, a pathogenic element in his unconscious.

It worked. After two to three minutes of silence, C stammered
through a memory of when he was about 5, and his father still
alive. It was the early afternoon of a hot summer day, the family
had been riding through the lake and, after lunch, the boat was
anchored at a buoy in the middle of the lake. Father was on deck,
fishing, mother, in a bathing suit, was in the shade on a deck
mat, a smile on her face, looking at father invitingly. Suddenly,
father laughed, put his fishing gear away, took mother by the
hand and went below deck with her. C felt "funny," excited, hot,
dizzy. A few seconds later, with a slightly trembling voice, C said
that he "may have gone below deck myself." After this last statement (which was quite a statement: as we shall see, six months

later he remembered that he did go below deck, trying to hear and *see* what his parents were doing in their little cabin), C was silent for a few minutes. It was now close to the end of the hour. I said, "I am glad you remembered more. And I have another hunch: that one day soon you will be able to remember more about that hot afternoon on the lake." He said, "Do you get that from the dream?" I said: "Yes, from the dream; and from the many things you have been saying over the last several months" (see Sharpe [1978, p. 151] regarding the use of a dream to stimulate recollection of earlier memories).

Theoretical Appendix: Some of the Dream Work Defenses

From the dream's manifest content:

A huge, big man: concrete pictorial representation of power, potency, and powerful drives; displacement from father; condensation into one image of mother's new male friend, therapist, father, and grandiose oedipal child.
Really big: secondary elaboration; defensive in that, by emphasizing the "realistic" bigness, it underplays its psychological bigness.
Running: concrete pictorial representation of urgency of drives and of the accelerated "urgency" of the premature ejaculator's drives.
Running recklessly: concrete pictorial representation of the energy, impulsivity, and recklessness of instinctual drives.
Chicken without a head: concrete pictorial representation of the unreasoning, unthinking, visceral, feeling-based nature of instinctual impulses; symbolism for castration; condensation of the two concepts (unreasoning, unthinking, etc., and castration) into one image.
Businessman: displacement from father and condensation into one image of mother's new, male friend, therapist, father, and grandiose oedipal child.
Not a kid: denial, but to the extent that the businessman is also the grandiose oedipal child, the businessman is indeed a kid.
Boat: symbolism for mother.
Jumping into boat: concrete pictorial representation of urgency of drives.

Both feet: concrete pictorial representation of decisiveness and lack of ambivalence.

Feet: symbolism for penis, metaphor for aggressiveness (in anger, one kicks with one's feet).

The boat tilted dangerously: concrete pictorial representation of "rocking the boat," disturbing the status quo, doing something forbidden and therefore dangerous.

From the associations—one listens to the dream's sessions as if it were a dream:

An American Tragedy (the story): allusion to the wish to kill Mary so he could be with mother or to kill mother so he could be with Mary.

A tragedy: displacement from his own personal "tragedy," his Oedipus complex.

"The Tranquilizer"

This dream was dreamed in C's sixth year of therapy, about two years after the dream just discussed. C had continued coming three times a week. What occurred in this two-year span could be roughly divided into three subperiods:

1. A subperiod, about six months long, which culminated with C revisiting "the scene of the incident" (as he came to call it), the time when he was 5, his father and mother had gone below deck, and C did go below deck himself.
2. A subperiod, also of about six months in duration, during which C recovered important memories of positive and negative feelings about father, a subperiod culminating with C revisiting a second time the "scene of the incident."
3. A subperiod, about twelve months long, during which C talked mainly about his mother, a subperiod culminating with "The Tranquilizer."

During the first of these three subperiods C had been uncharacteristically morose, snappish, and impatient and had difficulty falling asleep. He himself remarked that he was acting and feeling just as his mother had told him he had been acting and feeling right after his father's death. During these six months, there were several dreams in whose manifest content C was underwater, underground, in basements and cellars, in subterranean rooms and understructures, and, once, the engine room, below deck, of course, of a large ocean liner. I thought that in those dreams he was both going into his unconscious and also going "below deck" to see and hear what father and mother were doing in their little cabin. Not wanting to say so openly, I only told him that he was dreaming about his subterranean, underground self, his unconscious. In the last of this series of underground dreams, he dreamed of being in a very large underground cave; he could not remember or tell me anything about the dream, except that the underground cave reminded him of "something of historic significance which he could not place or remember." But, having just said that, he found himself, without any prompting from me, going back to the "scene of the incident." (The expression, "the scene of the incident," is later connected with the last of C's dreams being discussed here.) In a small and shaky voice, he remembered that he had indeed gone below deck himself, had put his ear to the door of the cabin where father and mother were and had heard muffled sounds and hushed moans. Having told me that, he took only a few minutes to recompose himself, seemed relieved, and said, "Well, I guess the old man and Mom were having a real good time." Even though this was not truly a case of having witnessed a primal scene, its recollection was still a powerful event. Yet C was being somewhat casual about it. I thought that in the underground of his psyche there were still more feelings and thoughts that he needed to deny. Still, the recovery of this memory was important: it opened the way to other memories concerning his father.

In the second subperiod, also lasting about six months, C did indeed share with me significant material about his father. He told me that his father had been an experienced snorkeler and did underwater fishing. When C was about 5, the family had gone to Sicily and he and his sisters had watched father diving from a boat to fish underwater. It was "exciting and scary" to see father emerge "from the deep," with a fish still wiggling on his harpoon. His father was scrupulous about him or his sisters not touching his underwater gun because of the dangers inherent in doing so. C had wanted to do underwater fishing with father and father had promised that he would teach him when he was older. (He added: "My father was very serious about it; Dad was always serious when he made promises to me.") As he recollected these memories, he was clearly moved and told me how much he loved and admired his father.

Having remembered more of the positive aspects of his relationship to his father obviously strengthened his ego enough to enable him to go back to the "scene of the incident" and tell me more about it and his feelings about father and mother. He remembered that when he heard the faint sounds coming from within the cabin he felt "hot and excited and began rubbing his penis against the door"; that he felt angry at both father and mother and may have wished both of his parents dead. He was being much more emotional this time; he said he was feeling anger, fear, guilt, sorrow, remorse. In a shaky voice, breathing rapidly, he remained very tense for several minutes (no rapid recovery or quick shift to casualness, this time). He then added, very sadly, "Yes, I may have wished him dead; and he did die, about one year later. I wonder how guilty I felt when he did." Up to this time, he had not actually remembered that for several weeks after father had died he had been morose, grouchy, and cantankerous; he remembered it now. I asked him to think about the way he had felt then and the way he had been feeling during the previous six to nine months. He saw the similarity, and said, "I guess that by remembering the incident, remembering it with feeling this time, I am reliving the anger at my father but also the love I had for him and he for me, the guilt I felt for my bad wishes, and the feelings of loss I had, at least semiconsciously, when he died."

It was around this time that another unconscious memory became conscious. As he was, once again, reminiscing about "the incident," and, specifically, as he was recalling putting his ear to the door, he suddenly recognized the "underground cave of historical significance" of a recent dream. "Holy Cow!" he burst out, "It was L'Orecchio di Dionigi, 'Dionysius' ear'!" He remembered that in the year the family had gone to Sicily, they had visited, among other places, the town of Syracuse and one of its attractions, "L'Orecchio di Dionigi," the cave of Dionysius I, the ruler of Syracuse around 400 B.C. He remembered having been greatly impressed by the story his father told about the cave; he was then 5 years old. The cave was (still is) a large, deep, underground space, with a barely visible opening at the top. Dionysius kept his political prisoners in this huge cave. The cave's acoustic properties were such that even whispers by the occupants carried upward to the invisible opening, to which Dionysius kept his ear to hear what the prisoners might reveal. It was a few weeks after the trip to Sicily that "the incident" on the lake had occurred. I said: "When you were eavesdropping at the cabin door, maybe, you wished your parents were the prisoners and you the powerful ruler—and you may have accomplished exactly that in your dream. After all, the cave is of 'historical significance' and so was the incident on the boat when you were 5." (I wanted to say, "And who is the 'holy cow,' your Mom?" but virtuously restrained myself.)

Concerning his mother, in the second but especially in the third subperiod of this therapy span, C continued to remind me that mother was "stunningly" beautiful, but also told me that she was indeed a very determined woman, firm and decisive, gracious and charming, but resolute and single minded. She missed her dead husband greatly but still was able to resume schooling "only two years after his death," be a superior student, and, after receiving her advanced degree, perform brilliantly as a teacher. She did not marry again, not only out of devotion to her late husband, but also to devote herself to the children, "especially to me, her only son." He also told me that her being so devoted to him was, at the time, a burden to him; that she never thought his girl friends were good enough for him; that she could be possessive of him, and that her being critical of his girl friends was her way of trying to keep him all for herself. It was never a question of disobeying her, because she made no prohibitions that did not make sense to him too, but, rather, a problem of not disappointing her because he knew she wanted him to excel and that at times that was a burden too. He added that she was fairly quick with criticism when his performance was not excellent, but was not as quick with compliments when he had done very well.

"Sometimes I had to wait a couple of days to get some appreciation." Earlier on in this subperiod of therapy, critical comments about mother were expressed with many qualifications; for instance, in talking about her not remarrying to devote herself to him, he added, "I don't know whether she actually conveyed this to me or I imagined it all on my own"; in saying that he wanted to excel to please her, he further said, "but, then, I myself liked to excel"; in referring to her propensity to be critical, he softened the remarks by saying, "but she always expressed her criticism gently." Later on, the caveats diminished or disappeared altogether and he would say, for instance, "She was beautiful, and very sweet, really, with that breathless, ecstatic quality about her, but she could be a pain in the neck—a sweet pain in the neck but a pain in the neck nevertheless." C also told me that his mother wrote to him every two weeks and wanted him to do the same. She was quick to complain if he did not, and that irritated him as well as made him feel guilty; lately he had resorted to dashing off "a quickie" to her every two weeks, "nothing substantial, just enough to keep her happy"; she "pestered him" about getting a university appointment[7] and publishing some articles. Only once or twice did he refer to her seeing the wealthy "old goat" about whom he had talked just before the previous dream ("On the Lake"). Apparently the relationship had not progressed beyond three or four meetings a month for theater and dinner out, or a cocktail party, or a visit to a museum or art gallery. C did not believe it had become a romantic or sexual relationship, professed being open to it if it became that, did not seem too invested in the subject.

During this two-year period, C's feelings and behavior with me and with Mary fluctuated in parallel with the vicissitudes of the analysis. He and Mary were not living together but were "talking about it" more and more often. Early on in this period of therapy, his sexual difficulties with her had increased and he was as snappish and morose with her as he was in general. With me, he was curt, abrupt, and impatient through most sessions, more

---

[7]In Italy, a medical specialist has not truly "arrived" unless he or she is a "Libero Docente," that is, has a university appointment or, even better, is the head of a department within the university medical school.

restrained in his snappishness at the end of the session, and almost affable and actually "sweet" at the end of the last session of the week, as if he needed to end those sessions, or the therapy's week, on a good note. He remembered that as a child or adolescent, he had rarely been angry or annoyed at either father or mother; but if he had been, it was important to "get a good night kiss" and go to bed "at peace." Thus, his reaction to me was part of the transference neurosis. During this period, two or three times he expressed concerns about my health. Once he said, "I hope you exercise enough. But, then, so did my father and, still, he died young." Thus, these concerns too were part of the paternal transference, positive and negative, which was being overcathected by what he had been remembering better and better about his father. Later on in this period of therapy, and especially after he had remembered, this time with intense feelings, "the incident," he became again loving and attentive toward Mary and was sexually impotent less frequently (he also masturbated less frequently and rarely felt dizzy afterwards).

In the last six months or so before the dream, around the time in which he had become more openly critical of his mother, the time when the caveats which had previously softened his criticism had begun to disappear, he told me that Mary had difficulty climaxing, whether through intercourse or when he fondled her, and that this had always been a problem for her. While he told me about Mary's sexual disability in a very empathic manner, at the same time he had me know that because of Mary's "difficulty" he had to wait before he could climax himself, and that frequently caused him to lose his erection. Also in this period of time, he began to experience me as "too ambitious for him" and "demanding"; felt that I wanted him to teach and to publish[8], felt it was a burden to live up to my expectations of him. These criticisms were never experienced or expressed with strong feelings;

---

[8]Of course, his mother had been "ambitious" for him and "demanding" of him, and so was his internalization of her into his superego. But, he knew that I taught at Fordham University; once, when he had told me he enjoyed teaching at Grand Rounds, I had asked him whether he would enjoy teaching regularly; and once, after he had told me that he had given "a beautiful speech," I asked him whether he would like to publish it. While the first transference's contamination (his knowing of my teaching at Fordham) was inevitable, the other two (my asking him whether he would enjoy teaching regularly and whether he would like to publish his speech) were not, and are good examples of collusion between the analyst's and the patient's superego.

they were nevertheless experienced and expressed: the mother transference was, clearly, developing.

And then an interesting incident occurred, which was the final overcathecter for the dream soon to be dreamed.[9] About three weeks before the dream, I had to ask him to change the time of one of his three weekly sessions to a later hour. C lived in a suburb of New York City and on the evenings of the session in question, he came to see me just after leaving his office for the day and before heading back home. One realistic consequence, for him, of the change in time, was that he had to wait in town for about one hour between the end of his day of work and his session with me and his trip back home. Nevertheless, he agreed very readily (too readily, I thought) but then twice, in the three following weeks, he let me know (subtly, not angrily, with many caveats and qualifications), that the change had inconvenienced him. Thus was the intrapsychic, interpersonal, and transferential scene set for the opening of the curtain on the third of his quartet of dreams.

The dream's session was, again, on the first day of the analytical week. C entered the room with a happy, self-contented, slightly smug smile on his face and told me the dream as soon as he lay on the couch.

"The Tranquilizer"

> I was dispensing a tranquilizer, Rauwolfia Serpentina (you know, Reserpine) to a patient of mine, Joan. Actually I had reserved it for another patient of mine, Helen, she had insisted that I reserve it for her. But I thought, what the hell, Helen can wait.

C went on: "Reserpine, strange to dispense that nowadays—a derivative of Rauwolfia Serpentina, of course, an old-time drug, it goes back to the fifties, hardly used today as a psychotropic drug, it's mainly an antihypertension drug. Three tablets, three tablets of Rauwolfia, the brand name is Reserpine, as you old-timers may remember." In further elaborating about the dream,

---

[9]Another good example of how truly accidental (?) incidents are processed, by the unconscious, in highly personal, idiosyncratic ways and thus become unwittingly overcathecters of all sorts of unconscious material.

C told me that "the three tablets of Rauwolfia Serpentina were in a very messy drawer of my desk. I am getting better in that department too, cleaner and neater; but in the dream that drawer was like in the old days, a truly holy mess." Joan was a young patient of his, nice and attractive, "probably in love with me," he said. Helen was an older woman, "depressed and depressing, still stunningly attractive, haughty and demanding, the typical Park Avenue pain in the neck" (yes, he did say "stunning" and "pain in the neck," the same words he had been using about his mother). Helen intimidated him, so he was glad he was capable, in the dream, of keeping her waiting, "that too was a good sign." He then asked me, somewhat perfunctorily, what did I think the dream meant. When I deflected the question by asking him to go on with whatever came to his mind, he began to talk about matters ostensibly not connected to the dream. About ten minutes before the end of the session, he expressed thoughts and feelings that allowed me to respond with an interpretation on the level of the drives and within the context of the transference. But before that, let us follow the internal processes leading me to my intervention.

The first two tasks at this point were to understand the dream session and sessions before it, and to understand the session's dream, that is, to know what the dream says.

In response to the session's dream and in response to the dream's session, my internal soliloquy included these thoughts. Some of the words he used (*dispensing, tablets, psychotropic,* etc.) were stilted, "medical," "distancing," "retentive," not in keeping with the more flowing "what the hell," "holy mess" expressions or with the contented, slightly smug demeanor he had as he lay on the couch. Repeating the terms *Rauwolfia Serpentina* and *Reserpine* at least three times was probably a clue to the symbolic importance of those terms. "Rauwolfia" could be an onomatopoeic expression for C's sexuality, the raw, naked wolf inside him, and "Serpentina," another for the sneaky, snaky, phallic C; and the fact that there were *three* Reserpines (three being a common symbol of male genitals), strengthened the probability that the tranquilizer represented sexuality. "Reserpine" made me think, also onomatopoeically, of "reserved penis," the penis he had to reserve for mother (in the manifest dream he was supposed to reserve three Reserpines for Helen). In pointing out that Reserpine was an old drug and referring to me as an old-timer hinted at the infantile sources of the dream. I also felt that Joan ("young and attractive") and Helen ("stunning," "a pain in the neck," and "intimidating") stood for his mother and, through the transference, for Mary and me. In keeping Helen waiting, he was keeping his mother, and me, waiting. The wish to "dispense" the tranquilizer ("dispense" his naked self, his phallic self) corresponded to the latent wish to tranquilize mother, soothe mother, lower her anger. C saw his sexuality both as a soothing, tranquilizing agent but also as a provocative, dirty one. The messy drawer of the manifest dream may have stood for dirty pants, or diapers, in the latent dream. I finally conjectured that in deciding, "What the hell, Helen can wait," there was indeed, as he himself had said, a prognostication of improvement in his premature ejaculation, as there was in his decision to defy Helen, an auger of amelioration in his timidity.

In response to the sessions immediately preceding the dream, my soliloquy included the following thoughts. More and more, in the six months or so preceding the dream, he had been talking of his mother as "possessive," "obsessional" about his writing to her, "demanding" about his getting a university appointment and publishing. Also, he had told me that he had resorted to "dashing off a quickie (note) to her—to keep her happy"; and to "dash off a quickie" was a telling expression for someone with premature ejaculation. "To keep her (mother) happy" correlated with the giving of tranquilizers in the manifest dream. My soliloquy also included that more and more in the six months or so preceding the dream, he had been experiencing *me* as possessive, demanding, critical, too ambitious for him, wanting him to teach and publish, a burden. He had been experiencing me as ambivalently as he experienced Helen, Mary, and his mother in his current interpersonal world and his preoedipal mother in his unconscious and intrapsychic world. Thus, I reasoned internally, the negative maternal transference had indeed developed and it was a crucial overcathecter of the dream. I further thought that the material concerning Mary's keeping him waiting because of her difficulty with climaxing also connected with the dream where C is debating whom *he* is going to keep waiting. Memories of mother keeping him waiting for compliments and affirmation was also one of the sources of the dream. An immediate overcathecter of the dream (only three weeks before the dream) had been to change his therapy hour. It made him experience me as the authoritarian mother of his unconscious, one more person who had the power to inconvenience him, to keep him waiting.

And finally, in response to all the sessions in the two-year therapy span preceding this dream, my internal soliloquy included, again, all of which I found myself selectively remembering and selectively resonating with. As I listened to the dream, I found myself thinking that in the twelve months or so preceding this dream, he had mostly talked about his mother. He had subtly reproached mother for going back to school "only" two years after father's death. His anger at mother for being demanding, possessive, too ambitious for him, "a sweet pain in the neck but a pain in the neck nevertheless" had become increasingly less subtle and less softened with qualifications and caveats. He had openly said that being "special" to mother was a burden in that it made him feel he had to make mother also "special" to him, and indeed, "reserve" himself for mother. More and more, in those twelve months, he had been experiencing me as his mother.

My soliloquy temporarily terminated, I tentatively concluded that the dream's latent content had to do with libidinal aggressive drives about his mother and that many drives were condensed in the dream. There was the oedipal drive to give his mother his primitive, raw, wolflike ("rauwolfia"), snaky-phallic ("Serpentina") self. There was the anal drive to give to his mother a dirty fecal penis just gotten out of his dirty, messy pants ("drawer"). There was the oedipal and preoedipal drive not to deny mother, to give mother anything she desired, after all his penis was reserved ("Reserpine") for her. And, there was the oedipal and the preoedipal drive to give to mother both to please himself and to tranquilize her; the preoedipal drive *not* to give to mother, to deny mother, to tease mother, to frustrate mother. He still needed and wished to see his penis as dirty, messy, poisonous (i.e., as an excretory and hateful organ rather than as an ejaculatory and loving one), which confirmed my hunch that the dream had more preoedipal than oedipal sources. I also surmised that Joan and Helen in the manifest dream and Mary and myself in C's current life were all transferential condensations of mother.

The third task was to respond to the dream, and to know what to say to the patient about the dream. It was now about ten minutes before the end of the session, and I had to decide if the dream should be responded to with silence, an intervention, or an interpretation. And if an interpretation was warranted, should it be on the level of the drives—but, which of the many drives I had thought about in my soliloquy, the oedipal, the preoedipal? Or should it be on the level of the defenses and within the context of the transference?

My internal thinking now included that the therapeutic alliance was solid and so was C's ego. The paternal transference had become positive again. The negative maternal transference could be worked on with relative impunity because of the strong therapeutic alliance and the strong paternal positive transference. Thus it seemed that the cardinal rule should and could be applied, and that an interpretation on the level of the drives and within the context of the transference would be appropriate. But, again, which drives, oedipal or preoedipal? I found myself thinking that both in the dream and at least in the year preceding the dream, preoedipal material had been more prominent than oedipal material; and that preoedipal feelings about and against mother had been more conspicuous than oedipal anger at father or oedipal desires toward mother. This had been especially so since the time, about twelve months before the dream, when C had revisited a second time, and this time with much more emotion, the "scene of the incident." Having remembered the feelings of desire, rivalry, and anger he had experienced as he had heard father and mother making love, had helped him *temporarily* transcend the oedipal rivalry; helped him recover from his unconscious feelings of love for, and his positive identification with father; and enabled his thus strengthened ego to experience frightening preoedipal feelings about mother. Sexual difficulties, of course, although less severe, were still present; therefore, the oedipal rivalry had obviously been transcended only to an extent. Clearly both preoedipal and oedipal problems still precluded C's full entry into genitality. Because of the above facts, it seemed that preoedipal problems had to take precedence in our work before the oedipal problems could be worked on more fully. Thus, in working with the dream, I felt I would want to respond not so much to the unconscious wish to be sexually loving to mother, but to the unconscious wish to be angry and withholding with mother. Preferably, I would do that through the transference, that is, working on his need to be angry and withholding *with Mary*, and *with me*, or at most with the mother of his current interpersonal world, not on his need to be angry and withholding with the mother of his internal preoedipal world. What he said toward the end of the session, as it often happens when we wait for the patient to give us clues, changed my plan somewhat but made the analytical task easier.

As stated a few pages back, having just asked me, rather perfunctorily, what did I think the dream meant, C had begun to talk about matters seemingly not connected with the dream. Then, about ten minutes before the end of the session, he spoke of having gone to a Broadway show with Mary. "Had to wait five weeks for my seats, I had reserved them five weeks before, but it was a great play, worth waiting for." Then he said, "Things are better sexually with Mary, I am less and less premature. Still, she takes a long time coming." I said, "She keeps you waiting." He said, "Yes, but she is a great girl. Sometimes I think she loves me for my money, which is nonsense. She loves me, she is devoted to me, she is ambitious for me, that sometimes irritates me." I said, "That, and her keeping you waiting, irritates you. Who else has irritated you lately?" I had been expecting, hoping, I guess, for him to have said, "You, of course, changing my therapy hour, which makes me waste a whole hour." But to my surprise (and disappointment) instead he said: "I know, I know, my mother, of course. She too loves me and is devoted to me and is ambitious for me and still can be an absolute pain in the ass."[10] Not unfeelingly, he continued: "Look, until the old goat showed up, all those years since Dad died, there she was, young, beautiful, but lonely, very lonely. All she had were her children, and me, and she needed me, she wanted to keep me all for herself. I could

---

[10]"In the ass," not "in the neck" (penis?) as he had more delicately been saying all along. And of course, it is not the neck that is the obsessive–compulsive's Achilles' heel, another confirmation that at the time of this dream, preoedipal issues were closer to the surface than oedipal ones.

not, I would not, deny her anything, it was pleasurable when I was a young boy, later, maybe, there were too many strings attached."

I could have left it at that. My two interventions (asking him to go on with whatever came to his mind when he had asked me what the dream meant and my asking, "Who else has irritated you lately?") had triggered the above response and resulted in C's becoming more conscious about important thoughts and feelings concerning his mother. Moreover, C's response confirmed my assumptions about the dream's latent meaning and C's internal dynamics. C did feel he had to reserve himself (and his penis: "Reserpine") for mother. The wish to do so was ambivalent, hence the impotence and premature ejaculation. His mother did consciously irritate him and was "a pain," did make him angry, hence, again, the impotence and the anal regressions. His mother did love him and did need him, so he felt he could deny her nothing, but the feeling he could deny her nothing was ambivalent too; mother and Mary paid through C's ambivalence and passive aggressiveness (they were only given "quickies") and C, of course, through his neurosis and its pains, paid the most.

Yes, I could have left it at that. But, as indicated above, I was surprised and a little disappointed by his response. I had expected and hoped for him to say that it was I who had been irritating him with my "possessiveness," "ambitiousness," and "demandingness" of him; that it had been Mary and I who had been angering him by keeping him waiting. I wanted him to become more conscious of his ambivalent feelings about the preoedipal mother experienced as demanding, possessive, and the one "who kept him waiting"—to become conscious of all that through a fuller development of the maternal transference to Mary and me. So I said:

> Yes, you are telling me that you loved your mother, very much, and she loved you, very much, but that, nevertheless, she could be a pain. But you have been also telling me that you love Mary and Mary loves you and she too can be a pain; and that while things are better sexually between the two of you, she "keeps you waiting" with her difficulty in coming and I'll bet that is a pain too. And a few minutes back you told me that you had reserved seats for a Broadway play and you had to wait five weeks before you could finally see the play. And then, I, with my changing the hour I had originally reserved for you, caused you to be kept waiting and that,

too, was a pain. I believe you are angry at Mary and angry at me, that is
the "who else" who has irritated you lately, and angry at us for keeping
you waiting, and angry at us for being possessive and demanding and
ambitious for you. And I also believe you are angry at us for other, more
important reasons, and maybe some of this anger may very well go back
to your Mom. In your dream you are being both loving and angry, giving
and depriving, to Joan and Helen. I feel you are both loving and angry
toward Mary, and want to be both giving and depriving toward her; and
I believe that you both care for me and are angry at me.

It was an interpretation on the level of the drives and
within the context of the transference; a response aimed at
developing the maternal transference further in order to move
him still further down the royal road to the unconscious where
more preoedipal (and oedipal) feelings lay still unanalyzed. By
referring to the positive as well as negative feelings he had
toward me and Mary, I was aiming at the feelings of ambivalence he had toward the preoedipal (and oedipal) mother. I
referred to his having had to wait several weeks before finally
"*seeing*" the Broadway play, "which was worth waiting for,"
first to increase the credibility of the interpretation concerning
the theme of "waiting." This theme of waiting was elaborated
on the conscious level, in waiting for Mary to climax and
waiting for me when his therapy hour was changed; on the
unconscious level, in waiting for his mother to praise and
compliment him, and on a still deeper unconscious level, waiting for her to fully give herself to him. Second, I did this to
open the door for a later analysis of his voyeurism (voyeuristic
drives were an important infantile source of the previous dream,
"On the Lake," and of the famous "incident").

It was almost the end of the hour. C had visibly listened to
my interpretation attentively and intently. After a few seconds he
got up from the couch, looking pensive and reflective, made a
face at me (a very "Italian" face: half-wink, half-smile, composed
and controlled but definitely warm) and left saying, "Okay, will
see you tomorrow."

Theoretical Appendix: Some of the Dream Work Defenses

From the dream's manifest content:

Dispensing a tranquilizer: displacement and secondary elaboration. In the latent dream, C is not dispensing tranquilizers, he is pouring his heart (his semen, his feces, his preoedipal and oedipal feelings) out onto mother. Thus, this is a secondary elaboration, having the defensive purpose of intellectualizing and distancing the manifest content from the more primitive feelings associated with the dream's latent wishes.

Rauwolfia: onomatopoeia for "raw wolf."

Raw wolf: concrete pictorial representation for naked, primitive, angry, and hungry sexuality.

Serpentina: onomatopoeia for "snakelike."

Snakelike: concrete pictorial representation for phallic shapes and onomatopoeia and concrete pictorial representation for "sneakiness."

Reserpine: onomatopoeia and condensation for "reserved penis."

Joan and Helen: displacement from Mary, therapist, mother.

Patient: metaphor disguising the wish for Mary, therapist, and mother to be "patient" (not "impatient") with dreamer.

From the associations—one listens to the dream's session as if it were a dream:

Old time drug, you old-timers: reference to the infantile sources of the dream.

Three: symbolism for male genital organs.

Drawers: displacement from underpants.

Messy drawers: concrete pictorial representation of anal sexuality, displacement and symbolism for feces and anger.

Pain in the neck: displacement for anal tensions, discomforts, conflicts.

Having gone to a Broadway show: possible reference to preoedipal and oedipal voyeuristic drives.

Great play, worth waiting for: mother kept him waiting in many ways, but she was usually worth waiting for.

"On the 'Sin' of an Accident"

The fourth and last of this series of dreams, "On the 'Sin' of an Accident" was dreamed about eighteen months after "The

Tranquilizer,'' more or less in the middle of C's seventh year of therapy. The word *scene* is rendered, onomatopoeically, as *sin* because of a psychodynamically meaningful play on words C himself made as we worked with the dream.

C had been continuing to come three times a week. After almost eight years of analysis, he was much better: happier, more fulfilled, more capable of enjoying life, less obsessional, more productive, more *loose* (his word) with time and money. But, as we shall see in a moment, he regressed to being obsessional at his worst shortly before the dream we are about to discuss. He had obtained a teaching appointment in a medical school in New York. Of course he still labored in the more intimate, sexual and nonsexual aspects of his life and work.

In the eighteen months preceding the dream, C talked mostly about his mother: directly and, through Mary and me, indirectly. Because of all the work that had been done, up to and including the interpretation of "The Tranquilizer," the maternal transference had continued to develop. Many of C's conscious and unconscious feelings about his mother were being relived, acted out, and talked about through various experiences with Mary and myself. The observing ego being fully operational, after a burst of transferential feelings or after a particular transferential acting out, C would not infrequently connect the feeling or the experience (ruefully or delightedly, but, always, with wonderment) to his mother. More memories emerged concerning qualities in his mother that had been, for C, "difficult to stomach" or "a pain in the ass," memories concerning times when his mother showed that "the stunningly beautiful princess could be 'tough as nails.' " Mother, at her best, was determined, firm, decisive, resolute, and strong minded, but at her worst stubborn, dogged, unbending, and unwavering. When mother was "tough," she was at best coldly affable, at worst coldly unapproachable. She rarely raised her voice and C could not remember her ever shouting, but she too, as C did, had an incredible command of the language and, when opposed, "in her determined, cool, and collected way, would use biting, caustic, mordant words." At those times C was consciously afraid of his mother. "When she went into her 'staccato' mood, her biting words could cut one to the quick, wherever 'the quick' might be." More than once he called her "adamant," once he called her "ballsy." He continued to tell me that she could be possessive and demanding, and very ambitious for him. She continued to write to him every two weeks without fail and he continued to "dash her off a quickie just to keep her happy" every two weeks or so. As it had become the case before "The Tranquilizer," less and less, if at all, did C need to qualify or soften the negative statements he made about his mother with any kind of caveats.

A trait of mother's about which C had not complained before became very prominent in these eighteen months: his mother's "nosiness." He told me that his mother was not nosy in a very obvious or crude fashion, but "just the way she asked you, in her breathless, charming way, what you had been up to, or the way she looked at you with those wide-open, expectant eyes ... it made you feel you had to tell her all your secrets. There was, about her, a quality of subtle intrusiveness, or at least curiosity, probably loving but nonetheless a pain you know where." He added that she was being intrusive and inquisitive in her letters too, "dropping hints to make me tell her how things are going between Mary and me, if we are planning to get married, that sort of thing" or on the telephone. But he was learning, "I no longer fall in that trap, the little fly has learned how to avoid getting in the web, I have learned to cut her short." It was when he first spoke about his mother's "nosiness" that he jokingly told me that mother had a "beautiful but longish nose ... à la Lorenzo dei Medici" and, seemingly a logical non sequitur, that she had "fine, beautiful, very sharp-looking teeth." During this period, he spoke very little about his father.

Mary and he had moved in together. He was sexually impotent less and less frequently; masturbation had continued to diminish; dizziness after masturbation had become a "thing of the past." With strong support from C, Mary had started therapy at about the time of "The Tranquilizer." Her difficulty with orgasm had not changed, C's feelings about that oscillated in unison with the vicissitudes of the transference. He could be genuinely empathic and encouraging, or angry, or through reaction formations, compassionate. In the nonsexual dimension of their relationship, his feelings for Mary also varied with the fluctuations in the transference. He could truly enjoy her warmth, intelligence, wit, physical beauty, and the love she had for him; be testy, irritable, touchy, and *prickly* (his word), explode in fits of anger at her most loose, casual, less obsessive style and living tempo. His explosions were usually brief and he always apologized afterwards. As indicated before, he would frequently understand his excess of emotion as transferential in origin: "I guess I am being angry at the old lady, not at Mary."

A doubly significant incident in this period of therapy was Mary's becoming "accidentally" pregnant about two months before the dream. The incident was significant in itself, realistically and because of the pain, concerns, and self-examining questions about the future of their relationship it caused Mary and C; and significant because of its psychodynamic connections with the dream soon to be discussed. Mary and C had been preventing conception through Mary's using a diaphragm. With his typically obsessional, hair-splitting handling of conscious and unconscious guilt, C said, "It was definitely an accident, neither of us wants to make a baby at this point . . . in part it was Mary's fault, she was being lazy and did not want to put her diaphragm on in the middle of an impromptu love-making, in part it was my fault, I came too soon and did not withdraw in time." The couple consensually agreed that Mary should have an abortion. The pregnancy was terminated about a month later. C was warmly and tenderly supportive of Mary throughout the experience. C and Mary decided that until they both felt ready for marriage, they would be doubly careful with birth control.

In therapy, C continued to experience me as too ambitious for him and too demanding of him: he was less jocular and more intense about it. Expectedly, the theme of "nosiness," his and mine, became a significant dimension of our work. C told me that I was nosy and intrusive, just like his mother " and this is no transference, or whatever you want to call it, you *are* nosy and intrusive." He went on to justify his perception: my silence was a subtle way of making him open up more and more; I did not ask him many questions, but I wanted to know all about him; lately I had been asking questions about him and Mary, questions about him and the women physicians he worked with. He understood my questions were part of my job and also motivated by interest and care, but they also revealed that I was a very curious person. Of course, C had become curious about me; as he was obsessing about what kind of car he wanted to buy, he asked me what kind of car I had, expressed interest about the kind of patients I had, was openly curious about "the beautiful young thing" that came just before him on Tuesdays, and "the athletic guy" who came after him on Thursdays. He once sheepishly admitted having lingered by my door between the waiting room and the bathroom on a Tuesday to try to hear what was going on in my session with the young woman who preceded him. He once asked me if I ever got angry with patients because on a Monday, as he was waiting for his session, he could have sworn he had heard me yelling at the patient before him. He added, with a half-snicker, "Ha! I bet you have to cut down on your Sicilian temper on Monday mornings when no one else is in the suite and you could be more easily heard." Speaking of "cutting down" on my alleged Sicilian temper, C had become more interruptive. The few times I did ask him questions, he would "cut me down" before I had even completed the question. I once pointed out to him that he interrupted me the way he interrupted his mother. "To use your own words, you cut me short the way you do with your mother on the telephone." He agreed but heatedly told me that lately I was doing the same to him, interrupting him with my questions, "cutting him short in the middle of a sentence."

Two weeks before the dream, C bought himself a sports car. The weekend preceding the week of the dream, he went to visit Dr. P, a woman psychiatrist who had been his supervisor during his psychiatric residency more than ten years before. Both events were significant overcathecters of the dream soon to be discussed.

C's purchase of his first sports car was an event clinically and psychodynamically significant. Clinically, that he should decide to buy himself a luxurious sports car (as indicated at the beginning of his case history, he was, in his words, "a tight ass" about money) was a positive sign. Psychodynamically, the obsessional gyrations he went through in reaching his decision about the kind of car he would buy, and the conscious and unconscious reasons behind his final choice, spoke about the castration fears and wishes that were behind his sexual problems and his obsessiveness. For about two months before the purchase was consummated, C obsessed, not painlessly, as to whether he would buy himself a Porsche Carrera (this was in the late 1970s) or the two-seater Jaguar XKE. Back and forth he went, from the Porsche to the Jaguar and back to the Porsche and back to the Jaguar. He liked the Porsche, "swift and maneuverable, you can run a slalom with it, go around all kinds of obstacles, barely grazing them" but he liked the Jaguar too, "fast and elegant, and what a name! It makes you think of the fierce, stealthy, pouncing jaguars of equatorial jungles." The obsessing was mainly about the relative lengths of the Carrera and the XKE's hoods: "The Carrera's hood is so short, a front end collision will cause the driver to lose his legs . . . or worse. The XKE, on the other hand, has a long hood, it can get into all kinds of frontal scrapes with no danger for the driver." He went as far as obsessively measuring the lengths of the two hoods in the respective dealers' showrooms with a measuring tape; and using the metric system, even though he usually preferred doing his calculations in feet and inches. About two weeks before the dream, C bought, as it could have been expected, a Jaguar XKE, bright red. As he was telling me about the obsessive measuring of the two cars' hoods, an interesting memory came to his mind: being about 13 and obsessively measuring his height against marks he had made on the wall of his bedroom. "As you know, father had been a very tall man, especially for an Italian, almost 1 meter 90 centimeters [6'3"] and there I was, 12 or 13, a little shrimp of 1 meter 50 [5'] measuring myself every Sunday night to see if I was growing. But by the time I was 16, I was almost 6 feet."

The last significant overcathecter of the dream was the visit C paid to Dr. P the Sunday before the dream. Dr. P had retired and lived on eastern Long Island and C went to visit her with Mary in his newly purchased Jaguar. He spoke about the forthcoming visit on his last session of the analytical week, a Thursday. He told me that Dr. P, a supervising psychiatrist, had been his "boss" during his psychiatric residency in a state hospital in New York; that she was the highly respected head of admissions at the hospital and he had been assigned to her Service. At that time he was a young resident in his midtwenties and she was in her late sixties. "But she's still a formidable woman, her faculties intact, her mind sharp as a steel trap, a brilliant psychiatrist, everybody admired and feared her because of her sharp tongue." She "could cut a guy short with her cold, pointed criticism" but was fair, "would never praise you in a lavish manner but when she was pleased with your performance, you knew it." He added that she had a "funny mannerism . . . when presenting a case to her, she would just look at you through her steel-rimmed glasses without saying a word, gritting her teeth . . . we young male residents used to joke that we better cover our balls with our hands when we were in her office or she would bite them off." He also told me that although she was a "tough, difficult woman," he had been, and had remained, fond of her, had kept in touch with her through the years, and was looking forward to visiting her and introducing Mary to her the following Sunday. Thus was the stage set for the last of his four dreams.

The dream session was, again, on the first day of the analytical week ("The Tranquilizer" and "On the Lake" had also been told in his Monday sessions). C entered the office with a quizzical, puzzled expression on his face, said "What a strange dream, last night," lay on the couch, and told me the dream.

"On the 'Sin' of an Accident"

> A very strange dream, as I was saying, it makes no sense at all, but, then, you say all dreams are important and I should tell you everything, so here it is . . . I was driving my new car toward Eastern Long Island and I came upon the scene of an accident. A young woman was lying on the ground, one of her legs had been injured—I thought, what a shame, she has beautiful legs. The ground was covered with snow, very dirty snow, and that also made no sense because it was a hot summer day. The next piece makes even less sense. I said to myself, "Her leg is longer because she has been injured." I felt sorry for her, but I felt okay because I was innocent. Here is the last absurdity, the last contradiction in this stupid dream. I said to myself, "My car did not stop because I was not driving it." But, one, I was driving my car and, two, my car had not hit her, I had committed no sin. And that too is strange, I don't think in terms of sins, I haven't since my First Communion days.

Right after telling me the dream C repeated at least twice how "nonsensical" the dream was, but added that it still puzzled him because of its very absurdity. Then seemingly changing the subject, he told me that on the day before, he and Mary had visited Dr. P, it had been very pleasant, Dr. P was remarkable, must be in her late seventies now, and her legs were weak. She walked with a cane, but her mind was still perfectly sharp. She liked Mary and was very glad to see C. They had reminisced about the good old days at the hospital. That night, before falling asleep and dreaming the dream, he had reminisced some more about that period in his life and remembered with a chuckle Dr. P's teeth mannerisms and the joke among the male residents he had told me the previous Thursday. He told me how much he enjoyed his new Jaguar. On the way over to Dr. P he had gone way beyond the speed limit for a short stretch on the road and it was his good luck that there were no police around. The spring weather was very balmy and he had the top of the car down, and with Mary's long blond hair flying and with his touring cap from the 1930s on his head, he had felt as though the two of them were glamorous characters from a movie.

He added that in the little villages in the Hamptons, his beautiful bright red car slowed down by traffic, they had attracted a lot of attention, and he had felt as if he were a character from one of F. Scott Fitzgerald's novels, maybe the Great Gatsby himself. In another of those villages he had rakishly waved at a Southampton matron on Main Street. In a third of those villages, he had almost hit a woman who was crossing the intersection against the red light, but immediately corrected himself and told me that, no, he had not "almost hit" her, he was going at a snail's pace at the time and he had had no trouble not hitting her.

C was silent for several minutes, then told me that Dr. P had made him think of his mother; that Dr. P and his mother were very different in many respects (age, looks, personality) but similar in that they both are brilliant, both could be very cutting with words, and both were widows; mother, "just like you know who, and I mean you" is very inquisitive and nosy, whereas Dr. P is not. Mother, in her calmly expectant, seemingly passive fashion, "just like you, my dear Sigismondo, has a way of getting to know everything about you, know all your secrets, big and small." But, as he had been telling me, he is learning, and when mother, on the phone, gets too direct about him and Mary, he "just cuts her short." He mentioned that he had not said a word to mother about Mary's pregnancy and abortion. Finally, "Well, just fifteen minutes to go, what do you make of the dream? It's a really funny

dream, it would be a sin to let it go unexplained by the great
Sherlock Holmes of dreams, Vincenzo Sigismondo Conigliaro. By
the way, that's at least the third time I am using the word *sin,* and
it's a dream about being on the *scene* of an accident. If you ever
write a book on dreams, you should call this dream 'On the "Sin"
of an Accident'—how is that for wit, Herr Doctor?"

The first two tasks at this point were to understand the dream
session and sessions before it, and to understand the session's
dream, that is, to know what the dream says. In response to the
dream's session, my internal soliloquy included these thoughts.
The "young woman lying on the ground" in the semimanifest
dream was Mary, and the analyst in the semilatent dream, and
mother in the latent dream. "Lying on the ground" represented
one who is both the beloved receiver and the hated victim of
libidinal and aggressive drives; the young woman's leg stood for
the intrusive mother's and analyst's nose and penis. The leg may
have been longer in the manifest dream but was definitely shorter
in the latent dream because of the injury (castration) wished by
C. I also thought that the snow covering the ground stood for
the semen C had ejaculated prematurely in the other "accident,"
the one that had impregnated Mary three months before (and,
in his deeper unconscious fantasies, had impregnated his mother,
decades before), and the snow was "very dirty" because C in part
saw his genital sexuality as anal, as he had in "The Tranquilizer."

"The hot summer day" of the manifest dream represented
C's "hot" loving and angry feelings; the manifest dream's car
(i.e., penis) "did not stop because I was not driving it" was both
a denial and a representation of the psychodynamics of a sexual
disability such as C's, in which the penis is controlled not by the
conscious ego but by internal forces of which the person knows
nothing and whose ejaculation, similarly, is not within conscious
control. Finally I thought that the manifest dream's "I knew I was
innocent" was a denial. C was indeed guilty of a "sin" on the
"scene" of the accident, he had caused the accident.

In response to the dream's session, I thought that Dr. P did
make him think of his mother in many important respects: not
just in the fact they both were widows and brilliant, but in their
both being "tough" and "cutting" with their words. One, Dr. P,
gritted her teeth in a most upsetting way and the other, C's

mother, had very sharp teeth. Therefore, the visit to Dr. P was an important overcathecter of the dream in that it had overcathected powerful unconscious feelings of fear and anger concerning mother. His reminiscing, consciously, about "the good old days" with Dr. P at the hospital (including the jokes about her castrating mannerisms) corresponded to the overcathected unconscious memories about the good and bad old days with mother and the times C had experienced mother as castrating, a mother whose "biting, caustic, mordant words could cut him to the quick, wherever the 'quick' might be." I also saw that the theme of mother's (and analyst's) nosiness and inquisitiveness was, obviously, still a hot issue: "The dream makes no sense at all but, then, you say I should tell you everything," and "Mother, just like you know who, and I mean you, is very inquisitive and nosy . . . in her seemingly passive way she, just like you, my dear Sigismondo, has a way of getting to know all your secrets, big and small." I finally thought that it was very significant that in a session in which he told me a dream in which a woman's leg gets longer (i.e., shorter) because of an accident, he would tell me, *again,* that he had learned that the best way to deal with his mother when she was being inquisitive, was "cutting her short." Telling me that Dr. P's legs were weaker also connected with C's unconscious desire to weaken mother's inquisitiveness by cutting her nose (penis) and by blunting her sharp teeth (i.e., castrating her).

In response both to the session's dream and the dream's session, C's repeatedly telling me, both in the dream's manifest content and in the context of telling me the dream, that the dream made no sense, was absurd, was contradictory, the fact, that is, that so much secondary elaboration accompanied both the dream itself and the telling of the dream, suggested that he had a strong need to make the dream appear unimportant, not believable. His protestations also suggested that the secondary elaboration had not distorted the dream sufficiently. As pointed out in chapter 5, secondary elaboration aims at disguising the dream by making its manifest content logical, coherent, "grammatical." In C's dream the "illogical" parts of the dream (illogical only in terms of Aristotelian logic and conscious thinking), had not been sufficiently "cleaned up" by secondary elaboration,[11] had not been made logical, coherent, "grammatical," had not been rendered more understandable to the conscious ego. Those phrases, therefore, were less distorted and therefore more understandable psychodynamically. I also thought that the manifest dream's "the car did not hit her" was a denial: someone's car had hit the young woman. In the dream's session, before reassuring me (and himself) to the contrary, he had told me that he had "almost hit" a woman in the little village in the Hamptons, and that the woman he had "almost hit," who had crossed the intersection against the red light, represented C's mother, who ignored C's "red lights" about her inquisitiveness. I finally thought that the word *sin* had come up many times (twice in the manifest dream and twice more in the dream's session), and this strongly suggested guilt in the dream's semilatent content. Sinfulness and guilt were also suggested by the association in the dream's session about the police who might have gotten him for recklessness on the expressway, by the association about almost hitting the woman in the little village in the Hamptons, and by the association about his rakish salute to a Southampton matron.

In response to the sessions immediately preceding the dream, my internal soliloquy included these thoughts. The purchase of the sports car and all the obsessing that preceded his final choice were connected with the dream and were important overcathecters of the unconscious fears and wishes of castration that were part, respectively, of the semilatent and the latent dream. He bought the Jaguar XKE, the car with the long, steely, powerfully protruding hood, the better to "hood," to protect, his vulnerable penis from castration by the long-nosed, sharp-toothed, cutting mother, *and* the better to castrate (to cut-short) the mother's long, intrusive nose, and the better to blunt her sharp teeth. A jaguar was a good representation of the stealth and fierceness with which he wanted to pounce on mother; and his "hot" sexual and aggressive feelings truly belonged to the equatorial jungle of his unconscious feelings just as jaguars do.

---

[11]"Sleeping consciousness we may even imagine as saying to itself in effect: 'Here comes our master, Waking Consciousness, who attaches such mighty importance to reason, logic and so forth. Quick! Gather things up, put them in order—any order will do—before he enters to take possession'" (Ellis, 1911, cited by Freud, 1900, p. 501, n 2).

Similarly, the short-hooded Porsche was no protection from the mother who could castrate him and only a puny offense against the mother he wished to castrate. The Jaguar XKE could get "into all kinds of frontal scrapes" without any danger to its driver. With that kind of Jaguarlike penis, C could lovingly make love to mother and angrily castrate her without any danger. Anxiously and obsessively measuring the hoods of the Porsche and the Jaguar (and using the measuring system of the *mother* country, the decimal system) symbolized measuring the length of his penis, represented making sure, again, that his penis was big enough to castrate and big enough to avoid castration. Measuring the car's hood did correspond to the anxious and obsessive measurement of his height at puberty: was he going to be as tall as father, tall enough, big enough, largely endowed (penis-wise) enough, to make love and war with mother with impunity? And I thought that all the material concerning Dr. P that had come up in the session just before the dream, had indeed been an important overcathecter of unconscious material concerning his mother—along the lines of my soliloquy about the dream's session.

And, finally, in response to all the sessions in the therapy period being considered (the eighteen months or so between "The Tranquilizer" and this dream), my internal soliloquy included all which I found myself selectively remembering and selectively resonating with what seemed to connect with the dream. In those eighteen months we had been mostly talking about mother, a mother "stubborn" and "tough as nails"; and one surely needed a steely Jaguar to deal with her; a "biting, caustic, mordant" mother, who could "cut you to the quick." One surely needed a long-hooded Jaguar to protect oneself from that. There was a mother who had "a longish nose," such a long intrusive "nose-y" "nose" made C want to shorten it. There was a mother whom C had likened to Lorenzo dei Medici, and whom C had called "ballsy." If mother could be likened to a man, the young woman lying on the ground in the manifest dream, besides representing women, Mary, and C's mother, could also represent a man, the analyst. I also remembered that the themes of excessive ambitiousness and demandingness, on his mother's part and mine, had also been recurrent themes in those eighteen months.

The negative maternal transference had continued to develop; the theme of nosiness, his mother's and mine, and ways of dealing with it, had become a prominent (pun intended!) theme in our work, and one of the ways he had learned to deal with that was "cutting us short." I found myself resonating with the incident of Mary's unwanted pregnancy and abortion, which had occurred about three months before the dream. In C's interpersonal and conscious world, in C's extrapsychic world, that had "simply" been an accidental pregnancy. In C's unconscious and intrapsychic world, it had become a car accident. In C's extrapsychic world, C took responsibility for the accidental pregnancy by seeing it caused, at least in part, by his having ejaculated prematurely and not having withdrawn sooner. In C's intrapsychic world, C felt guilty (semilatent dream) and happy (latent dream) for having "hit" mother with his powerful penis, and spread semen all around her. In C's extrapsychic world, it was Mary's uterus that had been entered and wounded by sharp surgical instruments; in C's intrapsychic world, it was mother's body that had been hit and wounded by C's sharp, powerful, jaguarlike penis. I also thought that the theme of *his* nosiness had also become important. C had become curious about me and my patients and at least once had lingered by my door trying to hear what was going on inside. Somewhat peripherally, at the edge of my consciousness, this resonated in my mind not so much with this dream but with the major dream ("On the Lake") of the previous therapy period and his memory of having heard his parents making love on the boat. I felt, therefore, that this material was probably not too germane to this period of work and to "On the 'Sin' of an Accident" and that comments about it would not be timely and appropriate.

My soliloquy temporarily terminated, I tentatively concluded that this dream too, like "The Tranquilizer," condensed preoedipal and oedipal wishes and fears, but that the preoedipal elements were still closer to the surface. I felt that the dream's latent content had primarily to do with angry preoedipal drives about mother, the wish of doing to mother what he felt mother had done or could do to him, the wish to castrate mother both *before* she could castrate him and *because* she had tried to castrate him. These aggressive drives in the latent dream were distorted into

and represented in the manifest dream as the young woman being hit by a car and her leg being injured. The same unconscious
impulses were behind the associations, in the dream session,
about Dr. P and the women in the little villages in the Hamptons.
Equally primary, I felt, was the preoedipal drive to soil and defile
mother with dirty semen, semen, again, as fecal as it had been in
"The Tranquilizer" dream, semen not lovingly given to a woman's vagina but prematurely spread and wasted all around her. I
thought that this drive in the latent dream was distorted into and
represented in the manifest dream as dirty snow covering the
ground around the young woman. The dream's semilatent content, I believed, contained the counterdrives (the defenses) to
the above drives, the guilt about wanting to castrate, cut short,
soil, and defile mother and the fear of being castrated, cut short,
caught for wanting to do so. I continued to believe that C had
loving oedipal and preoedipal feelings and serious oedipal conflicts. I felt that these feelings and conflicts could not be worked
on until the aggressive preoedipal feelings had been worked
through; and believed that the more loving preoedipal and oedipal feelings which were part of the dream's latent content, were
secondary, not primary, and could not yet be worked with.

The third task was to respond to the dream, and to know
what to say to the patient about the dream. It was now about
fifteen minutes before the end of the session. C had just asked
me to be Sherlock Holmes and to tell him what I made of the
dream and I had to decide whether I should respond to the
dream with silence, an intervention, or an interpretation, and, if
an interpretation was warranted, whether it should be on the
level of the drives, of the defenses, and within the context of the
transference. My internal thinking in this regard included these
thoughts. Stage of analysis, quality of alliance, and C's clinical
and psychodynamic state certainly warranted interpretations on
the level of the drives. The maternal transference was quite well
developed and an interpretation within its context would have
been also clearly legitimate. If I opted for an interpretation, the
preoedipal drives and conflicts were more primary and more accessible than the oedipal drives and conflicts and, therefore,
should be the drives to respond to. I also felt as I had after "The
Tranquilizer," only more so, that preoedipal problems had to

be resolved before the oedipal problems could be worked on. I decided, therefore, that I would respond with an interpretation on the level of the preoedipal drives within the context of the maternal transference, but that I wanted some more association, first, if possible. So I said: "Yes, I will tell you what the dream makes me think about—but we still have time. Anything else you want to say?"

Angrily, he accused me of "doing it again." There he was, having given me a dream, having spoken nonstop for half an hour, having told me a great deal about himself and Mary and his mother and Dr. P, had even regaled me with a witty caption for a dream for a book that he now hoped I would never be able to write. And there I was, just like his mother, asking for more, being nosy and inquisitive. As was characteristic of C, he felt better after the outburst and more calmly told me that, yes, I was being just like his mother, actually worse, because I got him to tell me a lot, not just by asking questions but by being silent. We were both like spiders, silently waiting for him to get into our webs. Then he said that he would do with me what he also did with his mother. Besides cutting her short (not counting the manifest dream, this was the second time he used that expression in the session) he now diverts her by asking her questions. So he asked me "And what kind of car do you drive?" Without waiting for an answer, he said, "I bet you have an Alfa Romeo." I felt like being cute and saying, "The Alfa Romeo 'Spider,' right? Yes, you do see me like your mother, a spider," but, virtuously, again, restrained myself. Instead, I said:

Okay, I will tell you what the dream makes me think about. First, let me point out to you that "long" and "short" have been a matter of concern for you lately: how short is the hood on a Porsche, how long on a Jaguar; how short you thought you were at 13, how glad you were when you got to be over 6 feet. Then, you have been seeing me as nosy and intrusive as your mother, and have been angry at me for that. And you have felt that I have been interruptive and cut you short in the middle of a sentence, and have been angry at me for that too. Now, twice today you have told me that when your mother is too inquisitive, you cut her short; and you have been doing that with me too whenever you have felt I was being nosy. And in the dream, somebody gets hit by a car, and somebody's leg gets longer—or is it shorter? I think your dream is a dream of anger and fear. Somebody is getting cut short and you are cutting somebody short. I think you are angry at me and you are cutting me short and are making one of my legs shorter. And since you are putting me together with your mother, I bet this anger is an old anger, it goes back to beyond my nosiness, or your mother's *current* nosiness.

It was an interpretation mainly on the level of the drives: "I think your dream is a dream of anger, you are angry at me, you are cutting me short—you are making one of my legs shorter." It was on the level of the defenses only peripherally and allusorily: "I think your dream is a dream of anger *and fear*"; "Long and short have been a matter of concern to you lately"; "Somebody is getting cut short." It was within the context of transference, even though I did refer to his mother, I told him that both in his dream and in reality he was angry *at me*, cutting *me* short, was making one of *my* legs shorter. I was clear, I hope, about this being an "old" anger. I wanted him to connect the present to the past, to connect current aggressive impulses against his mother and me to old aggressive impulses against his mother, to connect current injuries and threats to his psyche and his boundaries to prelatency injuries and threats. I chose not to refer to the anal aspects of his anger, not only not to overwhelm him with too much at once, but mainly because the manifest dream only included one small reference (dirty snow) to anality, while the castratory aspects of the anger were much more prominent. Besides, the entire therapy period had been much more concerned with these than with anal concerns.

Of course, I did not use any of the "big words," such as castration or anal. I also ignored the association about waving at the Southampton matron and did not use any of the associations about the trip to Eastern Long Island: the bracing feeling of speeding in the open car; the proud, exultant feeling about Mary's long blond hair flying into the wind, the exhilaration of feeling as though he and Mary were two glamorous characters from Hollywood, and C, the Great Gatsby himself; the exalting feeling of being admired by all as his expensive, red sports car's powerful engine was rumbling in heavy traffic through the little towns of the Hamptons. These were all important parts of the dream's session and therefore of the dream itself. I chose to ignore them because they belonged to a different level of analysis, the level of preoedipal and oedipal positive feelings with mother: being in a luxurious, powerful, long-hooded car on a beautiful spring day, a beautiful woman, Mary (the good mother of his childhood) at his side; being about to visit Dr. P, an old, prominent psychiatrist who was fond of him because of the good old days together (again, the good mother of his childhood); . . . feeling flush and grand and a little hypomanic with the feelings of oedipal and preoedipal success. Again, my agenda was limited: I only wanted to help C become conscious of his preoedipally based anger at me, of his preoedipally based wish to cut me short, I only wanted to use the dream to proceed further onto the royal road to his unconscious where most of those impulses were still producing pathogenic effects.

C was silent for a moment, then said, softly, full of feeling, thoughtfully: "Dr. P comes to mind, and the joke I told you we had among ourselves about the way she gritted her teeth. You are talking of castration, man, castration fears, Freud called them. Yes, you cutting me short, you interrupting me, you being nosy, Mom being nosy . . . but also, me cutting you short, uhm? and me cutting Mom short. I am kind of shivering inside, yet I also feel good, like I am on the verge of discovering something important, something that will make me feel really free." He got up and left.

Theoretical Appendix: Some of the Dream Work Defenses

From the dream's manifest content:

A very strange dream; It makes no sense at all; And that also makes no sense; The next piece makes even less sense; Here is the last absurdity, the last contradiction in this stupid dream; And that too is strange: secondary elaborations.
Driving my car: displacement; or symbolism for "driving" (directing) his impulses.
Driving my new car: secondary elaboration and turning into the opposite: it's his *old* prelatency impulses that are animating the car.
Scene: onomatopoeia for "sin."
Accident: displacement from Mary's accidental pregnancy; concrete pictorial representation of wish to inflict harm.

Young woman: displacement from Mary, analyst, mother.
Lying on the ground: displacement from lying in bed; concrete pictorial representation of sexuality.
Lying: symbolism and concrete pictorial representation of any kind of intimate interpersonal activity, being nursed, having sexual intercourse, etc., onomatopoeia for laying, "getting laid."
Leg: displacement from nose and penis.
Snow: symbolism of, or displacement from, semen.
Dirty snow: symbolism of, or displacement from, feces.
Hot summer day: concrete pictorial representation of passion.
Car did not stop: denial or turning into the opposite, the car did stop.
I was not driving: denial or turning into the opposite, he was driving the car. Also, concrete pictorial representation of lack of conscious control over one's sexual functions.

From the associations—one listens to the dream's session as if it were a dream:

Nonsensical, Absurdity: more secondary elaborations.
Dr. P: displacement from analyst and mother.
Dr. P's legs: displacement from analyst's and mother's nose, teeth and penis.
Dr. P's teeth mannerisms: representation of castratory attitudes.
Jaguar: symbolism of, and displacement from, penis and sexual and aggressive energies.
Going beyond speed limit: concrete pictorial representation of wish to act out.
The police: symbolism for superego and parents.
The flush, grand feelings during the trip: displacement from, and representation of, hypomanic feelings of child whose preoedipal and oedipal impulses have been gratified.

Postscript

C terminated analysis three years after "On the 'Sin' of an Accident"; he was close to 45 and had been in therapy for almost ten years. This last period of therapy was a very fruitful one, the first two years of the three years was a subperiod filled with important insights, new memories, and memories which had been shared with me before, being "revisited," being seen under a new light, and understood differently. The last year was mostly devoted to working through and to the resolution of the transference.

As I had been hoping, the interpretation given to "On the 'Sin' of an Accident" furthered our progress down the royal road to his unconscious preoedipal castration wishes and fears concerning his mother. The week after the session of the dream, he shared with me a new preconscious memory that he had never before brought to therapy. Two or three times a year, C's father, mother, and two older sisters went skiing. C and his younger sister remained at home with C's paternal aunt, a loving and warm single woman. C was told this occurred even before C was born, but he himself remembered being 4, and maybe even 3, and his parents leaving. He remembered being a small child and his aunt showing him photographs of his parents on the ski slopes. He remembered that he missed his parents, especially his mother, and that he had been fearful that his mother would fall and hurt herself. He did *not* remember any dreams of mother falling and hurting herself, but wondered whether he dreamed of his mother "having an accident skiing and injuring a leg—after all, there had been snow in the dream he had just had—wouldn't that be something, if the dream I just had, I had also had it almost forty years ago?"

The more aware C became of the fact that, as a child, he may have feared and wished (and dreamed?) of "castrating" mother, of cutting her short, the more his castration fears abated. He became less and less vulnerable to, and annoyed at, his mother's intrusiveness, more and more capable of seeing mother's inquisitiveness as just curiosity. "Look, she may have a rich and interesting life, but, still, she lives alone, must get lonely, so she wants to keep in touch." He became better able to accept the way she was when he was a child. "Yes, she could be a pain; yes, she made you feel she could cut you to the quick; but she did not, and besides, she was also lovely and she did love me." Last and not least, he had dreams whose latent content suggested diminishing fears of potency, sexual and otherwise. Simultaneously, in the transference, I became less and less the intrusive, ambitious, and demanding mother I had been before the dream.

Clearly, his castration fears had been to a large extent the product of castration wishes projected onto mother. Also, he had become somewhat less obsessional and compulsive ("somewhat": Is character destiny, after all?) or, more accurately, his obsessive–compulsive propensities had become less and less maladaptive. As I had also hoped, the partial, but pretty satisfactory resolution of his preoedipal problems, made it possible to work further on the oedipal problems that had been shielded up till now by the anal regressions. These oedipal problems were still pathogenic, pain-producing: although better sexually, C did still have problems with Mary, sexual and nonsexual. In the one to two years after the "On the 'Sin' of an Accident" dream, C resumed talking about the glamorous, tall, powerful father of his childhood (who had died when C was 6), thus resuming work on still unworked-through oedipal feelings concerning his father (and mother).

It became more and more apparent that between ages 5 and 6, typically and age-appropriately, C loved his father but was also afraid of him, competitive with him, and angry at him. As we started again working on the oedipal feelings concerning his father, castration fears reappeared, but were now largely centered on father. Memories he had shared with me before resurfaced, but with a different feeling and a different kind of recollection. He talked again about the snorkeling vacation in Sicily when he was 5. His father's underwater gun did awe him; father's prohibitions about touching it, intrigued him; he did wish to touch it and to touch the gun's trigger. To see father emerge from underwater with a big fish wiggling at the end of his harpoon fascinated him. He did fantasize aiming at "some big fish" in the sea; he *now* wondered whether "*the big fish in the sea*" was his father. He did remember wondering *then* what it would be like to aim the gun at father and have father wiggling at the end of the harpoon. But he also remembered how much, at that young age, he also loved and admired his father, which I believe to be true. He also talked, again, of the trip to Syracuse and to the cave of Dionysius' Ear; told me that he still remembered the dream about the cave that he had told me about five years before. While Dionysius had "spied" on his political prisoners, he, C, in the famous "scene of the incident" (when he had gone below deck and put his ear to the door of the cabin where father and mother were making love), had "spied" on his parents making love. "Yes, we children can be little tyrants to our parents!" he said. Finally, thinking of the "scene of the incident," he remembered the sexual and angry feelings he had felt then and had described to me five years before, right after the "On the Lake" dream, and again, more feelingly, about six months after that. He reminded me that he had told me that he may have wished his father dead, then, and he believed that, but that he still also loved his father very much.[12]

With the same awed wonder which had accompanied his considering the *possibility* of having had two dreams about accidents injuring his mother's leg at an almost forty-year interval, C mused about any possible connections between having referred to the cabin on the boat in which father and mother had been making love as "the scene of the incident" and having baptized his last dream "On the 'Sin' of an Accident"; and saw the psychodynamic connections between the two "incidents," sexual and angry feelings in both, castratory impulses and castration fears in both. As he recovered more and more thoughts and feelings concerning the oedipal father, the paternal transference came to include the same ambivalent feelings of the Oedipus complex. As the Oedipus complex was being resolved, both intrapsychically and within the transference, C began to experience father (and me) more and more realistically as he had been doing about the preoedipal mother, right after our work on the "On the 'Sin' of an Accident" dream. At the same time, he became more consistently potent, sexually and nonsexually. As the aggressive components of the oedipal feelings, including the wish to castrate father, were becoming more integrated, he became more consistently assertive and less fearful of being punished for "cockiness." Castration fears (by father) had also been the product of castration wishes projected onto father. Also, he no longer said of himself, "I can play a mean game of tennis," but, "a strong game of tennis, as Dad did." He identified more and more with father and more and more appreciated physical and psychological traits

---

[12]This was in a very emotional session during which C had also told me once more of the underwater dreams that were so frequent in this period of therapy, the eighth or ninth year of our work together. When C told me, "I may have wished my father dead, then, this was true, but, still, I loved him very much," I interjected, "And, I believe that that, too, is true." C burst into tears and asked me if I would hold his hand for a minute. I did.

within himself that he traced to "Dad." He realized, contentedly, that his father had been fourteen years older than his wife and he was ten years older than Mary.

C's tenth year of therapy was mainly a working though year. It was in the last year of analysis that he and Mary began to make plans to get married: "I am 45 and Mary is 35, it's finally time (I have been waiting long enough, haven't I?) to imitate the old man all the way and start having children myself." He married a few months after terminating analysis.

At termination, C's feelings for me were warm and affectionate. What Freud called "affectionate feelings" of the positive transference, "admissible to consciousness and unobjectionable" (1912a, p. 105)—a somewhat cautious and edgy metaphor for "love"—were plentiful and reciprocal; and many were the ways in which C had shown tendencies to identify with me, as well as with his father. Yet, C never decided to become a psychoanalyst, never decided to imitate the transferential "old man" that way. I am not conscious of being disappointed at that, but I did and still do wonder why he did not. To the extent that the psychoanalyst is a voyeur of the psyche (one hopes a sublimated voyeur), to the extent that the psychoanalyst must be curious (not nosy and intrusive, but curious in the sense of "Nihil humanum mihi obstat," "Nothing human is alien to me" [Publius Terentius Afer, 190–159 B.C.]); to that extent, maybe C did not become a psychoanalyst because his voyeurism and nosiness had not been analyzed to the point of sublimating unhealthy, intrusive voyeurism and nosiness into healthy, life-giving, inquisitiveness and curiosity.

8

Dream Interpretation, 3

In their internal soliloquies, that is, through their own internal conjectures and speculations, and in listening with the third ear, analysts travel the royal road to a better knowledge of the unconscious activities of their patients' minds with each and any of their patients' dreams and utterances. But analysts may also gain this knowledge together with the patient, through interventions and interpretations, guiding the patient at the right time and in the right way: a twentieth century Virgil and Dante going through the hell and purgatory of painful symptoms to, one hopes, a paradise of realistic serenity and self-possession (i.e., possession by one's conscious ego and ego ideal, not by one's id and superego).

In working with dreams in a Freudian fashion, the basic principles guiding the analyst are, again, *ultimately one must analyze the latent, not the manifest, content* (Sharpe's *"cardinal rule of dream analysis"* [1978]) and, *one can respond to dreams on the level of the defenses or on the level of the drives and within the context of the transference* (chapter 6). To apply the cardinal rule of dream analysis is the same as analyzing the dream's latent content and responding to the dream on the level of the drives. All three approaches are valid, because the dream's latent content is in the unconscious, and the drives that form that latent content are in the unconscious. To apply the cardinal rule, to analyze the latent content of a dream, and to respond to a dream on the level of the drives, is to enter the royal road to a better knowledge of the unconscious activities of the mind.

As previously emphasized, to apply the cardinal rule is a powerful response and therefore a response to use only when therapy is no longer in its early stages and the therapeutic alliance is solid; when the patient has been in analysis long enough and the defenses sufficiently understood and analyzed; when the patient has the ego strength and capacity to tolerate, absorb, and utilize this type of response. One is reminded again of the difference between the science of the theoretical and technical principles directing the analyst's response to dreams, and the art of dream interpretation. When is therapy no longer in its early stages? When is the therapeutic alliance solid enough? When have the defenses been understood and analyzed sufficiently? When is the ego strong enough to tolerate, absorb, and utilize the full application of the cardinal rule? It is the art of dream interpretation that answers these questions. The analyst's clinical skills and sixth sense, that intangible and immeasurable something that is part of the art of psychotherapy and dream interpretation, are always needed to supplement, complement, modify, and temper all theoretical and technical principles.

In one possible scenario, the patient is in the middle–late or later stages of analysis, the therapeutic alliance is solid, the defenses have been sufficiently understood and analyzed, the patient's ego is strong. The analyst has been listening to the patient and to the patient's dream psychoanalytically with a third ear, and has engaged in the internal soliloquy. The dream's session and the session's dream have been understood, the analyst knows what the patient's dream says. Ultimately, we have said, one is supposed to apply the cardinal rule, to analyze the dream's latent content, and respond on the level of the drives. Not too soon, but at the right time, appropriately, as theoretical and clinical principles warrant, and as the analyst's clinical skills and sixth sense suggest. In this first scenario, the analyst believes that the analytical situation warrants a full application of the cardinal rule, that a path to the royal road has opened, and further progress down that road is safely possible. The analyst decides to apply the cardinal rule. The dreams worked with in chapter 7 were dreams dreamed in the middle–late or later stages of therapy and were illustrations of this scenario, dreams with which I did apply the cardinal rule.

In a second scenario, analysis has just begun, the therapeutic alliance has barely been formed, the patient has not yet revealed very much. The analyst has only an imprecise estimate of the patient's ego's strength, only a theoretical textbook understanding of the patient's defenses, only an approximate knowledge and understanding of the patient's problem. The analyst's internal soliloquy, therefore, can only be based on the analyst's skill, intuitiveness, and third ear, or on the analyst's imaginativeness, which can be an asset or a liability. The cardinal rule cannot be applied. This is the case with first dreams, dreams dreamed in the early stages of therapy, the so-called "simple dreams," and "need" dreams. The dreams worked with in this chapter are illustrations of this scenario and were dreamed in clinical situations in which the cardinal rule was not applied, situations where a path onto the royal road had opened but had been traveled only a small part of the way, if at all, with the patient. In these cases, my patients and I safely remained in the psychic territory of the preconscious ego, the unrepressed past, and the ego's mechanisms of defenses. Dreams were responded to with silence, or interventions and interpretations solely on the level of the defenses. To this scenario one may add dreams told in consultation interviews, which of course, will be first dreams, "first" at least with regard to the patient–therapist dyad within which these dreams were told.

In a third scenario, the cardinal rule is not applied because the analyst's agenda is to use the patient's dream for purposes other than traveling the royal road with the patient. This is the case with dreams dreamed at times of severe psychic crises, and the "special purpose" dreams. With these dreams too, I did not apply the cardinal rule.

To reemphasize the important point made at the onset of this chapter: whether one does or does not apply the cardinal rule, one will still engage in the internal soliloquy, but one's conjectures, reflections, and resonances will not be shared with the patient, or shared only minimally; and if interpretations are made, the interpretations will be strictly only on the level of the defenses.

FIRST DREAMS AND EARLY DREAMS

Stages of therapy may be classified in various ways. A clinical classification breaks stages of therapy down to an initial phase, in which the relationship and rapport between analyst and patient are being formed and the therapeutic alliance is built; an early middle phase, during which common patterns are discovered, psychogenetic themes are uncovered, psychodynamics are formulated; a late middle phase, the working through stage; and a final phase, termination.

One may also think of stages of therapy in terms of prevailing defenses: superego defenses (guilt, self-punishment, ingratiating maneuvers toward the analyst) are prevalent in the early stages of analysis. Ego defenses (whichever defenses the ego utilized to disguise the drives that had become part of the neurotic conflict) are found throughout analysis, id defenses are found in the later stages.

In working with dreams that are brought in during the earlier stages of therapy, including first dreams, an initial theoretical–technical guide to follow is to respond to dreams according to the characteristics and requirements of the early stages of therapy, which is to say, in ways that will facilitate the development of the relationship between patient and therapist, the development of the therapeutic alliance, the development of the transference, and the analysis of the superego defenses. A second theoretical–technical rule in working with these dreams is to think about the following formula: *Not much can be said*—we hardly know the patient, we cannot have very much to say. *Not much should be said*—we hardly know the patient, what we do say could be wrong, could contaminate the transference, could precipitate a premature termination. *Just enough should be said*, to help patients continue to want to tell us their dreams. The analyst's clinical skills and sixth sense will have to supplement and complement all such theoretical–technical guidelines, rules, principles, or formulas.

With the following material, the dream session, and the session or sessions preceding the dream, will not be presented in as much detail as in chapter 7. Only those early clinical and historical details will be given that were relevant to the way I understood the dream and worked with it. My silent thinking as I was listening to my patient's dreams, my internal soliloquy, will still be presented at some length.

"Late for the Concert"

At the time of this dream, Father X was a 45-year-old Roman Catholic priest who came to see me from a nearby state once a week. His dream was brought into therapy in the fifth session. Father X was an "order" as opposed to a "diocesan" priest: a Vincentian father. In the first five minutes of his first session with me, he told me that he had traveled hours to come to see me; that he wished my office was more conveniently located; that the armchair where he was asked to sit was "abominable and not very comfortable"; that the lighting in my office was "execrable." He also told me that his religious order's patron saint was St. Vincent de Paul and that he hoped I was named after St. Vincent Ferrer because, in his opinion, Vincent de Paul was not a great saint at all, and actually was a prick. I told him that we, he and I, were both lucky, as I was indeed named after Vincent Ferrer.[1] He told me he was "vastly relieved," but he should have known, after all de Paul worked with and for the poor, and considering "the outrageous fees" I charged, I could not have been named after de Paul. Yes, Father X was caustic, sarcastic, hostile; but also a pathetic man, terrified about much, and most of all, terrified of human contacts. He was also brilliant and spoke beautifully: he was fluent, articulate, had an unbelievable command of English, and when he "sermonized" me (which he did frequently), he would do so with eloquence and elegance. I had to caution myself against a positive countertransference of enjoying too much his verbal pyrotechnics and virtuosity.

Father X's symptoms included depression, loneliness, a feeling of isolation, and the sense that life was passing him by. He was a tormented man who spoke of his pain briskly and matter of factly. He did not expect or accept sympathy or understanding. No one liked or respected him, but then he neither liked nor respected anyone. Perfectionistic and scrupulous, by the end of the day he was exhausted: "I am very conscientious and work

---

[1]One's sense of humor must be used sparingly in psychotherapy, especially in the first session. It can be offensive, frightening, narcissistically hurtful, and may contaminate the transference. My flip response may have been motivated by a countertransference triggered by his opening salvo. If so, it could have contributed to the dream that he was going to tell me five weeks later; shooting was part of that dream's manifest content.

hard, not that anyone notices it . . . but, then, I don't care. In your jargon, Doctor, you might say that I am obsessional." Overtly homosexual, he had never had any sexual experiences. He was contemptuous of women; he once dreamed of a "brutish woman," her face, in his words, a composite of Bella Abzug, Betty Friedan, and Martha Raye, in whose grotesquely exaggeratedly made-up mouth he ejaculated, through masturbation, a brown-colored semen. He taught philosophy and theology at the graduate level and was extremely well read in both; but he was, primarily, a musician, which was surprising for a person as rigid and mentally compartmentalized as he was. In fact, he had already composed several masses and liturgical songs which had been performed at Catholic churches and centers throughout the United States. My working diagnosis was obsessive–compulsive character neurosis, with schizoid and depressive features.

In the fourth session, the one session before the dream session, he told me that he was the eighth of nine children; his mother was a volatile, loud, hysterical woman who threw dishes and glasses at her family and was physically abusive of her husband and of her children. His father was a weak, submissive, passive man. His younger brother was the only child his mother liked. He, Father X, grew up in a huge, chaotic house. All his siblings were married and he had over thirty nephews and nieces whose names he hardly knew. When he visited his parents as he had recently for his mother's birthday, the experience was one of total chaos. He asked me in that session how long did I think psychotherapy would take. I said, rather tersely, that it was, of course, up to him, but that it would "take long."

Father X told me his dream in the fifth session, as soon as he had sat in his chair. With a sardonic smile, he said, "Well, I had a dream. Not that dreams mean a darn thing. You told me it's better not to write down one's dreams, but I would have forgotten it, it's a long dream, so I decided to disobey you. Here it is."

"Late for the Concert"

A huge stone house or mansion. I was standing outside. Rifle shots are being exchanged between two groups of opponents: I was right in the middle. The mansion is fantastic, huge, sprawling: hundreds of rooms, architecturally crazy, many wings, jutting protrusions, abutments, patios. I finally get inside. I am supposed to meet a woman conductor. I am either going to play the piano in her orchestra or direct a choir of hundreds. I fear I will be late. There are many locked doors. There is a watchman or janitor but he is not very bright and is so slow, he is no help at all.

I have to go to the bathroom to defecate. I am wearing many layers of clothes and taking them off will retard me even more. The bathroom is painted yellow and is very filthy. I ask the watchman-janitor to clean it up, he does, but with a dirty mop and he is so slow!

I finally make it to the auditorium. I am forty minutes late, instead of 3:30 P.M., I got there at 4:10 P.M. The woman conductor has given my part to a younger musician who is a "technician of the piano" at best, not a true musician. I am resigned, it was my fault in a way, but the slow janitor did not help either.

I told you I do not believe in dreams . . . this dream does not mean a thing. I still think the answer to mental problems is in chemistry and Aristotelian logic . . . you analysts better put your act together!

That janitor . . . reminds me of some Italian bricklayers I saw working near my house when I was a child, how slowly they worked! But then I realized that they lift bricks eight hours a day and had to pace themselves and go slow.

Father X showed no interest in continuing to talk about the dream. After the broadside about chemistry and Aristotelian logic, he did not return to the dream. My soliloquy was very tentative, of course, because I barely knew the patient, and included these thoughts. The house stood for his mother: "stony" or impenetrable; "huge," a giant for the child within the dreamer; "architecturally crazy," hysterical, possibly psychotic. The latent wishes were, among others, the wish to masturbate (he is going to play the piano), the wish to be angry (he has to go to the bathroom to defecate), the wish to be more important than the eighth of nine siblings (he is going to direct a choir of hundreds). I also thought that the "not so bright janitor" represented his father and me; that he had not gotten much help from his father in the past and was not very hopeful he would get much from me now. His inner drives were very well defended (the "many layers of clothes"). He did believe that his mother preferred his younger brother to him (the woman conductor gave Father X's part to the younger musician).

Having come tentatively to understand the dream's session

and the session before it, and, I hoped, the session's dream (the analyst's first two tasks, leading to knowing what the patient's dream says), I had to decide how to respond to the dream (the analyst's third task, knowing what to say to the patient about the dream). Should I remain silent, or make an intervention or interpretation?

This being a first dream, I decided ("not much can be said, not much should be said") to ignore the dream's latent content. Interpretations on the level of the drives (application of the cardinal rule) were out of the question. I decided I would focus on those elements of the manifest dream, of the dream session, and of the sessions preceding the dream which would help me accomplish what I wanted to accomplish at the time, which was to begin to form a relationship with a very resistant patient, a man who felt no one liked or respected him, a man who made light of his pain but was nevertheless tormented. To that end, I wanted to show some empathy, but only some. Too much might have offended and frightened him. I wanted to show him too that there are continuities between what we think and feel during the day, and what we "think" at night while dreaming. If I could help him see those continuities, he might share his dreams with me again. Silence, therefore, was not advisable ("just enough should be said"). So I said:

> In this dream, Father X, you might be revisiting the past, the old past but also the recent past. There is the huge, chaotic home of years ago, but also of recent time. Only last week you told me of your visit there on the occasion of your mother's birthday and how awful that visit was. You see, there is continuity between waking life and dreams. And your dream also tells us how difficult things are—there are worries and concerns, in the dream, and confusion—and you have been telling me how difficult your days are and how exhausted you feel at the end of each day.

It was an intervention in that I "gave" him something (empathy, support), something having nothing to do directly with the dream; and it was an interpretation on the level of the defenses in that I said nothing about the dream's sexuality, rage, and anality. I omitted any references to the precariousness of Father X's position in life (intrapsychically and extrapsychically, present and past), a precariousness clearly alluded to in the manifest dream (rifle shots; standing outside, i.e., isolation; being between conflicting parties). Concerning his internal, conscious, and semiconscious feeling state, I used such words as *confusion, worries,* and *concern* not to risk frightening him with such words as *anxiety* or *fear.* And I used the pronoun *us* ("your dream tells *us*") because this sometimes helps in building the therapeutic alliance. His dreaming the dream and his sharing it with me were successfully used to help us in terms of my agenda at the time, which was to build the therapeutic alliance and help him want to bring in more dreams.

Theoretical Appendix: Some of the Dream Work Defenses

From the dream's manifest content:

House or mansion: symbolism for mother.
Huge: concrete pictorial representation of psychological size of mother.
Hard: concrete pictorial representation of mother's anger, brutality, savagery.
Standing outside: concrete pictorial representation of feeling of alienation.
Rifle shots: displacement from, simile, and symbolism for wounding, hurtful words.
Two groups of opponents: displacement from and simile for opposing factions within the family.
Further descriptive words and adjectives for the mansion: concrete pictorial representation of mother's various psychological characteristics.
Woman conductor: displacement from and symbolism for mother.
Play the piano: displacement from and symbolism for masturbation.
Not very bright: turning into the opposite.
Defecation: undisguised representation of anal drives; concrete pictorial representation of anger.
Yellow: simile or symbolism for fear.
3:30 P.M., 4:10 P.M.: displacement from corresponding life cycle's age periods.

Younger musician: displacement from and symbolism for younger brother.

From the associations—one listens to the dream's session as if it were a dream.

No associations were given

But let us continue with another first dream, one which had the added quality of belonging to the categories of the "simple" dreams and "need" dreams.

"I Was Very Thirsty"

The "simple" dreams, of course, only appear to be "simple" (in orthodox Freudian thinking, a cigar is never just a cigar), and seem simple only in their manifest content. The simple dreams include (1) dreams that are believed to be "simple" because they seem directly, indeed "simply," related to current external life circumstances ("Doctor, this dream is very simple . . . it really means nothing: it's an exact replication of what happens at work every day!"); or dreams are believed to be simple because they were simply provoked by life concerns ("Of course I dreamed about examinations . . . I am having my midterm exam tomorrow!"); (2) dreams that look simple because they seem to have been simply produced by sensory stimulations occurring during sleep (the alarm clock ringing, sounds from the street). These dreams appear simple to patients and analysts because of resistance and counterresistance. For these reasons, simple dreams can be very deceptive and escape analysis.

In addition, some "simple" dreams are also "need" dreams, that is, dreams dreamed in association with a wish experienced consciously on the day before and then dreamed about and gratified directly in that night's dream. Or they are dreams dreamed in association with a physiological need (hunger, thirst, urination, defecation, etc.) experienced the night of the dream. Again, the dreams may have been dreamed in association with the conscious wish from the day before or in association to the physiological need in the dream's night, but it is resistance and counterresistance that make patients and analysts believe that those dreams had been dreamed *only because of* those conscious wishes and physiological needs. These dreams, too, therefore, can be very deceptive and escape analysis.

To return to some basic Freudian theory on dream formation. As discussed more at length in chapter 4, in 1900, when the first edition of *The Interpretation of Dreams* was published, and in 1909, when Freud gave five lectures on psychoanalysis at Clark University, he believed that in some dreams dreamed by children the latent and manifest content could be identical, that those dreams were undistorted. Early on, therefore, even Freud believed that some dreams could be "simple" (that "a cigar could be just a cigar"). As the years went on, however, Freud qualified those earlier statements more and more and eventually ended up believing that, of all the "sources" of dreams, "infantile material" is the most important and one never absent. Thus, in orthodox Freudian thinking, very few dreams, if any, are "simple"; very few dreams, if any, are ever totally undistorted, that is, have a manifest and latent content that are exactly the same. Few, if any, dreams are ever related, solely, to current, external life circumstances, are ever caused only by current life concerns, or are ever purely the result of sensory stimulations occurring during sleep. Few are ever uniquely linked to wishes experienced consciously the day before, are ever exclusively produced by physiological needs experienced during the night.

At the time of his dream, G, an intelligent, cultured, psychologically sophisticated, successful businessman in his late thirties, was coming once a week. The dream was brought into therapy in the fourth session of treatment. His wife was a busy and successful pediatrician in her midthirties; they had been married almost ten years, loved each other, and went along well with one another. They had no children. G had come to therapy because of mild depression, which appeared mainly in the form of, "I can't really enjoy life with total abandon and insouciance unless I am a little drunk," and "excessive timidity in asserting myself." In love making he liked to wait for his wife to "give the signal," to take the initiative, but, after she had, he was "appropriately active." He was not an alcoholic but tended to drink too much too often:

"It's self-medication: it's better than taking tranquilizers or mood-elevators." Drinking did relax him, made him more amorous, and helped him take the initiative. The relevant history gathered thus far included bouts of upper gastrointestinal distress bordering on duodenal ulcer pathology; there was some early evidence of well-covered dependency on his wife. I thought that G was an oral character with passive-dependent propensities, whose character condition decompensated, now and then, into episodes of mild, subclinical depression or psychosomatic gastrointestinal dysfunctions.

Our fourth session started as usual: he greeted me with his customary warm, courteous, and gracious demeanor and sat in his chair with a relaxed and jovial expression on his face. Early in the session, he told me, in a hearty and bluff manner, that, the night before, he and his wife had not eaten together because she had had to go to a professional meeting. He had eaten "all alone," a salty pizza with anchovies; and just before going to sleep, he had had a salty midnight snack. He then added, "and I had a dream, my very first dream, very understandable, considering the junk I had eaten."

"I Was Very Thirsty"

> I was in a cool, tropical forest high in the mountains. Plenty of water everywhere: streams, water falls, little ponds, droplets of water on leaves . . . water, water everywhere. There was a water fountain set high on a wall. I drank and drank to my full satisfaction.

He continued: "Freud was right, as the good Herr Doctor said, we do dream to preserve sleep. I went to sleep thirsty and dreamed of drinking and drinking because I had not drunk enough before going to sleep." He then spoke of a trip to Puerto Rico he had taken with his wife a few weeks before, of having visited El Yunque, Puerto Rico's tropical rain forest, of how taken he had been with the forest's richness in water and moisture and said, "In my dream I was back in El Yunque—plenty of water there!" Both times, he pronounced "El Yunque" as if it had been written "El *J*unque" (i.e., making it sound like "junk"). He did not overtly return to the dream.

My soliloquy included the following thoughts. Being in a "cool" and yet "tropical" forest could be a concrete pictorial representation of "hot" feelings and thoughts ("hot" with anger, hunger, or sexuality). "Water fountain set high on a wall" could represent a penis but, more likely, breasts. If so, "wall" could be a concrete pictorial representation of a wife experienced, the evening before the dream, as neglectful and hard as a wall. He had told me that the evening before the dream he had eaten "all alone." Anger at his wife was also suggested by his pronouncing the word *Yunque* (not just once but twice) as if it were spelled *Junque.* This correlated with his using the word *junk* to refer to the food he had had to eat "all alone" the night before the dream because of his wife's professional commitments. The pronunciation slip suggested that when he was "hot," that is, angry at his wife, he thought of her, or of what she fed him as "junk." (No, G did not speak Spanish, but he prided himself on being able to pronounce foreign words the way they are supposed to be pronounced. He did not speak French either, but had pronounced the word *insouciance,* early on in therapy with the correct French pronunciation.) I also wondered about the "Herr Doctor" in reference to Freud. I wondered whether "Herr" stood for "her" (the feminine pronoun) and was an onomatopoeic reference, again, to his wife, a doctor. There were suggestions of dependency on his wife, and he was somewhat timid with her. I thought, therefore, that his wife probably represented, through displacement, his mother. But I knew nothing about his family background, so I did not let myself go any further with this thought. Of course his insistence, at the very beginning of the session and then again right after telling me the dream, that this dream was a "simple" dream, doubly alerted me to the fact that the dream was not. I tentatively concluded that the dream's latent drives represented thirst and hunger, not for water, but for milk and nurture, and anger at his wife for being, at least the night of the dream, ungiving and ungenerous. Thus, the dream's latent content was oral. This initial conclusion was consistent with the history of mild depression, overdrinking, and upper gastrointestinal distress bordering on ulcer.

Having come to understand, albeit tentatively, what G's dream said, I had now to decide how to respond to his dream.

This being a first dream, the latent content was to be ignored and interpretations on the level of the drives excluded. Unlike Father X, G was a cooperative, highly motivated patient, resistant only to the extent to which all patients resist. Since he would probably continue to tell me dreams, silence would have been appropriate. But at the end of the session he did say: "So, what do you think of the dream?" It would probably still have been appropriate to answer by saying that I did not really know (which was not an untruth) or by asking him if he had any further thoughts about the dream. But it was almost the end of the hour and I did want to "give" him something, to be nurturing, maybe, to some infinitesimal degree. So I said:

> You did go to bed very thirsty . . . I wonder what else you may have been thirsty for.

It was an *intervention*, in that I "gave" him something more relevant to his general clinical status than to the dream, an intervention on the level of the defenses, the defenses making him want to see his dream as a "simple" dream of thirst only for water. It was maybe also an *interpretation*, in that I alluded to factors other than his realistic thirst as being behind the dream. My acknowledging his realistic thirst contributed to the therapeutic alliance; and it was not an untruth. His realistic thirst did contribute to the dream, it was a day's residue that had overcathected, or resonated with, other kinds of thirsts, it corresponded to two of Freud's three sources of dreams (Freud's "recent and indifferent material in dreams" and "somatic sources" of dreams; see chapter 4). Alluding to other kinds of thirst was a soft tap on one of the doors opening onto G's royal road to his unconscious, a tap that I hoped would encourage him to open the door a little further and permit us further progress.

Theoretical Appendix: Some of the Dream Work Defenses

From the dream's manifest content:

Cool: turning into the opposite.
Tropical: concrete pictorial representation of hot, passionate, feelings.

Forest: Displacement from dreamer's id; indirectly, concrete pictorial representation of a tangled mysterious place with primitive, wild feelings.

High: turning into the opposite (feelings are "low," they "reside" in one's "heart," or "guts," or genitals; ideas, thoughts, ideals are "high," they "reside" in one's head). But, also: concrete pictorial representation of ecstatic feelings.

Water, streams, ponds, etc.: displacement from milk.

Water fountain: displacement from and symbolism for breast.

High (on a wall): concrete pictorial representation of inaccessibility.

Wall: concrete pictorial representation of wife's (and mother's?) imperviousness.

From the associations—one listens to the dream's session as if it were a dream:

Herr Doctor: "her," a woman doctor.
El Yunque (pronounced "El Junque"): "junk."

"Time for a Change"

At the time of this dream, the patient, E, was in her early forties. She had been my student at Fordham University Graduate School of Social Service and had entered psychotherapy three years after having earned her master's degree in social work. She was a medical social worker in a hospital in New York City. The dream occurred around the fifth month of therapy; she had just begun to come twice a week and to use the couch. She was a Dominican nun and had stopped wearing her black-and-white habit about ten years earlier.

E was attractive and personable. She was timid and reserved but hid her seriousness and somberness under a jovial and friendly demeanor and consistently impeccable good manners. Most of the time she related to me in a cordial, warm, manner. She was slightly overweight and had been grossly overweight before puberty. She was the oldest of three children, her two sisters being respectively two and five years younger. Her parents were Irish-American. Her father was a "good and gentle man," her mother, "warm and fair, but irascible and strict, demanding, especially of me." E was intelligent and conscientious. She was serious about her religious commitments in an authentic, mature, "post-Vatican II" manner. She had entered the Dominicans in her teens and had never been sexually active; she masturbated infrequently and did not make "a big deal" about it, at least consciously. She had more difficulty with the vow of obedience than with the vows of poverty or chastity. She could be angry inside, but never became openly angry. Through her adult years, she had learned to stand her ground and win arguments with persons in authority through a determined, pertinacious stance and with the help of cool, brisk, and impeccably good manners.

E came for psychotherapy because of "feelings of sadness," social isolation, and various interpersonal difficulties. Winning arguments with authority figures was costly to her: she would feel guilty afterwards, or compelled to "make up" to those persons by being extra solicitous and sometimes haunting them in a persecuting way, with kindliness and agreeableness. Diagnostically, I saw her as depressed and orally fixated, with passive-aggressive but also obsessional character propensities and tyrannized by a superego rigidly expecting her to be serious, good, and self-sacrificing, to control her anger, to be sexually inhibited, to be always fair, not to be playful, and to love her neighbors more than herself.

E was a "good patient." She never missed a session and always came on time. She was "serious" about therapy, a self-inquiring person who was curious about what "made her tick," and who wanted to make inroads "into her subconscious." Unconsciously, of course, it was different: she did not tell me dreams very frequently. "Time for a Change" was after about twenty sessions of therapy, only her third dream. The transference was positive but had not developed fully and was still diffuse. The therapeutic alliance was excellent. There had been no changes in E's personality by the time of the dream, except that, because of the influence of the positive transference, because of the therapeutic alliance, and because of beginning changes in her superego, she had become slightly less serious, slightly more playful, slightly less hard on herself. The session before the dream session she had spoken about a "mini-argument" with the Superior in her convent, who had scolded E about the somewhat spirited liturgy E had arranged for the Sunday Mass and about E's playing jazz on the convent piano.

E began the session by commenting on the "nice weather outside." She exhibited her usual jovial and friendly demeanor. She spoke about enjoying herself a little more at work, of having less of a "work-work-work" attitude, of being able to "give herself a break" from time to time, of bantering more with her coworkers. She played with her Fordham graduation ring by sliding it off and on again, not a characteristic behavior of hers. She told me that a few days before she had visited Sister C in a hospital. Sister C was a fairly close friend of hers, the sister with whom she had entered religious life many years before, an Italian-American woman of whom she was fond. "By the way," she said, "I had a dream of visiting a nun in a hospital last night. I am sure it was triggered by my visiting Sister C a few days ago." At this point she told me the dream,

"Time for a Change"

> I was visiting a sister (another nun) in a hospital. She was convalescing from some kind of surgery on her back: something like "dura mater" had been removed from her back? I am not sure about that: it had been removed? It was going to be removed? I am not sure. I offered to change her bedsheets and she accepted. Instead of white sheets, I put on the bed a nice set of sheets with a flowery pattern. Then the scene changes. I am with my mother, in a bathroom? Again, I am not sure of this. I see two baby elephants, one black, one white, splashing water all over the place with their trunks.

Having told me the dream, E repeated that she was "positive" the dream had to do with having visited her friend in the hospital. The fidgeting with the ring had continued through the telling of the dream. She then told me that in childhood her mother used to tease her about being overweight by calling her "Ellenfant," a play of words on E's first name. E wondered whether the elephants in the dream stood for her. She told me that Sister Superior, in her convent, had "practically apologized" to her for her comments about E's playing the piano in the convent: "It pleased me, but it made me feel guilty, too." Then, returning to the dream, she said, "Those bedsheets, with all those flowers, really, really pretty, I was so glad!" The fidgeting with the ring on her finger had slightly increased in frequency and intensity; throughout the session so far, she had been lying on the couch in a perfectly composed fashion but with her legs under her long skirt slightly apart. At this point in the session, she stopped talking, stopped fidgeting with the ring, put her arms by her sides on the couch, crossed her legs, and asked me what did I think of the dream.

My internal soliloquy included these thoughts. The nun she was visiting in the manifest dream could be a displacement from E, and maybe, me (same surname initials; both Italian). The surgery being performed in the manifest dream (removing the "dura mater"—the meningeal sheath around the brain) could be a concrete pictorial representation of therapy, through which her superego was beginning to relent, her "strict, demanding" mother was being taken off her back. I also thought that changing the bedsheets from white to flowery sheets represented (through symbolism and, again, concrete pictorial representation), a desire for less seriousness and rigidity in behavior, less lily-white "purity," more playfulness, more sexuality, a desire that was being gratified, in the dream, precisely because her "dura mater" was relenting. I thought that this desire appeared also at the end of the dream, where she (elephant = Ellenfant) was being playful and aggressive with her mother. I also felt that the elephants being black and white represented (concrete pictorial representation) the black-and-white, all-or-nothing, dimensions of her personality, as well as the black and white of the Dominican habit. Her playing, with her mother, *in a bathroom* and the elephants splashing water *with their trunks,* hinted at anal and phallic dimensions in her character structure. In "resonating" with the material presented in the dream's session and in the sessions preceding it, I felt that the gratifications represented in the dream correlated with her uncharacteristic behavior in the dream's session—the classic masturbatory equivalent of playing with the ring on her finger—and with her changing behavior in her waking life. In the dream's session, she had told me she had been enjoying herself more at work; in the session before the dream, she had told me that she had been playing jazz on her convent's piano (using her hands to give herself pleasure: a possible sublimation of masturbation). In preceding sessions she had been telling me that she had become less serious, more playful, less hard on herself. I tentatively decided that the dream's latent drives included phallic, and possibly anal, autoerotic drives and aggressive drives, as well as desires for greater autonomy (having less of a hard mother on her back).

Having come to understand, tentatively, of course, what E's dream said, I had to decide what to say to E, if anything, about her dream. Should it be an intervention or an interpretation? We were still in the earliest stages of therapy, this was not a first dream, but it was only the third in about twenty sessions of therapy. Even though E was not fragile and the therapeutic alliance was already strong, there was no question but that the cardinal rule should not be applied, and no interpretation on the level of the drives should be given. But, should I be silent, even though E had asked me what I thought about the dream? Because she had only recalled three dreams in about twenty sessions, something should be said to help her remember her dreams more. Also, I wanted to strengthen the therapeutic alliance more: there was hard work ahead (plenty of "dura mater" still to "remove," plenty of superego defenses still to analyze) especially considering that she had just begun coming twice a week and had just begun using the couch. I thought that to say something mildly supportive and superficially interpretative would further those two aims of my internal agenda (help her remember her dreams more and strengthen the therapeutic alliance). Thus, even though it was not the end of the session, I decided not to deflect her question about the meaning of the dream by turning it back on her or by asking for any associations to the dream. I said:

> You began the session by saying, "Nice weather outside." There seems to be "nicer weather" in your world too, both your external world and your internal world. In your external world, the Superior in the convent is less on your back, she even apologizes to you, and you are enjoying yourself more, are being more playful. In your internal world, you feel you are becoming less serious, and again, more playful, less hard on yourself. And even in the internal world of your dreams there is "nicer weather": there are flowers, the flowery patterns of the bedsheets for Sister C, the successful surgery, and playfulness in the latter part of the dream. And I agree with you: the elephants in the dream could stand for you, since your mother at times called you "Ellenfant."

It was mainly an *intervention*. By connecting the dream to the dream's session (when I referred to her opening statement, "Nice weather outside") and to the sessions before the dream (when I referred to what she had been telling me about her overall functioning), I was demonstrating to the patient continuity between thinking while awake and thinking while asleep (i.e., dreaming) and I thought that this could further her dream recollection. I was also showing E that I did indeed listen to her, and did remember what she said: even patients who are not paranoid will understandably feel better when they realize that the powerful parent–therapist does listen to what they say and remembers it, and this might help with the therapeutic alliance. It was an intervention entirely on the level of the defenses, since I said nothing about drives: the masturbatory equivalents in the dream session (i.e., playing with the ring) or in the sessions preceding it (i.e., playing the piano in the convent), or anger at the Superior (i.e., mother). To the minimal and superficial extent to which my response was interpretative, it was an interpretation entirely on the level of the defenses, because I did not try to "analyze away" any of the defenses distorting the underlying drives. I did not contradict her about who Sister C, the nun she visited in the manifest dream, really was. If I had told her that Sister C stood for me, it would have been an interpretation on the level of the transference. I did not connect the "dura mater" to her mother, or surgery to therapy, or flowers and playfulness to sensuality and sexuality, and, of course, made no reference to the dream's latent drives.

With this dream too, as with Father X's and G's dreams, there were many doors offering an entry to the royal road to the unconscious; with this dream too, the offer was declined and the road was not entered (not with the patient); I did not even gently tap on one of the doors, as I did with G's dream. Confirming the connection "elephant = Ellenfant" was done to help the patient see the continuities between one's history and one's dreams; it did not "analyze away" any defenses, or puncture any bubbles of repression. The memory of mother calling her "Ellenfant" was a preconscious memory she had communicated to me herself in the dream's session.

Theoretical Appendix: Some of the Dream Work Defenses

From the dream's manifest content:

Sister: displacement from dreamer herself.
Hospital: displacement from psychotherapy room, symbolism for a place where one goes to get well when one is ill.
Surgery on her back: displacement from and simile for psychotherapy.
Back: displacement from "back of the head," the unconscious. (Therapy works on the unconscious, on the "back of the head.")
Dura Mater: onomatopoeia for her hard, difficult mother and her superego.
Not being sure about the dura mater being removed: secondary revision.
Changing the bedsheets: displacement from or simile for therapeutic changes.
White sheets: symbolism for purity.
Flowery patterned sheets: symbolism for sexuality, playfulness, freedom.
Baby elephants: displacement from dreamer, and, possibly, symbolism for dreamer's phallic wishes.
Black and white: concrete pictorial representation of dogmatic, simplistic thinking; and displacement from Dominican habit.
Dominican habit: concrete pictorial representation of dogmatic, simplistic thinking.
Splashing water with trunks: concrete pictorial representation of playfulness, phallic activity, and urination.

From the associations—one listens to the dream's session as if it were a dream:

The only associations were *nonverbal,* spoken through *body language* (*fidgeting with the ring on her finger*). They symbolically represented masturbation.

Two more examples, working with the first and second dreams of the same patient, B, "Swimming Underwater" and "Animal Trap."

"Swimming Underwater"

B told me this dream, his first dream, during his eighth session of therapy; he was coming, at the time, once a week.

B was a handsome and elegant man in his midforties, athletic and tall. He was a high-level executive with one of the major Wall Street investment houses. He came into therapy on his wife's insistence: "She is a psychiatric social worker and sees things that I don't see." In his first session of therapy, he told me that he loved his wife, was very happy with her, and she was his best friend; and that she loved him very much too, but was unhappy about some aspects of his behavior. He added that he "guessed" he did have "some small problems, nothing to write home about, but still mildly disturbing; I could be happier, and I should be less of a loner and I have a problem which I am very ashamed of, masturbation." He added that his problems did not make sense: he was very successful, had a lovely wife and two wonderful children: he should be very happy. He had a "fabulous" sex life. Why should he masturbate?

B had a very open, trusting, engaging face which frequently broke up into an open, trusting, engaging smile. In his third session of therapy, he told me that he called that, "the buddy smile." The truth of the matter, he said, was that he did not often feel like smiling and that he was not a very trusting person. ("There are plenty of sharks in my field . . . I trust no one, not my business associates, God forbid, or my clients; not even my secretary, who has been with me for over ten years.") Interestingly, after he told me about the "buddy smile," I was treated to it only at the beginning and at the end of the session, not so much during the session, and less and less as our work went on.

B was popular and had a reputation for being "very sociable, the life of the party," but he really liked best being home reading or playing competitive golf. Elaborating on his marriage, he told me again that he loved and trusted his wife, "She is my best friend, she is my buddy," and that his wife loved him, but she was not happy with his "buddy smile." She barely tolerated it when he used it at corporate parties or dinners, openly disliked it when he engaged in it at gatherings attended by no business associates or clients, and was enraged by it if he broke into it at home, with her or with their two children. He was unhappy about his wife's unhappiness about that, believed she was right in being upset with him about it, and felt "sad about it, I don't need it with her . . . with her, I do it from sheer force of habit . . . I trust her . . . I told you, she's my buddy." He added that earlier in the marriage, his wife had also been unhappy with his difficulty in enjoying her companionship in "typically female kinds of things like shopping, decorating the house, buying flowers." With this too, he had been unhappy about his wife's unhappiness, believed that she was right in being upset about this "quirk of his," and felt, again, "sad . . . I cannot help it . . . I am a typical man's man. She is still slightly unhappy about this, but she is such a buddy, she has adjusted to it and does not complain about it much any more. And she appreciates my strong cards, I make a very nice living for both of us, we have two luxurious homes, and a great sex life."

B had told me that he and his wife made love frequently and both enjoyed it very much, but in the seventh session (the one before the dream's session), he told me that his wife was "slightly unhappy" with him about something else: his difficulty in remaining in bed with her and cuddling up with her after lovemaking was over. In that session (I learned the "gory details" of his behavior much later), he told me that as soon as they had both climaxed and she had assured him that she did not wish to continue making love, he liked to get out of bed, and, no matter the hour, do "something else." The "gory details" were not gory at all, just bizarre, as human behavior can often be. B would literally bolt out of bed as soon as lovemaking was over; the "something else" he wanted to do was not something "conventional," such as reading, taking a shower, having a cup of coffee. (What is "conventional" in our culture, after making love?) No, he would feel compelled (again, no matter the time of night), to cook himself a bowl of pasta—and he was not even Italian. This behavior was completely ego syntonic; when he eventually told me about it, he said, "Well, you are Italian, I'm sure you do the same thing." With this third problem too, B was unhappy about his wife's unhappiness with him, but could not really understand her feelings. "I don't like her being unhappy with *anything* I do, but, with this, I am really puzzled. It isn't that I haven't pleased her sexually, but after lovemaking I feel kind of antsy in bed, not quite claustrophobic, but wanting to get up and out of bed."

B called these problems between him and his wife "miniproblems," but he was concerned with his wife's concerns with his behavior, and had become more and more aware that his wife wanted more from their marriage than being his buddy, having two luxurious homes, and having a "fabulous" sexual life. His unhappiness over his wife's unhappiness was undoubtedly one important reason why he had acceded to her request that he enter therapy. Concerning masturbation, he told me that he masturbated almost every other morning, whether he had or had not made love to his wife the night before. This "bad habit" disturbed him on two grounds: "It feels childish, immature, almost perverse"; and "it keeps me from making love to my wife," because the evening after the mornings on which he had masturbated, "For whatever reasons, hormonal or whatever, I do not feel amorous." (For B to have said "make love *to*" rather than *with* his wife was accurate: he served his wife with his penis rather than sharing it with her.).

Diagnostically, I saw B as a high-functioning schizoid personality. I thought he had serious problems with trust and intimacy, probably especially where women were concerned. He could not even trust a secretary who had worked with him for years, and his behavior with his wife, both sexual and nonsexual, and his protestations about her being his buddy, suggested that unconsciously he feared closeness with her too. There were also passive-dependent and passive-aggressive traits. Hunger for nurture and dependency were behind his social skills, his capacity to be accommodating, his need to be "buddy" to his wife, his need to seem "buddy" to those he did not like, and his need to serve his wife with his penis, his money, and the two luxurious homes. The buddy smile also served the purpose of hiding his anger. Passive-aggressiveness and aggressiveness projected outward were behind his ingratiating techniques and his schizoid mistrust of people. Up to the time of the dream, I knew nothing about B's childhood or family history. Concerning his wife's feelings and reactions to him and about him, it may be important to add that at no time in those first eight sessions had I felt that she was a demanding or controlling person or a "nagging" wife. As I came to know her better through my work with B, I had no reason to change my mind about her. I thought that she was a woman of courage and psychological integrity, that she did love B, wanted the best for him, and wanted him to want more and better for himself.

Our eighth session, the dream session, started out as usual: B sat in his chair and flashed "the buddy smile" at me. After that, he loosened his tie a bit, he had never done that before; it was not a particularly warm evening. Then he told me that he had had a dream, his first dream since he had come to see me.

"Swimming Underwater"

> I had a dream, last night, a very brief dream. It does not make sense at all: there is no plot, no story. This is the dream: I am swimming underwater, in a pool, maybe.

B said, "As I said, it does not make any sense at all, the dream has no story line, no plot." I encouraged him to go on, to just say anything coming to his mind, whether it seemed it had to do with the dream or not. He said the dream reminded him of a movie he had seen a few evenings before, *The Graduate*, and of the Dustin Hoffman character in the swimming pool of his parents' house, "with the scuba equipment, spear gun and all" he had just received as graduation gifts. He repeated that the dream did not seem to make any sense; but his next three associations (he thought, of course, that he was changing the subject) gave me an intimation of what the dream might be about.

He first talked of his masturbation. He told me that he had masturbated that morning, which meant he would not feel like making love with his wife that night. He said that his wife had no idea he masturbated at all, let alone that he did it almost every other day. He could not understand what it did to his sexual desires: "I can make love to my wife, and come more than once in a night, and masturbate the next morning just five or six hours later. But I might not even have an erection tonight, because I masturbated this morning. It cannot be only shame and guilt." Next, he spoke about Miss X, a woman on Wall Street, a successful investment banker, with whom he had had lunch the day before. He found her "cold, demanding, obnoxious," did not like or trust her. He added that she could be good looking, but dresses "almost like a nun, a Mother Superior kind of nun—I wonder what it would be like to sleep with her—well—I would not touch her with a ten foot pole." During the lunch he had been very charming, of course, "buddy-smiled her so much that my face ached afterwards." He then said: "Strange, but something comes to mind that goes back to my high school days, more than thirty years ago. Talking of Miss X dressing like a nun, long skirt and all, brought it to mind—God, thirty years ago and I can still get all steamed up about it." "It" concerned a priest who had taught him religion in high school, "and in those days priests wore the full habit, a long skirt." He described the priest as "a very obnoxious man . . . I feared him and I hated him. He thought he had my number, he thought that I was a liar, he thought I concealed a lot, he called me 'submarine.' " In talking about this man, he became agitated, as I had never seen him become before. A few seconds later, he composed himself, gave me the buddy smile and said, "Well, it's almost the end of the hour. I would never have thought that I would ever think of that again."

My very first thought, right after he had told me the dream, was that the dream, of course, had to do with concealment of feelings, with keeping feelings "underwater," so to speak, hidden. His first association to the dream (*The Graduate* and the Dustin Hoffman character in his scuba outfit) seemed to confirm this thought. After all, the theme of concealment, the theme of hiding negative feelings about associates and clients through spurious sociability and the buddy smile had been a prominent theme. So, I thought, B was swimming underwater to hide feelings of anger and mistrust. I also thought he could be underwater to express anger and mistrust, to spear "the sharks" he had referred to in his third session. My soliloquy also included the thought that loosening his tie at the beginning of the hour suggested that matters were getting psychically hot for him; and, from his association to *The Graduate*, that maybe, he was about to "graduate" to a new level of interaction, with me and within himself. Of course, his repeatedly protesting that the dream "did not make sense at all," was revealing in and of itself.

When B had first mentioned *The Graduate*, I had found myself thinking of the character Mrs. Robinson, and her seducing the character played by Dustin Hoffman, who was young enough to be her son. That is, I had found myself thinking of B's oedipal feelings about his mother; since I knew nothing about B's mother, I did not let myself trust that thought. But as I listened to B's three associations (concerning masturbation, Miss X, and the priest from high school), I found that those associations were suggesting to me a number of speculations about B's still unconscious feelings about his wife and at least one other woman, Miss X. Because of those associations, my internal soliloquy now included these thoughts. Through compulsive masturbation, B avoided intercourse with his wife, and thus escaped intimacy with her and indirectly expressed his fear of her and his anger at her. B believed that his wife "had no idea" that he masturbated. His masturbation, therefore, and all that masturbation expressed about B's unconscious feelings, his anger and fear, were indeed concealed, were "underwater." I further thought that there were connections, based on predicate thinking similarities, among B's wife, Miss X, and the high school priest; and connections among the three of them on the one hand, and, if not B's own mother (I knew nothing about her), then at least "mother figures" on the other hand.

Thus, I thought that B's associations about masturbation, Miss X, and the high school priest, spoke about his unconscious preoedipal and oedipal conflicts about his mother or a mother figure. The dream was very well defended. In its manifest content, there was indeed "no story, no plot," and, except for swimming, no action. Its latent content was not simply distorted through the dream work, it had been totally hidden, was indeed, "underwater," was, in fact, so submerged, that there was nothing in the manifest content (condensed, displaced, represented pictorially, or symbolized), that could be traced back to its latent antecedents. Intimations about the dream's latent content had come, not through retracing of dream work operations from manifest to latent, but from the patient's associations about masturbation, Miss X, and the high school priest, associations that the patient did not, consciously, consider associations to the dream. He consciously thought he was changing the subject. Those associations suggested that the latent dream contained precisely those preoedipal and oedipal drives.

Having come to a tentative understanding of what B's dream said, I had now to decide what I would say to B, if anything, about his dream. These were the thoughts that guided my response to B's dream: that the dream was, indeed, very well defended; that after telling me (three times) that the dream made no sense at all, and sharing with me his two direct associations to his dream (*The Graduate* and Dustin Hoffman in the pool), B had asked me no questions about the dream and had seemed to leave the dream and change the subject. Therefore, B was not ready to work on the dream. I also thought that this was a first dream, that the therapeutic alliance was tenuous, and that the transference was largely undeveloped. All this recommended utmost prudence and discretion in responding to the dream. I also thought that, notwithstanding all these factors, the patient was "working" in therapy relatively well. He had always come on time, was verbal, was reasonably spontaneous, and did have a dream, strongly defended as the dream was, and that the "regressive drift"[2] had started. This was another indication that the patient, resistance and all, was indeed "working." I decided that the cardinal rule, of course, would not be applied; and that my response would consist of an intervention that would not refer to the dream at all and would, instead, support the regressive drift and strengthen the therapeutic alliance. So I said:

> I am glad you went back to that memory. It must be important, if, as you said, it can get you all steamed up, more than thirty years later.

---

[2]With a patient who is "working" relatively well in therapy, one will observe, after a number of sessions, a going back to *preconscious* memories belonging to earlier and earlier times: the "regressive drift." Each regressive drift goes on for a while, then suddenly stops, and the patient goes back to more current events, only to go into another regressive drift whenever the defenses allow it. *Where* the regressive drift stops usually corresponds to fixation points in the unconscious; the *preconscious* memory at which point the regressive drift stopped is usually the screen of a particularly powerful *unconscious* memory (thus regressive drifts are valuable also diagnostically). Regressive drifts are produced because of the dynamic influence of the unconscious and are facilitated by free associations and by the very nature of psychoanalytical treatment, which is of a regressive nature. B's regressive drift had gone from masturbation the morning of the dream session, to the lunch with Miss X the day before, and to his religion teacher more than thirty years before, at which point the drift stopped and B propelled himself back to the present. The teacher calling him "submarine," I conjectured, may have corresponded to a fixation point about some activity he wanted to conceal from his mother; the *preconscious* memory of the teacher labeling him a liar may have been a screen for an *unconscious* memory of an experience in which his mother accused him of being a liar.

I did not refer to the dream at all: hence, there was no inter-pretation, either on the level of the drives or the defenses. The intervention was not about the dream, but about the preconscious memory. Support was given, quite directly, to the importance of bringing in preconscious memories and, indirectly, to the idea that it may be all right "to get steamed up" about something. I thought and hoped that the intervention would help him with future regressive drifts, would strengthen the therapeutic alliance, and would be a step in superego analysis.

As already indicated, the dream was so well defended that the only dream work operation was a massive repression of the latent content: the latent content was "sent underwater." Since none of the other dream work defenses (displacement, concrete pictorial representation, symbolism, etc.) were in operation, we shall not have the usual "Theoretical Appendix on Dream Work Defenses."

In the next session, B brought up his second dream.

"Animal Trap"

The session started as it usually did. B flashed his buddy smile at me and made himself comfortable in his chair. He did not, this time, loosen his necktie. He launched into a good-humored, gen-tly phrased tirade about his secretary, how she meant well but drove him crazy with her perfectionism and with her blushing if he complimented her about her good looks. "She is kind of repressed, I never compliment her in a vulgar way (some men can be very crude, I never am), or in a way that might be construed as coming on to her." He spoke, at some length, about a difficult deal he was trying to negotiate, about feeling he was being "caught between a rock and a hard place" and "caught in a hole." He referred to Miss X, with whom he had spoken briefly on the telephone. "I bet she could 'hear' my buddy smile through the wire." He said, "Maybe I am not talking of any heart-rending problems, but I like to be able to talk to you about . . . whatever. I told you, except with my wife, I am guarded with people, appear-ances notwithstanding." Having mentioned his wife, he told me that they had made love a couple of times since he had seen me, and, once, he had been able to remain in bed with her afterwards for a little while, but had felt "antsy, a little claustrophobic, not relaxed." "The next morning I masturbated," he added. He then briefly reminisced about sexual experiences going back to his college years; he always liked to get out of bed "as soon as the sex part was over. I feel a bed is only to sleep and make love." He spoke of relationships he had before meeting his wife, "Very attractive ladies, nice, too, but I did not let myself get attached to any of them. Those girls I did not love; but with my wife, whom I love very much, I don't understand why I shouldn't like to remain in bed next to her and cuddle up." Then, just a few minutes before the end of the session: "By way of absolutely nothing, I had a dream, last night. There is a little more, in this, than in the previous one, but this too makes no sense, seems to come from nowhere, and seems hardly connected with anything in my current life."

"Animal Trap"

> I am trying to get out of a tight hole . . . I was in it with both feet . . . some kind of an animal trap? . . . a bear trap, maybe.

He added: "Well, it's time to go. I am a hunter, but I have never seen animal traps. I suppose some are just camouflaged holes in the ground, but I hear that some are really vicious, with teeth and stuff." And, "But what about dreams? This dream too seems so unconnected to anything going on in my life!"

Up to the time when, toward the end, B had told me his dream, my internal soliloquy about the dream's session had included the following thoughts. The regressive drift had momentarily stopped, except for the brief reminiscing, and that reminiscing had only drifted to his college years, concerning previous sexual experiences. He had not loosened his necktie, this time, at the beginning of the session, because no dynamically very significant unconscious derivatives were about to come up. Unconscious derivatives, of course, come up all the time, the only question being how threatening they are to one's defenses, and this is determined by the dynamic equilibrium of one's neurotic conflict at any particular time. Indeed, B may not have been talking of any "heart-rending problems," but the material being verbalized was, nevertheless, still important. I had also been thinking that well defended anger at women, maybe especially at "repressed" women, was seeping through in the tirade about his secretary, in his mentioning having given the buddy smile to Miss X on the telephone, and in his referring to the young women he had dated in college as "ladies." It again made me wonder whether there had been, in his childhood, a mother or a mother figure who had been "a lady," who had "driven him crazy" with the same kind of perfectionism and repressed behavior as his secretary exhibited and the same kind of demeanor as Miss X did. I also thought that his mistrust and intimacy problems with women were confirmed by his postcoital behavior with the "ladies" he had dated before meeting his wife; by his telling me again about feeling "antsy, a little claustrophobic, not relaxed," after sex with his wife; and by his asserting that he never let himself get "attached" to anyone before his wife (by the way, he had not married till he had reached his midthirties). But it was only after he told me the dream that some of the dream's session material took a sharper psychodynamic focus.

I first thought that, although well defended enough for a dream of a nonpsychotic patient, this dream was more revealing than the previous one. Its latent material was distorted through the basic operations of the dream work. It was possible to speculate about its latent content by simply retracing the steps of the dream work's defensive operations from the manifest level to its latent antecedents. It was possible "to know what the dream said," just from the dream, none of which had been true in the previous dream. The latent dream, I thought, was about *very aggressive* phallic and oral erotic wishes against a mother figure (again, I still knew nothing about his mother, so I could not more simply say "against his mother"). The semilatent dream was about the castration fears and anxiety those aggressive wishes elicited. More specifically, my internal soliloquy about the dream included these thoughts. The "tight hole" represented a woman's vagina, a vagina tight around a man's penis, or, more broadly, the embracing, enfolding, encircling, entwining, and engulfing behavior by a woman toward a man. On the level of the dream's semilatent content, B believed that a woman's vagina can be as vicious as an animal trap and that a woman's embrace is not to be trusted. On that level, he believed that a terrible fate could befall men who were not wary of women, men who were willing to jump into the hole "with both feet." He thought that one better not be "bare" ("bear" in the manifest dream), that is, physically naked (sexual) and psychologically naked (trusting). I also thought that B might have, in his unconscious, a "vagina dentata" fantasy, the fantasy of a vagina with teeth that will tear apart the unwary man's penis, a fantasy not uncommon in the unconscious of men suffering with sexual disabilities. On a deeper level, the level of the dream's latent content, I thought that B wanted to jump into women's (mother's?) vagina, and, more broadly, into mother's body, heart, mind, soul, with all his rage, unambivalently, and be a wild animal, a bare bear, and tear women (mother?) apart with his teeth. The vagina dentata fantasy of impotent men is usually a projection; a man who is sexually impotent because of preoedipal biting rage against his mother, projects his wish to bite and castrate mother, onto mother; and then sees mother as biting and castrating.

Having fantasized in this fashion about the session's dream, my thinking about the dream's session included psychodynamically deeper conjectures. I thought that I understood better B's feeling "antsy, a little claustrophobic, not relaxed," after love making was over, because cuddling up with his wife was like being in the tight hole, was like being in a bear trap. He had masturbated, after having forced himself to stay in bed after love making, to relieve himself of the anxiety caused by having forced himself to do that. His telling me, his only association to the dream, that he was a hunter, connected with my fantasy that there was anger in his latent dream and in his unconscious. Telling me twice that the dream hardly connected with anything in his *current* life confirmed that the dream, of course, had infantile sources. Finally, I thought that, during the session, unbeknownst to him, at least consciously, he had indeed been talking of heart-*rending* matters: "vicious" traps, "with teeth and stuff," do "rend" the heart, and other organs. In business, talking of being "between a rock and a hard place . . . caught in a hole," was also an unconscious derivative of being in the tight hole he had dreamed about. I also wondered whether in telling me about his secretary, and his never being "crude" to her, was a way of telling me that he was never "an animal." As long as he was not an animal and respected women, he did not have to be afraid of being caught in an animal trap.

On a general, clinical–psychodynamic plane, I also thought that B could be sexually potent with women for two reasons, in spite of how loaded his unconscious was with rage at women and with fear of that rage. One was that his potency was more phallic than genital, more "anatomical" (organ-connected, penile potency), than total or existential (person-connected, general potency). His sexual behavior, I believed, was more the case of a part (the penis) of a man's total self, being massaged by a part (the vagina) of a woman's total self, than the case of a truly interdependent, interpersonal, object-related interaction between two human beings, as in genital sexuality. He was only able to enjoy his wife's or previous partners' sexual parts, not the entire woman or a woman's "womanly" pursuits ("I guess I am a man's man," he had said early on). The second reason was that he needed his penis to serve and appease women, to assure them that he was "their buddy," a peaceful and gentle teddy bear, not an angry and hungry, powerful and dangerous, big bear.

Having come to understand, tentatively of course, what the dream said, was I going to say anything to B about the dream? An interpretation on the level of the drives was out of the question. These were the thoughts that guided my decision. I had a patient who was working relatively well in therapy, who had begun to remember his dreams, who had, indeed, brought in two dreams in two subsequent sessions, who had already been capable of a very productive regressive drift in the previous session and of a fairly productive one in his last session. The therapeutic alliance was still tenuous, but he had just told me that he liked "to be able to talk" to me "about . . . whatever." On the other hand, yes, he had had two dreams in two succeeding weeks, but he had told me this dream almost at the end of the hour (telling me, in effect, that he did not want to work on it), had disparaged the dream's value, and had twice declared that the dream had no connection whatever to his current life concerns. Also, I had felt a twinge of countertransferential anxiety when he had seemed to disparage the value of *all* dreams, not just this last dream of his ("What about dreams? This dream too seems so unconnected to anything"). I had felt tempted to make a connection between

the dream's "tight hole" and having felt "caught in a hole" in
trying to negotiate a difficult deal, "to prove" to him the continuities between daily concerns and dreams. But I was able to resist
the temptation: I felt I should respect his need to separate the
"hole" he consciously experienced in his business life, from the
much more frightening ones he thought about unconsciously and
had dreamed about in this dream. I decided that my response
would be an intervention, rather than an interpretation on the
level of the defenses. It would not refer to the dream at all and
would, as I had done the week before, further strengthen the
therapeutic alliance and support the regressive drift. I said:

> I am glad that you like to talk to me about . . . whatever, especially because
> you are able to talk about the present, but are also able, quite spontane-
> ously, to go back to the past like when you were telling me, today, about
> girl friends going back to your college years.

I did not refer to the dream at all, hence, no interpretation.
The intervention was not about anything he had said in the manifest dream, or about his one association to the dream (being a
hunter), but about what he had said about talking to me and
what he had said about his college women friends. The fact that
there was no time left for a different, or lengthier kind of response was not instrumental, I believe, in my choice of response.
I would have responded as I did regardless of the amount of time
left. I would not even have wanted, had I had more time, actively
to ask for associations. I thought and hoped, again, that the intervention would help with more regressive shifts and would further
strengthen the therapeutic alliance. But this dream, too, I felt,
was a dream to file and remember. As many early and first dreams
do, this dream did encapsulate the core dynamic of the neurosis.

Theoretical Appendix: Some of the Dream Work Defenses

From the dream's manifest content:

Tight hole: symbolism for female genitals; concrete pictorial representation of any harrowingly and dangerously constricting, en-
trapping, imprisoning situation; any situation causing "anxiety"

in the etymological sense of the word *anxiety* (*angustia*, a narrowing, confining, contracting, tightening of one's self. When we are anxious, our chest feels constricted, confined, tight and we breathe deeply to relieve the "angustia").

Feet: displacement from and symbolism for penis.

Animal: concrete pictorial representation of primitive, "animalistic" feelings.

Bear: onomatopoeia for bareness; concrete pictorial representation of vulnerability and cuddliness if it is a "teddy-bear"; concrete pictorial representation of power and ferocity, if it is a grown bear.

Maybe: secondary revision.

From the associations—one listens to the dream's session as if it were a dream:

Hunter: allusion to aggressive feelings within the dream.

We shall now continue with a second occurrence in which the cardinal rule of dream interpretation is not applied, that is, in working with dreams in consultation interviews.

DREAMS PRESENTED IN CONSULTATION INTERVIEWS

Dreams may be told to analysts in consultation interviews by patients who will not continue in therapy with that analyst. To ask for dreams in consultation interviews and to respond to them appropriately may be useful diagnostically and therapeutically.

As it was indicated at the beginning of this chapter, we may travel to our patients' unconscious *with the patient*, which is what we do when we engage in interventions or interpretations, or *only within ourselves*, in our internal soliloquy of conjectures and speculations. Traveling to the patient's unconscious *within ourselves* can be helpful (tentatively, of course) diagnostically, because it will enrich our understanding of the patient's deeper psychodynamics. Traveling to our patient's unconscious *with the patient* may be helpful diagnostically and therapeutically (to the patient), because in reaching some of the deeper roots of our patients' pains and symptoms, we may be able to relieve our patients of those pains and symptoms. With dreams presented in consultation interviews, since the cardinal rule is not applied, the analyst can travel to the patient's unconscious only through the internal soliloquy of conjectures and speculations. When the consultant's impressions about these dreams are shared with the analyst with whom the patient will ultimately be working, the consultant's hypotheses (if, of course, they were on target), may be helpful to the analyst in understanding the working of that patient's unconscious.

In my practice, I encounter three kinds of possibilities. Patients may call me and tell me that they wish to be in therapy with me. If I can take new patients, I tell the caller that I will see her or him once (or a very limited number of times), after which the two of us will decide whether we want to, or can, work with each other. If I cannot take any new patient, I tell this person so, offer to see her or him once, and say that I will make a referral after the consultation. If the person prefers it, I may say that I will make a referral right then and there. Finally, persons may call me who have not decided that they want to start therapy and only want to explore the possibility. Here I shall discuss only situations where both the patient and I knew that the patient would be referred to another therapist.

Are there transferential and countertransferential dimensions in consultation work? Of course. Transferential and countertransferential processes are part of life. More specifically, if a patient calls a therapist to enter therapy, even if the patient had never heard of this particular therapist before, the very fact that the patient makes that call, indicates that, amidst whatever fears or despair he or she may experience, there is at least a degree of expectant hopefulness and optimistic expectations. A generalized, nonspecific, positive transference is usually behind those positive feelings. There is the unconscious hope and expectation that this therapist will be a better parent, a parent who will make things better. If the therapist whom the patient has called is highly recommended, or recommended by a former patient of that therapist, someone the prospective patient trusts and respects, the generalized, nonspecific, positive transference will be even stronger. The patient may unconsciously feel that this new thera-pist, like the all-powerful preoedipal parent could have done, will effortlessly transform all of the patient's inadequacies into perfection, provide peace and happiness forever, and hand over to the patient the keys to the kingdom. Dreams told in consulta-tion interviews, of course, will be first dreams, thus, the general technical rules applying to first sessions and first dreams will apply here too, and even more stringently. There will be no future sessions to make up for serious technical errors, or for anything that may have been facile, cavalier, or disrespectful to the patient. Specifically, interpretations on the level of the drives are out of the question. There should be no interpretations within the con-text of the transference, both out of respect toward the patient and out of respect to the patient's prospective therapist. Only mild, nonspecific interpretations or interventions on the level of the defenses are indicated: tentative interpretations or interven-tions, and openly acknowledged as such. The formula, "Not much can be said, not much should be said" should be followed very strictly. "Just enough should be said" should be applied with the greatest discrimination. Only if patients tell us that they very rarely dream or remember dreams, and are genuinely surprised at having had this dream just the night before the consultation, and only when we do have a clear sense that these patients have no belief in, or "feel" for dreams, the imaginary, that which can-not be seen, touched, and measured, only then may it be appro-priate to make some brief and temperate comments about the dream. Of course, there should be no extravagant and indiscreet expressions of enthusiasm about patients having had their "first dream in decades." That the patient "finally" remembered a dream, must not be taken personally, has nothing to do with the patient consulting *with us.* That "first dream in decades" was remembered only because of the patient's transferences and the patient's anticipated skirmishes with the unconscious. Generally the analyst will have to measure carefully the degree of reassur-ance and support to give: not so much support and reassurance that the patient may have a "flight into health," and not so little that the patient may not follow up with the referral. Too much reassurance and support may be seductive and certainly contami-nate the transference, which would be grossly unfair to the patient and the next therapist.

"I Stood Up"

The dream, "I Stood Up," was dreamed by N, who was the son of a business associate of Y, who had been a patient of mine. N called, told me that his father had been given my name by Y, and said that he was calling me "to get into therapy, or maybe analysis." On the telephone, I "heard" the voice of an educated, cultured young man whom I assumed to be in his midtwenties, a voice with the shaky decisiveness of someone who is not very decisive. I told him that I had no time open for new patients but could see him for a consultation, if he wished to, and then make a referral. He said he would not mind coming in. I saw N within one week from the phone call.

N came in on time. He was a handsome, tall, thin young man with a sensitive, delicate face. He was dressed appropriately in an unremarkable, slightly crumpled business suit. He stooped when standing and had a slouched posture also when sitting. He appeared mild mannéred and gentle looking, did not seem happy, spoke softly and with a slightly depressed affect, chose his words carefully, made a visible effort at appearing strong and determined. As is my custom, I told him that we had forty-five minutes, but that I might want the last five to ten minutes for myself to say something which I hoped might be helpful. I asked him to tell me, in whatever sequence he wished, what he thought I should know. He told me he was 24, had graduated from an Ivy League college three years before, and had majored in English because he had "some vague ideas about becoming an academician." Since graduation, he had not been able to decide "what to get into." He had been working at a record store and then at a prestigious bookstore in Manhattan. But he realized that he could not do that for the rest of his life, besides he was getting pressure from both his parents, especially his father "to get into something more permanent." His father wanted him "to get into" the investment business (his father's business), his mother would not mind it if he went to graduate school and into an academic career, but he just could not decide, and he did want "to get his father off his ass." That was the only time in the entire interview when his restrained and decorous manner of speaking gave way to a "vulgar" colloquialism. At this point, he stopped and looked at me expectantly. I asked him to tell me more about himself.

He told me that he was born in New York City, where he had spent the first five years of his life. His parents divorced when he was 5; he and his two-year younger brother stayed with mother. Shortly after the divorce, the three of them moved to the small town in New England where mother came from. He and his brother saw father every other major holiday and for a month each summer. In New York, N had his own apartment. Now N saw father (who had never left New York) maybe once a month for dinner, and his mother at least twice a month on weekends, and on most holidays. He added that he was very fond of his mother and spoke with her on the telephone several times a week. She was very loving, but a little helpless and dependent. He and his brother worried over her: she tended to be overweight, had no social life, had never dated. His father, on the other hand, had started dating shortly after his divorce and remarried when N was 9. N said that his father was a successful businessman, that father was "all right, but always very busy with his work." He also told me that his father's second wife was younger than father, glamorous, very beautiful, successful in business. N did not like her: she tried to play "great stepmother," meddled in his affairs, gave him unsolicited advice.

N told me that he did not date; that his father, who was the one who suggested psychotherapy, wondered whether N was homosexual, "which shows how little Dad knows me." He said that he did not date because he was timid with girls, felt he was not good looking, was too "cerebral," not "a regular guy," preferred books and intellectual pursuits to sports and parties. But he knew he was not homosexual; with considerable embarrassment he added that he masturbated "a little too often, at least once a day," and that he only thought of women when he did. He told me that he had been in psychotherapy for about two years shortly after puberty, "obsessive–compulsive condition, they called it," so he guessed his masturbation now could be called "compulsive." Some obsessional symptoms returned during his freshman year in college, and he saw a psychologist in school for about a year. He had been reading about this condition, and felt he still tended to be "kind of obsessive, about things and about myself," and especially and most worrisome to him, one who "cannot make up his mind about things, big things, like what I should get into, jobwise, I mean, as well as small, everyday things." It was at this point, about half an hour into the session, that I asked him if he usually remembered his dreams. He said that he did not, but he did remember a dream he had had about two weeks before; it was a very short dream, and it was amazing to him that he still remembered it. He hesitated and seemed to need encouragement to tell me the dream. I showed interest and he told me the dream.

"I Stood Up"

> Well, this is my dream . . . a very constipated production, I must say. I don't even know I can call it a dream, it's just one sentence . . . some dream! Well, this is the dream: I stood up. I can't even say I saw myself standing up, or saw myself standing up as opposed to sitting down . . . it's just a sentence, "I stood up," as if I read it, or heard it. Some dream!

Having told me the dream, N said that he was "almost ashamed" at the "intellectual poverty, lack of substance, terseness, almost epigrammatic nature" of his dream. I said, "You have such a rich vocabulary, and, you told me, you like so much books and intellectual pursuits, I can understand your being upset about the shortness of your dream." N seemed pleased by my remarks and told me that he had not wanted to say that before, "It felt like bragging," but he had graduated summa cum laude and had been a Phi Beta Kappa, so maybe he was underachieving. He looked at his watch, saw that it was about ten minutes to the end of the hour, and looked at me expectantly.

Up to the moment N told me his dream, my soliloquy of conjectures and speculations had included the following thoughts. His shaky decisiveness suggested timidity, unconscious anger, and conflicts about that anger. This anger seemed to be against his father. It had already been suggested by his terse description of father, "he is all right, but always very busy with his work," and could have been further inferred by the paucity and poverty of N's contacts with him. His effort at appearing strong and determined suggested the need to please father, to show father that he was not an effeminate homosexual. I further thought that to have said that he wanted to "get his father off his ass" suggested anal fixations. N had appeared a little shaken when he had said that. I thought that his sudden, fleeting lapse from his restrained and decorous manner of speaking to the anal colloquialism, was a break in his characterological armor against anal impulses; and that was why he had seemed shaken when he had used that locution. Also, I reasoned within myself, N had used a number of times the expression, "to get into." I thought the expression suggested phallic–oedipal drives and conflicts about those drives; and I thought that he did not date, not because of latent homosexuality, but because of those phallic–oedipal conflicts. Along these lines, I also felt that his negative feelings about his stepmother were not simply related to loyalty to his own mother, but also to unconscious, oedipal, erotic feelings toward stepmother and unconscious, oedipal, competitive feelings against his father for having married this "glamorous, very beautiful, successful" younger woman.

I conjectured, therefore, that N's difficulty in settling down, his procrastination about giving a final direction to his career, his having only "vague ideas" about what to do, were not only related to anal conflicts about productivity but also to phallic conflicts about assertiveness. I concluded that, quite obviously, N still suffered from an obsessive character neurosis. My major diagnostic and psychodynamic hypotheses were that beneath N's conscious feelings of loving and concerned protectiveness toward his mother, there were unconscious oedipal feelings toward her. Beneath N's anger against his father, there were unconscious feelings of oedipal rivalry and rage. The anal fixation which manifested itself in N's obsessive character neurosis, had been reached regressively from an oedipal conflict made more troublesome by a divorce at the height of the oedipal age. Therefore, both anal and phallic–oedipal dynamics were condensed behind N's difficulties.

Then N told me the dream. Conjecturally, I saw the dream too as a condensation of anal and phallic drives. The dream seemed to confirm my major diagnostic and psychodynamic hypotheses. My internal soliloquy about the dream included these thoughts. All the secondary revisions, all the denials and caveats ("It's just one sentence." "Some dream!" "I don't even know I can call it a dream.'') showed the dream was very well defended. At the same time, the fact that N had remembered it after almost two weeks, showed that the dream was important, was emanating from some highly overcathected place in his unconscious. I thought that, yes, the dream was "very constipated," very well defended, and that even the use of that word strongly suggested its anal content. In this regard, "I stood up" in the manifest content could have represented, through a turning to the opposite, "I sat down." It could have represented the anal desire to sit down on the potty and not produce, the anal wish to sit down on the toilet seat and express rage and obstinacy through procrastination and anal retention. But I also thought that "I stood up," could have represented at the same time the phallic desire to stand up, to be "erect" (rather than stooped, which was the way he "stood" when standing and the way he lived figuratively), the wish to be an erect penis, the better to compete with father, to be as successful as father, to have a woman as beautiful as father's second wife. "I stood up," in other words, could have also represented the competitive, aggressive, phallic–oedipal desires he was conflicted about.

Having come to a tentative understanding of what N's dream said, what would I say to him, if anything at all, about his dream? He had told me he rarely remembered dreams, and that made me feel I should say something to him about this dream. He thought little, consciously, of this dream. This too made me feel that, without "explaining" the dream, I could try to instill some conscious respect in him for dreams and dreaming. Finally, he appeared unhappy, and was actually more dispirited and dejected than he allowed me to see. That made me feel I should be a little encouraging, a bit supportive. He had seemed buoyed by what I had said about his rich vocabulary and his interest in books and intellectual pursuits; it had "given him permission" to tell me he had graduated summa cum laude and was a member of Phi Beta Kappa. This made me feel I could safely be encouraging and supportive. I said:

> Yes, I have been listening to you and I have heard how upsetting it is for you, not to know what you want to get into in life, careerwise, especially considering your intellectual talents and academic credentials. Yes, the

idea of getting into therapy or maybe analysis is a very good idea indeed. And I find your dream, actually, quite interesting. It looks like maybe in real life you have been wanting to "stand up" but, for all kinds of reasons, you have been "sitting down," so to speak, in unchallenging, unexciting jobs. But in the dream you are "standing up." The dream might indicate a resolve, a determination, to do precisely that—a self-incitement, a self-exhortation to do that.

The first part of my response was a supportive intervention, the second part, a supportive interpretation on the level of the defenses. The intervention was supportive because, in it, I empathized with N's discomfort and affirmed his intellectual capacities. In reference to his presenting problem, I used the words, "*getting into* life, careerwise," cognizant of the fact that the expression, "getting into" had a phallic ring. It connected with my conjecture concerning the phallic psychodynamics behind that problem. I felt that to use those words was safe, he himself had repeatedly used that expression, and possibly helpful toward connections he might make later in his analysis between that problem and those phallic psychodynamics. I thought I would make using that expression extra safe by adding the word *careerwise.* The intervention was supportive because it reflected the possibility that the dream suggested such positive emotions as resolve and determination, which should have been encouraging to someone as irresolute and unassertive as N. I was aware of the possibility that this kind of support could have intensified superego defenses, but I felt the risk was minimal. The interpretation was strictly on the level of the defenses, because I referred to "standing up," which was in the dream's manifest content, that is, in the dream's "defended," distorted content. I referred to "standing up" as being a metaphor *only* for greater assertiveness in leaving unexciting and unchallenging jobs, and finding a more rewarding career. I never even hinted at or alluded to the anal and phallic latent contents I thought were behind "standing up."

I believe that in this consultation, both through the session and through the session's dream, I had entered and traveled a few steps closer to N's unconscious, not with N, of course, only in my internal soliloquy. I also thought that the small journey had been helpful diagnostically and, to a small extent, therapeutically, if, indeed, I had succeeded in helping N be more open to remembering his dreams in the future, and succeeded in making him feel a little less depressed and less hopeless. Of course, only if N had continued with me in analysis, would I have known if my support had or had not been excessive and had or had not contaminated the transference, and would have known if my interpretation had or had not been too bold or imprudent. I did suggest a male analyst; N accepted the suggestion. I made the referral, N followed through and entered analysis with this person. I shared with this analyst my impression about the consultation session and the session's dream. I hoped my conjectures and hypotheses were helpful.

"A Crowd of Short Black Men"

I said previously that to ask for dreams in the consultation can be helpful to the patient diagnostically and sometimes therapeutically, both in the consultation session itself and later, when the consultant analyst's impressions are shared with the person who becomes the patient's analyst. The work done in the consultation session with GS's dream was helpful diagnostically, but, I believe, not helpful to GS herself.

GS was referred to me by her parish priest, Father L. He told me that she was a woman in her early forties, a devout churchgoer, a scrupulous daily confessant and communicant. She tormented herself, and her husband, with the belief that her husband was sexually unfaithful to her. Father L told me that he knew the husband very well too: he was a mild and good natured man, also a faithful churchgoer, a monthly confessant with Father L, who found the idea of his being unfaithful to GS not just absurd, but actually humorous. When GS called me for an appointment, I "heard" a woman with a tense, distant, and distancing voice. I told her I had no time open for new patients but could see her for a consultation, if she wished to, and then make a referral. She hesitated, then agreed. It was not easy to settle on an appointment: after three different times were offered and turned down for reasons that seemed legitimate, she accepted one for two weeks later.

GS arrived a few minutes late. She was an attractive, 43-year-old woman, was dressed appropriately and rather ordinarily, wore an unfashionable hairdo and much makeup. She was nervous, fidgeted, made eye contact briefly and tensely before quickly diverting her eyes, looked around the office, but it seemed as if she did not see or take in anything. She looked harassed, did not smile, frowned frequently, called attention to her body by obsessively pulling down on the hem of her skirt, smoothing her stockings, adjusting her undergarments.

I started the session as I did with N and as I do with most patients. She asked me if Father L had told me why she was there, she was sure he had. Without waiting for an answer and talking nervously and rapidly, she told me that she thought her husband was unfaithful to her, but then, he is a man, and all men carry on with women, her father had, and so do her brothers, and Father L does not believe her, and she does not have any real evidence, and maybe her husband is not unfaithful, but she cannot be sure he is not.

GS stopped and looked at me more defiantly than expectantly. When I asked her to tell me about herself, she asked me to ask her questions. I declined and urged her to tell me whatever she thought I should know; she snorted. Then, still talking "rapid fire," she told me that she had married her husband when she was 19 and he, 25. He worked in his father's hardware store in the neighborhood, she guessed she loved him when she married him, he was nice, still is. She always thought men carried on with other women, but somehow believed her husband didn't, "he was too fat," until about five to ten years ago. Nothing happened at that time to make her think that, the thought just began entering her mind, maybe he does not, after all he is in the store six days a week, and she works with him three of those days. The hardware store is now her husband's, he makes good money from it, they go on vacation to Florida every winter for two weeks and have a little house near the beach on Long Island. Again, she stopped, again looking more defiantly than expectantly; and then said that she was sure that I wanted to know all about her sex life.

When I simply smiled and said nothing, she told me that she does not enjoy "it," but knows what her duties are, so she always complies when her husband is interested in "it," her husband is very gentle about "it," he always asks her if "it" is okay with her. If her husband does not initiate "it," she will ask him if he is sure that he does not want "it" and sometimes she makes it double sure by asking him a second and sometimes a third time, "which drives him a little crazy." (She never used the words *sex* or *lovemaking*, but always "it," emphasizing the pronoun as if indeed it were in quotes.) They had no children, her husband had himself "checked" and he was "all right," she never wanted to have children, but she would have them, because she is "a good Catholic, and to please my husband." She was "checked too" and nothing was found wrong, so she guessed it's God's will. I did ask her if anything else bothered her and she told me that she is "a little fanatic" with the housework, has "a little craziness about faucets, like a compulsion." She has to touch the faucet in the bathroom, or in the kitchen, once or twice, and after she has done this, she has to wash and scrub her hands even if they are perfectly clean. This "habit" started when she was about 18, and had just "begun to develop into a woman." She also told me that she feels ill at ease out in the streets and "very frightened in crowds—things happen to women in crowds . . . you know, 'mashers,' or worse," and this goes back to when she was 18. Her husband loves baseball, and once, shortly before being married, she did go to the stadium with him, and as he was in line to buy tickets, she became anxious, short of breath, and sweaty, "very sweaty, all over, and I mean all over," she added suggestively.

I asked her to tell me about her parents and childhood. She was born to a middle-class Italian-American family in Queens, New York. She was the oldest of three children, had two younger brothers. Her father was a "happy-go-lucky Italian," he had a fierce temper, but "more bite than bark, no, I got it wrong, I mean, his bark was worse than his bite," enjoyed his large, extended family, loved drinking wine, playing cards, and telling dirty jokes, liked to pinch his daughter and nieces. "But, then, he also pinched his sons and nephews." He ran his own travel agency, flirted a lot with the women customers, and, no, she had no real evidence that he was unfaithful to her mother, but his secretary, an Italian-American widow, seemed to like him a lot. Her mother was "a good woman, but she suffered from periodic depressions and was sick a lot." I asked her when had she begun menstruating; she told me that she did not have her first period until she was 18 and that her "figure" did not really begin to develop until she was 20. She had said that her obsessions about faucets and phobias about crowds had started when she was about 18 and had just "begun to develop into a woman." My question seemed legitimate, not a countertransferential curiosity. I asked her if she remembered her dreams. She told me that she dreamed almost every night, most of her dreams were very vivid, and some frightening, with people chasing her and meaning harm, but usually she forgets them in a day or two. She volunteered a dream she had had shortly after she had called me; she wrote her dream down so she would not forget it, but she thought she would have remembered it anyway. "It was very peculiar, never had a dream like that." She told me the dream with about ten minutes to go before the close of the session.

"A Crowd of Short Black Men"

> I was kind of trapped at the bottom of a very small dead-end street, hiding under the stoop of a small apartment house. The street was filled with a crowd of black men; funny, they were all short men, shorter than me. They were cheering on two black men who were going to rape a young black woman. The young girl did not seem frightened, but perhaps she was. But I was frightened, very frightened: if they saw me, they might do it to me. I woke up in a sweat.

She said, "I have no idea what this dream means. But it was frightening. I have had frightening dreams before, I told you, people chasing me and meaning harm, but I never had a dream about people raping a woman. Anyway, do you think I could use some therapy? Maybe I am tormenting myself and my husband unnecessarily with this idea that he sees other women."

Up to the moment GS had told me the dream, I thought she suffered with mild agoraphobia, phobia of crowds, obsessions, compulsions, and sexual frigidity. My internal soliloquy of conjectures and speculations included that the idea of her husband being unfaithful had no basis in reality, was obsessional not paranoid, and was determined by GS's internal ideas about men. Her attitudes, demeanor, and verbal and nonverbal communication in the session, clearly indicated that she was not at ease with herself or with me. Her talking rapidly ("rapid fire" came to my mind as I was listening to her) was, in part, a derivative of unconscious anger (as if she unconsciously wanted to "fire" on me). In part, it was an agoraphobia-in-time, a symptom of wanting no open spaces in time, because open spaces could get filled with objectionable thoughts and feelings. On a more psychodynamic plane, my fantasies and hypotheses were that GS may have experienced her father as dangerously attractive, and "dangerous" in nonsexual areas as well (someone whose bite was indeed worse than his bark, as her slip of the tongue suggested). She may have been unconsciously angry at him for being so attractive and so dangerous. She may have married a less attractive and less "dangerous" man as a way of avoiding marrying a father figure. She might not have received much nurturing from her depressed, sickly, not strong mother (a nurturing that an older daughter with two younger male siblings in an Italian-American household may have especially needed).

On a deeper psychodynamic plane, I conjectured that strong, conflictual oral wishes and fears, caused by not having been nurtured the way she had needed to be, kept GS from being able to nurture (she was not a nurturing wife to her husband), and from being able to become a mother (I thought, in other words, that her inability to conceive was largely related to preoedipal problems). Strong, conflictual, oedipal wishes and fears could have been behind, not only GS's choice of spouse, but also behind the delayed menarche, the late development of secondary sexual characteristics, her frigidity, and her conscious and unconscious anger at men. GS's anger at men also appeared in the way she tormented her husband with accusations of infidelity and the way she "dutifully" offered herself to him sexually ("it drives him a little crazy"). Also, I speculated that the agoraphobia and the phobia of crowds were derivatives of unconscious wishes and fears that, being in an open space, she could be overtly exhibitionistic and be sexually attacked. In the panic attack she had had at the baseball stadium, she may have felt vaginally stimulated: "I was sweaty all over," she had said, "and I mean all over," she had added suggestively. The conscious fear of being sexually attacked, which manifested itself in the conscious feeling that this is what can happen to women in a crowd and in the manifest content of many of her dreams, was, in part, a projection of her wish to attack and to be attacked, sexually and nonsexually. Being compelled to touch faucets was a derivative of the unconscious fear and wish to touch her father's penis. The idea that her husband was unfaithful to her was, in part, a displacement from thoughts and feelings she had about her father, and "all men," and their behavior with women; and in part, a projection of her own unconscious wish to be sexual. Given this volcano of turbulent feelings within, she did need a fanatic, scrupulous religiosity: it provided an external armor of defenses, an additional external superego.

When GS told me her dream, I saw the dream, conjecturally, as a dream of angry sexuality. It confirmed my major diagnostic and psychodynamic hypotheses about GS. My internal soliloquy about the dream included these thoughts. The "small dead-end street" represented, in a narrow sense, her vagina, and in a broader, existential sense, her neurosis, the dead-endedness of her harrowing neurotic feelings. "The stoop" under which she was hiding might have represented her mother "stooped in" depression, and "stooped" under the "superiority" of her extraverted, effervescent husband, GS's father. I also thought that the "crowd of black men" represented, through condensation, the sexual and dangerous thoughts and feelings crowding her unconscious, "black" thoughts and feelings (i.e., as sexual and dangerous as African-American men are stereotypically supposed to be). The crowd of black men also represented her father, "black," that is, pagan and dissolute as African-American men are stereotypically presupposed to be. I opined that the diminutive stature of the black men was a way of representing her conscious, defensive, devaluation of men, ultimately of her father, since in her unconscious, father was represented by all men; and, by turning to the opposite, it was a way of representing her unconscious overvaluation of men, ultimately, of her father. And, of course, I thought that she was the "young black woman": the oedipal child, "black," that is, "bad," with forbidden sexual and angry desires, "black" with the desire of father ("the two black men") doing "it" to her. That the young girl "did not seem frightened, but perhaps she was," I speculated, was a good representation of GS's ambivalence about her oedipal wishes. No wonder she "woke up in a sweat." The dream's latent wish for angry sexuality had been acted out, she would be in a sweat, as much in a sweat (and "a sweat all over") as she had been when she had been in a crowd, mostly of men, at the baseball stadium.

Having come to a tentative understanding of what GS's dream said, what would I say to her, if anything, about the dream? She had told me that she remembered her dreams frequently; thus, there was no need to reinforce her capacity to remember dreams by commenting on this one dream. Also, she was a phobic person, an "avoidant" person, a personality who avoided all that which could further overcathect her already heavily charged repressed drives; a person who even avoided sustained eye contact, not to speak of open spaces, crowds, and truly genital sexual intimacy. She was a person who saw contact and connectedness as a "rape," or as an intrusive penetration that she both wished for and feared. I saw this as an additional reason for not volunteering any comments on the dream. Besides, after she had told me the dream, which she did only ten minutes before the end of the session, she seemed to dismiss it, and asked me, not about the dream, but whether I thought that she could benefit from psychotherapy. I opted for a comment which would only make the most indirect and, I thought, innocuous connection between the dream and one of her symptoms. I only said:

No wonder you fear crowds.

It certainly was not an interpretation on the level of the drives: because I did not even allude to the latent reasons why she feared crowds. It was not even an "interpretation" on the level of the defenses. She had told me herself why, consciously, she feared crowds: "Things happen to women in a crowd . . . you know, 'mashers,' or worse." It was a somewhat empathic intervention, or as empathic as I felt she could accept without feeling patronized and intruded upon, "penetrated." I told GS that, yes, I felt psychotherapy was indicated and suggested a woman analyst. In my own thoughts, I believed that she could benefit from psychoanalytically oriented psychotherapy, moderately reconstructive, and felt that with a female analyst, the erotic and sadistic dimensions of her ambivalent feelings about her father would not get in the way. I also thought that a warm and competent female analyst might provide her with the nurture that her depressed mother had not been able to provide. It is possible that counter-transferential dimensions affected my thinking when I thought that a woman therapist might be better for GS than a man. GS accepted the referral and followed through with it.

"My Old Apartment, Beautiful, But"

With this patient, the consultation session was only slightly helpful diagnostically: the absence of very overt, or severe, pathology caused my conjectures and speculations to remain very tentative. But working with the session's dream was helpful to the patient in that it contributed to her having a clearer idea of what she might want to work on in her subsequent therapy.

LR was referred to me by her new husband, R, a former patient of mine. R had been my patient in twice a week, psychoanalytically oriented psychotherapy for six years, and he had terminated therapy about five years before referring LR to me. LR introduced herself, told me that she had married R six months before. She was "happy in her marriage, mostly," but wanted to get into therapy, and R had suggested that she call me. On the telephone, I "heard" a friendly, upbeat, educated, elegant voice. I told her that I was not going to be able to take her as a patient but could see her for a consultation leading to a referral. She said that she did want to see me for the consultation. We made an appointment.

LR arrived on time. She was a very attractive 48-year-old woman who looked much younger than her age. She was dressed appropriately, casually but elegantly, and quite stylishly. She held a high executive position in one of Manhattan's most prestigious department stores. She was spontaneous, pleasantly self-assured, made good eye contact, seemed at ease. I began the session in my customary way. I learned that LR, an only child, was born and raised in a large Midwest city. Her father had been a successful architect. He "has always been and still is a very caring and loving father." Ten years older than his wife, he was now in his late seventies, was still very handsome, very elegant, and "very much with it." Her mother had been and still was "a socialite, member of a half-dozen or more civic organizations, loved to entertain, was very good at it, gave great parties." LR attended a prestigious

women's college in the East and settled in New York after graduation. She worked in fashion and design and was determined to
develop a successful career in that field. At 25, LR married a
successful businessman fifteen years her senior. "It was a mistake,
we married impulsively, we didn't talk enough about our individual goals and personality differences." A "caring, charming, elegant man," he was very much in love with her, but wanted to
settle down and raise a family while she wanted to wait at least
until she was 30 or 35 before having children. He objected to her
working late hours and sometimes having to travel on weekends,
"and he wanted sex a lot more than I did." They divorced three
years later; it was he who decided on the divorce, but she had to
admit that it was more painful for him than for her.

After the divorce, LR went to graduate school and obtained
a degree that combined fashion design and marketing. For the
next fifteen years or so, she "truly enjoyed" the single life. Her
career "took off." She received much affirmation and praise at
work, was known nationwide in her field, earned a great deal of
money. She owned an elegant apartment in Manhattan, gave
small and glamorous dinner parties, went to the theater, the op-
era, the ballet. She had four sexual affairs; two were "brief encounters" while on vacation abroad; the other two times, the
relationships lasted six months in one case, eight months in the
other; in both of these two cases, the men were "good persons,
and charming too," ten to fifteen years older than she, substantial
and successful, one widowed, one divorced. She never lived with
either of these men, nor either of them with her. Both relationships ended when she felt the man was becoming too serious
about her and wanted too much of her time. Sexuality was not a
problem, "I enjoyed it, I suppose, but usually they cared for it
more than I did." The men who accompanied her to social events
were "good friends," elegant, successful, and fun to be with, not
interested in marriage or in committed relationships. She occasionally felt lonely in the evening, "did not have a steady sexual
life, but did not really miss that, there were plenty of other plea-
sures I drew energy from." But over the last five years or so, she
had felt lonely more often. Even though she continued to be
very successful at her job, her work had become boring. She was
beginning to consider a second career in teaching or consulting.

The thought that she was "still a single woman, and in a few years a 50-year-old single woman, was a little scary." Then she met R, "at a time, perhaps, when I had begun to feel it was time to settle down, to finally live with someone, to be married."

LR and R had met at a fashion show in LR's store. They liked each other instantly and began to date. R was 59, had been divorced for over ten years, was the head of a very successful company, and LR found him "solid, charming, warm, caring, humorous." (From my own experience of R, he was all that.) They felt they loved each other and might want to spend the rest of their lives together. Sex was "okay, I guess; again, he wanted it more than I did, but we did not feel that was going to be a problem." The only potential problem they foresaw was that R intended to begin to delegate more of his work, and to begin to travel for pleasure, and he had told LR that he would insist on her winding down on her job and resigning in a couple of years. She had thought she could do that, she herself had felt her job was getting stale. They agreed to marry.

Six months into the marriage, she was not "entirely comfortable being married." She loved R, liked and respected him, but "after 20 years of being single, to live with another person, no matter now much you care for him, is not easy. Not infrequently, I feel itchy and antsy, and it is not that R is possessive or insensitive." Before marrying R, she had known she would sell her beautiful apartment and move into R's equally beautiful townhouse, but now that she had done it, she was "missing the old place . . . no, it is not the old place, I miss, it's the single life I miss, being totally independent, having to report to no one, being able to come and go as I please. But I want to make it with R, I just have to get adjusted." She hinted at "some sexual problems"; did not elaborate; and she was "getting cold feet" at the thought of leaving her job. But she also did not want to give up on being married to R without looking into and understanding what was making her "itchy and antsy." She had told R about her feelings and they both felt that she should see a therapist.

About ten minutes before the end of the hour, I asked her if she usually remembered her dreams and if she had had any

recent dreams. She told me that she thought she dreamed frequently but rarely remembered what she had dreamed. She remembered a dream she had had a few nights before. She
proceeded to tell me the dream.

"My Old Apartment, Beautiful, But"

> Kind of an obvious dream, I think, but perhaps it has some other meaning.
> I was visiting my old apartment, the one I just sold, the couple that bought
> it from me had invited me for cocktails. It definitely was that apartment,
> I recognized the doorman downstairs, but, and this is very strange, it was
> much, much larger, even the ceilings were higher. So large, so comfort-
> able! And here is the other bizarre twist: there was something slightly
> scary about the place: beautiful, large, comfortable, and yet . . . slightly
> scary. And my hosts were very charming and welcoming, at least the man,
> an old business acquaintance of mine, was, yet I did not feel fully com-
> fortable.

LR went on, saying: "Even with those two strange twists, the
dream seems kind of obvious. I miss—but in part, only in
part—my single life, and my old apartment stands for my single
life. I make it larger, and very comfortable, because in that apartment, as a single woman, I did not feel 'itchy and antsy.' I told
you, R is not a possessive man, he does not crowd me in the least,
if I feel a bit claustrophobic about being married, it's because I
have to get used to it, after having been single for so many years.
And about the other bizarre twist, there being something slightly
scary about my old apartment, that too is explainable: I told you,
in the last five years or so, I was beginning to feel lonely more
often and the thought of approaching 50 and still being single
was getting scary. I guess the dream tells me that, at least in part,
I miss the single life because, as a single woman, I was independent, foot loose and fancy free. But maybe it has some other kind
of meaning."

As I said before, my soliloquy, up to the moment LR told me
her dream, was very tentative. My conjectures and speculations
included these thoughts. LR had problems with intimacy; she
liked "being able to come and go" as she pleased, not "having
to report" to anyone. Maybe she equated intimacy with dependency or with being under someone's control. From the age of

28, when she had divorced her first husband, to the age of 45, when she had begun having second thoughts about her life-style, she had been happiest (or more accurately, had been least unhappy) as a career woman and having tenuous relationships with men. Wanting to be a successful career woman may have been, in part, wanting the "right" thing for the "wrong" reasons; that is, might have been an escape from, and a compensation for, intimacy. Her fear of intimacy, obviously, had continued into her second marriage: "to live with another person, no matter how much you care for him, is not easy. Not infrequently, I feel 'itchy' and 'antsy'. . . ."

On a deeper place, I tentatively wondered whether oedipal conflicts were interfering with her capacity to be intimate. She had been the only child of a caring, handsome, and successful father. The four serious relationships of her adult life had all been with men ten to fifteen years older, all men who had been as caring, handsome, and successful as her father. I felt even more tentative about the role her mother had had in LR's development. Did LR not want to mother a child because she herself had not been well mothered? Had her mother been too busy with civic activities and entertaining to be nurturing? Finally, and a little less tentatively, I thought that in the last five years or so, when she had begun to feel lonely more often, when the thought of being still a single woman who in a few years would be a 50-year-old single woman had become "scary," I thought that, in those last five years or so, her conflicts between independence and dependence, autonomy and intimacy, had become skewed toward letting herself consider "settling down, finally living with someone, to be married." And, if I was correct in my speculations about the role that oedipal conflicts played in her ambivalence about "settling down," those conflicts too, I thought, had become skewed toward giving in, to a degree, to the oedipal wishes, but not without some anxiety, as I thought the dream showed. Giving up on her cautious kind of relatedness, and an attendant life-style that had served her well for most of her adult life (and having to do that without the buffer of a demanding job, that inevitably reduced the amount and quality of time spent together with a husband) made her "itchy and antsy." Because of the above psychodynamics, LR was confused, perplexed, and afraid and had let herself at last seek professional help.

My soliloquy about the dream included, speculatively and conjecturally, these thoughts. The manifest dream's "old apartment" stood for what, in the latent dream, was a much older home, the home of her childhood. The manifest dream's "old apartment," therefore, stood for her childhood. When, before telling me the dream, she had said that, having just sold her beautiful apartment, she was "missing the old place," unconsciously she was referring to missing her childhood home and her childhood. The first of the two "strange twists," the fact that the manifest dream's apartment was "much, much larger, even the ceilings were higher," dated the dream, thus strengthening the hypothesis that the manifest dream's apartment stood for her childhood home. The rooms and furniture surrounding us when we are children, are scaled to adult size, not to children size; places of average size and ceilings of average height do seem "larger and higher" than they are in reality, and that is the way we "see" them, when, as adults, we dream about them. Thus, I thought, the manifest dream may have been about visiting the apartment of her single life over the recent past, but the latent dream was about revisiting her childhood, being a child again. The truly latent dream, I conjectured, was about oedipal drives and the joys and ecstasies of fulfilling the oedipal romance. The semilatent–semimanifest dream was about the anxiety and guilt accompanying the fulfillment of the wish. Thus, the manifest dream's "other bizarre twist," that there was something scary about the place, became understandable. Conflictual oedipal feelings were indeed being acted out (the oedipal father is being welcoming, the oedipal father is "downstairs"). If so, the manifest dream's "doorman" was, in the latent dream, her father; the manifest dream's "couple" corresponded, in the latent dream, to her parents; the manifest dream's "downstairs" ("the doorman downstairs") represented, in the latent dream, her genitals. Reinforcing these oedipal conjectures was the fact that, of the two hosts, only the man ("an old business acquaintance of mine") was charming and welcoming: the oedipal father was loving, the oedipal mother was not.

I further thought that LR needed to believe that she was *only* missing the good and bad single days of her recent past, not the good and bad days of her remote past. She needed to believe that she was being ambivalent about being married to R *only* because of feelings and conflicts going back to her recent past, not because of feelings and conflicts going back to her remote past. She needed to believe that she was feeling "itchy and antsy," married to R, only because she was missing the independence and freedom of being single, not because of the conflictual oedipal feelings that being married to R evoked in her unconscious.

Therefore, through the dream's two *but's* (the old apartment was beautiful, *but larger*, and, *yet* there was something *scary* about it), LR was making important statements about the "but's" not so much in her recent past but in her remote past. Consciously, LR was quite clear about the "*but's*" in her recent life's past: her single life as an adult had been very enjoyable, *but* had been occasionally lonely; it had been a life that had felt safe and secure, *but* it lacked sexual ecstasies; it had been a life in which she did not feel "itchy and antsy" *but* one that, in the few years preceding her marrying R, had become more lonely and sometimes "scary." But through her latent dream, she seemed to be alluding to the ecstasies and the problems of her oedipal, and possibly, preoedipal childhood, which, like most people's, had been "beautiful, but." The latent dream seemed to be stating that behind LR's ambivalence about marriage, there were not only external conscious reasons, but more important internal, unconscious reasons.

I also thought that the dream, of course, was important, but LR had unwittingly alerted me to its importance by attempting to diminish it by saying that it was "kind of obvious." Additionally, by insisting, several times, that the manifest dream's old apartment was the apartment she had just sold, she had also inadvertently alerted me to the probability that it was not. But at the same time as she was doing that, she had also added, "but maybe it (the dream) has some other kind of meaning." I admired the psychological strength that enabled her to do so. It spoke of her resolve to try and understand her ambivalence, of her determination to do something constructive, this time, about whatever caused her to feel "antsy and itchy" in being married to a second, good and loving husband.

The dream had been told to me with less than ten minutes to go before the end of the hour. Having come tentatively to

understand what LR's dream said, what was I going to tell her, if
anything, about what the dream said? I decided for an intervention that might strengthen her determination to start therapy and
to look for the internal reasons that made her uncertain about
the marriage (and also help her with remembering her dreams
more often). I said:

> I sense a real determination in you to do something to make your mar-
> riage work. The dream you just told me, of course, is important, as all
> dreams are. The dream does talk, as you yourself seem to be saying, about
> your single life, about all the years before you married R, what was good
> and not-so-good about all those years, what you miss about those years,
> what made those years "beautiful, but. . . ." My hunch is that the success
> of your marriage may very well rest on understanding better, more in
> depth, how you feel about your single life, about all those previous years,
> understand better, more in depth, what was good and not-so-good about
> your single life, about all those previous years.

LR listened attentively. After a thoughtful pause, she asked
me whether she should insist on continuing to work. I told her
that I was sorry if I sounded evasive, but I could not possibly
answer that question, and that all I could say was that she should
continue talking openly with R about whatever was on her mind,
continue articulating with him what she thought work meant to
her, continue discussing with him what teaching and consulting,
which she had herself thought about even before meeting R,
might be like for the two of them. I said, again, that her priority
should be to understand better what she missed about her single
life and previous years.

My response to the dream's session included no interpretations. Whatever progress I had made through the royal road to
LR's unconscious, I had made entirely within myself, in my internal soliloquy, and I had kept it for myself, sharing with LR none
of my conjectures and speculations about her unconscious. In my
response to the dream, I agreed with LR about the fact that the
dream spoke about her missing her single life. This could be seen
as an interpretation on the level of the defenses, or as an agreeing
with the patient's conscious feeling about the dream. But I made
sure always to add to the words *single life*, such words as *all the
years before you married R*, or *all those years*, or *all those previous years*,

as a hint, which was all that I felt I had the right to give, that those old days could very well include the days of childhood. Telling her that the success of her marriage depended on "understanding better, more in depth" how she felt about her single life, about all those previous years, was aimed at reinforcing her determination to start psychotherapy and to look for the *internal* reasons making her uncertain about her marriage. The "hint" was that those internal reasons might very well go back to the good and bad old days of childhood, the "not as beautiful, but okay" days of childhood. Finally, telling her that the dream was important was aimed at helping her remember dreams more often.

I asked LR if she preferred working with a male or female psychoanalyst. She said it did not matter. I referred her to a woman analyst.

Let us now conclude with the two exceptions to the cardinal rule of dream interpretation as specified by Ella Freeman Sharpe, who first coined that term. The two exceptions are in working with dreams dreamed at times of severe psychic crises and dreams in which "the whole dream seems to fulfill a specific purpose" (Sharpe, 1978, pp. 79–82).

DREAMS DREAMED AT TIMES OF SEVERE PSYCHIC CRISES

Sharpe suggested that in these dreams the latent content is practically manifest, and "it is possible to read the meaning without the latent content . . . the symbolism is straightforward and typical." She postulated that these dreams "can be partly interpreted without the latent content" (1978, p. 79).

I believe that even in these dreams the latent content, while less distorted, is not totally manifest. In these dreams, dreamed by patients in crisis, the depleted ego does not have at its disposal that much psychic energy to fully exercise censorship and to produce a fully distorted dream. But even in these dreams there still is some censorship, there still is some distortion, there still is, behind the manifest content, a somewhat latent content. Even in these dreams, the symbolism is not *entirely* "straightforward and typical." Analytical work can and should be done to retrace some elements of the dream's manifest content back to their latent antecedents.

With these patients and with these dreams, therefore, an exception is being made, the cardinal rule is not applied. This is done knowingly, consciously, by design. With these patients and with these dreams, since the latent content is almost manifest, their unconscious is almost on the tip of their tongue. The analyst's access to the unconscious of these patients will be much easier. The cardinal rule is suspended. Let us revisit two dreams which Sharpe used to illustrate her point and let us, with all due respect to a brilliant theorist, show that she could have gone a little further in retracing parts of the dream's manifest contents back to their latent antecedents.

"The Concert Was Like a Feeding"

> I was at a concert and yet the concert was like a feeding. I could somehow see the music pass before my eyes like pictures. The music pictures passed like ships in the night. There were two sorts of pictures, white mountains with softly rounded tops, and others following them were tall and pointed [Sharpe, 1978, p. 20].

This dream, Sharpe tells us, had been dreamed by a a patient "who had passed through a severe trauma, who was keeping contact with reality but struggling and finding it almost unbearable" (p. 79). Even though the dreamer's hunger for food and nurture is quite undisguised ("the concert was like a feeding"), it was not *totally* undisguised. Sharpe pointed out that the dreamer utilized a simile (one of Sharpe's secondary dream work defenses) to represent the feeding. But there were other dream work operations distorting the dream, and Sharpe herself recognized that the "white mountains with softly rounded tops" symbolized mother's breasts, and the "tall and pointed" pictures represented father's penis. I will add that the dreamer seeing the "female" images (mother) as white mountains (white: covered with snow?), as opposed to green mountains (green: covered with lush vegetation), might suggest that, on a more latent level, she, the dreamer, saw mother, and her breasts, as cold and unnurturing. Again, on a more deeply latent level, she might have wished to be fed also by the "male" images (father), to be fed also by father's penis, precisely because of the shortcomings in the breasts. Clearly, however, Sharpe understood the dream fully: "So we read the dream wish. The great parents like ships in the night are friendly to each other. The child is secure in the plenitude of supply from both. The poignancy of the dream lay in the fact that in reality the patient was suffering from the loss by death of a beloved one. This loss had stirred memories to the depth of infantile frustration and desire" (1978, p. 21).

Now a dream dreamed by another person in severe psychic crisis.

"I Was Being Wheeled in a Perambulator"

That is the dream is its entirety. This dream was brought to Sharpe by a patient who "was finding the effort to keep in touch with reality almost impossible" (1978, p. 79). The patient had just overcome a long-standing delusion of persecution, and the loss of such a powerful symptom, of course, necessitated many internal psychic readjustments. Sharpe saw the dream as simply expressing desires for passivity and total dependency and felt that it could be "partly interpreted without latent content" (p. 79). I will add: behind the facade of a delusion of persecution there usually are unconscious sadistic drives defended against through projection. The delusion having been overcome, if the patient still has those unconscious sadistic feelings, these feelings are now unprotected, and need to be dreamed about. I would speculate that the drives for passivity and total dependency (which Sharpe thought the dream was expressing simply and straightforwardly), actually constituted the dream's semilatent content. I would further conjecture that behind the facade of that passive and dependent content (being passively and dependently carried around in a baby carriage), on a more deeply latent level, the dream was expressing active and sadistic drives. The latent dream might have been: "I am actively killing people," the semilatent, "But I am not, I am a passive little infant who cannot walk, let alone kill."

SPECIAL PURPOSE DREAMS

Sharpe also referred to dreams "in which the latent content may be of significance, but not of such importance as the psychological purpose which the whole dream fulfills" (1978, p. 80). Freud believed that any dream's "purpose" is to be dreamed, that is, to relieve and give hallucinatory expression to overcathected intrapsychic drives. But there are interpersonal "purposes" in the remembering and telling of a dream. These interpersonal purposes are always transferential. In the Freudian belief system, nothing is only related to extrapsychic reality. Ultimately, therefore, these interpersonal, extrapsychic "purposes" are related to internal, intrapsychic dynamics.

At a particular point in therapy, a dream's interpersonal reason for being remembered and told may have a "special" purpose. At those particular times, to work on these dreams' interpersonal transferential "special purposes" may be of greater importance than working on the latent content, more fruitful than using the dream to travel, with the patient, toward their unconscious. In these cases, the cardinal rule is, again, suspended by design. If there is any movement toward the patient's unconscious, it occurs only in the analyst's internal soliloquy, and only peripherally, on the side of one's consciousness, so to speak. Most of the analyst's internal soliloquy will be focused on trying to fathom the dreamer's "special purpose" in telling the dream. Among these dreams are:

1. Very long, elaborate dreams, the telling of which takes most of the analytic hour. The special purpose here is resistance, and this is what will have to be addressed.
2. Very colorful, entertaining dreams. The special purpose here may be the need to impress the analyst with one's psychological potency, with the fertility of one's imagination, one's oneiric prolificity, a more transparently transferential form of resistance. Analyzing according to the cardinal rule may have to wait, analyzing the patient's need to impress the analyst may have to take precedence.
3. Dreams having the special purpose of unconsciously wishing not only to impress but also to confuse the analyst. A patient

of mine, a very gifted cinematographer, and the son of a prominent movie director, did humorously refer to such dreams of his as "one more of my Cecil B. DeMille, cast of thousands, dreams." With him the transferential resistance was even more transparent and important because of his father's occupation, and that was the special purpose that needed priority attention.

4. Analyst-placating dreams, gift dreams. A patient of mine with very strong superego defenses, after sessions in which she had been angry at me, or sessions in which she had spoken strongly and angrily against her parents, always, in the following session, brought a "dream for me," a dream whose manifest content was about positive feelings toward me, or complimentary thoughts about the therapeutic process. To work on her need to appease me, to work on her need to gain forgiveness from me, and whomever I represented transferentially, was more important than working on the dreams.

To conclude, a last, somewhat humorous example of, if not a special purpose dream, a special purpose dreaming which was the result of interesting machinations on the dreamer's part. (This story might make the dreamer appear a little silly, if not pathetic; but neither she, nor her husband, were that.).

The dreamer, P, was an attractive and elegant woman in her late fifties. She had been the daughter of a powerful father, a busy, glamorous, business tycoon, and of a gentle, mild, ineffectual mother. She was married, not unhappily (but not happily or ecstatically, either) to a wealthy and successful "but" gentle and mild husband (many women have affairs with their father, but marry their mother, it has been said). In the middle stage of therapy, she had an idealized father transference toward me and a mildly critical, moderately belittling mother transference toward her husband. In therapy she had been expressing subtly negative feelings about her husband, unfavorably and unfairly comparing him with me (i.e., unconsciously comparing her mother with her father). She had just gone through a period of several weeks in which she had been unable to remember dreams, which distressed her inordinately because she wanted to be the perfect patient (i.e., the perfect daughter), pleasing me by bringing in dreams "regularly" (an anal, as well as an oedipal gift).

P devised a "system" (a ritual, actually) that, she thought, would help her remember her dreams. She told me nothing about the system until it "worked." (It is important for the reader to know that P and her husband usually made love early in the morning, when they both woke up, around 6 A.M.; and that they slept in the same bed.) The system consisted of setting up her radio alarm at about 4:30 in the morning; waking up and thinking about dreams (and therefore, about me) for ten to fifteen minutes; setting the alarm again for about 6:00; happily and virtuously going back to sleep, which apparently she could do without difficulty. This was also true of her husband, but he was a very sound sleeper and rarely heard the radio alarm going off. The "idea" of the system was that, in that last sleep period early in the morning, she would dream, and it would be a cinch remembering the dream. After a week or two the system finally worked, she happily told me a dream, and proudly described the ritual which, she thought, "had produced it."

Amused, bemused, and slightly awed by the ritual (an intriguing reminder that oedipal hopes spring eternal), my soliloquy was almost entirely about the ritual, and not very much about the dream. I thought that the ritual was about unconscious wishes to wake up *for me*, and not just for the purpose of giving me a dream fresh from the oven of her psyche, unconscious wishes to be awakened *by me* (a twentieth century sleeping beauty awakened by her prince), and unconscious wishes to fall asleep *with me* inside her mind, if not inside her body—"me" being, in all instances, the father of her childhood. She had told her husband why she was doing that, and he had been slightly baffled, but had responded in his usually all-loving, all-forgiving, all-understanding way, which made her angrier and more contemptuous of him. The ritual, therefore, was also about unconscious wishes to create tensions between her husband and me (an oedipal wish to create animosity between her mother and father). I did not feel I could, or should, ignore her dream, her valiant attempt at remembering it (it was, after all, a gift; and it had been a "labor of love"). So, I said,

I know how happy it made you, to be able to remember dreams again, but I wonder what your 'system' is going to do to your sex life—and to your husband.

I said nothing about the dream, I only addressed myself to the act of dreaming it. The dream itself was mildly oedipal. While the latent content of the dream was important, what was more important at the time was the latent meaning of the ritual that (so P thought) led to dreaming the dream. In my internal soliloquy, I moved closer to P's unconscious through the doors opened by the ritual. The special purpose of dreaming the dream was indeed interpersonal (the characters on the stage of the present being P, her husband, and me) and transferential (the characters on the stage of the past being P as a child, her mother, and father). In my intervention I chose to work only on the P–husband interpersonal special purpose of the ritual. Therapy had begun to touch on her dissatisfaction with her husband. Commenting on what her "system" was going to do to her husband and to her sex life with him was in line with what was going on in therapy at the time. Focusing on her interpersonal transactions with, and feelings about, her husband, would, I thought and hoped, allow P and me to take a few steps along the royal road in her unconscious toward her interpersonal transactions with, and unconscious feelings about, her father and mother.

9

Dream Interpretation, 4

One may learn more about dreams and dreaming by showing how much richer a dream's interpretation can be when the dream is interpreted on the level of the truly latent drives, that is when the cardinal rule is applied. One may also learn more by showing what does and does not happen when the cardinal rule is inappropriately and unnecessarily suspended, and the dream is interpreted only on the level of the semilatent content (especially when the analyst is not aware because of countertransference or inexperience that the cardinal rule had not been applied, and that the dream's truly latent content had not been reached).

Concerning the implementation of the cardinal rule of dream interpretation, there are five possible scenarios.

1. The patient is in the middle or later stages of analysis, the therapeutic alliance is solid, the transference is well developed, defenses have been sufficiently understood and analyzed, the patient's ego is strong. (Analysts well versed in the science and art of psychoanalysis and dream interpretation and relatively free of countertransference will know this.) With this picture, the cardinal rule should be applied and is applied, knowingly, by design. *Results*: the royal road to a knowledge of the activities of the unconscious is being entered with the patient, not just in the analyst's internal soliloquy. The dream is fully analyzed; analytical and clinical progress can be expected.

2. The patient is in the early stages of therapy, the therapeutic alliance is feeble, the transference is undeveloped, the patient's psychodynamics are not clear, defenses have not been

sufficiently understood or worked with, the patient's ego is not strong; or some of the clinical exceptions to the application of the cardinal rule are present. Also, the dream's session and the session's dream have not been sufficiently understood. With this picture, the cardinal rule should not and is not applied by design. *Results*: the road to the patient's unconscious may have been entered, but only in the analyst's internal soliloquy, defenses are respected, the dream has not been fully analyzed, but the analyst knows that this is so. Continuing analytical and clinical progress can be expected.

3. The clinical picture is identical to the one just presented, but inexperience or countertransference prevents the analyst from recognizing that this is so and from knowing that the cardinal rule should not be applied. The cardinal rule *is* applied, knowingly or unknowingly, by design or inadvertently (this is what Freud called "wild psychoanalysis" [1910b, pp. 221–227]). *Results*: the true road to the patient's unconscious is not being entered, defenses are violated or are being threatened. Depending upon the patient's ego state, the patient might regress, decompensate, terminate prematurely, or at best will take in the inappropriately timed interpretation only intellectually. Resistance will increase, and the analysis will stall. The dream may have been analyzed fully, but it has been a purely intellectual analysis, a cerebral exercise that will have no beneficial therapeutic effect.

4. The clinical picture is identical to that presented in scenario 1, above, but inexperience or countertransferential timidity make the therapist decide not to apply the cardinal rule. The cardinal rule, which could have been applied, is not applied. *Results*: the road to the patient's unconscious could have been entered but it is not, defenses will not be analyzed as much as they could safely have been, time is being wasted. The dream could have been more fully analyzed, but it has not been: but this was done knowingly, by design.

5. The clinical picture is identical to the one just presented in scenario 4. The cardinal rule should be applied but it is not. Because of inexperience or countertransference the therapist mistakenly believes that it is being applied, erroneously thinks that what is being analyzed is the dream's latent content. In actuality, only the semimanifest or semilatent contents have been

worked on. *Results:* the same as those presented in scenario 4, above. The royal road to the unconscious is not being entered, defenses have not been analyzed as much as they could safely have been, time is being wasted. But, in addition, since the analyst mistakenly thinks that the dream has been fully analyzed, false conclusions will be reached about the dream. Since the analyst erroneously believes the road to the patient's unconscious has been entered, erroneous conclusions will be reached about the patient's psychodynamics or psychopathology.

In the following pages we shall revisit three dreams: "Medical Student and Hospital," dreamed by a young acquaintance of Freud's; "Irma's Injection," Freud's own dream about Irma, his patient; and "Three Theatre Tickets," dreamed by a patient of Freud's. The three dreams are discussed at various lengths in Freud's *The Interpretation of Dreams.* From Freud's own discussion of them, it is clear that the cardinal rule was not applied, and the dreams had not been fully analyzed. This section will include: (1) *Freud's thoughts and soliloquy about dream and dreamer,* how he understood the dream, how he fulfilled the analyst's second task in working with dreams, "knowing what the patient's dream says"; (2) *Freud's actual response to the dreamer,* how he fulfilled the analyst's third task in working with dreams, "knowing what to say to the dreamer about the dream"; (3) *my own soliloquy about dream and dreamer,* how I would have fulfilled the analyst's second task in working with dreams; (4) *my own hypothetical response to the dreamer,* how I would have fulfilled the analyst's third task in working with dreams. This will be done through my imagining working with and responding to each of the three dreams, as if the dreams had been told to me in the present time. The rationale of this is, again, to show how the analyst should think and work in responding to dreams.

Lest this chapter be mistakenly taken as an instance of attacking Freud for committing the error he was to warn against (thinking that a dream had been more fully analyzed than it had been in actuality), two points must be made. First, as we shall see shortly, with at least two of these three dreams ("Three Theatre Tickets" and "Irma's Injection"), Freud may have known that those dreams had not been fully analyzed. With "Three Theatre Tickets," it is at least possible that he did know; with "Irma's

Injection," that he did know is actually probable. Even in the first edition of *The Interpretation of Dreams*, several allusions by Freud hint that he did know. Second, Freud's work with these three dreams goes back to before 1900, much before he had refined his thinking on the theory and technique of dream interpretation, and almost two decades before he had written his major papers on the unconscious and the drive theory.

"MEDICAL STUDENT AND HOSPITAL" (Freud, 1900, pp. 125, 170)

Freud's Thoughts on Dream and Dreamer

We learn from one of Freud's letters to Fliess in March of 1895 (Freud, 1892–1899, p. 213), that Rudolf Kaufmann ("Rudi") was a medical student and a nephew of Dr. Josef Breuer, Freud's older and renowned colleague, and coauthor with Freud of an early work on hysteria (Breuer and Freud, 1893–1895). It is in this same letter that Freud first reported the dream to Fliess. We note that in the dream itself, as delineated in *The Interpretation of Dreams*, the dreamer is called "Pepi," and not by his name "Rudi." This may have been Freud's attempt to disguise the actual identity of the nephew of the prominent physician, Breuer. Comparably, Freud makes an important allusion in his correspondence with Fliess which he does not elaborate in the later account. In the letter, he notes that there is a hospital in Vienna, "the Ruldolfinerhaus," which bears a likeness to the dreamer's name.

At the time of the dream, "Pepi" (in actuality, "Rudi") was 22 and living away from home in a rooming house (Freud, 1900, p. 125). On the morning of the dream, Freud reports, that for this young student "Sleep seemed peculiarly sweet. The landlady called through the door: 'Wake up, Herr Pepi! it's time to go to the hospital!' " (p. 125). He added that, upon completion of the dream, the dreamer "turned over and went on sleeping. In this way he openly confessed the motive for his dream" (p. 125). This dream exemplified what Freud called "dreams of convenience" (pp. 125, 233). By this he inferred that the latent wish of the dream was the student's wish to see himself already at the hospital so that he could continue to sleep. But this wish, I submit, was the dream's semimanifest or semilatent wish, not the latent wish.

The Dream "Medical Student and Hospital"

[H]e had a dream that he was lying in bed in a room in the hospital, and that there was a card over the bed on which was written: "Pepi H., medical student, age 22." While he was dreaming, he said to himself "As I'm already in the hospital, there's no need for me to go there" [1900, p. 125].

The following are my thoughts on the dream and the dreamer. My soliloquy includes the following speculations and conjectures (italics: a paraphrase of what Freud wrote about Rudolf and Rudolf's dream in both *The Interpretation of Dreams* and his letter of March 4, 1895, to Wilhelm Fliess).

Pepi (Rudi) was 22 years old. On the morning of the dream, was he unhappy not so much about having to get up to go to the hospital, but with loneliness and sexual frustrations? *The landlady woke him up.* Did that resonate with earlier times when his mother woke him up? *Lying in bed in a room in the hospital.* One is usually lying in bed when having sex, in bed one may gratify erotic wishes. In a hospital bed one is taken care of, one may gratify dependency wishes. Was this element of the manifest dream a concrete pictorial representation of erotic and dependency wishes? *A room in the (Ruldolfinerhaus) hospital.* A hospital that incorporates his name—was that a concrete pictorial representation of childhood grandiosity? *Living away from home.* On the morning of the dream, was he feeling homesick? *A card on which was written, "Pepi H., medical student, age 22."* Was that a hint that in a large medical school, living away from home in a rooming house, he was also feeling anonymous, nameless?

As my soliloquy stops, I will tentatively conclude that the semimanifest and semilatent wish of already being in the hospital covered the more latent wish of being in a place where erotic and dependency wishes from the yesteryear rather than the yesterday, were being gratified; that these wishes were preoedipal wishes (dependency) and oedipal wishes (erotic) toward the mother of his preoedipal and oedipal years, the mother of whom the landlady of the present was a transferential displacement. Rudi was indeed "homesick" for the mother of his childhood and for a time and place (his childhood home) when and where he felt central, not peripheral, meaningful, not anonymous.

My Hypothetical Response to the Dream and Dreamer

Having come to a conjectural and tentative understanding of what Rudolf's dream said, what would I say to Rudolf about his dream, if anything? Now the task is much more difficult, because the possible responses one gives to an actual patient in a real life interpretation of a dream (silence, intervention, interpretation) depend on the psychoanalytical and clinical picture at the time of the dream, as spelled out in the five scenarios given at the beginning of this chapter. A clinical or psychodynamic picture of Rudolf at the time of his dream is not available. What follows, therefore, will be "iffy."

If this had been a first dream, or a dream told very early in therapy, a psychoanalytical and clinical picture akin to the one presented in scenarios 2 and 3, the cardinal rule would obviously be suspended, knowingly, by design. Likely responses could consist of sensitive, expectant silence, of encouraging the patient to associate to the dream, or of general, not too specific questions about the dream and the dreamer. Or, since with first and very early dreams, "not much can be said, not much should be said, and, with some patients, just enough must be said," an acceptable response could be a mild interpretation on the level of defenses. For example: "By dreaming of being in the hospital, and seeing your name on the card over the bed, you were trying to avoid some unpleasant feelings." This would be no more than an allusion to the unpleasantness caused by the frustration of the preoedipal and oedipal drives I had conjectured to be part of Rudolf's latent dream.

If the dream had been told later on, appropriate responses could consist of interventions on the level of the defenses and, probably, on the level of the transference; that is, thoughtfully chosen questions and requests for associations, chosen precisely for being on the level of the defenses or of the transference. Such interventions might include: "What else comes to mind about lying in bed, about a hospital, about the name of the hospital, about a card identifying you by name, about your landlady?" Or, "Do you, sometimes, feel lost in the crowd, anonymous, as if you are being treated impersonally? What does that make you think of?" Or, "Have you been feeling lonely? What does that make you think?'' Or, ''From what you have been saying in recent sessions, I think you are feeling homesick'' (or lonely, or sexually frustrated, or anonymous, depending upon what the fictional Rudolf had said to me). ''Tell me more about that, your dream could have something to do with that.'' Again, it needs to be emphasized that with a ''real'' patient, in a ''real'' analytical session, only one or two of those questions or interventions would be advisable, and which question or intervention would be preferable, would depend again on the psychoanalytical and clinical picture at the time of the dream.

If the dream had been told even later, with the psychoanalytical and clinical picture akin to that presented in scenarios 1, 4, and 5, the analyst might feel an interpretation on the level of the drives and within the context of the transference would be appropriate. Likely responses could consist of: ''You were telling me last week that you wished you could put your head on my shoulder and cry—are you dreaming of being ill in a hospital so you could do that, put your head on my shoulder, and be taken care of?'' Or, a more ''potent'' interpretation might be, ''Are you dreaming of being ill in a hospital so you could do that, put your head on my shoulder, and be taken care of, as with a good Mom (or Dad)?'' These last two interpretations would be particularly appropriate if the line in therapy, at the time of the dream, had been dependency and maternal or paternal transference.

Only by exploring beneath and beyond the semimanifest and semilatent dream and by speculating, conjecturing, and hypothesizing about the latent dream, can one apprehend the full richness of Rudolf's dream.

"IRMA'S INJECTION" (Freud, 1900, pp. 106–121)

This is a famous dream. Freud had described some attempts at the analysis of his own dreams before (Breuer and Freud, 1893–1895), but this dream about Irma was the first of Freud's own about which he wrote extensively. In a footnote added in 1914, he pointed out, ''This is the first dream which I submitted to a detailed interpretation'' (1900, p. 106, n 1). In an editorial note, Strachey refers to the letter to Fliess in which Freud conveyed his equally famous fantasy. ''[O]n June 12, 1900 (Freud,

1950a, Letter 137), Freud describes a later visit to Bellevue, the house where he had this dream. 'Do you suppose' he writes, 'that some day a marble tablet will be placed on the house, inscribed with these words?—In This House, on July 24th, 1895 the Secret of Dreams was Revealed to Dr. Sigm. Freud—At the moment there seems little prospect of it' " (Freud, 1900, p. 121, n 1). The dream of "Irma's Injection" was also the first dream after the analysis of which Freud first and unequivocally stated that "dreams really have a meaning and are far from being the expression of a fragmentary activity of the brain, as the authorities have claimed. *When the work of interpretation has been completed, we perceive that a dream is the fulfilment of a wish"* (Freud, 1900, p. 121).

Important as the dream about Irma is, it was an incompletely analyzed dream: Freud interpreted the semimanifest–semilatent dream, not the latent dream, analyzed the yesterday and the dream's recent sources, not the yesteryear and the dream's infantile sources in his own unconscious, brought into view only his semimanifest–semilatent thoughts and wishes, not his unconscious id wishes.

However, as briefly mentioned at the beginning of this chapter, it is probable that, privately, Freud carried the analysis of the dream to deeper ends than he did publicly. In *The Interpretation of Dreams*, Freud may not have analyzed the dream fully for personal reasons, including the fact that Irma, unlike any other of the patients whose dreams he analyzed extensively, was a friend of the family, as he humorously and perhaps cleverly informs us, as if wanting the reader to read between the lines (p. 106). The historical truth may never be known, but it is legitimate to think that Freud *did know* he had *not* analyzed his dream about Irma all the way to its latent level. In the last pages of his discussion of the dream, Freud acknowledged at least three times that his work on the dream was incomplete. Referring to the interpretation of the dream, he said: "While I was carrying it out I had some difficulty keeping at bay all the ideas which were bound to be provoked by a comparison between the content of the dream and the concealed thoughts lying behind it" (p. 118). In a footnote added in 1909, he wrote: "[I]t will be understood that I have not reported everything that occurred to me during the process of interpretation" (p. 118). And in the last page of the discussion of the dream, he said: "I will not pretend that I have completely uncovered the meaning of this dream, or that its interpretation is without a gap. . . . I myself know the points from which further trains of thought could be followed. But considerations which arise in the case of every dream of my own restrain me from pursuing my interpretative work" (pp. 120–121).[1] It is indeed probable, therefore, that Freud's approach to his dream about Irma was not what scenario 5 describes: Freud did realize he had not applied the cardinal rule. But the main purpose of this chapter is to alert the reader to the theoretical and clinical problems that arise from suspending the cardinal rule without realizing that one is doing so. Freud's analysis of his dream of "Irma's Injection" will be discussed as he presented it publicly in *The Interpretation of Dreams.*

Again, to recapitulate before moving forward, let us recall to mind the following basic points of Freudian dream theory, points previously discussed here and there in this book, but very relevant to our work with this dream now: All persons, objects, places, or situations being dreamed about, are dreamed about *only if and because* they have been overcathected with energy from the dreamer's unconscious drives. If these persons and objects are daily residue which had been preserved from the dream's day in the dreamer's preconscious, they are now being dreamed about *only if and because* they have been overcathected with energy from the dreamer's unconscious.

All dreams have one "leg" in the unconscious (the dreamer's yesteryear, the dream's infantile sources). Therefore, all persons, objects, and so on, which are found in the manifest, semimanifest, and semilatent dream (i.e., the dreamer's yesterday, in the dreamer's recent sources), are a transferential displacement from counterparts in the dreamer's unconscious (i.e., the dreamer's yesteryear, the dream's infantile sources), counterparts which will be found in the dream's latent content.

The dream's manifest content and the dreamer's yesterday are only magnets and triggers, so to speak, for the unconscious drives by which they are overcathected and which they, in turn,

---

[1]Additional insights on Freud's dream about Irma's injection are provided in Erikson's classic article (1954).

overcathect. They are only facades for those unconscious drives, facades that those same drives utilize to camouflage themselves. Nevertheless, the dream's manifest content and the dreamer's yesterday are still extremely important, especially in analyses on the level of the transference, because it is the dream's manifest content and the dreamer's yesterday that tell the analyst which current persons, objects, places, or situations have been overcathected with transferential energies.

Countertransference, positive or negative, is as inevitable as transference. The question is not whether the experience of countertransference is good or bad, but whether one is able to be aware of it and able to use it, especially diagnostically. Sometimes it is the analyst's countertransference to a patient's unconscious feeling about the analyst that makes the analyst aware of that feeling in the patient. The analyst can use such feelings, in order to gain insight into the patient's unconscious dynamics, and into how these psychodynamics resonate with the analyst's own unconscious. The analyst can use such countertransference feelings therapeutically, for the patient's benefit and for the benefit of the analyst's ongoing self-analysis. When analysts dream about their patients, as Freud did about Irma, those dreams are countertransferential. Of course, all the analyst knows about himself or herself in relation to that patient, is part of the dream and will be helpful in analyzing that dream. Therefore, in working with Freud's dream about Irma, all that Freud tells us about Irma and about himself in relation to Irma is essential in our work with that dream.

In a session in which a dream is told, anything the dreamer says, before or after telling the dream, can be an association to the dream, or at least a path, or a shortcut, to a greater understanding of the unconscious. For this reason, those words of the manifest dream to which Freud had associations, and all that he said about the dream, before and after telling us the dream, are important and reported verbatim.

The Dreamer (Freud) on the Dream and Dreamer—Before the Dream was Dreamed

At the time of the dream, July 24, 1895, Freud was 39. Three years before, he had moved away from hypnosis and toward free association. With a technique more and more "patient centered," his patients, who were increasingly left on their own, so to speak, more and more often told him their dreams.

Both in a preamble to his interpretation of this dream (p. 106), and in the initial paragraphs of his analysis following the dream (p. 108), Freud provides information which serves as a context for the dream. Irma (whose real name was Emma), Freud's patient, was a young widow suffering from hysterical anxiety. She had been referred to him by Joseph Breuer (Dr. M in the published dream). Freud tells us that she was "on very friendly terms with me and my family." Therapy had relieved Irma of her anxiety but not of her somatic symptoms. Shortly before treatment was interrupted for the summer, Freud had proposed "a solution to the patient which she seemed unwilling to accept." The Freuds spent that summer "at Bellevue, a house standing by itself on one of the hills adjoining the Kahlenberg," the Schloss Bellevue resort hotel in the hills near Vienna. "This house," Freud tells us, "had formerly been designed as a place of entertainment and its reception-rooms were in consequence unusually lofty and hall-like." Irma's family's country house was not too far from where the Freuds were staying. The day before the dream, Freud learned from his wife Martha that Irma would be among friends who were soon going to visit the Freuds on the occasion of Martha's forthcoming birthday. Also on the day before the dream, Otto (in actuality, Oskar Rie[2]), Freud's friend and younger colleague and the pediatrician of Freud's children, visited the Freuds at Bellevue. Otto had just left Irma's family's house. Freud reports that he made inquiry of Otto. "I asked him how he had found her and he answered, 'She's better, but not quite well.' " Freud felt annoyed by Otto's words; he "detected a reproof in them." That evening he wrote Irma's case history extensively, "with the idea of giving it to Dr. M. (a common friend who was at that time the leading figure in our circle) in order to justify myself." That night he had the dream.

---

[2]For a fuller elaboration of the actual persons depicted in Freud's dream of Irma's injection, see Peter Gay's detailed and informative *Freud: A Life for Our Time* (1988, pp. 80–87), although Gay renders a different interpretation of Freud's reticence about these persons. Also, Jonathan Winson (1985, pp. 94–102, 224–229) elaborates his neuroscientific hypotheses about dreaming with his understanding of Freud's dream about Irma.

Everything reported in the previous paragraph (excluding the actual identities of the personages in the published dream) is told us by Freud in *The Interpretation of Dreams*. In our work with this dream, his remarks will be treated as part of the dream session.

The Dream "Irma's Injection"

A large hall—numerous guests, whom we were receiving.—Among them was Irma. I at once took her on one side, as though to answer her letter and to reproach her for not having accepted my 'solution' yet. I said to her: 'If you still get pains, it's really only your fault.' She replied: 'If you only knew what pains I've got now in my throat and stomach and abdomen—it's choking me'—I was alarmed and looked at her. She looked pale and puffy. I thought to myself that after all I must be missing some organic trouble. I took her to the window and looked down her throat, and she showed signs of recalcitrance, like women with artificial dentures. I thought to myself that there was really no need for her to do that.—She then opened her mouth properly and on the right I found a big white patch; at another place I saw extensive whitish grey scabs upon some remarkable curly structures which were evidently modelled on the turbinal bones of the nose.—I at once called in Dr. M., and he repeated the examination and confirmed it . . . . Dr. M. looked quite different from usual; he was very pale, he walked with a limp and his chin was clean-shaven. . . . My friend Otto was now standing beside her as well, and my friend Leopold was percussing her through her bodice and saying: 'She has a dull area low down on the left.' He also indicated that a portion of the skin on the left shoulder was infiltrated. (I noticed this, just as he did, in spite of her dress.) . . . M. said: 'There's no doubt it's an infection, but no matter; dysentery will supervene and the toxin will be eliminated.' . . . We were directly aware, too, of the origin of the infection. Not long before, when she was feeling unwell, my friend Otto had given her an injection of a preparation of propyl, propyls . . . propionic acid . . . trimethylamin (and I saw before me the formula for this printed in heavy type). . . . Injections of that sort ought not to be made so thoughtlessly. . . . And probably the syringe had not been clean [1900, p. 107].

The Dreamer (Freud) on the Dream and Dreamer—After the Dream Was Dreamed

Early in his work with dreams, Freud believed that to analyze a dream, it should be broken down into its parts, and the dreamer should engage in free associations to each of those parts. He did so in the analysis of this dream. As he gives us his associations, these associations show us how they led him, the dreamer, to his thoughts about the dream, to his self-analysis of his dream, to his internal soliloquy about the dream, and ultimately, to his interpretation of the dream. Following are some of the thoughts that came to his mind as he struggled to understand his dream.

Free associating about Irma, Freud thought of a woman friend of Irma's of whom, he tells us, he "had a very high opinion"; of a governess, whose mouth he had once examined; of Martha, his own wife, who was usually pale and had once looked puffy; of Mathilde, his eldest daughter, and of a woman patient, whose name also was Mathilde, who had once developed dysentery; of a child ill with diphtheria, whom Freud had once examined. This made Freud realize that the manifest dream's Irma, through condensations and displacements, represented, as well, the six other persons he had thought about.

Thinking about Dr. M brought Freud to think of his elder brother, also clean shaven, who limped because of arthritis. Freud added, "There must, I reflected, have been some reasons for my fusing into one the two figures in the dream. I then remembered that I had a similar reason for being in ill-humor with each of them: they had both rejected a certain suggestion I had laid before them." Therefore Freud realized the manifest dream's Dr. M represented, through condensation and displacement, Dr. M and Freud's elder brother.

Trimethylamin brought to Freud's mind that this substance was a metabolic product of sexual activity. In his dream thoughts, then, Irma's lack of a sexual life (she was a young widow in Victorian Vienna) could be "an excuse for the failure of my treatment in her case," one more reason, he thought, why he could not be faulted for Irma's persisting symptoms.

Other associations were that the hall of the manifest dream was "unusually lofty"; that the governess, whose mouth Freud had once examined, had been resistant in opening her mouth because she had "plates," false teeth; that his own wife, of whom he had thought in free associating about Irma, was "bashful in my presence and I could not think she would make an amenable patient."

In free associating to his dream, Freud's conscious and pre-conscious mind was also occupied, of course, with the thoughts and feelings he had had about the various dramatis personae who were part of the manifest dream, the thoughts and feelings he had shared with us in the preamble before telling us the dream. These thoughts and feelings include the following. Otto, just the day before the dream, had said that he had found Irma "better, but not quite well." Freud had felt annoyed by his words and had "detected a reproof in them." The evening before the dream he had felt the need to write Irma's case history extensively in case Dr. M would be critical of his management of the case. Freud also lamented that if only Irma had accepted his advice about her condition, his "solution," then she might be better.

In the public discussion of his dream (i.e., in the published account in *The Interpretation of Dreams*), Freud's thoughts and associations led him to believe that the dream's wishes were the wish to exculpate himself of the fact that Irma was "not quite well"; the wish to put all the blame on Otto; the wish to take revenge on Otto, whose remarks about Irma's not yet being "quite well" had been construed by Freud as a criticism; and the wish to exonerate himself with Dr. M as well as within his own conscience. Through the dream, Freud thought, he was telling himself that he was not at fault for Irma's painful symptoms, all those symptoms were Otto's fault, not Freud's, the fault of the injection Otto had given her so thoughtlessly, and with a dirty syringe too. Furthermore, if Irma's condition was caused by "some organic trouble," as the dream was saying, Freud, a psychoanalyst, surely could not be faulted for not having made her well.

My Thoughts on the Dream and Dreamer

Freud's associations to this dream show us how these associations led him to his "soliloquy" about the dream and, ultimately, to his interpretation of the dream. They also led me to my soliloquy of conjectures, hypotheses, and speculations about the dream and, ultimately, to my understanding of the dream—all of which is precisely what our patients' associations do for us, when the dreamer is our patient. Here of course, a very significant difference is that the patient is Sigmund Freud himself: possibilities for countertransferential blocks and inhibitions on my part are infinite. Nevertheless, these are the conjectures, hypotheses, and speculations of my soliloquy about dream and dreamer. (Italicized words reflect what Freud wrote about himself and the dream.)

A large hall. In reality, the Bellevue villa did have large rooms; this notwithstanding, was this a displacement from childhood? A large room looks, to a child, as big as a hall; a ceiling of conventional height looks, to an infant, as high as a cathedral's ceiling. Was the *large hall* of Freud's manifest dream a normal size room in Freud's childhood, and did this date the dream to Freud's yesteryear? *Lofty and hall-like.* Was this a turning into the opposite, of "base" into its opposite "lofty," a defense against guilt-producing "base," "vile" feelings and mental representations belonging to the latent dream? *Numerous guests.* In reality, many guests were expected for Martha Freud's birthday; nevertheless, was this a displacement, or a projection onto the guests of the manifest dream from equally numerous thoughts and feelings in the latent dream?

The six persons Freud thought about in free associating to Irma included his *daughter* and his *wife.* Irma, Freud thought, was a displacement from his daughter and his wife. In other words, Freud went as far as his daughter and wife, but he did not go far enough. Beyond those two family members, I conjectured, there was one more family member, his mother. My conjecture, I thought, was supported by the fact that one more of the six persons Freud thought about was a "*governess,*" that is, someone who, through predicate thinking, is a mother figure; and another was "an intimate woman friend" of Irma's of whom Freud "had a very high opinion," that is, another potential mother figure. And what is happening with Irma-mother? She *looked unusually pale,* a concrete pictorial representation, I conjectured, of having gone through a powerful emotional experience. She "*looked puffy,*" a concrete pictorial representation, I thought, of pregnancy. Freud "looked down her throat," a displacement from vagina. And of her pain, Irma says, "*it's choking me.*" I speculated that this was a concrete pictorial representation of her being overwhelmed by oedipal-Freud's semen and penis, a concrete pictorial representation of Irma-mother having fellated a penis so large, in the oedipal child's grandiosity, to be choked by it. My speculation, I thought, was supported by the three following bits of data: there was a *"big, white patch"* (semen?) on her *"throat"* (vagina?); *"solution"* does appear in the manifest dream, and that, too, could be a displacement from or a symbolism of semen; and a *"syringe"* (penis) and an *"injection"* (coitus) do appear later on in the manifest dream.

When Freud free associated about Dr. M, he thought of his *"elder brother"* who was *"walking with a limp,"* that is, a displacement from his brother to Dr. M. Here too, I conjectured, deeper into Freud's unconscious, there was one more family member and one more displacement to Dr. M from that family member, his own father, who was already ill at the time of the dream. This conjecture too, I thought, was supported by Freud's adding: *"I then remembered that I had a similar reason for being in ill-humour with each of them"*—Dr. M and his brother—*"they had both rejected a certain suggestion I had recently laid before them."* This was a possible allusion to the oedipal father with whom little Oedipus-Freud is, of course, in ill humor. In line with this last speculation, I thought that Dr. M was *"clean shaven,"* *"very pale,"* and *"walked with a limp"*: all concrete pictorial representations of Dr. M (i.e., Freud's father) having undergone castration at the hand of Freud, the oedipal child.

My soliloquy continued. If behind the manifest dream's Irma was mother, and if behind the manifest dream's Dr. M was father, then behind Otto was Freud himself. My fantasy, therefore, was that *an injection of trimethylamin* was a metaphor for sexuality, and *injection,* as indicated a few lines above, a symbolism for coitus. Thus *"Otto had given her an injection of . . . trimethylamin,"* through displacement and projection, stood for Freud having done so. This conjecture was supported by Freud's association to trimethylamin as *"an immensely powerful factor of sexuality."* To continue with this particular line, *syringe,* I thought, was an obvious symbolism for penis, that *"the syringe had not been clean"* was a concrete pictorial representation of the idea that oedipal sexuality, in the eye of the superego, is reprehensible, is *not clean.* And, most central to the dream's latent content, the accusation against Otto, that *it was Otto's fault,* stood, through displacement, projection, and turning into the opposite, for *it was to Freud's credit.* It was the sexual potency of the grandiose oedipal child, his huge penis, the copiousness of his semen, the potency of this "*solution*," his sexual prowess, that *choked* Irma-mother, that made her "*puffy*" and "*pale*."

I also thought that the dream had a voyeuristic aspect. *Bellevue* could have been an onomatopoeia for "beautiful view"; *looking* "*down her throat*" was transparently scoptophilic, and Freud was *looking down* Irma-mother's throat-vagina precisely to get the "beautiful view." The "*big white patch*" being "*on the right*," I conjectured, was a turning into the opposite and a concrete pictorial representation of the idea that what the dreamer was up to was, after all, "right," not "wrong."

And finally, I thought, in the manifest dream, Irma showed "*recalcitrance*" in opening her mouth to have Freud examine her throat. When Freud associated to this, it reminded him of the *governess* whose mouth he had once examined, who had been resistant in opening her mouth because she had false teeth, and of his own wife who was "*bashful in my presence*," and not "*an amenable patient*." And my soliloquy was: Irma's recalcitrance (i.e., Freud's mother's recalcitrance) was a turning into the opposite. In the primacy of wish-fulfillment and magic thinking, Irma, the oedipal mother, is, of course, not recalcitrant at all about the oedipal child, her beloved Sigmund, feasting his eyes on her mouth, throat, vagina, and injecting his "*solution*" into her. On the level of the defenses, of course, castration fears hover in the background. Does she have strong teeth, with which she could bite off his daring penis? Or, on the contrary, does she have *false teeth* and is, therefore, harmless? Doubts also flicker on and off. Will she be a willing partner, or will she be difficult as Irma, who did not accept Dr. Freud's "*solution*," or not "*an amenable patient*" like his own wife who is "*bashful in* [Sigmund's] *presence*"?

As my soliloquy of fantasies, conjectures, and speculations comes to an end, I will tentatively conclude that the dream's semimanifest and semilatent wishes were exactly those wishes Freud had acknowledged in his public interpretation of the dream. These are: the wish to exculpate himself for his failure in treating Irma's illness (her real psychiatric illness, her anxiety hysteria, not the spurious illness represented in the manifest dream), the wish to put all the blame on Otto, the wish to revenge himself on Otto, and the wish to exonerate himself from any blame from Otto, Dr. M, and especially, his internal self.

About the latent dream, I will tentatively conclude that the dream wishes were phallic and voyeuristic oedipal desires toward his mother, and aggressive, castratory wishes toward his father. In the semimanifest and semilatent dream, those drives were disguised and distorted, mainly through displacement, projection, turning into the opposite, onomatopoeia, and symbolism. Mother was disguised as Irma and the six other persons whom Freud thought of in free associating about Irma; father was disguised as Dr. M and Freud's elder brother; Freud himself was disguised as Otto. Freud's penis was disguised as Otto's syringe, mother's vagina as Irma's throat, sexuality as trimethylamin, semen as solution and as white patches. Voyeuristic drives, finally, were disguised by locating the dream at Bellevue.

My Hypothetical Response to the Dream and Dreamer

Having come conjecturally to a tentative understanding of what Freud's dream said, what would I tell the dreamer about his dream? In working with Freud's dream of Irma up to this point, I have shared with the reader my conjectural understanding of that dream through my thoughts about the dream, as gathered from the conjectures and fantasies bubbling up to my consciousness in resonating to all Freud himself told us about the dream and about himself. My conjectural understanding evolved through my thoughts about the dream, based on the theory of dream formation, in terms of how various dream work operations can take us back from specific components of the manifest dream to corresponding specific counterparts in the latent dream. Arriving at this speculative understanding of the latent dream was made easy by Freud's prolific associations to the dream, and by his generosity in telling us about the dream's cast of characters, including himself, at the time of the dream. But now we have to imagine how to respond to the dream, which is much more difficult. In the case of Rudolf/Pepi, the difficulty was that the dreamer not being a patient, one lacked the clinical data one needs to decide whether to respond to the dream with silence, an intervention, or an interpretation. With Freud's dream about

Irma, the clinical data are abundant, but the difficulty is in trying to imagine being Freud's analyst, or a late twentieth century Fliess, Freud's confidant. Nevertheless, throwing all countertransferential concerns and inhibitions to the wind, we proceed.

Assuming that one's clinical sense makes one feel that a response other than silence is desirable, responses on the level of the defenses might include eliciting still more associations about Irma, or Otto, or Dr. M, or Freud's older brother, or the governess, or the syringe, or Bellevue, or the white patches. The intent of this exploration is to lead the dreamer further toward the yesteryear and the infantile sources of the dream, further toward the dream's latent content. Another appropriate intervention would be to ask questions about specific items that the analyst's clinical sense feels would be useful to focus on. For instance, "What else might have made you feel guilty, what else might you want to exonerate yourself from?" Or, "What else might you be angry at Otto about?" Or, "What else comes to mind about the 'ill-humor' you felt toward Dr. M and your brother?" Or, "What comes to mind about the woman friend of Irma's of whom you think so highly?"

Responses on the level of the drives could include references or allusions (more or less direct or indirect, depending on how long the patient has been working with us, and on the state of his ego) to oedipal and voyeuristic desires toward mother figures and to oedipal aggressive feelings against father figures. These could include any mother figure or father figure in Sigmund Freud's life in the summer of 1895, who might have been transferential representations of his parents.

Analyzing Freud's dream of Irma to a fuller extent, by applying to its interpretation the rules which Freud himself was later to formulate, deepens considerably our understanding of the dream.

"THREE THEATRE TICKETS" (Freud, 1900, pp. 415–416; 1901a, pp. 669–670, 673; 1916b, pp. 122–125, 219–221)

In this dream, as in the two previous ones, the dream was not fully analyzed and the thoughts and wishes that were believed to be part of the latent dream were actually part of the semilatent dream. Unlike his dream about Irma, with this dream Freud gives very few details about the dreamer; and the dreamer's associations were scarce. With dreamers whom analysts know well and who associate prolifically, the analyst's soliloquy will be based on actual facts about the patient, or about the persons or occurrences the patient dreamed about, as well as upon the patient's associations. We could easily do that with Freud's dream about Irma because of the abundance of details about the persons who were part of the dream, and because of the richness of Freud's associations to the dream. With "Three Theatre Tickets," because of the dearth of details, one's soliloquy will have to be based more on what one can fantasize about and resonate with from the few details available. This is a valuable exercise. Working with this dream is akin to what analysts must do with dreams dreamed by new patients, or patients they do not know well, or patients who have difficulty associating to their dreams.

Freud on the Dream and Dreamer—Before the Dream was Dreamed

"Three Theatre Tickets" was dreamed by a woman patient of Freud's. The dreamer was "still young" and "had been married a number of years" (1900, p. 415). It is not clear how long she had been Freud's patient or why she had entered analysis. A younger friend of the dreamer, who figures prominently in the dream and in the dreamer's few associations to the dream, was named Elise. On the day preceding the night of the dream, the dreamer's husband had told her that Elise had just become engaged. Also on that day, the dreamer had heard that her sister-in-law had received a gift of 150 florins from her own husband, and had spent it on jewelry for herself. "Three," the number of theater tickets in the manifest dream, was also the number of months by which Elise was the dreamer's junior. Some days before the dream, the dreamer had gone to some trouble in order to buy tickets for an upcoming play she did not want to miss and had paid some extra money for these tickets. But, when she and her husband had arrived at the theater, "they found that one side of the house was almost empty. There had been *no need to be in such a hurry*" (pp. 415–416). The dreamer's husband had teased her about her unwarranted haste and concern. The dreamer loved her husband.

The Dream "Three Theatre Tickets"

> She was at the theatre with her husband. One side of the stalls was completely empty. Her husband told her that Elise L. and her fiancé had wanted to go too, but had only been able to get bad seats—three for 1 florin 50 kreuzers—and of course they could not take those. She thought it would not really have done any harm if they had [1900, p. 415].

Freud on the Dream and Dreamer—After the Dream Was Dreamed

Freud thought that the dream's day residues were the news about Elise's engagement, the gift which the dreamer's sister-in-law had received, and the jewelry that her sister-in-law had purchased with it. He thought that the number "*three*" in the manifest dream was connected with Elise's being three months younger than the dreamer. He thought that "1 florin 50 kreuzers" was linked with the amount of money (150 florins) which the dreamer's sister-in-law had received as a gift. He thought that "one side of the stalls was completely empty" was linked with the experience of having actually gone to the theater and having found it almost empty. He noted that the sum of "150 florins is a *hundred* times as much as 1 florin 50 kreuzers" (p. 415).

Freud's soliloquy also included these thoughts. References to time in the dreamer's thoughts occurred frequently. "She took the theatre tickets *too early*, bought them *over-hurriedly* . . . her sister-in-law had been *in a hurry* to take her money to the jewellers . . . " (1916b, p. 123). The dreamer "was not always so dissatisfied with her early marriage as she was on the day when she received the news of her friend's engagement" (1916b, p. 120). One detail of the manifest dream seemed particularly absurd, "namely the *three* seats being taken by *two* people" (1900, p. 416). That seeming absurdity, Freud thought, probably covered something important.

Based on these thoughts, Freud concluded that the absurdity of *three* seats being taken by *two* people represented "the most strongly emphasized of the dream-thoughts, viz., 'it was *absurd* to marry so early' " (1900, p. 416). He believed that in her dream the patient was saying: " 'There was *no need to be in such a hurry.* I see from Elise L.'s example that I should have got a husband in the end. Indeed, I should have got one *a hundred times* better' (a treasure) 'if I had only waited. My money' (or dowry) 'could have bought *three* men just as good' " (1901a, p. 670). Having married too early, Freud thought, was the strongest of the dreamer's dream thoughts.

Freud also believed that a second dream thought was a devaluation of her husband. "The reduction of the actual 150 florins to 1 florin 50 corresponded to the *low value* assigned by the dreamer to her husband (or treasure) in her suppressed thoughts" (1900, p. 416). A third dream thought had to do with voyeurism: " 'Marrying' is clearly replaced by 'going to the theatre.' 'Taking the theatre tickets too early' is, indeed, an immediate substitute for 'marrying too early.' " (1916b, p. 220). Freud noted that young girls "after becoming engaged, are reputed often to express their joy that they will soon be able to go to the theatre, to all the plays which have hitherto been prohibited, and will be allowed to see everything. . . . Thus the dreamer, in her present anger at her early marriage, harked back to the time at which early marriage was the fulfillment of a wish because it satisfied her scoptophilia, and, under the lead of this old wishful impulse, she replaced marriage by going to the theatre" (1916b, pp. 220–221).

Thus, Freud saw the dream mainly as representing unconscious feelings the dreamer had about her husband, anger about having married him when she was too young, regret that the premature marriage had preempted her chances of marrying a better man. "The analysis led to the inevitable conclusion that she had a low estimate of her husband (cf. her idea that she could have got one 'a hundred times better'), that she regretted having married him, and that she would have liked to exchange him for another one" (1901a, p. 673). Elsewhere Freud again emphasized: "The dream expresses the *low value* assigned by her to her own husband and her regret at having *married so early*" (1916b, p. 124). Freud summarized the meaning of the dream by saying: "It is true that she asserted that she loved her husband, and that her emotional life knew nothing of any such low estimate of him, but all her symptoms led to the same conclusion as the dream. And after her repressed memories had been revived of a particular period during which she had consciously not loved her husband, her symptoms cleared up and her resistance against the interpretation of the dream disappeared" (1901a, p. 673).

Thus Freud understood this dream too in terms of current or recent problems, current dissatisfaction with her husband which was overcathected by the news of Elise's engagement, and getting married in the recent past which had gratified her voyeurism. This dream, therefore, is also an incompletely analyzed dream, a dream in which Freud interpreted the semilatent content, not the latent; in which he analyzed the yesterday and the recent sources of the dream, not the yesteryear and the infantile sources; in which he brought into light the dreamer's semilatent wishes, not the unconscious id wishes of the dreamer's deeper conflicts. In the analysis of this dream, Freud may have broken, without realizing it, the cardinal rule of dream interpretation.

In fairness to Freud, with this dream he also acknowledged gaps and flaws in his still growing understanding of dreams and dreaming. "[T]here is still much that is unintelligible about it. It really seems to me that we are not yet equipped for interpreting a dream and that we need first to be given some further instruction and preparation" (1916b, p. 125). And also in fairness to Freud, I believe that the truly latent wish in this dream, a wish that did go back to the yesteryear and to infantile sources, was voyeurism. Freud himself did consider voyeurism ("scoptophilia") one of this dream's wishes. But he weakened this insight by referring to it as the last and least important of the three dream thoughts, and by thinking that the dreamer's voyeurism only went back to when she had first married (i.e., early adulthood). But in a short, easy to overlook sentence of *Introductory Lectures on Psycho-Analysis* (1916b), he did refer to the infantile sources of scoptophilia, expressed in Victorian Vienna by young women being able to go to the theater once they had married. He said: "The pleasure in looking, or curiosity, which is revealed in this was no doubt originally a sexual desire to look [scopophilia], directed towards sexual happenings and especially onto the girls' parents..." (1916b, p. 220).

My Thoughts on the Dream and Dreamer

My soliloquy includes the following speculations and hypotheses. (Italicized words reflect what Freud wrote about himself and the dream.)

"*At the theatre.*" Theaters are places to which one goes to watch something entertaining, oftentimes moving and powerful. Was the dream's theater a displacement from a bedroom where parents are enacting something as exciting for the child as sexual intercourse? Might this be a displacement from anything else, equally exciting, to which the dreamer had been an awed spectator as a child or an infant? Since theaters are usually large and spacious, this feature too, like the large hall in the dream about Irma, could have been dating the dream to childhood, a time when ordinary rooms seem as large as theaters. "*With her husband.*" Was this a displacement from any other family member who was psychodynamically important in childhood, the dreamer's father, for instance? *Her husband had teased her.* Was this a displacement in object and time? Had her father, in the dreamer's childhood, teased her about something? Had her father been a "tease," a "tease" with words, a "tease" to her natural childhood voyeurism, a "tease" by showing off like an actor in a theater, or by parading around the house half undressed?

"*One side of the stalls was completely empty.*" Were the stalls a displacement from the parental bed? Was "*one side empty*" because mother was not there in reality in the child's memory, or just as likely, not there in the child's wish? Was mother not there, in reality or in fantasy, so that the voyeuristic and erotic child could jump into bed and have father all for herself? Or, on the other hand, was "*empty*" a concrete pictorial representation of an empty feeling in the dreamer's yesteryear? Or was it a turning into the opposite? The bed, the bedroom, far from empty, was full, full because the dreamer and her father were in it, full because the scene and whatever was happening was filling the dreamer, the child, with excitement? "*Bad seats.*" Was this, again, a turning into the opposite? The seats in the latent dream, in the dreamer's yesteryear, might actually have been quite good, so that the voyeuristic child could enjoy her eyeful of father's partly undressed body? "*Three.*" Is it her father's genitals (*three* is a classic symbol for male genitals) that the little child is feasting her eyes on? *"Elise L. and her fiancé."* Was this a displacement from father and mother? And finally, *"Elise L. and her fiancé . . . had only been able to get bad seats . . . and of course they could not take those."* Was this a concrete pictorial representation of the dreamer's wish to take revenge on her parents for the times in which they excluded her from watching them?

As my soliloquy of conjectures, speculations, and fantasies ends, I will conclude by saying that I understand the semilatent dream more or less as Freud did. The semilatent wishes are the wish to be at the theater with a man other than her husband, and the wish to exclude Elise from the voyeuristic pleasure which only married women in Freud's day had, the pleasure of going to the theater. In the manifest dream, thanks to the defensive distorting operations of the dream work, she was at the theater with her husband, the performance was not great at all (the theater was half empty), there is no dream consciousness of the wish to be married to anyone else or to be at the theater with anybody else, and there is regret rather than glee at Elise's not being there.

Freud stopped here and did not proceed further toward the dreamer's unconscious, her id drives, and the infantile sources of the dream. He did not relate to the latent dream. From the conjectures, hypotheses, and speculations bubbling up to my consciousness as I "heard" the dreamer's dream and to what Freud said about it, I believe that the dream's latent wishes included oedipal–voyeuristic wishes about father and oedipal–aggressive wishes against mother. In the semilatent dream these drives are still well disguised and distorted through displacement, symbolism, and turning into the opposite. Father is disguised as husband, as Elise's fiancé, and as any major actor on the stage. Mother is disguised as Elise and as any major actress on the stage. The parental bedroom is disguised as the theater. The dreamer's mother's absence is disguised as one side of the stalls being completely empty, the dreamer's father's genitals by the number *three*, and the glee at Elise's not being there, by regret.

My Hypothetical Response to the Dream and Dreamer

This is the analyst's final task in working with dreams, "knowing what to say to the patient about the dream." How would I have responded to the dream? Having reached tentative (and conjectural) conclusions as to the meaning of the dream, what should I say to the dreamer about it, if anything? On the one hand, to answer this question will not be as difficult as it was with Freud's dream. Here, we do not have to imagine being Sigmund Freud's analyst, we only have to imagine being the analyst of a former patient of Freud's, a much less daunting task. On the other hand, because of the dearth of details, and the paucity of associations by the dreamer (Freud and I each had more associations to the dream's manifest content and to the dreamer's story than the dreamer herself did), the task here is more difficult than it was with Freud's dream about Irma. But this is no greater than the difficulty all analysts have with new patients, or with patients the analyst does not know well, or with patients who have difficulty with free associations.

If one's clinical sense makes one feel that a response other than a benevolent expectant silence is desirable, and if the psychoanalytical and clinical picture is akin to that described at the beginning of this chapter in scenario 2 (early stages of therapy, feeble therapeutic alliance), then responses on the level of the defenses would be appropriate, and might consist of waiting for associations (waiting for associations rather than actively trying to elicit associations is generally preferable). Or the analyst might ask for associations to the theater, to the theater performance the dreamer did actually attend with her husband, to the empty stalls. Or the analyst's clinical sense might prompt questions which he or she feels would be useful to focus on. For instance, "What other feelings have you about your husband?" "How did you feel when he teased you?" "Who else used to tease you?" If the psychoanalytical and clinical picture is more akin to the one described in scenario 1, responses on the level of the drives might be appropriate. Such responses could include direct, or better, indirect, references, allusions, or even, if appropriate, statements about oedipal–erotic and voyeuristic drives toward various father figures or oedipal–aggressive drives toward mother figures in the dreamer's life.

Again, analyzing this patient's dream to a fuller extent, applying the cardinal rule to its interpretation, if only in our internal soliloquy, deepens our understanding of the dream and the dreamer considerably.

Appendix: Connections between and among Dreams, REM Sleep, Primary Process Functions, and States of Sensory Privation and Cortical Deafferentiation

There are important connections between and among dreams, the primary subject of this book, and other subjects such as rapid eye movement (REM) sleep, primary process functions, daydreams, hallucinations, and states of sensory privation and cortical deafferentiation. Some of these connections are clear and well established, others less so. All of these connections are intriguing, many are far reaching. For instance, the connections between primary process functions and the states of sensory privation and cortical deafferentiation (be these states self-generated or externally induced) may be seen in aspects of normative functioning and have also been implicated in the development of some forms of schizophrenia and senile psychoses. Many of these connections were addressed in overview in chapter 1. This appendix aims to make these connections more explicit, and to show how these subjects and their interconnections explain an important characteristic of the conscious ego, that is, its dependence on stimulation for optimal functioning. It will also illustrate how the

conscious ego adapts and protects itself in the absence of stimulation. In sum, this appendix will elaborate dream formation from
a neurological perspective.

In chapter 2 we said that the id's primary process functions
have several capacities: (1) the capability to perceive those objects
and object relations in the external world through which drives
essential for survival had previously been gratified; (2) the capacity to record those perceptions as memories; and (3) the faculty
to reproduce those memories as mental images. The primary process was defined as the process which produces a memory image
of those objects and object relations that are needed to reduce a
tension. In predicate thinking and magic thinking, the memory
image of a needed object or object relation, and the actual object
and object relation, are one and the same. The imagined gratification and the real gratification are also one and the same. Freud
called this "perceptual identity" (1900, p. 566).

Since primary process functions consist of and result in the
imagined gratification of a frustrated, ungratified drive, and since
primary process functions operate by flashing to our mind the
remembered *image* of needed objects and object relations, primary process functions are our first dream, pleasant or unpleasant, a beautiful dream or a nightmare. Dement and Kleitman
(1957) found that a great majority of images in dreams are visual:
even sensory stimulations of a tactile or auditory nature are represented in dreams as visual stimulations. To the extent that the
images we flash to our mind are visual, whenever our primary
process functions are operating in the state of sleep, our eyes
will function in a state of REM. Since the seminal discoveries of
Aserinsky and Kleitman (1953) and Dement and Kleitman
(1957), it has been clearly established that every dream is accompanied by a REM state and, in every dream, primary process functions are operating. However, sleep researchers have not ruled
out the possibility that dreams and primary process functions of
a kind other than visual (i.e., auditory, tactile, olfactory, or gustatory) might occur during a NREM state (for relevant references
to dream research, refer to chapter 1).

Let us address the connections between dreams, daydreams,
and hallucinations. Primary process functions consist of and result in the imagined gratification of a frustrated, ungratified drive.

Primary process functions operate by flashing to our mind the remembered *images* of needed objects and object relations. While our primary process functions are our first dream when we employ them in the state of sleep, primary process functions are our daydreams or our hallucinations when we employ these functions in the state of wakefulness. To explain this connection further, and to explain the connection between, on the one hand, primary process functions, daydreams, and hallucinations, and on the other hand, states of sensory privation and cortical deafferentiation, we need to discuss how sensory privation and cortical deafferentiation also trigger the operationalizing of primary process functions.

Empirical observation shows that when sensory (visual, auditory, tactile, olfactory, gustatory) or psychological stimulations diminish, consciousness undergoes a variety of changes. It becomes less sharp; its vigilance operations become less effective; it fades, it deteriorates; it may disappear altogether, as when we become unconscious or fall asleep. With nothing to see, as in deep darkness, with nothing to hear, as in the still of a very cold night in the country, with no one touching us, with no sharp odors or tastes distracting us, with no muscular efforts disturbing us (we are reclining or lying down; thus, we do not even need to exercise any resistance against the force of gravity), and with no thoughts or feelings distressing us, we fall asleep.

The sensory privation and the concomitant diminution or cessation of external stimulations can be caused by a variety of situations. It can be caused by realistic circumstances imposed from outside, as when one is imprisoned, put in solitary confinement, or shipwrecked on a raft or on a desert island. It can be voluntarily chosen, as when a person elects to become a hermit or chooses to engage in meditation; or more commonly, when one decides to close one's eyes, ears, and conscious mind to anything external, and goes to sleep.

Unstimulated or understimulated, in a state of deafferentiation from without and within, the conscious mind, the ego of consciousness, the cortical centers responsible for the more highly adaptive responses, fade and "die," that is, fall asleep, "dead" asleep. This process is accompanied by parallel physiological "fadings": 9 to 13 cycles per second EEG alpha waves are gradually replaced by slower, 5 to 8 cps theta waves, and eventually even slower 2 cps delta waves. Blood pressure, heart rate, respiratory rate, muscle tone, and other physiological telltale signs slow down too. To be sharp, brisk, and lively, to function at optimal capacity, to be capable of the alertness, quickness, and accuracy of highly adaptive responses, the conscious ego needs to be exposed to a reasonable amount of sensory stimulations from without and from within. And the cortical centers responsible for the most highly adaptive responses need to be equally afferentiated. When nonstimulated and in states of cortical deafferentiation (of whatever kind or origin, whether self-generated or externally induced), the conscious ego decays and becomes nonfunctional or dysfunctional.

If the conscious ego needs stimulations to survive, how does it protect itself from dissolution in the absence of stimulations? It adapts by creating its own stimulations; by producing memory images of objects and object relations from the past, that is, by regressing to primary process functions, and by flashing to its own consciousness the images of those objects and object relations. In the absence of external stimulations, the conscious ego protects itself from dissolution and deterioration by stimulating itself with its own daydreams and fantasies.

The regression to primary process functions in which the ego engages adaptively and defensively is possible because of previous ontogenetic and philogenetic events. Ontogenetically, in infancy and early childhood, we have all employed primary process functions and have experienced the relief that these functions procured for us. As infants and small children, we succeeded in getting those *indispensable objects* and in entering into those *crucial object relations* that were capable of relieving all our needs, because of the help of a loving caretaker. Whenever we could not, we engaged our primary process functions, which did it for us by providing the memory image of those objects or object relations. Since infancy and early childhood, we learned that the next best thing to having "the real thing" (the actual indispensable object, the actual crucial object relation) was to *imagine* that we were having it. Since infancy and early childhood, we learned that if we cannot fill our body with those indispensable objects or crucial object relations, we can at least fill our mind, our consciousness, with their image.

But the capacity to regress adaptively and defensively to primary process functions in the absence of stimulations is also possible because of previous philogenetic events, that is, the fact that primary process functions became operational not only in our own individual infancy, but also in the infancy of the species. Just as the person is neurogenetically prompted to periods of rest and sleep, periods in which he or she is closed to stimulations, the person is also neurologically activated to wake up, so to speak, from his or her period of rest and sleep, to stimulate himself or herself with self-generated stimuli, the primary process functions. During REM sleep, human beings are not as fully asleep as during NREM sleep. As Grey Walter hypothesized (1953), eons ago a self-awakening pacemaker probably developed through genetic mutations, and only those ancestors of ours survived in whom that pacemaker had been preserved through natural selection. These periods of full wakefulness eventually became the periods of "rest-activity" (partial wakefulness, less deep sleep), of REM sleep (i.e., sleep with dreams), periods during which rudimentary vigilance operations are possible. While asleep and dreaming, one may be awakened by the sound of an intruder entering one's home or the smell of a fire next door, stimulations one may not perceive during NREM sleep. During NREM sleep, sleep is more restful than during REM sleep. There is more complete exogenous deafferentiation than during REM sleep. Ephron and Carrington believed that the REM state periodically revitalizes those cortical centers responsible for highly adaptive responses (1966; see also 1967, 1970).

Thus, from the crib to the grave, from infancy and early childhood to old age and death, whenever reality, morality, or social considerations prevent us from getting what we wish or need, we regress to primary process functions. In situations of minor deprivations, with an ego still relatively intact, we do so automatically, almost by reflex, but are free to do so or not to do so through fantasies and daydreams. In situations of major deprivations, with an ego more damaged by the protracted lack of stimulations, we do so instinctually and regressively and without any freedom of choice, through hallucinatory and delirious states.

Depending upon the gravity of the deprivation to which the regression to primary process functions is trying to adapt, the regression may be adaptive and in the service of the ego, only partly adaptive, or maladaptive.

In cases of mild and temporary deprivations due to realistic, moral, or social considerations, we do regress to primary process functions, we are fully aware that we are doing so, and the regression is quite adaptive. This is the case with the simplest and most elemental daydreams and fantasies. If we are frustrated in our hunger or thirst, we will find ourselves fantasizing about our favorite food or beverage; if we are sexually frustrated, we will daydream about a favorite sexual companion; in the absence of our beloved, we will carry him or her in our heart; if starved for companionship, we will find ourselves stimulating ourselves by talking to imaginary friends and by imagining we hear their answers; if work has been particularly exhausting and unrewarding, we may daydream of being in our favorite foreign city. The more intense or prolonged the states of deprivation to which the primary process functions are affording us adaptation, then the more intense will be the regression to primary process functions, and the more one-track minded will our fantasies and daydreams become. The fantasied food will be imagined so vividly that we can almost taste it; the sexual daydreams may seem so real that ejaculation and orgasm will follow without any actual self-fondling. We almost smile as we imagine being in that most delightful place on earth we have always wished to return to. But the ego is still in charge, its critical capacities are intact, and we know that the fantasied gratification, the daydreamed object, the imagined object relations are just that, fantasies, daydreams, and mental images.

The regression to primary process functions is less adaptive and less functional in situations of greater deprivation or more severe sensory privation. In these cases, the ego is less capable of retaining its critical faculties, and daydreams and fantasies become hallucinations. Sailors marooned on a barren island, travelers lost in the desert, shipwreck survivors drifting in rafts for days on end, will see land, drink water, hear people, and so on. Their conscious ego has deteriorated so much, it can no longer tell the difference between what is real and what is hallucinated. Ephron and Carrington (1966) described the effects and functions of sensory deprivation: "Hallucinations (usually either visual or auditory) have been reported to occur in certain persons under conditions of experimental sensory deprivation. . . . It would seem that with diminished stimulations, stimulation of *any kind* may be avidly sought" (p. 511). They added: "We might wonder whether those hallucinatory experiences which are greeted with relief or pleasure under conditions of reduced sensory input have this effect because they perform a necessary *replacement function.* If so, an organism deprived of sensory input might be regarded as creating its own input, to which it subsequently attends" (1966, p. 511).

An interesting situation is the sensory privation occurring with boredom. Boredom may be externally or internally induced. Externally induced boredom can be the result of being exposed to repetitive, monotonous, external stimulations. Workers confined to too many hours of assembly line work consisting of continuous, repetitive, and meaningless motion will become bored. Their conscious ego may deteriorate to the point of causing them to lose concentration, or even to fall asleep, or cause harmful accidents. Most of these workers protect themselves from ego deterioration through fantasies and daydreams that keep them awake and alert without causing them to lose concentration. The assembly line activities in which they engage may be regarded as innately dull.

On the other hand, a situation may be experienced as boring, as distinguished from simply being dull. Internally induced boredom is the by-product of repression, and is the result of being exposed to psychodynamically threatening stimulations. A dinner party, a conversation, a lecture, a joke, a book, a novel, a film, a visit to a museum consciously experienced by a person as "boring" are actually not boring at all, but threatening because they resonate with and overcathect forbidden and conflictual, erotic and aggressive thoughts and feelings in the unconscious. These persons' conscious egos may honestly find these experiences "boring," but their unconscious egos and superegos experience them as psychodynamically dangerous. When that is the case, the state of the dynamic equilibrium of the person's neurotic conflict at that moment will demand that the stimuli coming from the threatening environmental or interpersonal experience be repressed to a minor or major extent; and that the stimuli be prevented from further agitating the person's psyche. Thus a state of self-induced sensory privation is created. These persons will feel bored and be prone to fall asleep.

Falling asleep may be quite adaptive on a purely psychobiological plane. In the state of sleep, the conscious ego is "not there," the higher centers of the cerebral cortex are in a state of deafferentiation; thus, the input of threatening stimuli is temporarily suspended. But adaptive as this response might be on that plane, it will probably be quite maladaptive on a realistic, social, and interpersonal plane. It may not be good form to fall asleep while attending the class of a possibly narcissistic professor, or while listening to the presentation given by a superior at work, or while watching a film with one's first date. These psychodynamically "bored" persons will protect themselves from falling asleep by stimulating themselves with their own daydreams and fantasies. While seemingly listening with rapt attention to the "boring" professor, the "boring" presenter, the "boring" film, they are actually taken with their own primary process functions.

A transcultural illustration in which extreme, externally imposed sensory privation causes primary process functions to stimulate ego consciousness and cortical centers, is found in the way that religious communities in the Far East screen their candidates. Religious orders in the West screen candidates before admission by means of the Rorschach Ink Blot, the Thematic Apperception, and other projective tests. In Buddhist communities in Tibet, a young postulant seeking admission to the community is sent to lonely caves in the high Himalayas where he remains in complete isolation. The postulant is kept there until he begins to hallucinate, at which point he is taken back to the congregation. His auditory and visual hallucinations are then "analyzed" by the head of the order and the young postulant's personality is declared suited or not to the rigors of monastic life (E. K. Schwartz, personal communication).

Self-induced sensory privation and the resulting regression to self-stimulating primary process functions has been implicated as a pathogenic factor in some forms of schizophrenia (Rosensweig, 1959). Let us consider stimulations of the conscious ego and the higher cortical centers from within and from without. There is clearly a complementary relationship between exogenous and endogenous stimulations. The less we are stimulated by sensory stimulations from without, the more we regress to being stimulated by primary process functions from within. The more stimulated we are from without, the less we are from within. When the conscious ego and the higher cortical centers are less stimulated by thoughts and feelings originating in the external and interpersonal world, the conscious ego and the higher cortical centers will be more open and more vulnerable to stimulations originating from the internal world. Psychodynamically, the conscious ego will be more open and vulnerable to stimuli from the unconscious, the id and the superego. In neurobiological terms, the higher cortical centers will be susceptible to input from limbic structures, hippocampus, and brain stem.

Searles (1963) addressed the extreme isolation of schizophrenic patients from their environment, obliterating their perceptions of persons or things in external reality. From this perspective, hallucinations may be regarded to some degree as the result of sensory deprivation (or privation, when little or no stimulation is afforded from infancy). Ephron and Carrington suggest that if this is so, then "hallucinations might represent a pathologic attempt to counteract the deprivation through creating an illusory world of the senses"(1966, p. 512).

Burnham, Gladstone, and Gibson (1969) have regarded schizophrenia as being caused, in part, by self-induced sensory privation related to what they term the *need–fear dilemma* and the *basic affective position*. In this theory, the basic affective position is a set of powerful, ego alien feelings of longing and rage which schizophrenics experience as small infants toward a mother they desperately need and long for, and whom they simultaneously fear and dread. Schizophrenics, therefore, are strongly ambivalent about their mothers, the need–fear dilemma. This ambivalence is seen in particular dramatic form in catatonics, who, in their catatonic stupor, are indeed almost immobile. They are "suspended," between the need-pole, wanting to move toward needed objects, and the fear-pole, wanting to run away from the feared objects. The basic affective position, repressed in the intervening years between childhood and the onset of psychosis, presses onward toward consciousness. When it breaks through, it blanks out the ego; it closes the ego to the external world and its stimulations; it makes the ego autistic, and in effect, produces a state of self-induced sensory privation. In this state, what the authors call *the psychotic position*, the ego becomes more vulnerable to the very same basic affective position which had caused it to blank out the external world to begin with. Then this greater "openness" to the internal world "closes" the ego further to the external world. This makes the ego more open to the internal world and thereby more closed to the external, and so on. This vicious cycle, according to the authors' hypotheses, contributes to the progressive deterioration of ego functions typical of the schizophrenic process, its thought and perception disorders.

Something similar may occur in senile psychoses. Here the sensory privation is produced by the set of psychological and cultural attitudes characteristic of ageism, a set of values creating an invisible but no less impervious chamber of sensory privation. The ghetto of significantly reduced or threatening sensory stimulations to which ageism confines old people is a ghetto which is either a desert of intellectual, emotional, and sexual privations or a frightening environment in which old people only experience fearsome stimulations. In this state of culturally induced privation, old people's conscious ego and higher cortical centers, less and less stimulated from the external world, are more and more stimulated from the internal world, the internal world of primary process functions going back to infancy, the internal world of repressed memories accumulated through a lifetime. The segregation of old men and women to this ghetto of sensory, emotional, intellectual, occupational, and sexual retirement contributes to their progressive cerebral deterioration much more than cerebral arteriosclerosis or normative aging.

Glossary

alpha waves. A 10 cycles-per-second rhythm recorded in the EEG of the neocortex while resting, awake, and with eyes closed.

amygdala. Almond-shaped neural structure part of the limbic system. It plays a significant role in emotions, especially aggressiveness; and as part of the temporal lobe, it plays a role in memory functions.

anaclisis, anaclitic. Terms which Freud used to designate the initial dependence of the sexual instincts on self-preservative physiological functions.

anal character. The character of a person fixated in the anal stage of development.

anal stage. Stage of development originally anaclitic on the physiological functions of the recto–anal organs and characterized by special interest in the anal erotogenic zone.

beta waves. A 15 to 25 cycles-per-second rhythm recorded in the EEG of the neocortex while resting, awake, and with eyes open.

brain stem. The brain structures just below the cerebrum and in front of the cerebellum.

cabalism. Esoteric theosophy and mystical method to interpret sacred mysteries; it also dabbled with foretelling the future and interpreting dreams.

cardinal rule of dream analysis. Ultimately, one must analyze the dream's latent content, not its manifest content.

cathexis, to cathect. The investment of the energy of a drive in an activity, object, idea, person, or body part. To attach oneself emotionally to an activity, object, idea, or body part.

371

censorship. The functions censoring unacceptable unconscious contents, preventing them from gaining access to consciousness as such. Also: the unconscious ego's defensive operations protecting the conscious ego from too direct an experience of id and superego. In the state of wakefulness, censorship censors and modifies unacceptable unconscious contents through the ego's defense mechanisms; in the state of REM sleep, it censors and modifies unacceptable dream wishes through the psychological operations of the dream work.

concrete pictorial representation. One of the defensive operations of censorship of the dream work. The representing of abstract, verbal dream thoughts and wishes through concrete, sensorial (mainly visual) images. Sometimes called *dramatization* and *plastic representation*.

condensation. One of the operations of censorship and of the dream work. In the state of wakefulness, the compression of many mental representations in the unconscious to one or fewer representations in consciousness; in the state of REM sleep, the compression of many latent dream wishes into one element of the manifest dream.

conscious. The level of thinking that encompasses all of which one is momentarily aware of.

content of dreams. According to Freud, the content of dreams includes unconscious memories of events going back to infancy and prelatency childhood, i.e., the unconscious leg of the dream, the "yesteryear" of dreams; and preconscious memories of events going back to the day or days preceding the dream, i.e., the preconscious leg of the dream, the "yesterday" of dreams, the "day's residues" or psychic remnants of daily experiences.

corpus callosum. Band of transverse white fibers uniting the two halves of the cerebrum.

cortical vigilance. A state of vigilance which includes a sense of orientation in space and time, the capacity to process sensory inputs, goal directedness. It is absent in NREM sleep, present to varying degrees in REM sleep.

countertransference. The analyst's unconscious reactions to the patient's overt behavior and conscious and unconscious feelings and thoughts; more or less related to the analyst's unconscious or the patient's unconscious.

day's residues. See CONTENT OF DREAMS.

deafferentiation. A neurophysiological (or, through somatization processes, psychological) state in which sensory stimuli from outside the body are not reaching the central nervous system.

decathecting. Withdrawing of a cathexis from an activity, object, idea, person, or body part.

defense mechanisms. Psychological operations protecting the conscious socialized ego from too direct an experience of id, superego, and unconscious processes.

delta waves. A 2 to 5 cycles-per-second rhythm recorded in the EEG of the neocortex while deeply asleep.

displacement. One of the defensive operations of censorship and of the dream work. A shifting of emphasis and focus from one element in the unconscious to another element in consciousness in the state of wakefulness; in the state of REM sleep, the shifting of emphasis and focus from one element in the latent dream to another in the manifest dream.

distortion. The result of the defensive operations of censorship.

dramatization. Spitta's (1882) and Sharpe's (1978) word for Freud's plastic representation and concrete pictorial representaion.

dream formation. The process in which unacceptable, overcathected dream wishes which are part of the neurotic conflict spill over into the person's REM sleep consciousness as compromise products. These compromise products may partake of more or less of the dream wishes and of more or less of the defense components of the neurotic conflict (i.e., the defensive operations of the dream work). Also: the process in which unacceptable, overcathected dream wishes spill over into the person's REM sleep consciousness as minimally distorted, mostly painful, unconscious derivatives (nightmarish dreams) or as maximally distorted, mostly painless, unconscious derivatives (pleasant or indifferent dreams). Also: the process in which the dream wishes become the latent dream, and, through the defensive operations of the dream work, the latent dream becomes the semilatent, semimanifest and manifest dream. The process of dream formation parallels that of symptom formation.

dream phobia. A conscious fear to sleep, psychodynamically related to the unconscious forbidden wish to dream and act out unconscious forbidden wishes through the dream's wish fulfillment process.

dream work. The whole of the operations transforming the latent dream into the manifest dream. The defensive operations of the ego and of censorship while asleep and dreaming.

dream work operations. Condensation, concrete pictorial representation, displacement, secondary revision, and symbolism. Also: simile, metaphor, metonimy, onomatopoeia, and synecdoche. Also, any of the ego's defense mechanisms may be enlisted in the transformation of the latent dream into the manifest dream.

drive and **instinct.** Often used interchangeably in psychoanalytic literature. Instinct in animals is an innate capacity to respond to stimuli with a state of excitation and a stereotyped behavior. Drive in human beings is also an innate capacity to respond to stimuli with a state of excitation, but its activation results in a much less stereotyped behavior. Only at the earliest id stages, is the resulting behavior as stereotyped as the one activated by instinct; at the later id stages and from then on, the behavior is variously mediated by a mind which has developed an ego and a superego. See also PRIMARY PROCESS FUNCTIONS and MIND.

drive theory. The Freudian belief that psychic life is energized by drives which impart motion and direction to all psychological processes. See DRIVE.

dynamic equilibrium of the neurotic conflict. The state in which, although conflictual drives and countercathecting defenses shift and change in energy endowment, the system remains stable and the conflicted drives continue to be prevented from spilling over into consciousness or behavior.

dynamic psychology. A theory explaining personality and behavior in terms of the psychic energy apportioned to id, ego, and superego.

EEG. Electroencephalogram, the electric potentials generated by the neurons of the neocortex measured by electrodes placed over the skull.

ego. The umbrella term, or abstraction, for a number of cognitive and perceptual processes including memory, problem-solving, reality-testing, inference-making, and the like that are conscious and in touch with reality; it also includes specific defense mechanisms that serve to mediate between id, superego, and the external environment. The agency of personality dealing with both internal and external reality.

ego alien, ego dystonic. Wishes, thoughts, impulses, and actions which the conscious ego and ego ideal do not recognize or accept as their own.

ego ideal. What a person would like to be or prefer to accomplish in terms of that which is positive and good.

ego syntonic. Wishes, thoughts, impulses, and actions acceptable to the conscious ego and ego ideal.

Electra complex. Jung's (1913) term for the feminine Oedipus complex.

endogenous. Originating from within the person.

Eros. The whole of the life-preservative instincts, including the sexual instincts.

erythrophobia. The conscious fear of blushing, psychodynamically related to conflicted, unconscious exhibitionistic drives.

exogenous. Originating from outside the person.

extrapsychic world. Consciousness, the preconscious, the external, interpersonal and sociocultural world and the conscious ego's mental representations of the external world.

fixation. A defense mechanism in which eros or thanatos remains attached to the modes of gratification characteristic of a specific psychosexual stage.

forebrain. The anterior part of the embryonic brain (in front of midbrain and hindbrain) which later divides into telencephalon and diencephalon. The telencephalon develops into the cerebral cortex, the basal ganglia, and the limbic system.

hebephrenic schizophrenia. A malignant form of schizophrenia.

hippocampus. A sea-horse shaped structure of mostly gray matter. In more primitive species, it is involved in olfactory and visceral processes; in humans and higher mammals it also plays a role in emotion, motivation, long-term memory, and learning. It may be very important in dreams and dreaming.

hypnagogic phenomena. Images experienced while first falling asleep.

hypnopompic phenomena. Images experienced while waking up.

hypothalamus. A peanut-size but extremely complex structure at the base of the brain. The site of survival-related functions such as temperature control, heart rate, blood pressure, and emotional and sexual behavior. Insofar as the id is personality's biological metaphor and the driving force behind man's emotional and sexual behavior, correlations have been made between the hypothalamus and the id.

id. The umbrella term or abstraction for the primitive, animalistic, instinctual elements of libidinal and aggressive energies demanding immediate gratification; the deepest component of the psyche, entirely self-contained, bent on achieving its own aims and solely governed by the pleasure principle.

identity of perception, perceptual identity. The memory image of an object, which had been previously able to reduce a tension, being identical with the perception itself; the perception of the object or object relation being identical to the object. (For the id, the memory image of food is identical to food itself.)

instinct. See DRIVE and INSTINCT.

intrapsychic world. The unconscious, the id, the superego, the unconscious ego.

latent dream. The dream as first dreamed, before the distortions effected by censorship and dream work.

left brain. Left half of the cerebrum characterized by secondary process, analytic and linear modes of thinking.

libido. The psychic energy of Eros.

limbic system. Evolutionarily old structures of the forebrain lying in an arc below the corpus callosum. It includes the hippocampus and the hypothalamus. The site of emotional and impulsive actions. Insofar as the id is personality's biological metaphor and the representative of man's impulsive, primitive, instinctual self, correlations have been made between the limbic system and the id.

magical thinking. The thinking at the id and primary process level of thinking; the belief that thinking and feeling are the same as doing.

manifest dream. The dream as remembered, after the distortions effected by censorship and dream work.

metaphor. One of the defensive operations of the dream work. A compressed simile in which words such as *like* or *as* are omitted.

metonimy. One of the defensive operations of the dream work. In metonimy, "the part," that is, an objectionable element in the latent dream, is rendered as "the whole," in the manifest dream.

midbrain. Mesencephalon, the middle of the three primary divisions in the brain of vertebrates.

mind. The abstraction representing the psychological component of the psychosomatic whole that man is. The mind is developed, philogenetically and ontogenetically, the better to assure man's adaptation and survival.

mirror relationship. The reciprocal, mutually overcathecting relationship between the unconscious and preconscious legs of a dream. Also see CONTENT OF DREAMS.

monotreme. Oviparous member of the lowest order of mammals, comprising duckbills and echidnas.

neocortex. The frontal, parietal, temporal, and occipital lobes of the brain. The evolutionarily most recent and complex of neural tissues. The site of the highest level of sensory and mental functions. Its expansion within the limited space of the skull caused the neocortical sheet to fold upon itself to form convolutions. Insofar as the ego includes high-level cognitive and perceptual functions, correlations have been made between the neocortex and the ego.

neo-Darwinism. Theories of evolution as expounded by later students of Charles Darwin; for instance, one believing in the evolution of man's social characteristics.

neurotic conflict. A conflict between a tendency striving for discharge and a countertendency trying to prevent that discharge.

neuroses and neurotic states. According to Freud and Fenichel, conditions in which only the defense components of the neurotic conflict spill over into the patient's consciousness and/or behavior.

NREM sleep. Those stages of sleep not characterized by REM sleep; sometimes called non-REM sleep.

numinous experience. Alterations of consciousness caused by a numinosum.

numinosum. Visible object or invisible presence causing, through magical thinking, alterations of consciousness.

oedipal stage. Age 3 to 5, the peak period, according to Freud, for the experience of the Oedipus complex.

Oedipus complex. The loving and hostile wishes the child experiences toward its parents; in its *positive* form, it appears as in Sophocles' *Oedipus Rex*, a desire for the death of the parent of the same sex, and a sexual desire for the parent of the opposite sex; in its *negative* form, there is love for the parent of the same sex and jealous hatred for the parent of the opposite sex; in its *complete* form, the two versions are found in varying degrees.

onomatopoeia. One of the defensive operations of the dream work. In onomatopoeia, the latent dream's verbal representation of an objectionable dream wish is rendered in the manifest dream with a word that echoes or resembles that representation.

ontogenesis. The development of individual organisms.

oral character. The character of a person fixated at the oral stage of development.

oral stage. Stage of development originally anaclitic on the physiological functions of the mouth and characterized by special interest in the oral erotogenic zone.

overcathexis. Strong investment of a cathexis upon an activity, object, idea, person or body part.

paleocortex. The "old brain," as opposed to the neocortex, the "new brain."

para-oedipal. Near oedipal, not quite oedipal, almost oedipal and, of course, the derivative of truly oedipal happenings.

perception. The mental representation of an object.

P.G.O. Pontine-geniculate-occipital cortex spikes, random signals from the brain stem instigating dream formation.

phallic character. The character of a person fixated on the phallic stage of development.

phallic stage. Stage of development originally anaclitic on the physiological functions of the phallic organ (penis and clitoris) and characterized by special interest in the phallic erotogenic zone.

phylogenesis. The development of a species.

pineal body or gland. A tiny structure so close to the center of the brain that Descartes hypothesized that it was the locus of interactions between body and mind.

plastic representation. See CONCRETE PICTORIAL REPRESENTATION.

pleasure principle. One of the two principles which for Freud govern mental functioning. It determines behavior aiming at immediate and undelayed quiescence, gratification, and pleasure.

preconscious. The level of thinking whose components are not a part of one's consciousness but which may be retrieved by a simple exercise of memory.

preconscious leg of dreams. See CONTENT OF DREAMS.

predicate thinking. Reasoning whereby two objects are seen as identical because they share the same attribute or predicate. It is part of magical thinking.

preoedipal stage. The period of psychosexual development preceding the formation of the Oedipus complex; during this period, attachment to the mother predominates in both sexes.

prelogical thinking. Any mode of thought that does not follow the principles of logic.

primary anxiety, guilt, disgust, shame. In Fenichel's (1945) triple stratification conceptualization, these feelings are experienced on the earliest tier, the "trauma" tier. Primary feelings are intense, occur automatically, and are experienced by the ego passively.

primary process. Mental functions of the id, unconscious, nonrational, taking no account of time and space, governed by the pleasure principle.

primary process functions of the id in hallucinations and dreams. Produce the mental image of an object or object relations needed to reduce a tension by reproducing the memory of

those objects and object relations which had previously gratified a drive. The mental images thus reproduced are multi-
sensorial. In dreams these multisensory memory images are
primarily visual. The reproduction of these mental images
produce wish fulfillment through what Freud called *perceptual identity,* sometimes referred to as *identity of perception.*

primary transference. The transference ideally experienced during psychoanalytical treatment toward the patient's analyst.

primitive perception. The perception found at the level of the
id's primary process perception. It uses prelogical thinking,
predicate thinking, and identity of perception. It perceives
that which is perceived, not in terms of the intrinsic qualities
and characteristics of that which is perceived, but in terms
of how that which is perceived affects the percipient.

principle of constancy. The principle according to which the psychical apparatus tends to keep the quantity of excitation
within itself at as low a level, or, at any rate, as constant a
level, as possible; constancy is achieved through discharge
of the energy already present, and, on the other hand, by
avoidance of whatever might increase the excitation.

psychic remnants of daily experiences. See CONTENT OF DREAMS.

psychodynamic assessment. Evaluation of a person's strengths
and weaknesses in terms of the psychic energies of his or her
id, ego, and superego and in terms of the kinds of defense
mechanisms in his or her stabilized personality.

psychoneuroses and psychoneurotic states. According to Freud
and Fenichel, conditions in which the symptoms are a compromise product partaking of both the drive components
and the defensive components of the neurotic conflict. Both
the drive and defense components of the conflict spill over
into the patient's consciousness and/or behavior, but the
drive components are better defended than in psychoses and
psychotic states, and the symptoms exhibit more of the defense components than of the drive components.

psychoses and psychotic states. According to Freud and Fenichel,
conditions in which the symptoms are a compromise product partaking of both the drive components and the defense
components of the neurotic conflict. Both the drive and
the defense components of the conflict spill over into the

patient's consciousness and/or behavior, but the drive components are less well defended than in psychoneuroses and psychoneurotic states, and the symptoms exhibit more of the drive components than of the defense components.

reactive personality traits or symptoms. Those developed through defense mechanisms other than sublimation.

reality principle. One of the two principles which for Freud govern mental functioning; it modifies the pleasure principle; it regulates behavior so that gratification is delayed according to the conditions imposed by reality.

regression. A defense mechanism characterized by a reverting to an earlier more primitive pattern of behavior—frequently to a previous fixation.

REM sleep. A stage of sleep characterized by rapid movements of the eyes under closed lids, irregular breathing, and other tell-tale signs.

reticular formation. A complex system of over 90 nuclei of neurons and very extensive nerve fibers in the central core of the brain stem; it functions in a number of processes including sleep.

right brain. The right half of the cerebrum, characterized by primary process, wholistic, globally impressionistic, and circular modes of thinking.

secondary anxiety, guilt, disgust, shame. In Fenichel's (1945) triple stratification conceptualization, these feelings are experienced on the middle tier, the "danger" tier. Secondary feelings are mild, are triggered by the ego's defenses and are experienced by the ego actively.

secondary process. Mental processes which are conscious, rational and logical, linked with the ego and governed by the reality principle.

secondary revision. Rearrangement of a dream so as to present it in the form of a relatively consistent and comprehensible scenario. One of the defensive operations of the dream work.

secondary transference. The transference ideally experienced during psychoanalytical treatment toward the patient's other extrapsychic life's significant figures.

semilatent dream. A not totally latent dream.

semimanifest dream. A not totally manifest dream.

simile. One of the defensive operations of the dream work; the equation of one element in the latent dream to another in the manifest dream by means of a common attribute; the similarity between the two dissimilar elements is expressed by means of such words as *like* or *as*.

sources of dreams. According to Freud, a dream is conceived whenever the unconscious drives which are part of a person's intrapsychic world have been overcathected by intrapsychic or extrapsychic processes.

stabilized personality. One in which a clinical equilibrium has been established around and because of a particular defense mechanism, or a particular cluster of defense mechanisms, or a particularly strong identification; not the same as a "stable personality."

structural theory. The Freudian belief according to which functionally related mental processes and contents can be grouped together as "structures." Freud distinguished three functionally related groups or structures and called them id, ego, and superego.

sublimation. Diversion of a drive toward a nonsexual aim and toward socially valued objects.

sublimative personality traits. Those traits developed through sublimation of drives.

superego. Agency of personality capable of judging, censoring, and inhibiting the ego.

symbolism. One of the defensive operations of censorship and of the dream work; consciously representing an unconscious content through its symbol in the state of wakefulness; in the state of REM sleep, representing an element of the latent dream through its symbol in the manifest dream.

symptom formation. The process in which unacceptable, overcathected unconscious drives which are part of the neurotic conflict spill over into the patient's consciousness and/or behavior as compromise products. These compromise products may partake of more or less of the drive and of more or less of the defense components of the neurotic conflict (i.e., the defense mechanisms of the ego); see NEUROSES AND NEUROTIC STATES, PSYCHONEUROSES AND PSYCHONEUROTIC

STATES, PSYCHOSES AND PSYCHOTIC STATES. Also: the process in which unacceptable, overcathected derivatives of the unconscious spill over into the patient's consciousness and/or behavior, either as mostly painful, reactive, ego alien compromise products or as mostly painless, sublimative, ego syntonic compromise products. The process of symptom formation parallels that of dream formation.

synecdoche. One of the defensive operations of the dream work. In synechdoche, "the whole," that is, an objectionable element in the latent dream, is rendered as "the part" in the manifest dream.

technique of dream interpretation. It is not directly based on the theory of technique of dream interpretation, is more an art than a science, it cannot be learned solely through books and in a classroom, it can best be learned through psychoanalytically supervised clinical practice and from dream analysis in one's personal psychoanalysis. It tells the analysts what to say to the patient about his or her dream.

tertiary anxiety, guilt, disgust, shame. In Fenichel's (1945) triple stratification conceptualization, these feelings are experienced on the latest tier, the "panic" tier. Tertiary feelings are very intense, occur automatically, and are experienced by the ego passively.

thanatos. The whole of life-destructive instincts.

theory of technique of dream interpretation. The theoretical roots and rules of dream interpretation. It is directly based on the theory of dream formation and it flows directly from this theory, because it deciphers dreams by retracing and reversing the steps of dream formation. To an extent it is a science, not an art, it can be learned through books and in the classroom. It tells the analyst what the patient's dream says.

therapeutic drift. Patients' wandering, in sessions not characterized by undue resistance, from the present to recent memories and toward earlier and earlier preconscious memories. When the drift stops, patients catapult themselves into the present. The last recollected preconscious memory is usually a screen memory of an unconscious event which the patient is not ready to recollect, usually an event at which important fixations had occurred.

theta waves. A 5 to 6 cycles-per-second rhythm recorded in the EEG from groups of neurons located in the hippocampus.

the yesteryear of dreams. See CONTENT OF DREAMS.

the yesterday of dreams. See CONTENT OF DREAMS.

topographic theory. The Freudian belief according to which psychological processes may occur at any of three levels of awareness, conscious, preconscious, and unconscious.

transference. The universal tendency to see the present in the light of the past.

triple stratification. The three tiers (trauma, danger, and panic) upon which anxiety, guilt, disgust, and shame are arranged in Fenichel's conceptualization of symptom formation (1945).

unconscious. Impulses, desires, memories, and images too anxiety-provoking to be accepted into consciousness. Impulses, desires, memories, and images which, if accepted into consciousness, would provoke intense anxiety, guilt, disgust, or shame. Also: that which is not conscious, does not readily become conscious, and is kept unconscious through a variety of defense mechanisms.

unconscious leg of dreams. See CONTENT OF DREAMS.

undercathexis. Weak investment of a cathexis upon an activity, object, idea, or body part.

References

Artemidorus of Daldis (2nd cent. A.D.), *Oneirocritica,* tr. F. S. Krauss. Vienna, 1881.

Aserinski, E., & Kleitman, N. (1953), Regularly occurring periods of eye motility and concomitant phenomena during sleep. *Science,* 118:272–274.

Augustine (397 A.D.), *Confessions,* tr. J. Ryan. Garden City, NY: Image/Doubleday, 1960.

Bettelheim, B. (1983), *Freud and Man's Soul.* New York: Alfred A. Knopf.

Bonaparte, M., Freud, A., & Kris, E., Eds. (1954), *The Origins of Psychoanalysis: Letters to Wilhelm Fliess, Drafts and Notes (1887–1902) by Sigmund Freud.* New York: Basic Books.

Botez, M. I., Olivier, M., Verzina, J.-L., Botez, T., & Kaufman, B. (1985), Defective re-visualization: Dissociation between cognitive and imagistic thought/ Case report and short review of the literature. *Cortex,* 21:375–389.

Brenner, C. (1973), *An Elementary Textbook of Psychoanalysis,* rev. ed. New York: International Universities Press.

Breuer, J., & Freud, S. (1893–1895), Studies on Hysteria. *Standard Edition,* 2. London: Hogarth Press, 1955.

Burnham, D., Gladstone, A., & Gibson, R. (1969), *Schizophrenia and the Need–Fear Dilemma.* New York: International Universities Press.

Busch, F. (1994), Some ambiguities in the method of free association and the implications for technique. *J. Amer. Psychoanal. Assn.,* 42:363–384.

Büschenshütz, B. (1868), *Traum und Traumdeutung im Altertum.* Berlin.

Cicogna, P. (1994), Dreaming during sleep onset and awakening. *Percept. & Motor Skills,* 78:1041–1042.

——— Cavallero, C., & Bosinelli, M. (1991), Cognitive aspects of mental activity during sleep. *Amer. J. Psychology,* 104:413–425.

Crick, F., & Mitchison, G. (1983), The function of sleep. *Nature,* 304:111–114.

Damasio, A. R. (1994), *Descartes' Error.* New York: Grosset/ Putnam.

Dement, W. (1960), The effect of dream deprivation. *Science,* 131:1705–1707.

——— Kleitman, N. (1957), The relation of eye movements during sleep to dream activity: An objective model for the study of dreaming. *J. Experiment. Psychology,* 53:339–346.

Edelman, G. M. (1992), *Bright Air, Brilliant Fire: On the Matter of the Mind.* New York: Basic Books.

Ellis, H. (1911), *The World of Dreams.* London.

Ephron, H. S. (1972), Dreams by Late-Life Dreamers. Research project.

——— Carrington, P. (1966), Rapid eye movement sleep and cortical homeostasis. *Psycholog. Rev.,* 73:500–526.

——— ——— (1967), Ego functioning in rapid eye movement sleep: Implications for dream theory. *Sci. & Psychoanal.,* 11: 75–102.

——— ——— (1970), The dream as "guardian of sleep": Indications for further research. *Internat. Psychiatry Clin.,* 7:344–351.

Erikson, E. H. (1954), The dream specimen of psychoanalysis. *J. Amer. Psychoanal. Assn.,* 2:5–56.

Fenichel, O. (1945), *The Psychoanalytic Theory of Neurosis.* New York: W. W. Norton.

Fisher, C. (1965), Psychoanalytic implications of recent research on sleep and dreaming, Part I: Empirical findings; Part II: Implications for psychoanalytic theory. *J. Amer. Psychoanal. Assn.,* 13:197–303.

Fosshage, J. L. (1987), New vistas in dream interpretation. In: *Dreams in New Perspective,* ed. M. L. Glucksman & S. L. Warner. New York: Human Sciences Press, pp. 23–43.

Foulkes, D., & Vogel, G. (1965), Mental activity at sleep onset. *J. Abnorm. Psychol.*, 70:231–243.

Frazer, J. G. (1911), *The Perils of the Soul.* London.

Freud, A. (1936), *The Ego and the Mechanisms of Defense.* New York: International Universities Press, 1966.

Freud, E., Ed. (1960), *Letters of Sigmund Freud,* tr. T. Stern & J. Stern. New York: Basic Books.

Freud, S. (1892–1899), Extracts from the Fleiss papers. *Standard Edition*, 1:173–280. London: Hogarth Press, 1966.

———— (1895), Project for a scientific psychology. *Standard Edition*, 1:281–397. London: Hogarth Press, 1966.

———— (1900), The Interpretation of Dreams. *Standard Edition*, 4 & 5. London: Hogarth Press, 1953.

———— (1901a), On dreams. *Standard Edition*, 5:633–686. London: Hogarth Press, 1953.

———— (1901b), The Psychopathology of Everyday Life. *Standard Edition*, 6. London: Hogarth Press, 1960.

———— (1905a), Fragment of an analysis of a case of hysteria. *Standard Edition*, 7:1–122. London: Hogarth Press, 1953.

———— (1905b), Three essays on the theory of sexuality. *Standard Edition*, 7:123–243. London: Hogarth Press, 1953.

———— (1910a), Five lectures on psycho-analysis. *Standard Edition*, 11:1–55. London: Hogarth Press, 1957.

———— (1910b), "Wild" psychoanalysis. *Standard Edition*, 11:219–227. London: Hogarth Press, 1957.

———— (1911), Formulations on the two principles of mental functioning. *Standard Edition*, 12:213–226. London: Hogarth Press, 1958.

———— (1912a), The dynamics of transference. *Standard Edition*, 12:97–108. London: Hogarth Press, 1958.

———— (1912b), A note on the unconscious in psychoanalysis. *Standard Edition*, 12:255–266. London: Hogarth Press, 1958.

———— (1914), On the history of the psychoanalytic movement. *Standard Edition*, 14:1–66. London: Hogarth Press, 1957.

———— (1915), The unconscious. *Standard Edition*, 14:159–204. London: Hogarth Press, 1957.

———— (1916a), A mythological parallel to a visual obsession. *Standard Edition*, 14:337–338. London: Hogarth Press, 1957.

—— (1916b), Introductory Lectures on Psycho-Analysis. *Standard Edition,* 15 & 16. London: Hogarth Press, 1961.

—— (1919), The "uncanny." *Standard Edition,* 17:217–252. London: Hogarth Press, 1955.

—— (1920), Beyond the pleasure principle. *Standard Edition,* 18:1–64. London: Hogarth Press, 1955.

—— (1921), Group psychology and the analysis of the ego. *Standard Edition,* 18:63–143. London: Hogarth Press, 1955.

—— (1922), Medusa's head. *Standard Edition,* 18:273–274. London: Hogarth Press, 1955.

—— (1923), The ego and the Id. *Standard Edition,* 19:1–59. London: Hogarth Press, 1961.

—— (1926a), Inhibitions, symptoms and anxiety. *Standard Edition,* 20:75–172. London: Hogarth Press, 1959.

—— (1926b), The question of lay analysis. *Standard Edition,* 20:177–250. London: Hogarth Press, 1959.

—— (1927), The future of an illusion. *Standard Edition,* 21:1–56. London: Hogarth Press, 1961.

—— (1932), The acquisition and control of fire. *Standard Edition,* 22:183–193. London: Hogarth Press, 1964.

—— (1933), New introductory lectures on psycho-analysis. *Standard Edition,* 22:1–182. London: Hogarth Press, 1964.

—— (1939), Moses and monotheism. *Standard Edition,* 23:1–137. London: Hogarth Press, 1964.

Fromm-Reichmann, F. (1948), Notes on the development of treatment of schizophrenics by psychoanalytic psychotherapy. *Psychiatry,* 11:263–273.

Gabel, S. (1987), Information processing in REM sleep: Possible neurophysical, neuropsychological, and clinical correlates. *J. Nerv. & Ment. Dis.,* 175:193–200.

Gaer Luce, G. (1974a), The effects of sleep deprivation. In: *The New World of Dreams,* ed. R. L. Woods & H. B. Greenhouse. New York: Macmillan, pp. 409–415.

—— (1974b), The effects of dream deprivation. In: *The New World of Dreams,* ed. R. L. Woods & H. B. Greenhouse. New York: Macmillan, pp. 415–418.

Galin, D. (1974), Implications for psychiatry of left and right cerebral specialization: A neurological context for unconscious processes. *Arch. Gen. Psychiatry,* 31:572–583.

Gay, P. (1988), *Freud: A Life for Our Time.* New York: W. W. Norton.

Gazzaniga, M. S., & Hillyard, S. A. (1971), Language and speech capacity of the right hemisphere. *Neuropsychologia,* 9:273–280.

Glover, E. (1968), *The Technique of Psychoanalysis.* New York: International Universities Press.

Greenberg, R. (1987), The dream problem and problems in dreams. In: *Dreams in New Perspective,* ed. M. L. Glucksman & S. L. Warner. New York: Human Sciences Press, pp. 45–57.

———— Perlman, C. (1975), REM sleep and the analytic process: A psychophysiologic bridge. *Psychoanal. Quart.,* 44:392–393.

Greenson, R. R. (1967), *The Technique and Practice of Psychoanalysis.* New York: International Universities Press.

Greenwood, P., Wilson, D. H., & Gazzaniga, M. S. (1977), Dream report following commisurotomy. *Cortex,* 13:311–316.

Grey Walter, W. (1953), *The Living Brain.* New York: W. W. Norton.

Hall, C. S. (1982), *A Primer of Freudian Psychology.* New York: Harper & Row.

Harth, E., & Unnikrishnan, K. P. (1985), Brainstem control of sensory information: A mechanism for perception. *Internat. J. Psychophysiol.,* 3:101–119.

Hawkins, D. R. (1966), A review of psychoanalytic dream theory in the light of recent psycho-physiological studies of sleep and dreaming. *Brit. J. Med. Psychol.,* 39:85–104.

———— (1969), A Freudian view. In: *Dream Psychology and the New Biology of Dreaming,* ed. M. Kramer. Springfield, IL: Charles C Thomas, pp. 39–56.

———— (1990), Dreaming, neurobiology, and psychoanalysis. *Psychiatric Annals,* 20:238–244.

Head, H. (1923), The conception of nervous and mental energy. II. Vigilance: A physiological state of the nervous system. *Brit. J. Psychology,* 14:126–147.

Hobson, J. A., & McCarley, R. W. (1977), The brain as dream state generator: An activation-synthesis hypothesis of dream process. *Amer. J. Psychiatry,* 134:1335–1348.

Jung, C. G. (1913), The Theory of Psychoanalysis. In: *Collected Works,* Vol. 4. Princeton, NJ: Princeton University Press, 1961.

———— (1938), Psychology and Religion: West and East. In *Collected Works*, Vol. 11. Princeton, NJ: Princeton University Press, 1969.

Kerr, N. H., & Foulkes, D. (1981), Right hemispheric mediation of dream visualization: A case study. *Cortex*, 17:603–609.

Khan, M. M. R. (1978), Introduction. In: E. F. Sharpe, *Dream Analysis*. New York: Brunner/Mazel.

Labruzza, A. L. (1978), The activation-synthesis hypothesis of dreams: A theoretical note. *Amer. J. Psychiatry*, 135: 1536–1538.

Lee, P. (1994), Is that all there is? Capital Records/CEMA Markets.

Loomis, R. (1957), Cerebral states during sleep as studied human brain potentials. *J. Experiment. Psychol.*, 21:127.

Lorand, S. (1974), Dream interpretation in the Talmud. In: *The New World of Dreams*, ed. R. L. Woods & H. B. Greenhouse. New York: Macmillan, pp. 150–158.

MacLean, P. D. (1963), Phylogenesis. In: *Expressions of the Emotions of Man*, ed. P. H. Knapp. New York: International Universities Press.

Maury, L. F. A. (1878), *Le sommeil et les rêves*. Paris.

McCarley, R. W., & Hobson, A. J. (1977), The neurobiological origins of psychoanalytic dream theory. *Amer. J. Psychiatry*, 134:1211–1221.

Miller, S. C. (1962), Ego-autonomy in sensory deprivation, isolation, and stress. *Internat. J. Psycho-Anal.*, 43:1–20.

Müller, J. (1826), *Über die phantastischen Geischtserscheinungen*. Coblenz.

Ostow, M. (1954), Psychodynamic disturbances in patients with temporal lobe disorder. *J. Mt. Sinai Hosp.*, 20:293–308.

Otto, R. (1917), *Das Heilige. Oxford Annotated Bible* (1962), New York: Oxford University Press.

Pavlides, C., & Winson, J. (1989), Influences of hippocampal place cell firing in the awake state on the activity of these cells during subsequent sleep episodes. *J. Neurosci.*, 9:2907–2918.

Plato. *The Republic.* tr. H. Davis. The dream theory of Socrates. In: *The New World of Dreams*, ed. R. L. Woods & H. B. Greenhouse. New York: Macmillan, 1987, pp. 166–167.

Penfield, W. (1938), The cerebral cortex in man: The cerebral cortex and consciousness. *Arch. Neurol. & Psychiatry*, 40: 417–442.

Publius Terentius Afer (190–159 B.C.), *Macmillan Dictionary of Quotations.* New York: Macmillan, 1989.

Rechtschaffen, A., & Kales, A. (1968), *The Manual of Standardized Technology for Sleep Stages of Human Subjects.* Bethesda, MD: National Institute of Health, Publication #204.

—— Vogel, G., & Shaikun, G. (1963), Interrelatedness of mental activity during sleep. *Arch. Gen. Psychiatry*, 9:536–547.

Roffwarg, H. P., Herman, J. H., Bowe-Anders, C., & Tauber, E. S. (1978), The effects of sustained alterations of waking visual input on dream content. In: *The Mind in Sleep*, ed. A. M. Arkis, J. S. Antrobus, & S. J. Ellman. Hillsdale, NJ: Lawrence Erlbaum Associates.

—— Muzio, J. P., & Dement, W. C. (1966), Ontogenetic development of the human sleep-dream cycle. *Science*, 152: 604–619.

Rosensweig, N. (1959), Sensory deprivation and schizophrenia: Clinical and theoretical similarities. *Amer. J. Psychiatry*, 116: 326–329.

Rousseau, J.-J. (1781), *Confessions*, tr. J. M. Cohen. London: Penguin Books, 1953.

Sacks, O. (1990a), *Awakenings.* New York: Harper Perennial.

—— (1990b), The neurology of the soul. *NY Rev. Books*, 37: 44–50.

—— (1991), Narrative and medicine. Alpha Omega Alpha Lectures. *Mt. Sinai J. Med.*, 60:127–131.

Searles, H. F. (1963), The place of neutral therapist-responses in psychotherapy with the schizophrenic patient. *Internat. J. Psycho-Anal.*, 44:42–56.

Sharpe, E. F. (1978), *Dream Analysis.* New York: Brunner/Mazel, Inc.

Silberer, H. (1909), Bericht über eine Methode, gewisse symbolische achten. *Jb. Psychoanal. Psychopath. Forsch.*, 1, 513.

Solms, M. (1995), New findings on the neurological organization of dreaming: Implications for psychoanalysis. *Psychoanal. Quart.*, 44:43–67.

Sperber, H. (1912), Über den Einfluss sexueller Momente auf Entstehung und Entwicklung der Sprache, *Imago*, 1, 405.

Spitta, H. (1882), *Die Schlaf- und Traumzustande der menschlichen Seele*, 2nd ed. Tübingen.

Stafford-Clark, D. (1965), *What Freud Really Said*. New York: Schocken Books.

Stekel, W. (1911), *Die Sprach des Traumes*. Wiesbaden.

Tuchman, B. (1985), *The March of Folly*. New York: Ballantine.

Vogel, G., Foulkes, D., & Trosman, H. (1966), Ego functions and dreaming during dream onset. *Arch. Gen. Psychiatry*, 14:238–248.

Vogel, G. W. (1978), An alternative view of the neurobiology of dreaming. *Amer. J. Psychiatry*, 135:1531–1535.

Wasserman, M. D. (1984), Psychoanalytic dream theory and recent neurobiological findings about REM sleep. *J. Amer. Psychoanal. Assn.*, 32:831–846.

Winson, J. (1985), *Brain and Psyche*. Garden City, NY: Anchor Press/Doubleday.

——— (1990), The meaning of dreams. *Sci. Amer.*, November: 86–94.

Name Index

Subject Index

Abstract concepts, 97
  transforming, into concrete representation, 99–104
Activation-synthesis hypothesis, 25–26
Adaptation, 57–58
Affectionate feelings, 267
Ageism, 370
Aggressive drive, 34
  about mother, 241–245
  beautification of, 213–214
  distortion of, 258–259
  undisguised representation of, 212
Aggressive feelings
  allusion to, 303
  metaphor for, 232
Agricultural societies, dreams in, 9
Allusions, 232, 303
Alpha waves, 363–364, 371
Amphetamine addicts, overdreaming in, 14
Amygdala, 29, 371
Anaclisis, 371
Anal character, 371
Anal drive, 277
Anal fixation, 309
Anal stage, 371
Analysis
  early stage of, 271, 335–336
  middle-late stages of, 270, 335
  stages of, 271–272
Analyst

dream work by, 125–132, 141–156
tasks of, 127, 130–131, 143–144, 146, 154, 159–160, 167–168, 177–181, 187–191, 199–202, 209–212, 219–221, 239–245, 254–262. *See also* Internal soliloquy; Interpretation; Intervention
Anger
  expression of, 206–208
  unconscious, 197, 315–316, 356–357
  well defended, 299
Anorexia, 65
Anus, symbolism for, 109
Anxiety
  equivalents of, 63
  primary, 52, 53–54, 55, 379
  secondary, 56–57, 381
  spillover of, 61, 62–63
  symbolism for, 302–303
  tertiary, 383
Anxiety dream, 72, 213
Anxiety hysteria, 57
Anxiety neurosis, 60–61
  case example of, 62–63
Aristotelian logic, 116–117
Artists, dream interpretation by, 4–5
Associations, 127, 134, 137, 149, 201, 287, 295, 302
  defenses from, 162–163, 172, 181, 192, 203, 213, 232, 246, 263,